# ASP.NET Core Recipes

A Problem-Solution Approach

Second Edition

John Ciliberti

Apress®

*ASP.NET Core Recipes: A Problem-Solution Approach*

John Ciliberti
Sparta, New Jersey, USA

ISBN-13 (pbk): 978-1-4842-0428-3          ISBN-13 (electronic): 978-1-4842-0427-6
DOI 10.1007/978-1-4842-0427-6

Library of Congress Control Number: 2017953377

Cover image by Freepik (www.freepik.com)

Managing Director: Welmoed Spahr
Editorial Director: Todd Green
Acquisitions Editor: Todd Green
Development Editor: Anne Marie Walker
Technical Reviewer: Damien Foggon
Coordinating Editor: Mark Powers
Copy Editor: Kim Wimpsett

Distributed to the book trade worldwide by Springer Science+Business Media New York, 233 Spring Street, 6th Floor, New York, NY 10013. Phone 1-800-SPRINGER, fax (201) 348-4505, e-mail orders-ny@springer-sbm.com, or visit www.springeronline.com. Apress Media, LLC is a California LLC and the sole member (owner) is Springer Science + Business Media Finance Inc (SSBM Finance Inc). SSBM Finance Inc is a **Delaware** corporation.

For information on translations, please e-mail rights@apress.com, or visit www.apress.com/rights-permissions.

Apress titles may be purchased in bulk for academic, corporate, or promotional use. eBook versions and licenses are also available for most titles. For more information, reference our Print and eBook Bulk Sales web page at www.apress.com/bulk-sales.

Any source code or other supplementary material referenced by the author in this book is available to readers on GitHub via the book's product page, located at www.apress.com/9781484204283. For more detailed information, please visit www.apress.com/source-code.

Printed on acid-free paper

*Dedicated to my daughter Katrina who never takes my iPad so she can watch Netflix.*

# Contents at a Glance

# Contents

# About the Author

**John Ciliberti** is a principal software engineer at Express Scripts. He has 16 years of professional experience in software engineering and architecture. After four years at Express Scripts, seven years with KPMG's Enterprise Architecture practice, and five years of solutions architecture consulting, he has acquired strong business and communications skills backed up by a broad range of technical knowledge. He specializes in machine learning, enterprise architecture, and web application development technologies.

# About the Technical Reviewer

**Damien Foggon** is technical director and lead developer for Thing-E Ltd., a company specializing in the development of dynamic web solutions for the education sector. He was responsible for the development of several ASP and ColdFusion web sites, and he's now in the process of moving most of them to ASP.NET. In addition to coauthoring *Beginning ASP.NET 4.5 Databases* (Apress, 2013), Damien is a regular technical reviewer for numerous .NET books. After several false starts, he's busy assembling his personal site.

# Acknowledgments

I would like to thank my family, especially my wife Kathy for her endless patience; my kids, Katrina and Maria; and everyone else in my life who helped me to complete this project.

# Introduction

ASP.NET Core is the biggest change in the Microsoft web development ecosystem since the introduction of ASP.NET in 2002. ASP.NET Core is not an incremental upgrade to ASP.NET MVC. ASP.NET Core is a rewrite of the entire ASP.NET platform from the ground up. ASP.NET Core is a modular, cross-platform, open source, high-performance, Internet-scale framework designed for full-stack developers. ASP.NET Core can easily be used in tandem with advanced front-end development workflows such as those needed to develop single-page web applications using frameworks such as React and Angular 4.

The journey to ASP.NET Core has been a long one. I first started writing this book in June 2014 shortly after the first community technology preview (CTP) of ASP.NET Core was released. Over the next few years the contents of this book evolved along with the evolution of ASP.NET Core. Some chapters had to be rewritten several times because of the constant steam of breaking changes that came with each preproduction release. Writing this book so early in the development process of ASP.NET Core forced me to peer deeper into the framework and in some cases become directly involved in finding and correcting design issues and defects in ASP.NET Core.

ASP.NET Core was the first version of ASP.NET to be developed out in the open with full participation from the community. This openness allowed the community not only to witness the development but also to contribute and shape its direction. Since ASP.NET Core is open source, you can understand the inner workings of the framework better than ever before.

In many recipes, after showing how to use a feature of ASP.NET Core, I include pointers and explanations of the ASP.NET Core source code on GitHub. This allows you to learn how to solve the development problem discussed in the recipe as well as truly understand how the solution works.

You can find the source code for this book on GitHub at `https://github.com/johnciliberti/AspNetCoreRecipes`.

The GitHub repository will be continuously updated as ASP.NET Core evolves. The code for the examples in this book will remain in the master branch of the repository. Updates to the source code in response to changes in ASP.NET Core will be placed into new branches. If you have questions or find issues with any of the examples in this book, please reach out to me on GitHub by posting an issue on the repository. You can find information on how to set up Git and download the source code in the appendix of this book.

# CHAPTER 1

■ ■ ■

# ASP.NET Core MVC Fundamentals

ASP.NET Core MVC is a cross-platform, open source development framework for building web applications and services using the Model View Controller (MVC) pattern. It is a successor to several legacy Microsoft web development frameworks and merges the functionality previously found in ASP.NET MVC, ASP.NET Web Pages, and ASP.NET Web API in a single modular framework. ASP.NET Core MVC offers orders of magnitude better performance than legacy ASP.NET and can be deployed almost anywhere including Windows Server, Microsoft Azure, Linux, and macOS. It also has built-in tooling that simplifies packaging ASP.NET Core MVC applications for use with container architectures such Docker and Pivotal Cloud Foundry.

This chapter contains a series of recipes that will help you master the fundamentals of ASP.NET Core MVC development. The recipes in this chapter are primarily intended for people who are new to ASP.NET Core MVC. This includes people who are new to development in general, as well as those who are experienced developers but are not familiar with ASP.NET Core MVC. It will also discuss the new features and benefits of ASP.NET Core MVC, including POCO controllers and view components.

This chapter covers the basic theory and patterns used in ASP.NET Core MVC and goes over the technical architecture of ASP.NET Core MVC.

These recipes are less practical than the recipes in the rest of the book, but they do teach foundational knowledge that will help you understand more complex recipes presented in other chapters. The recipes in Chapter 1 are also designed to help you gain insights that will aid in root-cause analysis and troubleshooting.

The code examples for this chapter are available from the Apress web site as well as on GitHub in the following repository:

```
https://github.com/johnciliberti/AspNetCoreRecipes/tree/master/Chapter01
```

## 1-1. Understanding the Microsoft Web Development Ecosystem

### Problem

You are new to the Microsoft platform and need to know how to get started. You are confused by the myriad of product offerings. You are interested in using ASP.NET Core MVC because of its use of proven development patterns and support for automated testing but are unsure of how it relates to other Microsoft web developer products including WebMatrix, LightSwitch, ASP.NET Web Forms, and Silverlight. You want to understand all these tools and determine whether you should focus on ASP.NET Core MVC alone or become familiar with the rest of the product stack as well.

© John Ciliberti 2017

J. Ciliberti, *ASP.NET Core Recipes*, DOI 10.1007/978-1-4842-0427-6_1

# Solution

Microsoft offers several products and frameworks for developing web applications. Before getting started with ASP.NET Core MVC, it is helpful to have a general understanding of the available development platforms, productivity suites, and programming frameworks and how ASP.NET Core MVC fits into the ecosystem.

In general, ASP.NET Core MVC is the best fit for developers looking to build scalable, modern, standards-based web applications. ASP.NET Core MVC makes it easier to write robust testable code and allows complete control of client-side HTML. In addition, ASP.NET Core MVC has a new project format and new build process that make it easier to use in conjunction with modern front-end application frameworks such as Angular and React.js.

ASP.NET Web Forms, on the other hand, is still a popular framework that trades some of the flexibility of ASP.NET Core MVC for developer productivity by hiding the details of HTML and JavaScript behind a suite of built-in user interface (UI) components that can be dragged and dropped into a design surface. ASP.NET Web Forms was designed to be easy to learn for developers transitioning from Visual Basic and uses similar development workflows such as double-clicking a button to create an event handler.

# How It Works

The Microsoft web development ecosystem consists of not only frameworks such as ASP.NET Core MVC but also server operating systems, highly scalable web servers, and powerful feature-rich development tools, all of which I discuss next.

## Microsoft Application Hosting Platforms

Microsoft has several platforms for hosting applications including Windows Server and Microsoft Azure. Windows Server is typically used for traditional deployments in corporate datacenters. This option offers a great amount of flexibility but is usually more expensive to scale and maintain. Microsoft Azure is a platform as a service (PaaS) that allows you to host your application in the Microsoft Cloud. With Azure, you can quickly deploy your application and scale up and down as needed. A drawback of the PaaS solution is that you do not have direct control over the server operating system, which can limit your ability to deploy some applications.

While Windows Server and Microsoft Azure are good choices for hosting your application, they are not required for running ASP.NET Core MVC applications. ASP.NET Core MVC has been designed so that it can be deployed on many platforms including Linux and Docker.

Windows Server and Internet Information Services (IIS) are required for legacy ASP.NET applications and ASP.NET Core MVC applications that rely on the full Windows Server distributions of the .NET Framework. Full versions of the .NET Framework for Windows Server and Desktop, such as .NET Framework 4.6, contain not only web application components but also components used for Windows desktop applications. If you are porting an existing ASP.NET application to ASP.NET Core MVC, you will likely still need to deploy your application on Windows Server.

## Microsoft Web Development Platforms and Frameworks

Since the late 1990s, Microsoft has created several web development platforms and frameworks. Some of these, such as the first-generation Active Server Pages and ASP.NET, are shipped with Windows Server and can be enabled from Server Manager and run on IIS, Microsoft's web server. Others, such as Web Matrix, can be installed using the Microsoft Web Platform Installer. These tools and platforms are discussed in subsequent sections.

## First-Generation Active Server Pages

Active Server Pages (ASP) was a Microsoft web development framework released in 1998 as part of the Windows NT 4.0 Option Pack. It was extremely successful, and even though it has been superseded by ASP.NET, it continues to power hundreds of thousands of web sites. It can still be installed in all versions of Windows Server, including Windows Server 2016.

ASP was also implemented on UNIX and Linux systems by ChiliSoft (later acquired by Sun and now part of Oracle).

The popularity of ASP was driven by the fact that it was simple and easy to learn. It allowed developers to use either VBScript or JavaScript as the programming language.

A major criticism of ASP was that it mixed business logic with presentation and often led to applications that became impossible to maintain. It was also difficult to debug. Many teams attempted to remedy ASP's shortcomings by putting the business logic into COM components written in C++ or VB. This practice was later officially recommended by Microsoft in what was called Windows DNA.

Ultimately, the rise of Java technologies and the growing complexity of business requirements led to the development of Microsoft .NET and ASP.NET, which replaced ASP.

Although ASP is still officially supported on the Windows Server platform, I do not recommend using it for new projects.

## ASP.NET Web Forms

ASP.NET Web Forms, which was first released in 2002, is now in its tenth major release, starting with ASP.NET 1.0 and moving through 4.6.2 in 2016. ASP.NET Web Forms is not supported in ASP.NET Core MVC. ASP.NET Web Forms has been the primary web development technology used on the Microsoft platform for more than a decade. Web Forms abstracts the Web and uses a programming model that is similar to programming Windows Forms and Visual Basic. It follows a model where a developer designs a screen by dragging controls such as text boxes and drop-down lists to the design surface and then double-clicking the control to create an event handler on a code-behind page. For example, double-clicking a button would create an OnClick event handler where you would put your code to be executed when the button was clicked.

Web Forms was designed to be easy to learn for Visual Basic programmers looking to transition from client-server programming to web applications. It also saved developers time with features such as form validation controls and web site security.

The main drawback of ASP.NET Web Forms is that its design assumed that most UI manipulations would result in a full round-trip to the server. Microsoft remedied this with some success in 2008 with the release of ASP.NET Ajax, but developers who attempt to create rich UIs might find themselves fighting the framework.

Web Forms might still be ideal for teams that need to rapidly put together a small application that does not need a highly sophisticated UI.

## ASP.NET MVC

ASP.NET MVC was first released in March 2009. It provided a Model View Controller–based approach to developing web applications on the Microsoft ASP.NET platform. The Model View Controller pattern is well suited for enterprise applications because it decouples application components and makes it easier to write unit tests that can be executed independently.

Early versions of ASP.NET MVC shared common infrastructure with ASP.NET Web Forms. As ASP.NET MVC evolved, it became increasingly decoupled from core ASP.NET and was eventually factored out into a stand-alone library distributed independently of ASP.NET.

ASP.NET MVC requires that the developer invest time into understanding the MVC pattern (see recipe 1-2). Compared to some of Microsoft's other frameworks, ASP.NET MVC might not be as easy for inexperienced developers to learn.

ASP.NET MVC has been replaced by ASP.NET Core MVC.

## ASP.NET Web API

ASP.NET Web API was introduced in 2012. ASP.NET Web API simplified the creation of REST-based APIs using the MVC pattern. Web API can be used in conjunction with ASP.NET MVC and front-end libraries such as Angular to simplify the development of Ajax-driven, rich end-user experiences. ASP.NET Web API is no longer distributed as a separate library. It is now part of ASP.NET Core MVC.

## ASP.NET Web Pages

The functionality of ASP.NET Web Pages has now been merged into ASP.NET Core MVC. Before the merger, ASP.NET Web Pages was a simple web development framework that provided a mechanism for creating custom web applications with the WebMatrix integrated development environment (IDE). It shared some underpinnings with ASP.NET MVC, including page routing and the Razor view engine.

## ASP.NET SignalR

ASP.NET SignalR is a framework built on top of ASP.NET Core that makes it easier to create applications that feature bidirectional communication between the web browser and the server. SignalR can automatically detect the capabilities of the web browser and select the best communication pattern. For users accessing your application using a modern web browser, SignalR can use the W3C-standard Web Sockets protocol. For older browsers, it will fall back to another method such as long polling.

A common example use case for SignalR is creating a web browser–based chat application.

## LightSwitch

LightSwitch is a rapid application development (RAD) tool that simplifies the creation of data entry–centric applications. The initial release of LightSwitch used Silverlight to create the end-user experience. It exploited Silverlight's rich data-binding capabilities to create data-driven applications with minimal or no coding. LightSwitch applications can be run either as browser Silverlight applications or as out-of-browser applications that run on the desktop. The latest version supports project output in HTML5 as well as Silverlight.

LightSwitch is a good solution for simple applications. It has several major limitations, such as the inability to support forms that need to update data from multiple database tables. These limitations prevent it from being used for anything other than simple applications that act as front ends to a database.

## Silverlight

Silverlight is a rich Internet application (RIA) tool that competes with the Adobe Flash plug-in. It is used primarily for creating rich media streaming experiences by web sites such as Netflix.

Even though Microsoft has pledged to continue supporting Silverlight until 2021, Microsoft's RIA strategy has shifted to HTML5. Silverlight still has some advantages over HTML, such as the ability to run on legacy enterprise desktops that have standardized on browsers such as Internet Explorer 8, which does not support HTML5 and has poor JavaScript performance. It also is superior to HTML5 in that it can deliver richer streaming experiences with an extensible media codec framework. Silverlight can run outside the browser and be granted permission to access the local file system.

You should avoid using Silverlight for new applications. If possible, you should either opt for a single-page web (SPA) application built using a combination of ASP.NET Core MVC and a front-end library such as React.js or consider using a native Windows desktop technology such as Windows Presentation Foundation (WPF).

## SharePoint

SharePoint is one of Microsoft's most successful products. It provides a portal that teams can use to share files and has document and records management capabilities. It also offers the ability for end users to create simple applications, including simple forms and workflows, using nothing but a web browser. Advanced users can use SharePoint Designer to create more advanced forms and workflows.

The underpinnings of SharePoint are ASP.NET Web Forms, Windows Workflow Foundation, and other Microsoft technologies. SharePoint is very extensible, and there are many places for developers to add customized functionality.

Some corporations have adopted SharePoint as an application platform where many teams can deploy their custom solutions onto a shared SharePoint infrastructure. In many cases, the value-added functionality of SharePoint can dramatically reduce the amount of code that is required to create the solution.

There are several drawbacks to using SharePoint as a development platform. The largest is the overall complexity of the product. Tracking down bugs and performance problems in a SharePoint application can be extremely painful. In other cases, adding what would be trivial functionality in other Microsoft web technologies would require weeks of pasting globally unique identifiers (GUIDs) into 900-line XML files and having to reset IIS every time you make a minor change.

SharePoint can be a powerful tool, but be sure to have a firm understanding of SharePoint development before selecting it as a development platform. Also, be certain that your application is using enough native SharePoint functionality to offset the complexity of development in the SharePoint ecosystem.

Starting with Office 2013, which included SharePoint 2013 and Office 365, Microsoft has created a new application mode, which simplifies the development experience by allowing you to use HTML, JavaScript, and Cascading Style Sheets (CSS) to create your front end, and to use C#, PHP, and VB.NET to create server-side code. The new framework supports RESTful APIs, which allow you to develop your service using the platform of your choice and then use the Office JavaScript API to create a UI to consume your service.

## ASP.NET Core MVC

ASP.NET Core MVC shares many of the same programming constructs as ASP.NET MVC classic but has been rewritten from the ground up on top of Core CLR. It is more lightweight and significantly faster than ASP.NET MVC classic. Benchmarks conducted by the ASP.NET team have shown that ASP.NET Core can process more than 1.15 million requests per second with 12.6Gbps throughput. This is a 2,300 percent improvement over ASP.NET 4.6.

# Microsoft Web Development Tools

Microsoft has several tools available for creating web applications. Figure 1-1 shows the major Microsoft web development tools and the targeted audience for each. The tools listed on the left side of Figure 1-1 were designed for a broader audience, which includes relatively nontechnical business power users. The tools on the right side were designed for professional developers and architects.

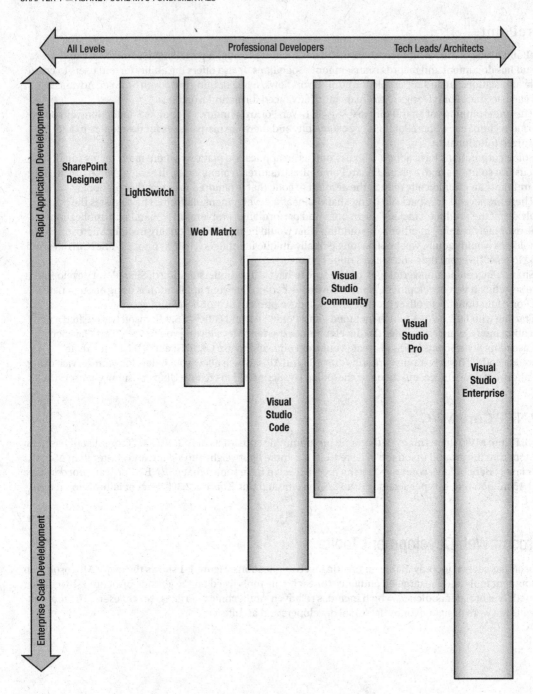

*Figure 1-1. Microsoft web development tools matrix*

Figure 1-1 also makes a distinction between RAD and enterprise-scale development. On the RAD side, the tools are optimized to quickly develop a solution but are less optimized for creating highly scalable, reliable, and maintainable applications. There are many situations in which a RAD tool is "good enough." For example, you have a customer who wants to build a web site for his small business; in addition to his marketing capital, he would like a way to collect some customer information on his web site. In this case, tools like WebMatrix are a good fit. On the other hand, if you are developing a trading floor application for a major brokerage firm, you would want to use the more robust tool set offered by Visual Studio. The Visual Studio products span the entire vertical axis of Figure 1-1 because they allow developers to target the entire Microsoft stack.

Table 1-1 describes the various tools from Microsoft that can be used for web development and the pricing of each product at the time of this writing.

*Table 1-1.* *Microsoft Web Development Tools*

| Tool | Description | Price (December 2016) |
| --- | --- | --- |
| SharePoint Designer | SharePoint Designer is a free addition to Microsoft Office. It allows power users to build and enhance web sites hosted in Microsoft SharePoint. Users can create and customize SharePoint lists, create InfoPath Forms, and create workflows. They may also alter the look and feel of the SharePoint sites. | Free with Microsoft Office |
| | With this tool, a SharePoint power user can create somewhat sophisticated departmental-scale applications without needing to write code. Advanced users who understand some basic HTML programming can create interesting user experiences. | |
| | There are several limitations that prevent SharePoint Designer from being a true enterprise development tool.<br><br>• It does not really support the concept of environment propagation. It is possible to export a SharePoint .stp file and then publish that file to another environment, but it is not a completely reliable method because the .stp file may have external dependencies not available on the target site.<br>• It does not support source control systems.<br>• It cannot unit test workflows.<br>• It is limited in flexibility and has no mechanism for writing custom code. | |

*(continued)*

***Table 1-1.*** (*continued*)

| Tool | Description | Price (December 2016) |
|---|---|---|
| Expression Blend | Expression Blend was initially developed as a stand-alone tool for creating XAML-based Silverlight, WPF, and Windows Phone applications. It is now included with Visual Studio and no longer offered separately. | Free with Visual Studio 2017 |
| | Expression Blend 5 also allows you to create touch-friendly HTML5 applications that run as full-screen native applications on Windows 8. It does not allow you to create HTML5 applications that target web browsers. | |
| | For web developers, Expression Blend is useful for creating the UI of Silverlight applications, usually in conjunction with Visual Studio. | |
| LightSwitch | LightSwitch is a RAD-based tool that can be used to create applications in Microsoft Silverlight and HTML5. It exploits Silverlight's rich data-binding capabilities to create data-driven applications with minimal or no coding. LightSwitch Silverlight applications can be run either as in-browser applications or as out-of-browser applications that run on the desktop. | Included with all versions of Visual Studio 2017 |
| | HTML5 support for LightSwitch was added with Visual Studio 2013 and, at the time of this writing, was not as robust as the support for Silverlight. | |
| | LightSwitch is a good solution for simple applications. It has several major limitations, such as the inability to support forms that need to update data from multiple database tables, which would prevent it from being used for anything other than trivial applications. | |
| WebMatrix | WebMatrix is an IDE introduced in 2011 as a lightweight alternative to Visual Studio. It is integrated with the Web Platform Installer. It allows developers to select an open source application from a gallery and use that as the starting point for the application. The WebMatrix IDE is available for free at http://bit.ly/1tRFgMv. | Free |
| | Microsoft has ended support for WebMatrix in November 2016. If you are still using it, you should consider moving to Visual Studio Community or Visual Studio Code. | |

(*continued*)

*Table 1-1.* (*continued*)

| Tool | Description | Price (December 2016) |
| --- | --- | --- |
| Visual Studio Community | Prior to Visual Studio 2017, Microsoft offered several free Express editions of Visual Studio. Each of the Express editions offered a subset of functionality. For example, Visual Studio Express for Web provided tools for web development.<br><br>In 2017 Microsoft discontinued the Express editions, and Visual Studio Community is now the only free edition of the Visual Studio IDE. Visual Studio Community offers a feature set like Visual Studio Professional but is free for students and independent developers.<br><br>Visual Studio Community's licensing does not allow it to be used in the enterprise. | Free |
| Visual Studio | There are three commercial versions of Visual Studio 2017. They can be purchased as a cloud subscription or a standard subscription. The cloud version gives you IDE, Team Services Access, and Team Foundation Server access. The standard version provides a perpetual software license that never expires and includes training and access to additional Microsoft products through MSDN for one year.<br><br>• *Test Professional*: Manual testing tools, Team Foundation Server support, collaboration tools, lab management, and $50 of Windows Azure cloud services per month.<br><br>• *Professional*: Platform development support including tools for Windows, Windows Server, and SQL Server. It also offers Microsoft Office, Dynamics, and other Microsoft Server development support, advanced testing and diagnostics tools, code clone, basic architecture modeling tools, PowerPoint storyboarding, release management, and $50 Windows Azure cloud services credits per month.<br><br>• *Enterprise*: Includes all the Professional features plus additional architecture and modeling tools, load testing, web performance testing, IntelliTrace features, and $150 worth of Windows Azure cloud service credits per month.<br><br>A full feature comparison can be found at http://bit.ly/1oD2V1r.<br><br>Apart from Community, all versions of Visual Studio are packaged with MSDN subscriptions. MSDN subscriptions give you access to a large percentage of the Microsoft product catalog, including servers such as SQL Server and SharePoint, operating systems, and desktop software.<br><br>A comparison of different MSDN subscription levels can be downloaded from http://bit.ly/1tRGwzh. | Professional Cloud: $539 per year<br><br>Professional Standard: $1,199 per year<br><br>Enterprise Cloud: $2,999 per year<br><br>Enterprise Standard: $5,999 per year<br><br>Test Professional Cloud: $539 per year<br><br>Test Professional Standard: $1,199 per year |

After reviewing Table 1-1, you can see that Microsoft has a large variety of tools available at many different price points. Most of the examples in this book work in all versions of Visual Studio 2017, including Visual Studio Community.

## Understanding the Variations of the Microsoft .NET Framework

First released in early 2002, the Microsoft .NET Framework has fragmented into many different implementations. Variations of .NET include the following:

- *Microsoft .NET Framework*: This is the full version of .NET Framework for Windows and Windows Server. This version is used for creating most desktop and web applications that run on Windows.

- *.NET Compact Framework*: This is intended for use on Windows CE and early versions of Windows Mobile. It implements a limited number of APIs.

- *Silverlight*: .NET for Silverlight is used for creating rich Internet applications and sandboxed desktop applications. It contained a subset of common .NET APIs but also implemented libraries unique to Silverlight.

- *Windows Phone Silverlight*: Like Silverlight, but contains a specialized set of APIs for Windows Phone.

- *Windows Phone*: .NET for Windows Phone 8 contains another set of APIs targeting Microsoft's phone platform but was largely incompatible with Windows Phone Silverlight.

- *Universal Windows Platform*: Introduced with Windows 10, the Universal Windows Platform supports a wide variety of Windows devices including PC, Phone, Xbox One, and HoloLens. It is compatible only with Windows 10.

- *Mono*: This is an open source implementation of .NET based on the ECMA-335 standard. Before .NET Core, Mono was the only implementation of .NET that ran on Linux and macOS.

- *Mono/Xamarin Platform*: This is a fork of the Mono framework used to allow developers to build iOS and Android applications using .NET. Xamarin was acquired by Microsoft in 2016.

- *.NET Core*: This is a new cross-platform open source implementation of .NET created by Microsoft. ASP.NET Core MVC is built on top of .NET Core. .NET Core 1.0, released in 2015, implemented only a small subset of the APIs exposed in the full framework but is rapidly being developed. .NET Core 2.0, expected to be released in 2017, will implement almost all major .NET APIs.

Each variation of the framework shares common design principles and language features but lacks consistency in APIs. This makes it difficult to port an application across the various platforms that support .NET. It usually requires the developer to implement some sort of cross-compilation strategy and often leads to duplication of efforts.

To combat this fragmentation, Microsoft has begun implementation of two major initiatives, .NET Core and the .NET Standard. .NET Core is a new open source, cross-platform implementation of .NET, which, as it matures, will likely replace most versions of the .NET base class libraries. The .NET Standard is a set of APIs that all versions of .NET should implement. This will allow developers to share code and use the same APIs regardless of which platform they target.

If you want to learn more about the .NET Standard, David Fowl has an excellent post at `http://bit.ly/2gfZhbz` that shows the features implemented in each version of the standard. He also shows what variants of the .NET are compatible with each version of the standard. I also recommend reading the MSDN blog post on the .NET Standard at `https://blogs.msdn.microsoft.com/dotnet/2016/09/26/introducing-net-standard/`.

# 1-2. Understanding the MVC Pattern

## Problem

You want to begin working with ASP.NET Core MVC, but you do not understand the MVC pattern and why it is beneficial.

## Solution

The MVC pattern is a popular design pattern used in many software systems. The pattern was first documented in 1978 by Trygve Reenskaug in regard to a project at Xerox PARC in which the MVC pattern was implemented for the Smalltalk-80 class library. MVC separates a software module into three distinct layers, each with a specific role (see Figure 1-2):

- *Model*: Models represent data. A model can be a single object or a complex type with many collections of objects within it. The model should not include implementation details. A model may have many associated views.

- *View*: The view typically represents a UI component that is bound to a model. The view can display the data and allow a user to modify the data. The view should always reflect the state of the model.

- *Controller*: The controller provides a mechanism for the user to interact with a system by defining how the UI reacts to user input. It is responsible for exchanging and interpreting messages between the view and the model.

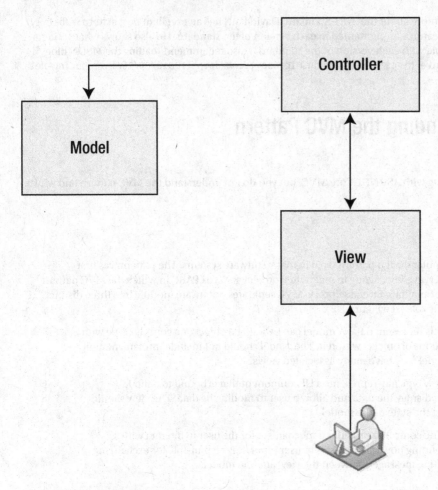

**Figure 1-2.** *Model View Controller pattern*

## How It Works

In addition to defining the layers, the MVC pattern provides rules on how the layers are allowed to communicate.

The allowed communication patterns include the following rules:

- Users may interact with a view.

- Views may interact with controllers.

- Controllers may interact with views.

- Controllers may communicate with other controllers.

- Controllers may communicate with the model.

The restricted communication patterns include the following rules:

- Users may not interact directly with controllers.

- Users may not interact directly with a model.

- Views may not interact directly with other views.

- Views may not directly modify the model.

- Models may not modify other models.

# Benefits of the MVC Design Pattern

If this is your first time reading about the MVC pattern, you might be saying to yourself, "Why bother with this approach? It seems like a lot of extra work."

The first benefit is that your view and model are decoupled. This means you can have many views associated with a given model. For example, with one model, you may have a separate view for each create, read, update, delete (CRUD) operation.

- A read-only view that displays the record but does not allow it to be changed

- A view for creating new records

- A view for modifying a record

Visual Studio has built-in features that simplify creating applications that follow the MVC pattern. By using the scaffolding features in Visual Studio, you can generate views based on a model class or Entity Data Model.

In addition to your standard CRUD views, you might want to create views that target specific devices. Perhaps you may need another view that returns the data as an Excel spreadsheet or a mobile view designed to run on a smartphone. In addition to views created for humans, you can also provide views that are accessed by other applications or client-side scripts.

The second main advantage is the view/controller decoupling. This allows you to change the way an application responds to user input without changing the view. It also allows the UI (the view) to be changed without changing the way the application responds to user input. In web applications, the UI will likely change more often than the business rules. By keeping the controller logic separate from the presentation, you can reshuffle your page layouts as often as your customer requires, without inadvertently breaking your business logic.

Another advantage of using the MVC pattern is that separating concerns allows different team members to focus on the part of the application that best aligns with their respective skill sets. For example, very few people both possess the skills for creating an attractive front-end interface using HTML and CSS and know the intricacies of C# programming. It also allows team members to simultaneously work on their respective parts of the page, as the code and the presentation are in different files. For the team that engages in test-driven development, the MVC pattern lends itself well to creating automated unit tests.

## Other Technologies That Use the MVC Pattern

ASP.NET Core MVC is not the only product that uses the MVC pattern, and it is not the first web development framework to utilize it. There are thousands of frameworks and applications that implement the MVC pattern. The following list describes several of the most popular frameworks that use the MVC pattern:

- *Apple iOS Development*: If you plan on creating a native application for the iPhone or iPad using Apple Xcode, you need to implement the MVC pattern. Xcode employs a drag-and-drop interface that allows you to define the various UI components and then drag a connector to the controller to define its relationship to the view.

- *Apache Struts*: First released in May 2000, Apache Struts is an open source framework that extends the Java Servlet API for creating Java Enterprise Edition web applications. Struts is probably the most mature MVC-based application framework. It has been used on thousands of enterprise-scale applications at Fortune 500 companies.

- *Spring Framework*: Spring is another Java framework that features an MVC framework in addition to its inversion of control (IoC) container and aspect-oriented programming features. The Spring Framework's MVC Framework was created to address architectural deficiencies in Apache Struts by providing better separation between the MVC layers.

- *Yii*: The Yii framework is one of the most popular PHP frameworks. It is noted for being fast, secure, and well-documented. The framework has a web-based code generator that turns a database table into a model class. The code generator will also generate PHP code to perform CRUD operations that follow the MVC pattern. You can then modify the generated code to meet your needs.

- *Ember.js*: Ember.js is a JavaScript MVC framework and templating engine. It has support for UI bindings, has support for composed views, provides a web presentation layer, and plays nicely with other JavaScript libraries. Ember can be used in conjunction with a server-side MVC framework to extend the MVC benefits to the ever-increasing complexity of the modern web application presentation tier.

- *Ruby on Rails*: Ruby on Rails is a popular MVC web development framework used by thousands of web sites. In Rails, the model is implemented as the `ActiveRecord` that maintains the relationship between the model and the database. Ruby method names are generated automatically based on the field names in the database. The view is implemented by the `ActionView` library and the `ActionController` subsystem that implements the controller. Much of the Microsoft MVC framework was inspired by Ruby on Rails, including its dynamic data scaffolding technology. In Rails, scaffolding generates major pieces of the application based on a model definition that includes the model class, forms, CSS style sheets, and tests.

# 1-3. Understanding the Differences Between MVC, MVVM, and MVP

## Problem

In addition to the MVC pattern, you often hear a lot about Model View ViewModel (MVVM) and Model View Presenter (MVP) patterns, but you are confused about the differences between them and where they should be applied.

# Solution

The three patterns—MVC, MVVM, and MVP—have many similarities but also are very different. All three patterns have an underlying goal, which is to separate the view from the model. All three patterns contain the concepts of the model and the view. The main difference between the patterns is the way changes are propagated between the view and the model. The view model, the presenter, and the controller all share the responsibility of communicating state changes between the view and the model, but they employ a different mechanism to do it.

# How It Works

I discuss each of the three patterns and how they work in the following sections.

## The MVC Pattern

In the Model View Controller pattern, events fired in the view result in actions being called on the controller. In ASP.NET Core MVC, this is implemented by HTTP requests routed to the appropriate controller by the ASP.NET request routing subsystem. Each unique URL is mapped to a special method in the controller, known as an *action*. Inside the action method, the view data is processed, and the model is updated. MVC controllers also have the additional responsibility of determining which view should be displayed.

## The MVP Pattern

In the Model View Presenter pattern, the controller has been replaced by the presenter. The presenter is similar to the controller in that it is the only entity that should manipulate the model. Presenters differ from the controllers in three ways.

- They do not play the role of the traffic cop as controllers do but instead are instantiated by a view.

- The view and the presenter are completely decoupled and communicate by way of an interface.

- The presenter handles all UI events on behalf of the view.

The MVP pattern is commonly used by enterprise ASP.NET Web Forms developers who need to create automated unit tests for their code-behind pages but do not want to run the tests inside a web server process. By modeling the properties and events defined in the Web Forms page into an interface, a mock implementation of the page can be used when running unit tests. Figure 1-3 shows a conceptual diagram of the MVP pattern implemented in an ASP.NET Web Forms application.

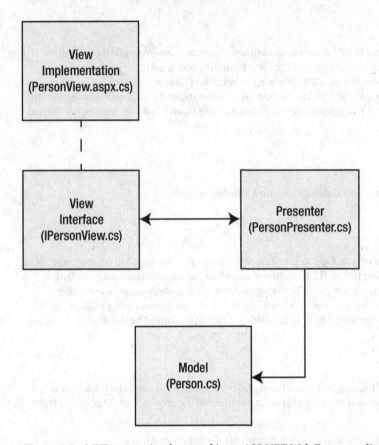

*Figure 1-3.* *MVP pattern implemented in an ASP.NET Web Forms application*

## The MVVM Pattern

In the Model View View Model pattern, two-way data binding is used to communicate state changes in the view to the view model. Many UI frameworks, such as Windows Presentation Foundation (WPF), Silverlight, and Knockout.js, employ a concept called *data binding* that use declarative syntax to bind data to a user interface. In application frameworks, such as WPF and Silverlight, this is done by setting the view model as the data context on the view. Because the data binding is bidirectional, when the view model's data is changed, the updated value is automatically propagated to the view, and changes to the view are automatically propagated to the view model.

The view model is a special model that typically contains properties for each user interface element. This differs from the model that abstracts a pure data entity and does not contain properties related to user interface components.

The view model typically uses the Observer pattern, in which an event is fired every time an exposed property is modified, notifying subscribers that a change has occurred. This allows the user interface to be updated automatically each time the view model changes.

The main advantage of this pattern is that it eliminates the need to explicitly write code such as `PersonNameTextbox.Text = myViewModel.Person.Name` to update the UI with data from the view model. It also removes the necessity of writing code such as `myViewModel.Person.Name = PersonNameTextBox.Text` to update the model with changes made by the end user in the view.

# 1-4. Discovering the Features of ASP.NET Core MVC

## Problem

You are an ASP.NET MVC developer looking to adopt ASP.NET Core MVC. You want to understand what new features and enhancements exist in the new framework over ASP.NET MVC. You also want to know whether there are breaking changes in the new version.

## Solution

The entire Microsoft development stack, which includes the Microsoft .NET Framework, ASP.NET, and ASP.NET MVC, has undergone a substantial architectural transformation. ASP.NET and ASP.NET MVC have been rewritten from the ground up. The changes can be broadly grouped into five major categories.

- *Performance:* ASP.NET Core and ASP.NET Core MVC are highly modularized. This design allows you to explicitly customize what framework components are deployed with your application. This makes your application start up faster and requires less memory. It also has been optimized to use asynchronous programing that eliminates most blocking I/O. Benchmarks show that ASP.NET Core MVC is many orders of magnitude faster than ASP.NET 4.6. A deep dive into the new architecture can be found in recipe 1-5.

- *Deployment:* ASP.NET Core is cross-platform. It can be deployed on Windows, macOS, and all major Linux distributions including Red Hat Enterprise Linux, Debian, openSUSE, Centos, and Ubuntu.

- *Consolidation:* There is one development platform for both cloud and on-premises deployments. ASP.NET MVC, ASP.NET Web API, and ASP.NET Web Pages have been consolidated into a single framework, and all redundant capabilities have been removed.

- *.NET compilation services:* .NET Compiler Platform (code name Roslyn) compiles your application automatically every time it is changed. The compilation occurs so rapidly that you are able to save your changes and then refresh your browser and almost instantly see the results of your change. This provides a no-compile developer experience without losing the performance benefits of compiled code.

- *New functionality:* In addition to the architectural changes, several new capabilities have been added, including simplified route mapping syntax, POCO controllers, view components, Tag Helpers, and simplified claims-based authorization.

It should be noted that since ASP.NET Core is a new platform, direct upgrades of projects created in ASP.NET MVC, which includes ASP.NET MVC 5, are not supported. However, since many of the code constructs and patterns of ASP.NET MVC have been ported to ASP.NET Core MVC, most of your existing code will be compatible.

## How It Works

In this section I provide a brief description of each of the features of ASP.NET Core MVC that did not exist in ASP.NET MVC 5. Detailed explanations and examples of how you can use these features can be found in Chapter 5.

# Performance

Performance is possibly the most significant advantage of ASP.NET Core MVC. Microsoft has invested heavily in optimizing not only ASP.NET Core but also the runtime engine that ASP.NET Core is built on top of, the CoreCLR. ASP.NET Core has a new request pipeline and a high-speed lightweight HTTP engine that can be used instead of IIS. The Techempower.com benchmarks rank ASP.NET Core the fastest of the major frameworks for HTTP request routing. In Techempower.com's round 13 test, ASP.NET Core was able to handle more than 1.8 million requests per second from a single server. This was an 85,900 percent improvement over a previous benchmark. To learn more about these benchmarks, you can visit the following web sites:

- *Techempower.com Blog*: http://bit.ly/2gqjqMn

- *ASP.NET Core Benchmark GitHub*: http://bit.ly/2glHC4O

# Deployment

ASP.NET Core MVC is built on the foundation of a new version of the Microsoft .NET Framework known as the .NET Core runtime or CoreCLR. CoreCLR allows you to have a very fine level of control over what components are deployed with your application. It also allows you to deploy your application on many different hosts and even other operating systems such as Linux. These changes can make your application 100 percent self-contained with no dependencies outside of your application's bin folder.

In the past, deploying an ASP.NET MVC application meant that you needed to deploy not only your application code but also the full version of the .NET Framework that your application depended on, the full ASP.NET stack, and the entire ASP.NET MVC framework. In addition, deploying an ASP.NET MVC application usually required that you use IIS on Windows Server. This was problematic in cases where you did not have full administrative control over your deployment environment or when deploying to a multitenant infrastructure such as GoDaddy. In many cases, this limited your ability to adopt the latest and greatest versions of ASP.NET and MVC until your IT department or hosting provider offered official support. With ASP.NET Core MVC, this is no longer the case. You as the developer have now been empowered to use whatever version of ASP.NET Core MVC that you require and can even deploy different versions of ASP.NET Core MVC on the same server without worrying about compatibility issues with the other applications.

To enable the flexibility and performance improvements in ASP.NET Core, many changes needed to be made to the underlying framework to break hard-linked dependencies between components and provide layers of abstraction. The architectural changes also required CoreCLR to provide a new way to resolve dependencies, a new configuration system that was not coupled with IIS or Windows, and a new way to start an application that can load the needed dependencies and configuration.

# Consolidation

Prior to ASP.NET Core MVC, ASP.NET MVC, Web API, and ASP.NET Web Pages were all different frameworks. With ASP.NET Core MVC, the three frameworks have been combined, and overlapping functionality and APIs have been eliminated.

Of these changes, perhaps the most impactful is the elimination of many of the WebAPI-specific classes and interfaces. In ASP.NET MVC 5.*x* and earlier, Web API routes were configured separately, and Web API controllers used a different base class. In ASP.NET Core MVC, this distinction has been eliminated.

Figure 1-4 and Figure 1-5 demonstrate this consolidation. In Figure 1-4 you can see that filters, dependency injection, model binding, controllers, and HTML Helpers had all been implemented independently in the three frameworks.

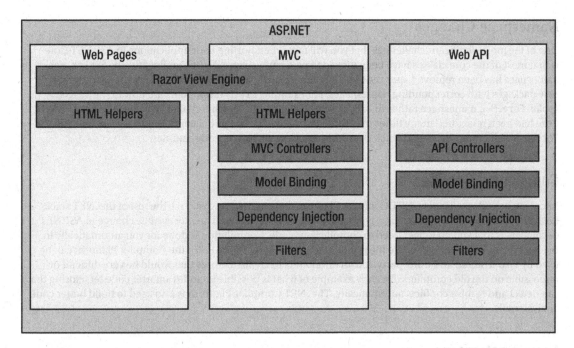

***Figure 1-4.*** *ASP.NET classic with three frameworks*

Figure 1-5 shows the components in ASP.NET Core. In the new architecture, all the components are shared in a single framework that contains the functionality of the three frameworks used in ASP.NET MVC.

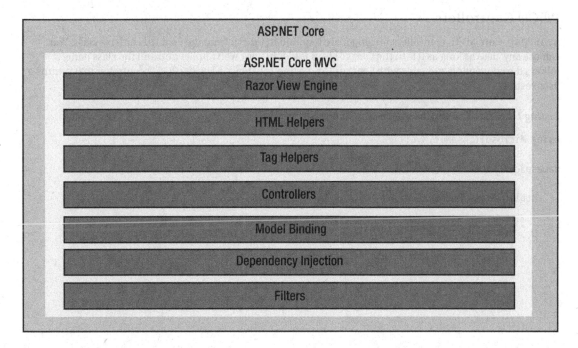

***Figure 1-5.*** *Components of ASP.NET Core*

## Namespace Changes

One of the most significant challenges that you will face when porting your applications to ASP.NET Core is that most of the core classes have been moved to new namespaces. Most significantly, the System.Web namespace has been removed, and the classes that previously were found under it have been moved to new packages with corresponding namespaces. For example, MVC components are now in the System. AspNetCore.Mvc namespace rather than System.Web.Mvc. Adding to this challenge is the fact that ASP.NET Core had been refactored many times over three years between the initial community preview and release. For this reason, many blogs and Stack Overflow pages have incorrect code samples.

## Compilation Services

Microsoft has adopted a new .NET Compiler Platform code named Roslyn. Like the rest of the .NET stack, Roslyn is open source. It enables new types of developer experiences. The most visible change to ASP.NET developers is that you no longer need to compile your code. Compilation is done for you automatically in the background each time a source file is modified. In addition, new APIs in the Compiler Platform can be used by Visual Studio and third-party add-in developers to create features that would be very difficult or impossible on the old compilers. An early example of what is possible includes smarter code refactoring that can detect and resolve conflicts automatically. The .NET Compiler Platform is also used to build better code analysis tools.

## New Functionality

In addition to the architectural changes, several new capabilities have been added, including simplified route mapping syntax, POCO controllers, view components, and Tag Helpers.

## POCO Controllers

In ASP.NET Core MVC, controllers no longer are required to inherit from the Controller base class. You can use any class as long as it is in the Controllers folder in your web application and the class name follows the convention and ends with Controller. Listing 1-1 shows a simple POCO controller that returns a JsonResult.

*Listing 1-1.* Plain Old C# Class Used as a Controller

```
using Microsoft.AspNet.Mvc;

namespace Chapter01.Controllers
{
    public class PocoController
    {
        public IActionResult Index()
        {
            return new JsonResult("{Poco:True}");
        }
    }
}
```

## View Components

View components are like child actions, which were used in earlier versions of the ASP.NET MVC framework. They can be useful for creating simple reusable components. They differ from partial views in that they are implemented as code rather than as a view page. For an example that shows how to use a view component to create a tag cloud, see recipe 5-4.

## Tag Helpers

Tag Helpers are a new feature that are like HTML Helpers in function but are easier to use. They appear in your Razor views as regular HTML tags but with one or more custom attributes added. For example, a Tag Helper that adds a form validation summary message when an incomplete form data is submitted will resemble the following code:

```
<div validation-summary="ModelOnly"></div>
```

You can find more information about Tag Helpers in Chapter 4.

## New Configuration System

.NET Core applications that include ASP.NET Core MVC no longer require `app.config` and `web.config` files. .NET Core uses a new more flexible and extensible configuration system. The new configuration system is no longer limited to a single XML-based file format. It comes with several supported file formats out of the box, including XML, JSON, and INI. In addition, it also allows your application to consume configuration information from nonfile sources such as environmental variables and command-line arguments.

---

■ **Note**    If you are planning to deploy your application to IIS, you will still need a `web.config` file for the IIS-specific settings found in `system.webServer`.

---

.NET Core's configuration system is extensible. It allows you to create your own configuration providers and sources. The .NET community has already started using this capability for creating additional providers such as YamlConfig, which can be found in NuGet. The YamlConfig package allows you to use the popular YAML Ain't Markup Language (YAML) format to configure your application.

.NET Core allows you to mix different types of configuration sources in a single application. For example, you can have some configuration information in one or more JSON files but also get configuration information from environmental variables and command-line parameters.

When creating a new ASP.NET Core project in Visual Studio, it will add a file named `appsettings.json`, as shown in Listing 1-2.

***Listing 1-2.*** appsettings.json Generated by Visual Studio

```
{
  "Logging": {
    "IncludeScopes": false,
    "LogLevel": {
      "Default": "Verbose",
      "System": "Information",
      "Microsoft": "Information"
    }
  }
}
```

In Listing 1-2 you see the new configuration information using JSON notation. The configuration controls the behavior of the Microsoft logging extensions.

## Missing Features

ASP.NET Core is a complete rewrite of ASP.NET. The level of change is analogous to when Microsoft moved from classic ASP to ASP.NET. You are seeing many new features and capabilities that were not possible in past versions. At the same time, though, not all the functionality from past versions will be available in the new release. Some of these features will become available in future releases based on community feedback, but others will be permanently discontinued. Here are some examples of missing features:

- No support for the VB programming language. Support for VB is planned in a future release.

- No support for HTTP modules directly in ASP.NET Core applications.

- Katana middleware will not be supported beyond version 3 released in August 2014.

- No support for the Web Forms view engine.

# 1-5. Understanding the Architecture of ASP.NET Core MVC

## Problem

You are new to ASP.NET Core MVC and want to know more about how it is architected, how ASP.NET Core MVC processes HTTP requests, and what extensibility points are available.

## Solution

ASP.NET Core MVC is built on the foundation of .NET Core and ASP.NET Core. .NET Core provides rich programing interfaces and compiler services. ASP.NET Core provides core HTTP processing capabilities, a flexible hosting model, security infrastructure, and request routing capabilities.

ASP.NET Core MVC adds a patterns-based programming model for creating web applications and RESTful web services. It offers several layers of abstraction that provide opportunities for extensibility and simplify the use of test-driven development (TDD) strategies.

The ASP.NET Core MVC framework architecture can be logically divided into the following components:

- *Route handlers*: These match incoming URLs with server code to execute. The routing infrastructure is part of ASP.NET Core and not the ASP.NET Core MVC framework. ASP.NET Core MVC provides a default route handler aptly named MvcRouteHandler to provide the linkage between the routing infrastructure and an ASP.NET MVC Controller class.

- *Action invokers*: These manage the execution of controller actions and filters. Whereas the route handler determines what code needs to be executed, the action invoker uses a controller factory to create an instance of the controller and then executes the correct action method and associated filters.

- *Action result*: These describe the objects returned from the action invoker and help ASP.NET Core MVC to call a rendering strategy and stream the results back to the caller.

- *View engines*: These provide mechanisms for binding data to server-side templates known as views that are typically rendered as HTML.

- *Model binders*: These provide a mechanism for tokenizing data in an HTTP request and converting it into a Common Language Runtime (CLR) type. For example, you may have a `Controller` action that expects a `Person` object and a `View` that shows a form for entering the properties of that object. A model binder automatically transforms the form data into a `Person` object. Without the model binder, you would be responsible for creating an instance of a `Person` object and then pulling the name-value pairs from the `Request` object and writing the data to the appropriate properties of your object.

- *Filters*: These contain shared functionality such as authentication, authorization, and exception-handling logic. The ASP.NET Core MVC framework offers several types of filters that can be executed before and after the controller action.

- *HTML Helpers and Tag Helpers*: These can be used inside views to encapsulate view logic. The ASP.NET Core MVC framework comes with many useful HTML and Tag Helpers and allows you to create custom helpers.

The ASP.NET Core MVC framework offers default implementations for each of these components but also allows any of them to be replaced or used in conjunction with alternative implementations.

## How It Works

In this section, I explore the inner core of ASP.NET Core MVC and its supporting components, starting with ASP.NET Core.

## ASP.NET Core

The new version of the core infrastructure for ASP.NET is collectively known as ASP.NET Core. ASP.NET Core is a completely modular system. It allows you to select only the components you require to run your applications. This is a significant architectural change from ASP.NET 4.6. In ASP.NET 4.6 all the core functionality was contained in the `System.Web` assembly, and hosting an ASP.NET application required loading all of it, even if you needed only a few functions contained in it. For example, in ASP.NET 4.6 an `HttpContext` object was instantiated with each request, and it required 30kB of memory. With ASP.NET Core, `HttpContext` is now optional, and a single request can use as little as 2kB per request.

Another important architectural change in ASP.NET Core is the full decoupling of ASP.NET and the Windows operating system and Microsoft's web server IIS. Although it was possible to run older versions of ASP.NET outside of IIS, you could not always rely on consistent behavior when moving between platforms. With ASP.NET Core, this has been mitigated with a new set of HTTP abstractions and OWIN-compatible middleware. OWIN was a predecessor to ASP.NET Core that defined standard interfaces between .NET web servers and applications. You can find out more about OWIN at `http://owin.org/`.

Figure 1-6 shows the overall architecture of ASP.NET Core and ASP.NET Core MVC. This architecture is divided into four primary layers, including native hosting, which hosts the native process for your application; the runtime, which is responsible for loading and initializing the .NET Framework and hosts the core .NET CLR including hooks for the Roslyn compilation services; the application host; and finally the components of ASP.NET Core and ASP.NET Core MVC.

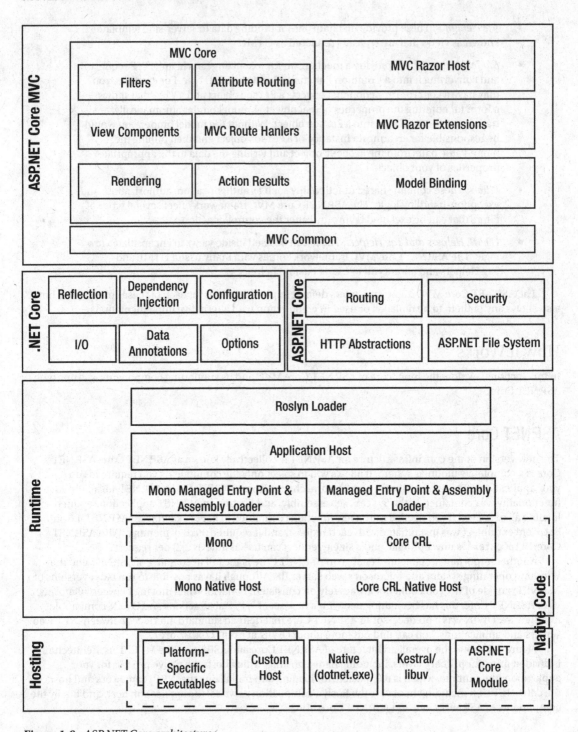

*Figure 1-6. ASP.NET Core architecture*

## Hosting: Native Process

At the bottom of Figure 1-6 is the hosting layer. Hosting is a small layer of native code that is responsible for finding and invoking the native host.

Several hosts are available, including the ASP.NET Core Module, Kestral, and dotnet.exe. The ASP.NET Core Module allows ASP.NET Core applications to be hosted in IIS. dotnet.exe is a command-line tool that can be used to build and run your ASP.NET applications for development and testing purposes. Kestrel is a high-performance cross-platform HTTP server based on the libuv asynchronous I/O library. It offers the best performance for hosting your ASP.NET Core application. Kestrel does not offer the same level of functionality as IIS, however. For example, if your application needs to use Windows authentication, you will need to use Kestrel in conjunction with IIS.

If you needed, you could create a custom host for hosting your ASP.NET application. This could be a WPF application, a command-line tool, or a Windows service.

## Runtime: CLR Native Host

The runtime layer configures and starts the CLR and creates the application domain for managed code to run inside of. When the hosting application shuts down, the runtime layer is responsible for cleaning up resources used by the CLR and then shutting it down.

In the runtime layer, Windows machines will have a core native code implementation of the CLR. You also have the option to run the Mono implementation of the CLR. The Mono project offers native hosts for macOS, Linux, and Windows.

## Runtime: Managed Entry Point

The managed entry point is written in native code. The main purpose of this layer is to find and load the required assemblies. Once the assemblies have been loaded, the managed entry point is called, and the application begins executing.

## Runtime: Application Host

The application hosting layer of the runtime is the first layer where a web developer will typically get involved. The application host reads the project's .csproj file and determines your application's dependencies. It can locate assemblies from many sources including NuGet and assemblies compiled in memory by the Roslyn compiler services.

In an ASP.NET Core application, this layer will also create the ASP.NET Core pipeline and load the specified middleware components.

## Runtime: Roslyn Loader

The Roslyn loader is responsible for loading and compiling source files. With ASP.NET Core, the application code does not need to be compiled before it is deployed. It can be deployed as source code and compiled on demand.

## .NET Core and ASP.NET Core

Figure 1-6 shows some of the components of the .NET Core framework and ASP.NET Core that are required to run ASP.NET Core MVC. On the .NET Core side, you have the following:

- *Reflection*: This component provides the ability for your application to inspect the assemblies loaded in your application and the types defined in them. Reflection is used extensively in the ASP.NET Core MVC framework.

- *Dependency Injection*: This set of components, now part of the .NET Core, allows you to reduce dependency coupling by providing a set of generic factory classes that can instantiate an instance of a class via configuration. This is a powerful design pattern that adds both flexibility and testability to ASP.NET Core MVC.

- *Configuration*: .NET Core has a new more flexible configuration library that allows you to use many different sources for configuration. The possible configuration sources include command-line arguments, environmental variables, and files. When using a file as your configuration source, you can choose from a variety of built-in formats including JSON, XML, and INI files. The configuration system allows you to use many configuration sources in your application.

- Asynchronous *I/O*: This component provides classes for interacting with the file system, creating and reading streams, and communicating over a network.

- *Data Annotations*: This library is part of the .NET Standard library. Data Annotations allows you to decorate your model classes and its properties with descriptive attributes. The metadata contained in these attributes can then be read by other components by way of reflection to perform many useful tasks such as input validation within ASP.NET Core MVC and database creation by Entity Framework when using a "code first" design approach.

In the ASP.NET Core stack there are many components required by ASP.NET Core MVC. Some of the most important are shown in Figure 1-6.

- *Routing*: This component contains logic for mapping HTTP requests to the desired static resource or application component. It allows you to customize the URL scheme for your web application or service.

- *Security*: This component consists of a collection of OWIN-based providers known collectively as ASP.NET Identity. ASP.NET Identity supports several authentication and authorization standards including SAML, OAuth, and Windows authentication, as well as custom user databases with cookie authentication. This functionality allows you to quickly integrate your application with external identity providers such as Facebook, Microsoft, and Google or integrate your application with Active Directory. ASP.NET Identity also includes support for advanced security features such as two-factor authentication.

- *HTTP abstractions*: These are new components that are part of ASP.NET Core. They create an abstraction layer that ensures consistent APIs and behaviors regardless of where you host your ASP.NET Core application.

- *ASP.NET Core file system*: This provides static file handling for your web applications. This is required because unlike past versions of ASP.NET, which delegated loading and serving of static files such as images and CSS files to the web server, ASP.NET Core needed a standard set of abstractions that would be consistent across different web servers and operating systems.

Unlike ASP.NET MVC, which contained most of its functionality in a single NuGet package, ASP.NET Core MVC has been broken up into many subcomponents, each with its own NuGet package. This allows you to be very specific about what components you include in your application.

A good way to get an understanding of ASP.NET Core MVC's modularity is to create a new project in Visual Studio. After creating a new ASP.NET Core MVC project in Visual Studio, you can explore the components that are included with the template by expanding dependencies and then NuGet folders from inside Solution Explorer. Depending on the variation of the new project template you selected and what type of authentication you selected for your project, you will see between 10 and 20 packages. Of these, the most significant from a developer's perspective are the `Microsoft.AspNetCore.Mvc` and `Microsoft.AspNetCore.Mvc.Routing` packages. If you expand `Microsoft.AspNetCore.Mvc`, you will see that it is made of an additional ten packages.

Another worthwhile exercise is to explore the ASP.NET Core MVC source code on GitHub (`https://github.com/aspnet/Mvc`). Inside the `Microsoft.AspNetCore.Mvc.Core` folder is most of the functionality that you will interact with in your application code, including `ActionResults`, `Areas`, `Controller`, HTTP attributes, and output formatters. In the `Microsoft.AspNetCore.Mvc.Core/ModelBinding` folder, you will find the components that perform the magic of taking data posted from Ajax and HTML form submissions from the web browser and then binding it to a CLR type on the server. The GitHub repository also includes the Razor view engine located in the `Microsoft.AspNetCore.Mvc.Razor` subdirectory. It should be noted, however, that ASP.NET Core MVC contains only the Razor view engine, which allows Razor to hook into the ASP.NET Core MVC framework request execution pipeline. The core of Razor, which includes the template parser, tokenizer, editor integration, and utilities, is in a separate branch of the ASP.NET tree that is independent of ASP.NET Core MVC (`https://github.com/aspnet/`).

## The ASP.NET MVC Request Processing Pipeline

As an ASP.NET Core MVC developer, it is important to understand how the ASP.NET Core MVC processes requests. In the previous section I introduced many of the components of ASP.NET Core MVC. Now I will discuss how these components work together to process a request. This insight will aid in root-cause analysis as well as in helping you understand where you can inject custom code into the request pipeline. Figure 1-7 shows a high-level look at the ASP.NET Core MVC processing pipeline.

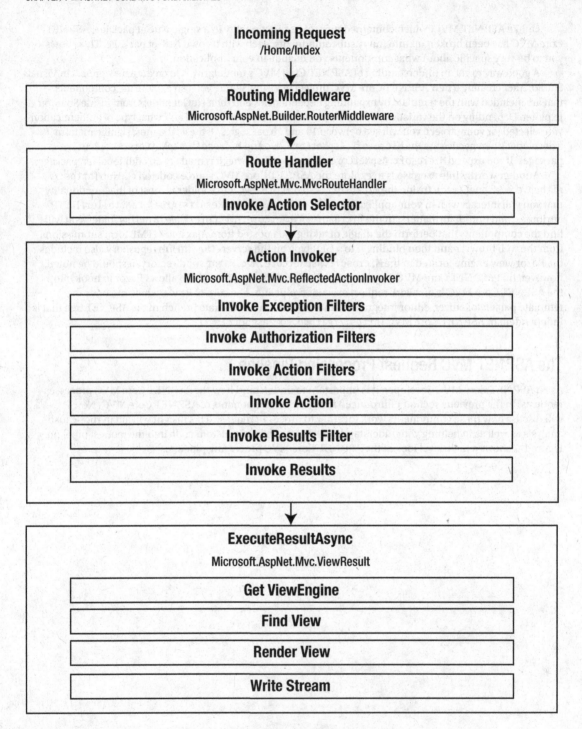

**Figure 1-7.** *ASP.NET Core MVC framework request processing pipeline*

Before ASP.NET Core MVC can process any requests, it must be initialized and configured. For ASP.NET Core, this starts with a host such as the ASP.NET Core Module or dotnet.exe starting and loading the base framework, instantiating a Startup class, and calling its ConfigureServices and then its Configure method. In an ASP.NET Core MVC application, the host will load the core ASP.NET services including HTTP abstractions, routing middleware, and other middleware components.

Once the application has been initialized and the routes have been registered, the application is ready to begin accepting new requests and passing them though the processing pipeline.

Request processing begins with the routing middleware component intercepting an incoming HTTP request and inspecting it to see whether it matches one of the patterns registered in the routing table. The default router middleware component in ASP.NET Core is a class called Microsoft.AspNetCore.Builder. RouterMiddleware. RouterMiddleware's constructor takes a route handler and a RequestDelegate instance as parameters. When the runtime calls the RouterMiddleware's Invoke method, it passes in an HttpContext object as a parameter. It then creates a new RouteContext object using HttpContext. RouterMiddleware then attempts to call the route handler's RouteAsync method. The route handler is the first extensibility point in the pipeline. Route handlers implement the IRouter interface, which exposes a single method called RouteAsync.

ASP.NET Core MVC comes with a route handler called Microsoft.AspNetCore.Mvc.MvcRouteHandler and is configured to use it by default. When RouteAsync is called, it uses an ActionSelector to inspect the incoming URL to see whether it matches a route pattern that has been added to the route collection. If a matching route is found, the route handler will create an instance of the configured action invoker.

The action invoker is another point of extensibility where you can supply your own implementation if needed. As with the route handler, ASP.NET Core MVC has a default implementation that is configured out of the box. The action invoker is called Microsoft.AspNetCore.Mvc.ReflectedActionInvoker. As its name implies, the action invoker uses .NET Core's reflection capabilities to inspect the matched controller class to determine whether it has a matching action method and then adds the appropriate filers to the execution pipeline.

The ReflectedActionInvoker constructor takes ActionContext, ReflectedActionDescriptor, IControllerFactory, IActionBindingContextProvider, and INestedProviderManager as parameters. It then uses the IControllerFactory parameter to create an instance of the controller. Once the controller is instantiated, ReflectedActionInvoker performs the following procedure:

1. *Creates a list of filters that need to be executed along with the action method*: This is a combination of global filters that have been registered as part of the application initialization process as well as filters added to the controller and action method declaratively using attributes.

2. *Invokes exception filters*: Exception filters contain code that is executed when exceptions occur. If any of the exception filters return a result, execution of the action will be short-circuited, and no other filters will be invoked.

3. *Invokes authorization filters*: Authorization filters check to see whether a user is logged in. If any of the authorization filters returns a result, execution of the action will be short-circuited. When an AuthorizationFilter has a result, it indicates that authorization has failed.

4. *Invokes action filters*: Action filters are the first item in the pipeline that has access to arguments via model binding. Action filters are typically used to encapsulate code that might otherwise be repeated in multiple action methods. As with the other filters, if a result is set, it short-circuits execution.

5. *Invokes the action method*: The action method is typically where you write your code. Internally the ASP.NET Core MVC framework sees the action method as a type of filter. The ASP.NET Core MVC framework uses the ReflectedActionExecutor class to execute the action method and to obtain the result.

29

6. *Verifies no unhandled exception has occurred*: All the preceding steps have been executed asynchronously and return `Task` objects. The tasks are examined to see whether any had uncaught exceptions and, if so, execution is short-circuited.

7. *Invokes ResultFilters, which will execute any result filters associated with the action*: Result filters implement the `IResultFilter` interface, which defines two methods—one that is executed before a result is generated and another for after.

8. *Invokes Result using ResultExecutedContext*: At this point, the pipeline can begin writing a response to an output stream directly or invoking a view engine. What action is taken here is directly related to the type of `ActionResult` returned by the action method.

In cases where the action method returns a `ViewResult`, then a view engine will be utilized to generate the result. In most cases a view engine will load a template file such as a `.cshtml` file for the Razor view engine and then begin the process of compiling the view, binding it with model data, and then writing a response to the output stream. The details of this process vary depending on what view engine is used, but the overall process from a Core MVC process flow perspective is the same regardless of what view engine is used.

1. The `ResultExecutedContext` is initialized with a service provider and a view engine. A service provider implements the `IServiceProvider` interface. Its job is to define a mechanism for receiving service objects. Service objects provide services to other objects. In MVC applications this is typically an `HTTPContext` object.

2. The view engine gets view names from the parameter passed to the `ActionResult` constructor or from the `ActionDescriptor.Name` property.

3. The view engine then attempts to find a view using the `ViewEngine.FindView` method.

4. The view engine then sets the `ContentType` header. By default, this is set to `"text/html; charset=utf-8"`.

5. The view engine creates a `StreamWriter` and a `ViewContext`.

6. The view engine then calls `View.RenderAsync`, which generates all of the content needed for the response and then writes it to the `StreamWriter`.

For more information on how view engines work, please refer to recipe 1-9.

# 1-6. Understanding Models in ASP.NET Core MVC

## Problem

You know that *models* are the *M* in MVC but are not sure how they differ from regular C# classes. You would like to get a better understanding of what models are.

## Solution

ASP.NET Core MVC can use any .NET class as a model. If you want, you could even use a simple primitive such as a `System.Int32` as your model. More often, the model is a complex class that contains many types and collections of types.

Although you could use any class, it is usually better to create classes that fulfil the model role. Although the primary function of the model is to describe your domain, it can also provide functionality such as calculations, perform complex validation logic, and manage the state of the entities it describes. You should avoid creating classes that perform a dual role and mix together model and controller logic. Please refer to recipe 1-2 and review the allowed communication patterns for general guidelines on how the model should interact with your application.

When you create a new ASP.NET Core MVC project using Visual Studio and use ASP.NET Core Identity, Visual Studio creates a Models folder and places several models in the folder for you. When you create your models, you can follow this pattern or, if the complexity of the model warrants it, you can place your model in a separate project.

There are several patterns that you can use when creating your models. Some of the most popular methods include

- Creating simple classes
- Creating composite classes
- Using the Entity Framework

# How It Works

In the following sections I demonstrate how to create a model in an MVC application using simple classes. The classes will make use of data annotations that are used by both the view engine to help generate HTML and the model binder to validate the model data on the server after a form has been submitted.

## Creating Simple Classes

A pattern used by the Visual Studio team creates a set of simple classes with no complex types that consist of nothing but public properties and data annotations. To see an example of this pattern, create a new ASP.NET Core Web Application project using the Web Application template and change the authentication type to individual user accounts. The project template includes a Models folder with a subfolder called AccountViewModels. The AccountViewModels folder contains a class called RegisterViewModel.cs. The RegisterViewModel has only enough properties to support the view that it is used with. Each property is decorated with a set of data annotations. These attributes—when used with the HTML Helpers or Tag Helpers—automatically generate the HTML needed to support form validation using jQuery validation. Listing 1-3 shows RegisterViewModel.

*Listing 1-3.* RegisterModel from MVC Template

```
public class RegisterViewModel
{
  [Required]
  [EmailAddress]
  [Display(Name = "Email")]
  public string Email { get; set; }

  [Required]
  [StringLength(100,
    ErrorMessage = "The {0} must be at least {2} and at max {1} characters long.",
    MinimumLength = 6)]
```

```
[DataType(DataType.Password)]
[Display(Name = "Password")]
public string Password { get; set; }

[DataType(DataType.Password)]
[Display(Name = "Confirm password")]
[Compare("Password",
    ErrorMessage = "The password and confirmation password do not match.")]
public string ConfirmPassword { get; set; }
}
```

RegisterViewModel is a simple class with three properties. It uses data annotations to apply certain attributes to each property. The advantage of this approach is that information such as the field name, whether or not the field is required, and validation error messages can be maintained in a single file and used with many views. For example, if this model has a view designed for a PC, another one designed for a tablet, and a web API for a native iPhone application, the information can be applied uniformly across all views.

## Creating Composite Models

If a simple model like the one mentioned in the preceding section will not meet the needs of your views, you can create a composite model. This method is useful in cases when you are displaying a view that needs data from several objects. It could also be useful in situations where you are working with an existing library defined in another assembly that does not map well to your view. In this case, the external library that defines your view is not in your project's model folder but in another project.

Rather than trying to use the external classes as your model or jamming random objects into the ViewBag, you can add a class that references one or more classes in your external library. Listing 1-4 shows a simple example of a model that describes items in a guitar case.

***Listing 1-4.*** The GuitarCaseModels

```
// Defined in the projects model folder
public class GuitarCaseModel
{
  public List<GuitarPick> Picks { get; set; }
  public List<GuitarCable> Cables { get; set; }
  public Guitar MyGuitar { get; set; }
}

// Defined in another assembly
public class Guitar
{
  public string Brand { get; set; }
  public string BodyStyle { get; set; }
  public string Finish { get; set; }
}

public class GuitarCable
{
  public string Brand { get; set; }
  public int  Length { get; set; }
}
```

```
public class GuitarPick
{
    public string Brand { get; set; }
    public string Thickness { get; set; }
}
```

One problem that might jump right out at you when viewing this example is that because the class does not use data annotations, you are not able to benefit from the declarative syntax used in Listing 1-4.

## Using the Entity Framework

Another way of defining a model is to use the Entity Framework or another object-relational mapper (ORM) to define the model. With this option, your model is also connected to your data abstraction layer. The Entity Framework provides several ways to design your model.

- *Model first*: This method uses a designer to define a model and then generates a database based on the model. It should be noted that this mode is no longer supported in Entity Framework Core.

- *Database first*: This method creates a model based on a database schema.

- *Code first*: This method allows you to use a plain old C# object (POCO) as a model and then connect it to the Entity Framework using a class derived from DbContext.

These options are discussed in more detail in Chapter 6.

# 1-7. Understanding Controllers and Actions in ASP.NET Core MVC

## Problem

You need some help understanding the role of the controller in an ASP.NET Core MVC application.

## Solution

Controllers are classes that either extend the System.AspNetCore.Mvc.Controller base class or are POCO classes that follow the naming convention. By convention, all controllers are placed inside a folder named Controllers inside the MVC web application project. The name of the controller must end with the suffix Controller, as in HomeController. Inside the controller are one or more methods that return an IActionResult object. These methods are known as *actions*.

The controller provides three roles in the MVC application.

- It selects what view should be displayed.

- It allows a clean separation between the view and the model by acting as an intermediary between the two.

- It processes data before it is passed along.

# How It Works

The main jobs of the controller are to perform some work on behalf of the user, such as creating an instance of a model and then passing the model data to an action result. The action result then takes that model data and converts it to an output format. In some cases, your action was called by a web browser that is expecting HTML content such as a form or a data grid. In other cases, this could be a client-side script that needs the model data in JSON format. The format of the result is determined by the type of action result returned by the action. ASP.NET Core MVC comes with more than 20 types of action results and allows you to create your own types. I will go over the different types of action results in detail later in this section.

The most common scenario is that you want your controller to pass the model data to a view and then have a view engine render the result, which can be sent back to the user in HTML format. In ASP.NET MVC this is accomplished by returning a special type of ActionResult called a ViewResult.

When you return a ViewResult and do not pass it the name of the view in its constructor, as shown in Listing 1-5, ASP.NET Core MVC will assume that you are looking for a view that matches the name of the action. ASP.NET Core MVC uses reflection to determine the name of the action and then attempts to find a view with the corresponding name in the Views folder for that controller. In the case of Listing 1-5, it will be looking for a view named Index in the folder Views/Home.

---

■ **Note** *Reflection* is a programming technique that uses information about loaded assemblies and the types defined within them. Code that uses this technique is looking at itself like a person looking in a mirror.

---

*Listing 1-5.* Returning a ViewResult Without Specifing a View Name

```
public class HomeController : Controller
{
    public IActionResult Index()
    {
        return View();
    }
}
```

If you pass in the view name as a string to the ViewResult constructor, as shown in Listing 1-6, it will base its search on the contents of the string. In this case, it will search for a view named about. When explicitly passing in the name of the view, the view name does not need to match the name of the action.

*Listing 1-6.* Returning a ViewResult with a View Name

```
// maps to About.chtml
// the view location logic will use refection to get
// the action name and then use it to find a matching view
// This version is more difficult to unit test
public IActionResult About()
{
    ViewBag.Message = "Your application description page.";

    return View();
}
```

CHAPTER 1 ■ ASP.NET CORE MVC FUNDAMENTALS

```
// also will map to About.chtml since we pass view name as an argument
public IActionResult About2()
{
  ViewBag.Message = "Your application description page.";

  return View("About");
}


// This one maps to OtherView.chtml
// the string in the argument gives the name of the view
// if OtherView.chtml does not exist an error will occur at runtime
public IActionResult About3()
{
  ViewBag.Message = "Your application description page.";

  return View("OtherView");
}
```

If you create a new ASP.NET Core MVC project using the Web Application template and select Individual User Accounts for authentication, Visual Studio will create a folder structure like the one shown in Figure 1-8. Each ASP.NET Core MVC project has a Views folder. Inside the Views folder is a subfolder with a name that matches the name of a controller. For example, as shown in Figure 1-8, the AccountController.cs has a corresponding views folder named Account.

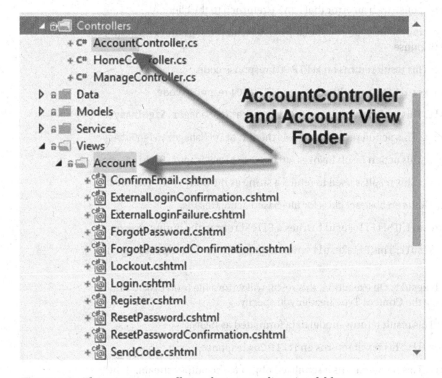

*Figure 1-8. The account controller and corresponding view folder*

Inside the account view folder are 12 views. Each of the views maps to an action inside the AccountController class. For example, the Login action maps to the view defined in the file Login.cshtml.

## Other Types of Action Results

Returning a ViewResult is probably the most common scenario, but there are other types of action results that come with the framework. These include the following:

- ChallengeResult: This result is used when you have a condition in your code that requires that the caller should be challenged for login credentials.

- StatusCodeResult: This action result produces a given response status code. Several other action result classes are derived from StatusCodeResult.

- BadRequestResult: When executed, this result will produce a Bad Request (HTTP 400) response.

- UnsupportedMediaTypeResult: This is a status code result that when executed will return an HTTP 415 result indicating that the request was for an unsupported media type.

- UnauthorizedResult: This is a status code result that when executed will return an HTTP 401 result indicating that the caller was unable to access the resource because the caller is not authorized.

- BadRequestObjectResult: When executed, this result will produce a Bad Request (HTTP 400) response with an error that can be returned to the client.

- OkResult: This is a status code result that when executed will produce an empty OK (HTTP 200) response.

- EmptyResult: This result returns an HTTP 204 response code.

- HttpNotFoundResult: This result returns an HTTP 404 response code.

- SignInResult: This action result invokes AuthenticationManager.SignInAsyc.

- SignOutResult: This action result invokes AuthenticationManager.SignOutAsyc.

- ForbidResult: This action result invokes AuthenticationManager.ForbidAsync.

- ContentResult: This result is used to return a string as the body of the response.

- FileResult: This is an abstract class for file-based action results.

- FileStreamResult: This FileResult writes a FileStream to the output stream.

- FileContentResult: This FileResult writes a binary file to the output stream as a byte array.

- PhysicalFileResult: On execution, this result will write a file from disk to the response using the Content-Type header you specify.

- JsonResult: This result returns model data formatted as JSON.

- NoContentResult: This result returns an HTTP 204 response.

- ObjectResult: This result returns a serialized object to the output stream. If the model is a simple string, this result will return the string as a text file; otherwise, it will convert it to a JSON object.

- OkObjectResult: This ObjectResult returns with HTTP status code 200.

- CreatedResult: This ObjectResult returns a created (HTTP 201) response.

- CreateAtRouteResult: This ObjectResult is similar to CreatedResult but also includes a location header.

- RedirectResult: This result redirects to the URL specified.

- RedirectToActionResult: This result redirects to a specified action method.

- RedirectToRouteResult: This result redirects to a specified route.

# 1-8. Understanding Page Routing in ASP.NET Core MVC

## Problem

You understand the basics of how MVC controllers work but are unsure about how the ASP.NET routing engine is able to map a URL to the correct controller and execute the proper action.

## Solution

The ASP.NET MVC routing system uses a series of rules listed in a routing table to determine which controller and action are executed in response to a request. The routing engine intercepts each request and determines whether the URL specified matches a pattern in the routing rules list. Each routing rule contains placeholders that can match a controller, an action, an area, and any number of variables and route constraints. When a URL is found to match a pattern, the routing engine attempts to match the text in the {controller} placeholder with a controller class defined in the web application. If it cannot find a match, the routing engine throws an error. The routing engine is also responsible for constructing URLs that can be used to create callbacks to the correct controller and action that are used in forms and Ajax calls.

## How It Works

Each ASP.NET Core MVC application contains a class named Startup in its root folder. The Startup class, like the global.asax file used in ASP.NET classic applications, is the place where all application initialization logic is performed. ASP.NET Core applications do not use the global.asax file.

The Startup class does not implement an interface nor does it inherit from a base class. It does, however, follow a pattern common to all Startup classes. Each Startup class includes a public property of the type IConfigurationRoot named Configuration. Startup also implements two methods, ConfigureServices and Configure. Startup's constructor is used to load the application's configuration data, which is used to initialize the Configuration property. The constructor typically accepts an instance of a class implementing the IHostingEnvironment interface as an argument. The IHostingEnvironment instance contains information about the host, such as the base path of the web application. This path information is used by the configuration builder to help locate the configuration files.

The Startup class's ConfigureServices method is used to register types with ASP.NET Core's dependency injection system. ASP.NET Core MVC comes with several extension methods to IServiceCollection to simplify registration. Shown in Listing 1-7 are the AddDbContext method, which registers an Entity Framework Core DbContext; AddIdentity, which registers ASP.NET Identity; and AddMvc, which registers the modules of ASP.NET Core MVC. In addition to using extension methods, you can register types manually. In Listing 1-7, two interfaces, IEmailSender and ISmsSender, are registered with AuthMessageSender as the concrete class that implements them.

The Startup class's Configure method is used to add modules to the request pipeline. This is done by calling extension methods on the objects passed as arguments, as shown in Listing 1-7. UseMvc is an extension method on the IApplicationBuilder argument. Invoking UseMVC adds ASP.NET Core MVC to the request pipeline. A lambda expression passed as an argument to UseMVC is used to define the default routes for the application.

***Listing 1-7.*** Routes Defined by the Visual Studio MVC Web Application Template

```
public class Startup
{
  public void Configure(
                IApplicationBuilder app,
                IHostingEnvironment env,
                ILoggerFactory loggerFactory
  )
  {
        // add default logging components
        loggerFactory.AddConsole(Configuration.GetSection("Logging"));
        loggerFactory.AddDebug();

        // Configure the HTTP request pipeline.

        // Add the following to the request pipeline only in development environment.
        if (env.IsDevelopment())
        {
            app.UseBrowserLink();
            app.UseErrorPage();
            app.UseDatabaseErrorPage(DatabaseErrorPageOptions.ShowAll);
        }
        else
        {
            // Add Error handling middleware which catches all application specific errors and
            // sends the request to the following path or controller action.
            app.UseErrorHandler("/Home/Error");
        }

        // Add static files to the request pipeline.
        app.UseStaticFiles();

        // Add cookie-based authentication to the request pipeline.
        app.UseIdentity();

        // Add other middleware to the request pipeline here.
```

```
// Add MVC to the request pipeline.
app.UseMvc(routes =>
{
    routes.MapRoute(
            name: "default",
            template: "{controller=Home}/{action=Index}/{id?}");

    });
  }
}
```

The code shown in bold in Listing 1-7 creates the default routing rule. It defines a routing template for "{controller=Home}/{action=Index}/{id?}" and declares the id parameter as optional using the ?. In addition, the route template sets default values for the controller and action parameters.

The settings defined in Listing 1-7 will result in the routes shown in Table 1-2.

*Table 1-2.* *Routing Rule Results*

| URL | HTTP Verb | Matching Controller | Matching Action |
| --- | --- | --- | --- |
| / | GET | Home | Index |
| /Home | GET | Home | Index |
| /Home/Index | GET | Home | Index |
| /Home/About | GET | Home | About |

It should be noted that because Web API and MVC are no longer two separate frameworks, there is no real distinction between an API route and a regular route. For both API and regular routes, an HTTP verb can play a role in deciding what action is called. There are two ways to match an HTTP verb with an action. The first is the name of an action. For example, an action named Post or PostMyActionName will be associated with the POST HTTP verb unless overridden by an attribute or other routing rule. This technique is more common for API routes that do not have an action name in the route. The second technique is to decorate the action definition with an attribute such as HttpPostAttribute.

Another important thing to note about routing rules is that they are processed in order. The first route that matches the URL is the one that is used. Any routes found after the matched route are completely ignored. When adding routes to the routing label, be sure to add specific routes prior to general ones. I cover this topic in greater detail in Chapter 5.

# 1-9. Understanding View Engines in ASP.NET Core MVC

## Problem

You have heard the term *view engine* used earlier in this chapter and perhaps in other media regarding ASP.NET Core MVC, but you do not really understand what it is and how it fits into ASP.NET Core MVC.

## Solution

ASP.NET Core MVC has a modular design and allows for each of the modules to be replaced or enhanced by a custom implementation. Of all the modules in ASP.NET Core MVC, the one that is the most interesting for developers is the view engine. Many view engines have been created by the community. Some of them emulate popular templating systems from other platforms, and others are unique to ASP.NET Core MVC.

## How It Works

A view engine is the ASP.NET Core MVC subsystem that defines the expressive syntax for authoring views and a rendering engine that converts the server-side template into HTML markup. ASP.NET Core MVC ships with the Razor view engine. Razor views have a .cshtml file extension, which stands for C# HTML. The initial version of ASP.NET Core MVC did not ship with the Web Forms view engine, but this may be shipped as an out-of-band update and made available via NuGet.

Each view engine has three main functional components.

- *View engine class*: This component implements the IViewEngine interface and provides a mechanism for locating view templates.

- *View class*: This component implements the IView interface and provides a method for combining the template with data from the current context and the model to output HTML markup.

- *Template parsing engine*: This component parses the template and compiles the view into executable code.

On other platforms, a view engine is sometimes referred to as a *template engine*. This is a component that takes a text file that usually contains a mix of HTML markup and scripts, parses the file, and then executes the code in the file to render the results. On development platforms that do not use the MVC pattern, the templating engine is the primary interface for developing the application. An example of a templating engine is classic ASP.

By making the view engine modular, the ASP.NET Core MVC team has made it possible to completely change the way views are constructed and rendered without impacting the rest of the infrastructure. For example, if you install the NHaml view engine, you could create views in a similar fashion to creating Haml views on Ruby on Rails.

The first component of the trio that makes up a view engine is a class that implements the IViewEngine interface. This interface is defined in Listing 1-8. The source code for IViewEngine can be found on GitHub at http://bit.ly/MvcIViewEngine.

**Listing 1-8.** The View Engine Interface

```
namespace Microsoft.AspNetCore.Mvc.ViewEngines
{
    /// <summary>
    /// Defines the contract for a view engine.
    /// </summary>
    public interface IViewEngine
    {
        /// <summary>
        /// Finds the view with the given <paramref name="viewName"/> using view locations and
        /// information from the
        /// <paramref name="context"/>.
```

```
    /// </summary>
    /// <param name="context">The <see cref="ActionContext"/>.</param>
    /// <param name="viewName">The name or full path to the view.</param>
    /// <param name="isMainPage">Determines if the page being found is the main page for an
    ///    action.</param>
    /// <returns>The <see cref="ViewEngineResult"/> of locating the view.</returns>
    ViewEngineResult FindView(ActionContext context, string viewName, bool isMainPage);

    /// <summary>
    /// Gets the view with the given
    /// <paramref name="viewPath"/>, relative to <paramref name="executingFilePath"/>
    /// unless <paramref name="viewPath"/> is already absolute.
    /// </summary>
    /// <param name="executingFilePath">The absolute path to the
    ///   currently-executing view, if any.</param>
    /// <param name="viewPath">The path to the view.</param>
    /// <param name="isMainPage">Determines if the page being found is the
    ///   main page for an action.</param>
    /// <returns>The <see cref="ViewEngineResult"/> of locating the view.</returns>
    ViewEngineResult GetView(string executingFilePath, string viewPath, bool isMainPage);

    }
}
```

The IViewEngine interface is simple. It consists of two methods, one for finding a view and another for getting the view.

The second component that the view class implements is the IView interface shown in Listing 1-9. This interface has a single method called RenderAsync. A major difference between MVC 6 and earlier versions of MVC is that all template rendering is done asynchronously. This increases the scalability of the ASP.NET Core MVC framework by preventing I/O latency from blocking threads.

***Listing 1-9.*** The IView Interface

```
namespace Microsoft.AspNetCore.Mvc.ViewEngines
{
    /// <summary>
    /// Specifies the contract for a view.
    /// </summary>
    public interface IView
    {
        /// <summary>
        /// Gets the path of the view as resolved by the <see cref="IViewEngine"/>.
        /// </summary>
        string Path { get; }

        /// <summary>
        /// Asynchronously renders the view using the specified <paramref name="context"/>.
        /// </summary>
        /// <param name="context">The <see cref="ViewContext"/>.</param>
        /// <returns>A <see cref="Task"/> that on completion renders the view.</returns>
        Task RenderAsync(ViewContext context);
    }
}
```

The RenderAsync method shown in Listing 1-9 takes a single parameter expecting a ViewContext.

The ViewContext contains all the data that needs to be passed to the template parsing engine component, including the controller context, the form context, the HTTP context, route data, view data, and information about any parent actions.

The final component, the template parsing engine, does not implement any predefined interface. This allows developers to do whatever they want. This component is typically by far the most complex of the three components and could consist of hundreds of classes. If you ever endeavor to create your own view engine, you will spend most your time with this component.

CHAPTER 2

■ ■ ■

# Getting Started with ASP.NET Core MVC

In this chapter, the recipes focus on getting your development machine ready for ASP.NET Core MVC development and increasing your understanding of the tooling provided in Visual Studio for developing web applications. The chapter also includes several recipes dedicated to preparing your application for deployment on IIS.

All examples in this book that feature Visual Studio will be using the Visual Studio 2017 Community edition on Windows.

## 2-1. Setting Up Your Development Environment

### Problem

You are new to ASP.NET Core MVC development and want to know what you need to get started. You are unsure if your current computer will make a good developer machine and what software you need to get started. If you need to upgrade, how do you justify the cost of this hardware to your management?

### Solution

With ASP.NET Core MVC, Microsoft has worked hard to broaden the types of machines that can be used to develop an ASP.NET Core MVC application. Microsoft has made it possible to develop your application in any text editor on any desktop platform including Linux and the Mac. In addition to the tooling in Visual Studio, Microsoft has also developed an SDK that contains powerful command-line tools that allow you to perform many of the actions that you would normally do in Visual Studio from a terminal or command shell.

While tools such as Sublime Text, GitHub Atom, and Microsoft's Visual Studio Code can offer great experiences, most developers would benefit from using the full-featured version of Visual Studio.

Visual Studio 2017 has an unparalleled feature set specifically targeted at ASP.NET Core MVC. It offers debugging, refactoring, and collaboration tools that are not available in other editors. It also comes with a rich ecosystem of third-party add-ons that extend its functionality and can improve both the speed and quality of your applications.

In the next section, I cover the ideal specifications for your developer machine, some recommended Visual Studio extensions, and software configuration.

© John Ciliberti 2017
J. Ciliberti, *ASP.NET Core Recipes*, DOI 10.1007/978-1-4842-0427-6_2

## How It Works

In this section, I discuss some of the more important aspects of what investments you should consider when selecting your developer workstation. I discuss several factors such as PC hardware, displays, and software configuration.

## PC Configuration

The minimum hardware requirements to run Visual Studio are a dual-core 1.8GHz processor with 2GB RAM and between 1GB and 40GB of disk space. While Visual Studio may run on minimal hardware, most developers will need something a bit more robust if they plan on being productive. I highly recommend that your PC has an i5 or better CPU and at least 8GB of RAM. To run Visual Studio 2017, you will need to be running Windows 7 SP1 or newer or Windows Server 2012 R2.

For the first time ever, Visual Studio is also available for the Mac. At the time of this writing, preview builds of Visual Studio for Mac did not offer the same feature set as Visual Studio on the PC. It should also be noted that Visual Studio for the Mac is a completely new code base. In general, MacBook Pros are great development machines, but for .NET development PCs still have an edge.

## Touch Screens

Because they are ubiquitous on tablets, smartphones, and new PCs, a large percentage of your software's customer base is likely accessing your web application with a touch-enabled device.

If you spend a significant amount of your time developing user interface components, having a touch-enabled device is a necessity. This does not necessarily mean that your main developer box needs a touch screen. You could have a secondary device like an iPad or similar device to ensure your application is usable in touch-only or touch-first use cases.

## Displays

Having a large enough display to see all the windows and toolbars of your development environment, to open web browsers, and to use other applications is essential to developer productivity. If your development PC is a laptop, I recommend a 15-inch display or larger. In addition to the laptop display, you should have a docking station that supports two or more external monitors.

Having the two or more large displays gives you a lot of real estate for all your windows. It allows you to have everything you need right in front of you. Multiple displays are an immediate productivity booster.

## Mouse and Keyboard

A quality mouse and keyboard are often overlooked components of the developer workstation. They should be ergonomic and comfortable to use for long periods. Wireless peripherals should be avoided in favor of wired devices that plug into your docking station or USB hub. Wireless keyboards require batteries that seem to always die at the worst times. They are also subject to interference, which can result in typos and latency.

## Getting Visual Studio Community Edition

The Visual Studio Community edition is free for students and individual developers. You can download the installer from the following URL:

```
https://www.visualstudio.com/downloads/
```

After you download the installer, you will be prompted to select which workloads you will use for Visual Studio. For the examples in this book, only the .NET Core and Docker workload is required.

## Visual Studio Extensions

Many third-party add-ons for Visual Studio can substantially improve your productivity and help reduce errors. Table 2-1 contains a short list of extensions that should be in every MVC developer's toolbox.

***Table 2-1.*** *Useful Visual Studio Extensions*

| Extension Name | Publisher | What It Does |
| --- | --- | --- |
| Web Extension Pack 2017 | Mads Kristensen | This substantially improves HTML, CSS, LESS, JavaScript, and TypeScript editing experiences inside Visual Studio. In addition to enhancing the built-in code editors, it comes with custom editors for editing `robots.txt`, HTML5 app cache files, an image optimizer, and more. In addition, it has code analyzers that aid in ensuring your client-side code conforms to best practices. |
| Code maid | Codemaid.net | This open source refactoring extension for Visual Studio offers code cleanup, formatting, and reorganizing tools. The code comment formatting feature is especially useful. |
| Trailing Whitespace Visualizer | Mads Kristensen | This helps you keep code files clean by helping you identify and clean trailing whitespace. Trailing whitespace will be flagged as a warning by many JavaScript code analysis tools. |
| Visual Studio Spell Checker | EWSoftware | This smart spell-checker for Visual Studio finds spelling errors in HTML, Razor, code comments, and more. |
| Resharper | JetBrains | This substantially improves the refactoring experience inside Visual Studio. It also provides code quality analysis that shows you how your code can improve as you type. This is also a great tool that can be used to enforce a coding standard for your team. Unfortunately, unlike the other add-ins, Resharper is not free. Personal licenses start at $149. |

# Other Software

In addition to Visual Studio, there are several other tools you will need for developing and testing your code.

## Web Browser Add-Ins

To ensure your web application functions as expected across all the browsers your end users might be using, you will need to have a version of each browser installed on your developer machine. Most browsers come with a set of developer tools out of the box that are helpful for troubleshooting layout issues and JavaScript errors. In addition, you might want to install one or more browser extensions that can enhance this experience.

- *Google Chrome*: The Chrome web store has many developer tools that you might find useful. The following are extensions that I recommend for ASP.NET MVC developers:

  - *Resolution Test*: This simplifies testing how your application will look at different screen resolutions. This is especially important if you are implementing a responsive web design.

  - *Firebug Lite*: In addition to JavaScript debugging support, this extension allows you to inspect and edit CSS and HTML elements.

  - *Advanced REST Client Application*: This extension allows you to create custom HTTP requests and inspect the JSON responses. This is very helpful for testing your Web APIs.

  - *Web Developer*: This extension adds a toolbar with quick access to many Chrome features, such as the ability to disable the cache.

- *Firefox*: Firefox has some of the best and most mature add-ins for web developers that can be used in conjunction with its excellent built-in developer tools.

  - *Firebug Lite*: This add-in offers similar features to the Google Chrome version.

  - *YSlow*: This add-in allows you to analyze a page for client-side download performance issues and offers a set of recommendations.

## Telerik Fiddler

Telerik Fiddler is a free network proxy tool that allows you to intercept, monitor, and fiddle with all HTTP traffic on your machine. The main advantage Fiddler has over the browser extensions is that it allows you to view all of the traffic from all your web browsers at the same time. It can even be configured to proxy traffic from Windows Store applications.

Some of the most useful features for ASP.NET Core MVC developers include the following:

- *Composer*: This feature allows you to construct HTTP requests that can be used to test your Web APIs. You can also record, modify, and replay sequences of request/responses.

- *Rules*: This feature allows you to simulate users with slow connections, disable the browser cache, and simulate user agents.

- *Decrypting HTTPS traffic*: This feature is essential when debugging a service that is using HTTPS.

## SOAP UI

Soap UI, available as a free download from https://www.soapui.org/, is an open source REST and SOAP testing tool that offers a complete API test automation framework.

## Business Justification for Adequate Developer Hardware

As an ASP.NET Core MVC developer, you are writing software that runs on the server or in the cloud. The software that you create might someday be used by thousands of people, and it could become an essential asset to your company. The tools that you use to create and test this software will put a much greater demand on your PC than a typical word processer or web browser. For certain development activities, you might need to run several OSs at once inside virtual machines (VMs). Your development tools will have many windows and toolbars, and you will often need to work with many open documents at once. To avoid the introduction of bugs that appear in production but can't be reproduced on your developer machine, your development environment should match your deployment environment as closely as possible.

Proper hardware for a developer is not difficult to justify. According to PayScale (www.payscale.com), the average salary for a .NET developer in the New York City area is around $98,000 per year. Assuming you work five days a week and eight hours a day, this works out to approximately $47 per hour. If having proper development hardware and software saves you two hours per day, your company would save $471 per week. For a large project that is scheduled to take six months, the savings would be more than $10,000. Because the delta between the laptops purchased for a standard laptop and a proper developer machine is less than $500, it should be a no-brainer for your company to approve a hardware upgrade, especially for senior developers and architects who are likely making considerably more than $47 per hour.

The following are a few other items that you can add to your nonstandard hardware acquisition justification proposal:

- Your deployment targets are 64-bit servers with dual six-core, hyper-threaded CPUs and 128GB of RAM. You plan to use advanced asynchronous and parallel programming techniques, but they are impossible to debug properly on your current machine.

- Your deployment target is a 64-bit OS. With the current 32-bit OS on your laptop, it is impossible for you to know how garbage collection will affect your application when it is consuming a large amount of memory.

- You would like to use Visual Studio's performance profiling tools, but the results of the profiling are inconclusive on your current environment.

# 2-2. Determining Which Operating System to Use for Your Development Machine

## Problem

Although Microsoft has worked hard to build layers of abstraction that shield developers from much of the drudgery of developing an application that can be deployed on different platforms, it is still possible for subtle differences between underlying implementations to cause a deployment to fail. In a perfect world, your developer machine uses the same OS and configuration as your production server. Unfortunately, this is not always possible. For example, if you are deploying your application to Windows Azure, there is no option for installing Azure on your desktop aside from the emulators needed for development. Another problem you could have is that you are supporting several applications that are running on several different versions of Windows Server or Linux. You might also be developing desktop or even Windows Store–style applications. What is a developer to do? You need to know which OS you should run on your development machine.

## Solution

The solution to this broader problem is OS virtualization. There are several products that allow you to run several OSs at the same time as VMs on top of Windows. However, you still need to choose a host OS. As an ASP.NET Core MVC developer, Windows 10 Pro is probably the best choice for the host OS on your development machine.

## How It Works

Windows 8 was the first desktop OS with a built-in hypervisor. Microsoft Hyper-V, which has been available on Windows Server, is now available on desktop Windows as well. The hypervisor allows you to run VMs on your local desktop computer at near raw hardware speeds. In the past, you could have a similar capability using VMware Workstation, Virtual PC, or Oracle VirtualBox. The difference with Hyper-V is that your VMs run closer to the metal and incur lower I/O overhead than user-mode applications such as Virtual PC.

If you are unable to run Windows 8 or later, the next best option is VMware Workstation on either Windows 7 or macOS. Even though VMware Workstation runs in user mode, meaning it is an application running on top of Windows, it does offer strong support for hardware-assisted virtualization and can even run 3D graphics.

In almost all cases, you should use a VM for your development environment. The following are the reasons why:

- You can have a virtualized version of the development environment with an OS that matches the configuration of your deployment target for all the systems you maintain.

- As you are going through the phases of development, you sometimes need to experiment with risky components and configurations that can potentially FUBAR your machine. Hyper-V and VMware both have snapshot capabilities. With snapshots, you can take a picture of your machine at a given time and then restore to that point later. For example, before starting a SharePoint installation, you take a snapshot. During the installation, you click the wrong button. SharePoint freaks out and wreaks untold havoc on your machine. Rather than rebuilding your entire machine from scratch, you can restore from the snapshot and everything is fine again. Another great use for snapshots is testing installation programs. You can run your installer, verify that it didn't work, fix the problem, roll back to the snapshot, and then try again.

- You can have a consistent developer machine image for all members of your team. VMware and Hyper-V both support creating machine templates. This allows you to create a base image with all the tools you need for a project. When a new team member comes on board, you can spin up a new VM and get him or her productive almost immediately.

- You can test across different versions of Internet Explorer. Because it is not possible to have two versions of Internet Explorer installed on the same machine at the same time, using VMs solves this issue. This technique can also be used with Microsoft Office or other tools with the same limitation.

- VMs also have the unique ability to use virtual hardware such as network cards and iSCSI. With iSCSI, for example, you can create Windows server clusters that require shared storage. Without virtualization, you would need to purchase expensive specialized hardware and software licensing for storage area network (SAN) packages such as EMC PowerPath.

- Most companies are virtualizing their production servers. This makes it very likely that your code eventually will be deployed to a VM. Developing and testing your code in an environment that is almost identical to production reduces the number of issues you may run into when you deploy your application.

## Enterprise Deployment Environments

For complex enterprise-scale applications, you should never deploy your code directly from your development desktop to production. Even if you are using a VM that is an exact match with your production server, chances are you are not going to be able to replicate the entire environment, which might include load balancers, firewalls, and more.

In most enterprises, a standard deployment process would consist of several environments that either can be scaled down or are full replications of the production environment. This usually consists of the following environments:

- *Development*: Servers shared by the entire development team during the development process can be continuously updated with fresh code.

- *QA*: This is a separate environment used by the quality assurance (QA) team that will only get QA releases.

- *User acceptance testing*: For applications critical to your organization, you might need a separate environment where important business stakeholders can test your application before releasing to production.

- *Staging*: For critical enterprise applications, a staging environment closely mimics production. This is your final quality check that could answer some questions like "What happens when I put my app behind a reverse proxy?" It can also be used for operations to test server driver upgrades and OS patches before installing them in production.

## Continuous Integration and Deployment

Most mature software development organizations employ a continuous integration and deployment (CI/CD) pipeline to help automate much of the drudgery associated with validating, testing, and deploying software. This pipeline can consist of the following components:

- A software configuration management and version control system such as GitHub Enterprise, Bitbucket, or Team Foundation Server/Visual Studio Team Services

- A code review workflow tool such as GitHub Enterprise, Atlassian Crucible, or Team Foundation Server

- A CI/CD server such as Jenkins, Team Foundation Server, or Atlassian Bamboo

- Static code analysis tools such as SonarQube

- Release management tools such as XL Release

When these tools are used in concert, it can allow you to continuously deploy code to production while ensuring a high level of quality and lower number of defects and security problems being introduced into your production environment.

# 2-3. Creating a New ASP.NET Core MVC Application Using Visual Studio 2017

## Problem

You are new to ASP.NET Core MVC development using Visual Studio 2017 and want to understand the options available for creating a new project using Visual Studio.

## Solution

Visual Studio 2017 has a new project wizard that will guide you through several steps for creating a new ASP.NET Core MVC project. The general process is as follows:

1.  Launch Visual Studio 2017.

2.  On the Start Page, select ASP.NET Core Web Application (.NET Core) under "New projects." Alternatively, from the Visual Studio File menu, you can select New ➤ Project ➤ Search Installed Templates for ASP.NET Core Web Application. Click ASP.NET Core Web Application (.NET Core) in the project list to select it.

3.  Choose a name for your project and a location on your computer where you want the project's files to be stored. Optionally, you can change the name of the solution. By default, the project and solution will have the same name, but in cases where you will have more than one project, it may be a good idea to use a different name for the solution.

4.  The wizard will prompt you to select from a number of ASP.NET Core templates. At the time of this writing, three templates are available, including Empty, Web API, and Web Application. If you want to create a web application that contains a user interface, Web Application is usually the best choice. This template is used for the majority of the examples in this book.

5.  By default Visual Studio will not add any security to your project. If you want to add security to your web site and require users to authenticate with a username and password or third-party authentication provider such as Facebook, you can click the Change Authentication button and select the option that best fits the needs of your application.

6.  If you are planning on shipping your application as a Docker image, you can select the Enable Container (Docker) Support box to add the required components to your application. This requires having Docker for Windows installed on your PC. This option will not work if you are using a virtual machine for development.

7.  If you have an Azure subscription and want to host your application in Microsoft Azure, select the Host in the Cloud check box. Note that this box will be disabled if you do not have an Azure account.

8.  Click OK to finish creating your project.

## How It Works

Visual Studio ships with several project templates. These templates have several components that first instruct Visual Studio on what UI should be displayed to collect the required information and then on what files should be copied into the new project. Project templates typically come with several item templates for the types of files that can be created in each project.

If you would like to learn more about how the templates work, I recommend exporting one of the built-in templates and exploring the content. To export a template, first create a project using one of the built-in templates. You can then export the template using the Export Template Wizard. The Export Template Wizard is an option available from Visual Studio's Project menu. The Export Template Wizard allows you to specify a name, description, and icons for the template. Once the export is completed, the directory containing the template file will be opened.

The template files are ZIP files. If you explore the ZIP file, you will see a file structure like the project but with a few additional files. The most important file added to the template is `MyTemplate.vstemplate`. This is an XML file that contains the metadata for your template. The metadata includes the information you entered in the description as well as a description of the files that should be included in the project and whether the file has replacement parameters that will be filled in with data collected during the project creation process. To see an example of a replacement parameter, open any of the `.cs` files inside the ZIP file and examine the namespace `$safeprojectname$`. When the project is created, `$safeprojectname$` will be replaced with the name of the project.

# 2-4. Creating a New ASP.NET Core MVC Application Using dotnet.exe

## Problem

You want to create a new ASP.NET Core MVC project, but you prefer not to use Visual Studio. This may be because you prefer to work on a Mac or prefer a more lightweight editor. You do not want to have to create the project from scratch and hope there is a way to do this from the command line.

## Solution

.NET Core ships with a set of command-line utilities known as the dotnet CLI. The CLI can be invoked via `dotnet.exe` on Windows and the `dotnet` command on other platforms. To create a new project from the command line, you can simply use the following command:

```
dotnet new
```

## How It Works

Just like Visual Studio, the `dotnet new` command has several options and templates to choose from. The best way to understand what options are available is to use the built-in help commands. To do this, follow these steps:

1.  Open a command or terminal window. On Windows you may also use PowerShell if you prefer.

2.  Enter the command `dotnet -help`. A list of commands and options will be displayed. Make note of the `new` command.

3.  Enter the command `dotnet new -help`. You should now see a list of options for the new command.

## Understanding the Options for dotnet new

dotnet new has three command options. All the commands have a long name and a short name. There is no functional difference between the log and short versions of the commands. The command options include the following:

- -h or –help: Displays help.

- -l or –lang <language>: Sets the programming language to use for the new project. The only valid options at the time of this writing are C# and F#.

- -t or --type <TYPE>: Allows you to specify the template that can be used to create the project. The following options are available for C# projects:

  - Console: A .NET Core console application

  - Web: An ASP.NET Core MVC application

  - Lib: A .NET standard class library

  - Mstest: A unit test project using the MSTest testing framework

  - Xunittest: A unit test project using the xUnit unit testing framework

## Creating a Project Using the Web Template

To create a new web project from the CLI, you will need to perform the following steps:

1. Open a command or terminal window and navigate to the directory where you want to create your project. Note that the CLI will not create a new directory for your solution. You must first manually create the directory. The project will be created in the local directory. dotnet new does not allow you to specify a path.

2. Enter the command dotnet new -t web.

After running the command, you will see a directory structure that contains all the files needed to start your ASP.NET MVC Core project. To run the project, you can simply enter these commands:

- dotnet restore: This command downloads the required packages from NuGet.

- set ASPNETCORE_ENVIRONMENT=Development: This sets the environment variables used by ASP.NET Core MVC. If you do not set this, the application will still function, but you may find that your CSS style sheets are not loading. I will review why this happens in recipe 2-5.

- dotnet run: This starts your application and lets you know what port it is running on. The default port is 5000.

You can view your app by opening a web browser and navigating to http://localhost:5000.

# 2-5. Understanding the Structure of an ASP.NET Core MVC Project

## Problem

You are an experienced ASP.NET MVC developer. You have just installed Visual Studio 2017 and have created a new ASP.NET Core MVC project. The project seems very different than ASP.NET MVC 5 projects. There are many new file types and class files that you are not familiar with. You want to learn more about the new project structure and the purpose of the files included in the template.

## Solution

The ASP.NET Core Web Application template creates a project with a very different structure than ASP.NET MVC 5 projects. The first difference is that at the top level of the directory tree is a folder named src that contains the other projects in the solution. This is the result of a convention that was developed as ASP.NET Core was being developed. In the convention, the root of the solution contained solution-level files, a folder named src that contained source files, and a folder named test that contained unit and integration test projects.

Another big difference is the existence of the wwwroot folder, which contains all of your static HTML, CSS, JavaScript files, and images. When you run your project, only files inside the wwwroot folder are directly accessible. Static files not under wwwroot cannot be accessed.

Other major differences are the absence of the global.asax file, a very minimal web.config file, and the existence of several JSON files and the Startup and Program class files.

## How It Works

In this section, I will walk you through each of the files and directories of your ASP.NET Core Web Application project and describe their purpose. The ASP.NET Core Web Application project shown was created with the Web Application template and the Individual User Accounts Authentication type selected. Listing 2-1 shows the directory tree of the project.

***Listing 2-1.*** Directory Structure of an ASP.NET Core MVC Application with Individual User Accounts Authentication

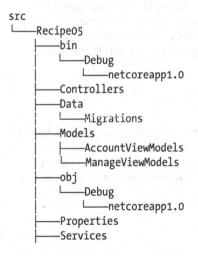

```
src
└────Recipe05
      ├────bin
      │     └────Debug
      │           └────netcoreapp1.0
      ├────Controllers
      ├────Data
      │     └────Migrations
      ├────Models
      │     ├────AccountViewModels
      │     └────ManageViewModels
      ├────obj
      │     └────Debug
      │           └────netcoreapp1.0
      ├────Properties
      ├────Services
```

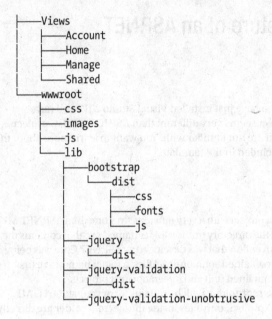

```
├───Views
│     ├───Account
│     ├───Home
│     ├───Manage
│     └───Shared
└───wwwroot
      ├───css
      ├───images
      ├───js
      └───lib
            ├───bootstrap
            │     └───dist
            │           ├───css
            │           ├───fonts
            │           └───js
            ├───jquery
            │     └───dist
            ├───jquery-validation
            │     └───dist
            └───jquery-validation-unobtrusive
```

## bin

Visual Studio does not display this folder in Solution Explorer, but you can view it by clicking the Show All Files button in Solution Explorer or by viewing the folder in File Explorer. The bin folder performs the same function as it did with earlier versions of ASP.NET. It contains the compiled artifacts for your application. Under bin you will find a subfolder for each build configuration. When you first create your project, only the Debug folder is available since no release builds have been created yet. Under Debug you will find a folder named netcoreapp1.0. This folder represents the target framework version for your application.

You should not modify the contents of the bin directory, and it should be excluded from source control.

## Controllers

Just like it did in ASP.NET MVC 5, Controllers contains your controller classes. The template added three controllers to your project: HomeController, which provides actions for the home page and about and contact pages; ManageController, which provides actions for managing user accounts; and AccountController, which provides actions for user registration and login. If you are not familiar with controllers, see recipe 1-7.

## Data

When you create an ASP.NET Core MVC project and select Individual User Accounts for registration, Visual Studio will add a Data folder with an Entity Framework Core DbContext class named ApplicationDbContext. Visual Studio will also create several database migrations. A DbContext class is used by Entity Framework Core to create a connection between your plain C# classes and the database you want to communicate with. Database migrations are how Entity Framework Core propagates changes in your model to the database. I will go over this topic in detail in Chapter 6.

# Models

The Models folder is another folder that should be familiar to you if you have worked with ASP.NET MVC 5. For ASP.NET Core MVC, this folder exists only when you choose to use the Individual User Accounts option when you create your project. The models are the *M* in MVC. To learn more about models, please refer to recipe 1-6.

The Models folder contains an ApplicationUser class that is referenced by the ApplicationDbContext class in the Data folder. ApplicationUser extends the ASP.NET Identity IdentityUser class and is used by ASP.NET Identity for storing data about the application's users. You can customize your ApplicationUser class by adding properties to it and then creating a new data migration.

The Models folder contains two subfolders: AccountViewModels and ManageViewModels. Both subfolders contain view models, which are models created specifically for the views they are associated with. One change you may notice from how this was done in the ASP.NET MVC 5 templates is that each class is now in its own file. In ASP.NET MVC 5 all the classes were defined in a single file.

# obj

The obj folder is not shown in Visual Studio and should not be stored in source control. It contains intermediate files generated by MSBuild. MSBuild will use the files in the obj folder to generate the final assemblies and before copying them to the bin folder. You should not attempt to manually modify the contents of the obj folder.

# Services

The Services folder contains the AuthMessageSender class. This is an abstraction that handles sending e-mails and SMS messages for the authentication system when two-factor authentication is enabled.

# Views

The Views folder contains the subfolders Account, Home, and Manage, which correspond to the controller with the same name. For example, HomeController has a folder under Views named Home. Inside each of the folders is one or more view files associated with each of the actions in the controller. The view files use the Razor view engine and consist of a mix of C# code and HTML.

The Shared folder contains UI components that are shared across all the views. These include the following:

- _Layout.cshtml: This is the primary layout file for the entire site.

- _LoginPartial.cshtml: This is the partial view used to show a welcome message when the user is logged in. For anonymous users, it will display links for the login and registration pages.

- _ValidationScriptPartial.cshtml: This file uses the Environment Tag Helper, which is discussed in recipe 4-8 to conditionally load the jQuery validation scripts based on the value of the ASPNETCORE_ENVIRONMENT environment variable.

- Error.cshtml: This is the default error page that is displayed when an error occurs and the ASPNETCORE_ENVIRONMENT environmental variable is not set to Development.

### _ViewImports.cshtml

The _ViewImports.cshtml file is a new feature of ASP.NET Core MVC. It allows you to add using statements that will be shared across all of your views.

### _ViewStart.cshtml

The _ViewStarts.cshtml file defines what view will be used as the default layout page for all views.

### .bowerrc

The .bowerrc file is a configuration file used by the Bower package manager. Bower is a package manager for JavaScript libraries that is very popular with front-end developers. The .bowerr file included with the project contains a single line of code, as shown in Listing 2-2.

***Listing 2-2.*** .bowerrc File Included with Project Template

```
{
  "directory": "wwwroot/lib"
}
```

The setting shown in Listing 2-2 tells Bower where to place the library files it downloads. For more information on the available configuration options for Bower, please refer to the following web site:

https://bower.io/docs/config/

### appsettings.json

appsettings.json is a configuration file that is loaded at startup. The file contains the default connection string for the database that is used with ASP.NET Identity. It also contains the configuration for the logging components. You can use this file to add your own custom configuration settings. You also have the option of creating your own separate configuration files.

### bower.json

The bower.json file defines metadata about the client-side application components used by your application or application module. The file also lists the JavaScript libraries that will be used by your project. When Visual Studio performs a package restore, it will look at this file and automatically download the required libraries and copy them to the folder specified in the .bowerrc file. Listing 2-3 shows the default bower.json file.

***Listing 2-3.*** bower.json

```
{
  "name": "asp.net",
  "private": true,
  "dependencies": {
    "bootstrap": "3.3.6",
    "jquery": "2.2.0",
    "jquery-validation": "1.14.0",
    "jquery-validation-unobtrusive": "3.2.6"
  }
}
```

## bundleconfig.json

The bundleconfig.json file is a configuration file that governs how the bundling and minification component will combine and compress the client-side JavaScript and CSS files in your solution. The file shown in Listing 2-3 has configuration nodes for the site.css file and the site.js file. It specifies the input file location and the path of the output file that will result from the combining and the files listed in the inputFiles array. The last section of the file sets options for the minification component and whether to create a source map file. Source map files allow JavaScript debuggers to show you display information in a human-readable format even though a compressed file is being downloaded by the web browser.

## Program.cs

ASP.NET Core MVC can be run inside IIS, but it can also be hosted in a console application. Program.cs is the console application that will configure and start the host.

## Startup.cs

Startup.cs contains the logic used to configure your ASP.NET Core MVC application and add middleware components into the ASP.NET Core pipeline. Startup.cs allows you to register types with the ASP.NET Core dependency injection system, load your configuration sources, and register the default routes for ASP.NET MVC. You can think of Startup.cs as a replacement for Global.asax used in ASP.NET MVC.

# 2-6. Using Visual Studio's Debugging Windows to Debug an ASP.NET Core MVC Application

## Problem

You want to watch how the value of a variable changes during the execution of your application. You are unsure of how to use debugging windows in Visual Studio, and you want to understand what each window does and how they work together.

## Solution

Visual Studio has six main debugging windows: the Locals window, the Watch window, the Call Stack window, the Immediate window, the Breakpoint window, and the Output window.

The Locals window shows all the variables that are in currently in scope. It shows the name of the variable, its current value, and the type of variable. For complex types, the value is displayed as a tree of objects. You can expand the tree to inspect the values of the nested types contained within the object.

If you have a complex page with many variables, tracking a value in the Locals window can become cumbersome. The Watch window helps solve this issue by allowing you to "add a watch" for a specific variable.

The Call Stack window allows you to view the functions that are currently on the stack. It displays the name of the function and the programming language in which it is written. The Call Stack window can be configured to show additional information, such as the byte offset, line number, parameter names, and module name. It also allows you to insert breakpoints on a specific call to a function.

The Immediate window allows you to execute code in the current context of a breakpoint. You can enter any code that is valid during that moment in the program. The statement will be executed when you press the Enter key.

The Breakpoint window shows all the breakpoints in the current open project and allows you to edit, delete, disable, or create new breakpoints.

The Output window shows the output of debug log assertions, compilation messages, and output from other Visual Studio components such as the JavaScript Language Service and Source Control.

## How It Works

Visual Studio has a powerful debugger. It allows you to set breakpoints in all your server-side code, including your models, views, and controllers. If you are debugging with Internet Explorer as your default browser, you can set breakpoints in your JavaScript files. Visual Studio also allows you to debug your SQL Server–stored procedures, native code, GPU code, DirectX graphics, Silverlight applications, and WCF services. It is unlikely that you will need to debug GPU or DirectX graphics in an ASP.NET Core MVC project, but in many cases, you might need to walk through a page execution that starts in a controller class, calls stored procedures in a SQL Server database, copies the data from SQL Server into a model, displays the data in a view, and then allows the user to interact with that data using client-side JavaScript. The Visual Studio debugger allows you to step through this page execution from cradle to grave. It allows you set breakpoints anywhere in the program flow and dig into the details of the application state.

The first step in debugging a project is setting breakpoints. A breakpoint is a place in your code where you want the debugger to pause your application's execution. The most common way to set a breakpoint is to click the margin in the left side of the code editor window. You can also set the breakpoint using the F9 key on your keyboard. You may also set breakpoints using the Call Stack window or by using the New Breakpoint dialog box. These alternative methods are sometimes required when it not possible to set a breakpoint on code that you are targeting because there is more than one statement in a single line.

Once your breakpoint is set, you can edit it by right-clicking the breakpoint. The breakpoint pop-up menu, shown in Figure 2-1, allows you to delete the breakpoint, disable the breakpoint, and change the position of the breakpoint. It also offers several options that can change when the breakpoint will cause the debugger to pause your application's execution.

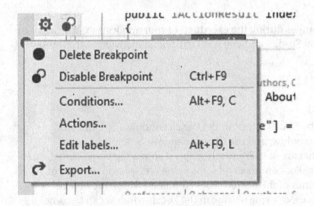

***Figure 2-1.*** *The Edit Breakpoint pop-up menu*

You can start debugging by clicking the Start Debug button in the main toolbar or by pressing the F5 key. After you start the debugger, it will open your application in the web browser. The debugger will attach itself to the IIS worker process, the web browser (if using Internet Explorer), and, if configured, your SQL Server database. It will pause execution when a breakpoint is hit.

In Figure 2-2, you can see the visual debugger in action. In this example, it has paused execution in the `HomeController` inside an action method called `GuitarCase`. In the code editor, the debugger will highlight the current line of code to be executed. The breakpoint icon will have a yellow arrow in its center, and the line to be executed is highlighted in yellow. You can view the values of the variables in the current view directly in the code editor by placing your mouse over a variable.

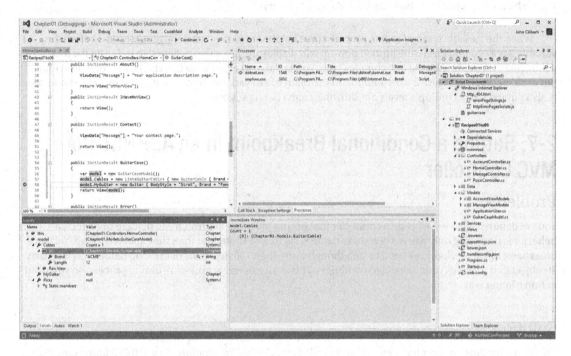

*Figure 2-2. Visual Studio debugging windows*

Figure 2-2 also shows the Locals window. In this example, you are viewing the details of the `model` variable, which is a custom complex type that contains a collection of `GuitarCable` objects and a `Guitar` object. Because `model` is a complex type, its value is shown as a tree view. The tree view has been expanded to view the contents of the variable.

In the Immediate window, you can enter any code that is executable in the current context. In Figure 2-2, `model.Cables` was entered in the Immediate window, and when the Enter key is pressed, you can see the contents of the collection.

The Immediate window is not limited to printing variables. You may also call methods and change values of objects. This can be handy when you want to see how changes in input will affect the operations you are debugging.

Also shown in Figure 2-2 is the process window. This window is not shown by default but can be shown by accessing it from the Debug ➤ Windows menu. Notice that it shows a yellow arrow next to `dotnet.exe`, which is in break mode. Also shown is `iexplore.exe` (Internet Explorer), which is also in the Break state. This demonstrates that both Internet Explorer and `dotnet.exe` are in scope of the debugging session.

Another feature worth mentioning is the ability to pin a mouseover pop-up in the code window. This allows you to make the pop-up window that appears when you mouse over something always visible while debugging. While debugging and stopped at a breakpoint (in break mode), mouse over a variable that you want to pin. On the right side of the pop-up, click the pin icon. You can then click the double down arrow icon to view or enter a comment about that variable. When you are done, it looks similar to Figure 2-3.

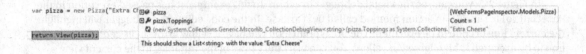

**Figure 2-3.** *Pinning a break mode variable on a complex type*

When the variable is out of scope, such as at the beginning of the next debugging session before the variable has been initialized, the pinned pop-up will display the last value assigned to it during the last debugging session. In the case of a complex type, you are able to expand each variable and then individually pin each member. In Figure 2-3, in addition to the main `pizza` variable, `pizza.Toppings`, one of its members is also pinned so that multiple levels are shown for each debug session.

# 2-7. Setting a Conditional Breakpoint in an ASP.NET Core MVC Controller

## Problem

You are debugging an issue inside a controller that occurs inside a loop. You think that the unexpected behavior is occurring only when a certain variable is set to a value greater than the expected range. You set a breakpoint inside the loop but need to step though more than 100 iterations of the loop before you loop over an object that matches your suspected condition. This is an extremely time-consuming process, so you need to find a better way.

## Solution

The Visual Studio debugger has a great feature called *conditional breakpoints*. To use this feature, create a new breakpoint by clicking in the margin on the left side of the code window. The breakpoint will appear as a red dot. When you mouse over the red dot, a small floating toolbar will appear. Click the Settings icon in the floating toolbar and select the Conditions check box from the inline Breakpoint Settings editor. After the Conditions check box has been selected, a form will appear directly below the check box allowing you to specify one or more conditions for the breakpoint.

## How It Works

Visual Studio supports three types of conditional breakpoints: conditional expressions, hit counts, and filters. In this section, I will demonstrate how you can use these three options for debugging a simple loop.

### Conditional Expressions

Conditional expressions allow you to add one or more expressions that can be evaluated each time a line of code is executed. When one or more of the conditions are met, the program can enter the Break state or perform a specified action, such as logging a statement to the debug log. The Breakpoint Settings dialog also allows you to log a message rather than break when the condition is met. To demonstrate this, you will set a breakpoint inside a loop that evaluates the expression $i > 5$. Here you will specify that you want a log message to be written only when this condition changes.

To do this, follow these steps:

1. Click the left margin next to the line of code where you want to place the breakpoint.

2. Mouse over the breakpoint and click the Settings icon from the pop-up menu. Alternatively, you can right-click the breakpoint and select Conditions from the context menu.

3. In the Breakpoint Settings editor, ensure that Conditional Expression is selected in the first drop-down box and "When changed" is selected in the second drop-down box.

4. Enter i > 5 in the text box to the right of the second drop-down box.

5. Select the Actions check box and enter **i>5 condition has changed** as the message.

6. Click Close to close the Breakpoint Settings editor and then press F5 to debug your application.

With your application running in Debug mode, navigate to the action. If you check the debug log, you should see the message written twice. It was written the first time when the loop began and the condition was false. It was written again after the fifth iteration of the loop when the condition became true.

## Counters

The hit count feature of the debugger keeps track of how many times a line of code is executed. This is useful in scenarios where you expect a line of code to be executed a specific number of times. If the counter goes above this threshold, you can have the breakpoint be hit. For example, let's say you have a function that should be called at the halfway point of your loop. This intention is to have this code called only once, but a defect in the code is causing it to be called many times. For this scenario, you can have the hit counter break when this code is called the second time.

To do this, follow these steps:

1. Click the left margin next to the line of code where you would like to place the breakpoint.

2. Mouse over the breakpoint and click the Settings icon from the pop-up menu. Alternatively, you can right-click the breakpoint and select Conditions from the context menu.

3. In the Breakpoint Settings editor, ensure that Hit Count is selected in the first drop-down box and = is selected in the second. Note the other options that are available in this drop-down box.

4. Enter 2 in the text box to the right of the second drop-down box. The breakpoint settings should resemble Figure 2-4.

5. Click Close to close the Breakpoint Settings editor and then press F5 to debug your application.

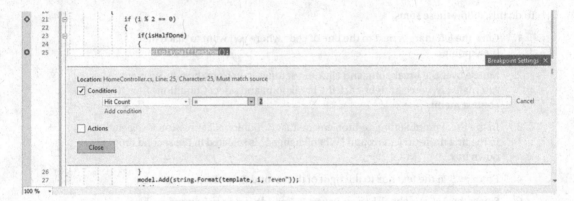

*Figure 2-4. Setting a conditional breakpoint*

## Filters

Filters are similar to conditional expressions but allow you to write expressions that involve data outside of your code such as the process name, machine name, or thread. In this example, you will set a breakpoint that will fire only when the application is running in the dotnet.exe process.

To do this, follow these steps:

1. Click the left margin next to the line of code where you want to place the breakpoint.

2. Mouse over the breakpoint and click the Settings icon from the pop-up menu. Alternatively, you can right-click the breakpoint and select Conditions from the context menu.

3. In the Breakpoint Settings editor, ensure that Filter is selected in the first drop-down box and "is true" is selected in the second. Note the other options that are available in this drop-down box.

4. Enter ProcessName == dotnet.exe in the text box to the right of the second drop-down box.

5. Click Close to close the Breakpoint Settings editor and then press F5 to debug your application.

This is a simplified example, but it should give you a general idea of how the feature works. It is extremely useful when you have a global variable that can be updated in several places in your code and you need to determine which one is causing an erroneous value to be written.

# 2-8. Testing Your ASP.NET Core MVC Application Across Many Browsers at the Same Time

## Problem

You are developing a web site that will be targeting the public and need to support Internet Explorer, Firefox, Opera, and Chrome. You find that you spend a lot of time switching between the different browser windows and clicking the Refresh button just to validate minor layout changes in your view. You wish there was a way to have all the browser windows updated automatically every time you click the Save button in Visual Studio.

## Solution

Starting in Visual Studio 2013, Microsoft introduced a new feature called Browser Link. With Browser Link, there is an active socket connection between your open web page and Visual Studio. Each time you save your page, the changes are updated in real time in all the open browser windows.

## How It Works

There are two steps required to enable Browser Link across multiple browsers. First, you need to set all the desired browsers as your default browser. Second, you need to enable Browser Link if it is not already enabled. Both settings can be accessed from Visual Studio's main toolbar.

## Enabling Multiple Default Browsers

To change the default browser, click the down arrow on the left side of the Start Debugging button, as shown in Figure 2-5.

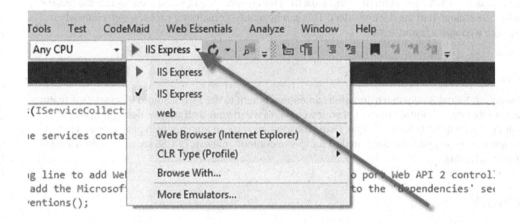

***Figure 2-5.*** *Selecting a browser*

In the menu you will see a list of browsers. The current default will have a check mark to the left. To change the default browser, select Browse With from the menu. This will open a dialog box listing all the browsers shown in the machine. Hold down the Control key and select the browsers you would like to set as your default; then click the Set as Default button. Now all the selected browsers should have the word *Default* in parentheses following the browser name. You can click the Browse button to launch all the selected browsers.

The Start button on the main toolbar should now say *Multiple Browsers*. One limitation is that if you click the Start button on the main toolbar, you will be prompted to select a default browser to use for JavaScript debugging purposes, and only the default browser will launch.

## Trying It

Now that you have Browser Link enabled, you can save all your changed files and update all the browsers at the same time by clicking the Browser Link refresh button. You can launch all your browsers at any time either by using the Browse dialog box available from the Start submenu on the main toolbar or by right-clicking a file in Solution Explorer and selecting View In Browser (Multiple Browsers) from the shortcut menu.

Now the only challenge is being able to view all the content in the browser windows at the same time. If only you had a few more 24-inch monitors!

# 2-9. Editing Your Views and Layouts from Inside Internet Explorer

## Problem

Visual Studio does not offer a graphical HTML editor for ASP.NET Core MVC views. Each time you need to modify static content or adjust a style, you need to locate the element you want to edit; determine what CSS file, partial view, or HTML file the element is in; make the change; save the file; and then refresh the browser to see whether the change had the desired effect. This can be a time-consuming process, especially when working through a complex layout issue.

## Solution

The Web Essentials Visual Studio extension offers an enhancement to the Visual Studio Browser Link feature that injects a toolbar on the bottom of each of your web pages when your web site has debugging enabled and Browser Link is enabled in Visual Studio. Using the toolbar, you can put your web page into edit mode inside of whatever browser you are using; make changes to content, markup, or CSS styles; and then save the changes to Visual Studio.

## How It Works

To enable Browser Link in browser editing, you must first install the Web Essentials extension using the Visual Studio Extension Manager. Once installed, you will be able to enable the editing functionality inside the web browser.

### Installing Web Essentials

To install Web Essentials, open the Visual Studio Extension Manager by selecting Tools ➤ Extensions & Updates from the main menu. In the left pane, select Online and then confirm that Visual Studio Gallery is selected. In the search box at the top-right corner of the Extension & Update Manager dialog box, type **Web Essentials**. After a few moments, you should see Web Essentials 2015 in the center pane.

If Web Essentials is already installed, you will see a green check mark next to the item; otherwise, you will see a Download button. Click Download to begin downloading the extension. In the Download & Install dialog box, click Install. After a few moments, the install will complete, and you will be prompted to restart Visual Studio.

After Visual Studio has restarted, verify that the Enable Saving F12 Changes option is enabled. This option can be toggled on or off by clicking the menu item found on the Browser Link toolbar icon, which can be found between the Start button and Solution Configuration drop-down on the Visual Studio toolbar.

## Editing a Web Page in the Browser

Now that you have the extension installed and enabled, verify that the ASPNET_ENV environmental variable is set to Development. You can do this by viewing the project's properties and viewing the Environmental Variables section of the Debug tab.

Next, launch your application by right-clicking the file that you would like to edit in Solution Explorer and selecting View in Browser from the shortcut menu. After the page loads, you will see the Web Essentials Brower Link toolbar being displayed semitransparently at the bottom of your web page, as shown in Figure 2-6.

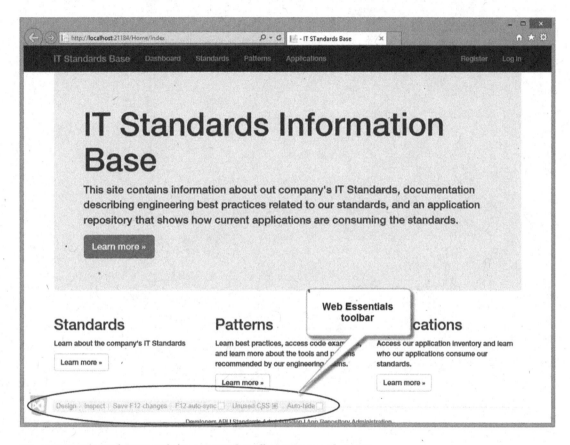

***Figure 2-6.*** *The Web Essentials Browser Link toolbar in your web page*

To begin editing your page, click the Design button on the Web Essentials toolbar. Once edit mode is enabled, your mouse cursor will be displayed as a crosshair, and a green border will appear around HTML elements as you hover over them. To select an element for editing, click it. You can now edit the content in the selected element. Try changing some text content. When you are done, click the Save F12 Changes button on the Web Essentials Browser Link toolbar. You should now see the changes applied to the file inside Visual Studio.

Try this again, but this time try to select an element that you know is being rendered from a partial view such as the web site header (if you are using the default Visual Studio template). When you go back to Visual Studio, you will see that _Layout.cshtml has been opened and the content that you changed has been modified.

# CHAPTER 3

■ ■ ■

# MVC Razor Syntax and HTML Helpers

The recipes in this chapter focus on fundamental programming constructs that you will use often when creating views using Razor. As an ASP.NET Core MVC developer, you will likely spend a significant amount of time creating views. Mastering basic Razor syntax and HTML Helpers is essential to becoming productive on the ASP.NET Core MVC platform. Recipe 3-1 is a Razor program that includes a bonus quick-reference guide when you run the sample web application associated with the recipe.

This chapter also includes a set of recipes dedicated to using the ActionLink HTML Helper. The ActionLink HTML Helper is a staple of everyday coding in ASP.NET Core MVC. Although the syntax for creating standard links using the ActionLink HTML Helper is reasonably straightforward, many people new to the platform struggle with it when they need to mix links with intricate markup. You will also learn how to apply the lessons learned from the ActionLink recipes to other HTML Helper methods.

Later part in this chapter, you will explore some of the other common HTML Helpers and see how to create your own.

You can access the sample code for this chapter on GitHub at https://github.com/johnciliberti/AspNetCoreRecipes/tree/master/Chapter03.

## 3-1. Understanding Razor Syntax

### Problem

You have decided that you want to use the Razor view engine for your new project but are intimidated by the new syntax. You want to gain a solid grasp of the fundamentals before jumping into coding.

### Solution

Razor was designed to be easy to learn. It builds on your knowledge of HTML and C# and includes simple syntax for adding variables and code blocks to your page. The easiest way to demonstrate Razor's syntax is to walk you through the basic syntax elements using a series of short examples. More advanced examples are presented throughout the book.

© John Ciliberti 2017
J. Ciliberti, *ASP.NET Core Recipes*, DOI 10.1007/978-1-4842-0427-6_3

## How It Works

Razor allows developers to mix C# with HTML markup to create dynamic web pages that are rendered on the server. In this section, will review Razor's major syntax elements including variables, control statements, loops, HTML Helpers, code blocks, code nuggets, explicit markup, and comments. If you download and run the code samples for this recipe, they will generate a web site that can be used as a quick-reference guide. The guide includes everything shown in this section.

## Variables

To include a variable in a view, simply prefix the variable name with the @ symbol. For example, if you want to print the date and time on the screen, you can use the following expression:

```
<!-- It is now 7/27/2014 9:19:28 PM -->
<span>It is now @DateTime.Now</span>
```

This syntax is not limited to variables. You can also use it to display the results of a method. For example, suppose you have an application that allows the end user to enter a year and then your application tells her whether it is a leap year. You could use syntax like the following to display your results:

```
<!-- 1973 was a leap year =  false -->
<span>1973 was a leap year =  @DateTime.IsLeapYear(1973)</span>
```

An important detail to note, especially when it comes to displaying dates, is that because Razor allows you to output the result of a method, you can exploit this capability to use format strings. Here is what the first example would look like if you used a format expression to print the date using the long date format string pattern:

```
<!-- It is now Sunday, July 27, 2014 -->
<span>It is now @DateTime.Now.ToString("D")</span>
```

In addition to variables and methods, you can use the @ symbol to print the results of an expression by enclosing the expression in parentheses. In this example, I am displaying the results of everyone's favorite math problem. Razor uses C# as its scripting language. Any valid C# expression is legal in Razor.

```
<!-- 2 + 2 = 4 -->
<span>2 + 2 = @(2+2)</span>
```

## Displaying Model Data

One of the most common activities you will do when creating your Razor view is to display data about your model. In most cases, you probably want to make your view strongly typed so you can take full advantage of Visual Studio's code statement completion. To do this, you first need to add a model directive to the top of the page.

```
@model Recipe01.Models.Guitar
```

Just like with variables, you use the @ symbol to prefix the directive followed by the Razor keyword model. You then enter the class name of your model's class. In this case, I am using the fully qualified name. This is required unless you register the namespace in the _ViewImports.chtml file in the Views folder. _ViewImports.chtml replaces the namespace section of the View folder's web.config file. Another important detail to point out is that the directive names are case-sensitive. As you will see in the next example, @model and @Model have completely different meanings in Razor.

For the next few examples, I use the model defined in Listing 3-1.

***Listing 3-1.*** Guitar Model

```
public class Guitar
{
    [Required]
    public string Brand { get; set; }

    [Required]
    public string Model { get; set; }
    public bool HasWhammyBar { get; set; }
    public string WhammyBarType { get; set; }
    public DateTime ManufactureDate { get; set; }
    public string Description { get; set; }
    public List<string> Strings { get; set; }
}
```

Model objects are created in controller actions and then passed to the view. The model data is accessible from the Model variable. Note that unlike the @model directive, the variable name begins with an uppercase letter. To display the Brand and Model properties of the Guitar object inside your view, you can use the following markup:

```
<!-- My new guitar is a Gibson Les Paul-->
<span>My new guitar is a  @Model.Brand @Model.Model</span>
```

Another important aspect to understand about Razor is that it uses the AntiXSS library to encode the output of your expressions. AntiXSS encoding replaces HTML markup and executable script code with harmless text by converting special characters into HTML escape sequences. For example, <h1>Hello</h1> would be converted into &lt;h1&gt;hello&lt;/h1&gt;. This is an important security feature that helps prevent you from introducing cross-site scripting (XSS) vulnerabilities into your application. In an XSS attack, a user or bot (automated attacker) will attempt to inject active content into your site. When other users access the site and run the active content, the attacker can steal information such as the contents of the user authentication cookie. By encoding the output, Razor ensures that only harmless HTML is displayed.

For example, suppose you had a form that allowed a user to enter a description about his guitar. On another page, you display the content using the following code:

```
My new guitar is a  @Model.Description
```

If a user entered some HTML in the comment form with the intent of enhancing the comment to include a bold typeface, Razor would automatically encode this content. If you view the HTML source generated by Razor, you would see that the angle brackets have been replaced with standard HTML escape characters.

```
<!-- comment = <b>Very cool guitar</b> -->
My new guitar is a  &lt;b&gt;Very cool guitar&lt;/b&gt;
```

If you need to output the raw HTML and do not want Razor to encode the output, ASP.NET Core MVC contains the Raw HTML Helper extension method. HTML Helpers can be accessed using the @Html variable, which maps to the HtmlHelper instance of the view. The Raw HTML Helper takes an object as a parameter and then outputs the value without encoding. Note that inside the parameters you do not use the @ symbol.

```
<span>My new guitar is a @Html.Raw(Model.Description)</span>
```

## Control Statements

Because Razor uses C# as its scripting language, any of the control statements that are legal in C# can be used in Razor. Listing 3-2 shows a simple if-else statement. Notice the lack of explicit code block delimiters. Razor's smart parser can automatically determine server-side script blocks from HTML. One item to note in Listing 3-2 is the placement of the curly braces. Curly braces should be placed on separate lines by themselves to avoid parser errors and to improve the readability of your code.

*Listing 3-2.* Using an if Control Block Inside of a Razor View

```
@if (Model.MyGuitar.HasWhammyBar)
{
    <span>My Guitar has a @Model.MyGuitar.WhammyBarType Whammy Bar</span>
}
else
{
    <span>No Whammy bars on this guitar</span>
}
```

In this statement, not only is the Razor engine able to detect the if statement, but it is also able to detect the variable embedded in the SPAN tag.

Listing 3-3 shows a switch statement inside a Razor view. Notice how it seamlessly switches back and forth between the control flow statements and HTML markup. As in the if-else statement, no explicit code block delimiters are required.

*Listing 3-3.* Using a switch Statement in a Razor View

```
@switch (Model.Brand.ToLower())
{
    case "gibson":
        <span>Slash loves his Gibson Les Paul</span>
        break;
    case "fender":
        <span>Stevie Ray Vaughan loved his Fender Stratocaster</span>
        break;
    case "charvel":
        <span>Warren DeMartini shreds on his Charvel San Dimas </span>
        break;
    default:
        <span>What kind?</span>
        break;
}
```

# Loops

Razor supports all the looping constructs in C# including for, foreach, while, and do. Listing 3-4 shows a foreach loop being used to display a list of Guitar objects. The model in this case is a List<Guitar> object. In this example, the built-in styles from the Bootstrap CSS library that is included with the ASP.NET Core MVC project templates are used to style a table. The styles add alternating row color to a table of items. The loop is started inside the table body and creates a new table row for each loop iteration. Notice as with the control flow statements that the curly braces are placed on lines by themselves.

*Listing 3-4.* Using a foreach Loop in Razor

```
@model List<Chapter3.Recipe01.Models.Guitar>
<table class="table table-striped">
    <thead>
        <tr>
            <th>Brand</th>
            <th>Model</th>
            <th>Has Whammy Bar</th>
        </tr>
    </thead>
    <tbody>
        @foreach (var item in Model)
        {
            <tr>
                <td>@item.Model</td>
                <td>@item.Model</td>
                <td>@item.HasWhammyBar</td>
            </tr>
        }
    </tbody>
</table>
```

# HTML Helpers

ASP.NET Core MVC comes with a number of HTML Helpers that work with the data annotations defined on your model to significantly reduce the amount of code your solution requires.

Listing 3-5 shows the Razor markup for a form that allows you to enter information about your new guitar. In this example, you can see several HTML Helpers in action. The first HTML Helper used is the @using (Html.BeginForm()){ //form content } construct. Html.BeginForm creates the beginning and end HTML form tags and uses route information to add the action properties. Next is the @Html.ValidationSummary() helper. This adds a section where form validation errors will be displayed. Finally, the form itself is shown. Here I am using templated HTML Helpers to display both the form label and the form field. Templated helpers are covered in detail in recipe 3-13.

*Listing 3-5.* A Simple Form That Uses HTML Helpers

```
@using (Html.BeginForm())
{
    @Html.ValidationSummary()

    <fieldset>
        <legend>New Guitar Form</legend>
        <ul class="list-unstyled">
            <li class="form-group">
                @Html.LabelFor(m => m.Brand)
                @Html.TextBoxFor(m => m.Brand)
            </li>
            <li class="form-group">
                @Html.LabelFor(m => m.Model)
                @Html.TextBoxFor(m => m.Model)
            </li>
            <li class="form-group">
                @Html.LabelFor(m => m.HasWhammyBar)
                @Html.CheckBoxFor(m => m.HasWhammyBar)
            </li>
        </ul>
        <input type="submit" value="Save" class="btn btn-primary" />
    </fieldset>
}
```

The @Html.LabelFor, @Html.CheckBoxFor, and @Html.TextBoxFor helpers take a lambda expression as a parameter. HTML Helpers use reflection to pull data from the data annotations that decorate the Guitar model and combine them with the data contained in the object passed into the lambda expression to generate the label and input HTML tags. For this to work, data annotation attributes must be added to the model that specifies the validation rules.

Listing 3-6 shows the HTML generated by the Razor code shown earlier in Listing 3-5.

*Listing 3-6.* HTML Code Generated by the Razor Markup in Listing 3-5

```
<form action="/Home/Helper" method="post">
<div class="validation-summary-valid" data-valmsg-summary="true">
  <ul><li style="display:none"></li>
  </ul>
</div>
<fieldset>
        <legend>New Guitar Form</legend>
        <ul class="list-unstyled">
            <li class="form-group">
                <label for="Brand">Brand</label>
                <input data-val="true"
                  data-val-required="The Brand field is required."
                  id="Brand"
                  name="Brand"
                  type="text"
                  value="Gibson" />
            </li>
```

```
        <li class="form-group">
            <label for="Model">Model</label>
            <input
              data-val="true"
              data-val-required="The Model field is required."
              id="Model" name="Model"
              type="text"
              value="Les Paul" />
        </li>
        <li class="form-group">
            <label for="HasWhammyBar">HasWhammyBar</label>
            <input name="HasWhammyBar" id="HasWhammyBar" type="checkbox"
                      value="true"
                    data-val-required="The HasWhammyBar field is required."
                    data-val="true">
        </li>
    </ul>
    <input type="submit" value="Save" class="btn btn-primary" />
  </fieldset>
<input name="__RequestVerificationToken"
            type="hidden" value="CfDJ8BIUrxdWIuxCmsL211uSFHI2Lzoa64xjRBikGoHpU5
            Amu1quiJbe4fx1OnzBehpTWVt45VJfEpzEOS991lzqP78JIquYMCtEfGtvKcVGInBUiP74wuOWx
            FtIXFGuAxfPczXmLsPONrkObvqQnR2wqvA">
<input name="HasWhammyBar" type="hidden" value="false">
</form>
```

## Code Blocks

Code blocks are sections of the view that contain only C# code and no markup. While inside a code block, all rules of the project's programming language must be followed. With C# projects, for example, a semicolon is required at the end of each statement.

Code blocks begin with @{ and end with }. There is no predefined limit on the number of lines of code in a code block. Keep in mind that the only code you should add to your views is view logic. You should not perform calculations or manipulate the model while in the view. The following is an example of a code block assigning a variable; then it shows how the variable can be used in the view:

```
@{
    var title = "Code Blocks";
}
```

```
<h1>@title</h1>
```

As smart as Razor is, it can get confused occasionally. For example, when you do attempt to use a variable inside an HTML attribute, Razor is not able to determine where the HTML ends and the code begins. Suppose that you had an image that used the ProductId of the model as the file name.

```
<img src="/media/products/guitars/@Model.ProductId.png" />
```

In this case, Razor will fail to recognize that @Model.ProductId is a variable name and will incorrectly render the variable name instead of the value.

This can be corrected by wrapping the variable with a set of parentheses. This convention is known as an *explicit code nugget*.

```
<img src="/media/products/guitars/@(Model.ProductId).jpg" />
```

## Explicit Markup

Sometimes you might want to have plain text mixed in with your code. Without the presence of angle brackets, Razor has a difficult time finding the end of your code block. To get around this problem, the Razor team invented the @: operator and the <text> block. The @: operator is used for single-line explicit markup. <text> is used for multiple lines of markup. Listing 3-7 shows an example of explicit markup.

*Listing 3-7.* Example of Explicit Markup

```
@if (12 == 12)
{
    @: I have @Model.Strings.Count in my guitar case
}
<text>
    Only the best guitar players play @Model.Brand
    and we know who we are.
</text>
```

The syntax allows code nuggets to be mixed with the explicit markup. It also allows you to mix in variables and other dynamic features just as you would in cases where angle brackets are present. In Listing 3-7, the @ symbol is used inside an explicit code nugget to allow a variable to be inserted.

It should be noted that the markup shown in Listing 3-8 will fail.

*Listing 3-8.* Example of Invalid Explicit Markup

```
@if(12==12)
{
    @: I have @Model.Picks.Count in my guitar case};
```

Because the @: symbol states that all content on this line is markup, the "};" is rendered as markup, and the page will have a validation error because the if statement is missing a closing brace.

## Comments

Every coding language needs a way to add comments. In Razor, you use the following syntax to create a comment:

```
@* This is my comment. *@
```

All code and markup between the symbols is commented out. This is useful for when you want to add a comment to your code but do not want it to appear in the markup sent to the client.

You can still use HTML, JavaScript, and CSS comments in your views, but keep in mind that HTML comments are sent to the client and can be read if someone views the source of your page. Here's an example:

```
<!-- this is an HTML comment. It will be sent to the client browser but is hidden on the page -->
<script>
    // this is a JavaScript comment
</script>

<style>
    /* This is a CSS Comment*/
</style>
```

You can also use C# comments inside code blocks. The C# comments do not get sent to the client.

```
@{
    // this is a comment inside of a code block

    /*
     * This is a multi-line comment inside a code block
     */
}
```

## Escaping the @ Symbol

As you saw in the previous examples, the @ symbol is used in Razor to identify variables, directives, code blocks, and even comments. So, what do you do if you need to display an @ symbol on your page? As shown in Listing 3-9, you can use double @@ symbols to escape the character and have it written to the screen.

*Listing 3-9.* Markup That Displays a Razor Code Sample Inside a Razor View

```
<pre>&lt;span&gt;It is now @@DateTime.Now&lt;/span&gt;</pre>
<span>It is now @DateTime.Now</span>
```

In Listing 3-9, the example code is displayed on the page, and then the output of the command is demonstrated directly afterward. The escaped @ character is shown in bold text.

# 3-2. Creating an Action Link

## Problem

You want to display a link in a view to another controller action on the same controller but do not want to hard-code the URL. Instead, you want to leverage information in the route collection to generate the link automatically.

## Solution

Displaying links to other actions using route data is the job of the ActionLink HTML Helper. The basic syntax for it is simple, as shown in Listing 3-10.

*Listing 3-10.* Example of an ActionLink

```
<h3>3-2. Create an Action Link</h3>
@Html.ActionLink("Link to about action in same controller", "About")
```

In the preceding example, the @ symbol is used to indicate that the text that follows it is server-side markup. Html is an instance of Microsoft.AspNetCore.Mvc.Rendering.HtmlHelper. I will discuss the details of what this class does in the "How It Works" section. ActionLink is a method of HtmlHelper that uses the route data to construct the link.

In the preceding example, the ActionLink method takes two arguments. The first is the text to be displayed in the link, and the second is the name of the action. The controller name is omitted in this example. When the controller name is omitted, ASP.NET Core MVC will use the current controller by default. The output of this helper is as follows:

```
<a href="/Home/About">Link to about action in same controller</a>
```

## How It Works

One advantage of ASP.NET Core being open source is that it allows you as a developer to peek under the hood and see how things work. In this section, I will walk you through the implementation of the ActionLink HTML Helper. This will give you a detailed understanding of the inner working of ASP.NET Core MVC. It also teaches you how you can explore the source code for ASP.NET Core MVC on GitHub.

In the solution, I used @Html.ActionLink to automatically generate the HTML for a hyperlink using information from the application's route dictionary. To understand how this works, you will start by examining the HtmlHelper class. The full source code of the HtmlHelper class is available at http://bit.ly/htmlhelper_cs.

Listing 3-11 shows the ActionLink method of HtmlHelper.

***Listing 3-11.*** ActionLink Method Source Code

```
public IHtmlContent ActionLink(
          string linkText,
          string actionName,
          string controllerName,
          string protocol,
          string hostname,
          string fragment,
          object routeValues,
          object htmlAttributes)
{
    if (linkText == null)
    {
        throw new ArgumentNullException(nameof(linkText));
    }

    var tagBuilder = _htmlGenerator.GenerateActionLink(
            ViewContext,
            linkText,
            actionName,
            controllerName,
            protocol,
            hostname,
            fragment,
            routeValues,
            htmlAttributes);
```

```
    if (tagBuilder == null)
    {
        return HtmlString.Empty;
    }

    return tagBuilder;
}
```

The first thing you should notice in Listing 3-11 is the ActionLink method signature. In addition to the two arguments shown in Listing 3-10, there are additional arguments for the controller name, protocol, host name, fragment, route values, and HTML attributes. The overload used in Listing 3-10 is actually defined in another class called Microsoft.AspNetCore.Mvc.Rendering.HtmlHelperLinkExtensions as an extension method of HtmlHelper. You can find the source for HtmlHelperLinkExtensions at http://bit.ly/ HtmlHelperLinkExtentions.

---

■ **Note**    Extension methods are C# programming constructs that allow you to add methods to an existing type without creating a subclass or modifying the original. For more information, please refer to recipe 3-7, which demonstrates this technique.

---

Microsoft.AspNet.Mvc.Rendering.HtmlHelperLinkExtensions provides six extension methods that overload the ActionLink method defined in Microsoft.AspNetCore.Mvc.ViewFeatures.HtmlHelper. Each of the overloads simply calls the base class's ActionLink method with a null value for the missing arguments.

You can learn more about how to use the overloads of ActionLink in recipes 3-3 through 3-10.

Even though the commonly used overloads for ActionLink are defined in an external class, all the business logic is defined in the base class implementation. With that in mind, let's walk through the code in Listing 3-11 to explore how it works.

## _htmlGenerator.GenerateActionLink

After validating that the linkText argument is not null, the code in Listing 3-11 calls the GenerateActionLink method on an instance of IHtmlGenerator. The purpose of this method is to generate the URL. To see how this is done, you need to refer to the default implementation of IHtmlGenerator. The default implementation used by ASP.NET Core MVC is defined in a class named Microsoft.AspNetCore. Mvc.DefaultHtmlGenerator. You can find the code for DefaultHtmlGenerator at http://bit.ly/ DefaultHtmlGenerator.

Listing 3-12 shows DefaultHtmlGenerator's GenerateActionLink method.

*Listing 3-12.*  GenerateActionLink Source Code

```
public virtual TagBuilder GenerateActionLink(
        ViewContext viewContext,
        string linkText,
        string actionName,
        string controllerName,
        string protocol,
        string hostname,
        string fragment,
```

```
            object routeValues,
            object htmlAttributes)
{
    if (viewContext == null)
    {
        throw new ArgumentNullException(nameof(viewContext));
    }

    if (linkText == null)
    {
        throw new ArgumentNullException(nameof(linkText));
    }

    var urlHelper = _urlHelperFactory.GetUrlHelper(viewContext);
    var url =
            urlHelper.Action(actionName, controllerName, routeValues,
            protocol, hostname, fragment);
        return GenerateLink(linkText, url, htmlAttributes);
}
```

As shown in Listing 3-12, GenerateActionLink does not actually do the work of generating the HTML, but rather it uses a factory method to get an instance of the UrlHelper, which in turn calls the Action method that generates the HTML. Although this may seem overly complex, this design helps to ensure maximuim performance by ensuring that only one instance of the UrlHelper factory is created for each ViewContext.

---

■ **Note**   The design of ASP.NET Core MVC avoids direct dependencies as much as possible. Rather than hard-code an implementation of the IHtmlGenerator interface, ASP.NET Core MVC loads an implementation that is dependency injected during the application initialization process. When the view engine creates an instance of HtmlHelper, it passes the IHtmlGenerator instance via the constructor.

---

## UrlHelper Action

The actual logic for generating the HTML can be found in the UrlHelper class. An instance of this class was retrieved using the UrlHelperFactory, as shown in Listing 3-12. You can find the source code for UrlHelper at http://bit.ly/UrlHelper. UrlHelper is somewhat complex, with more than 350 lines of code. For that reason, the code is not repeated in this book.

The Action method's first job is to get the path to the controller action. It does this by looking at the route data from the ViewContext and IRouter instances that have been passed to DefaultHtmlGenerator via the constructor. It then takes into consideration the four optional arguments that include protocol, host, path, and fragment. The fragment parameter represents an HTML anchor name, as in <a name="fragment">. This fragment markup is how an HTML author can create links to another section of the same document.

If the fragment argument is not null, the URL fragment will be prefixed with # concatenated with the value of fragment. It then checks to see whether protocol and host have values. If no value is found in either argument, then a relative URL is constructed. When Action builds relative URLs, it always ensures they begin with a forward slash. If a portal or host is given, then an absolute URL will be constructed. This behavior is demonstrated in the following examples.

Given the following `ActionLink`

```
@Html.ActionLink("Link with a fragment", "Profile", "Home", "", "", "Email", null, null)
```

the action constructs the relative URL /Home/Profile#Email.

```
@Html.ActionLink("Link with a fragment", "Profile", "Home", "https", "", "Email", null, null)
```

Because the protocol was specified, the absolute URL was constructed: https://localhost:50181/Home/Profile#Email.

```
@Html.ActionLink("Link with a fragment", "Profile", "Home", "", "myhostName", "Email", null, null)
```

When the host name is included but the protocol is omitted, an absolute URL is constructed with the host name provided and HTTP as the protocol: http://myhostname/Home/Profile#Email.

In the case of the example in Listing 3-11, protocol and host are both null. This results in the output being /Home/About.

# 3-3. Creating an Action Link to Another Controller

## Problem

You want to display a link in a view to another controller action on a different controller but do not want to hard-code the URL. Instead, you want to leverage information in the route collection to generate the link automatically.

## Solution

Displaying links to other actions using route data is the job of the `ActionLink` HTML Helper.

In Listing 3-13, `ActionLink` is invoked with three arguments: the link text, the name of the action, and the name of the controller. In this case, you want to create a link to the Somewhere action on the Away controller.

***Listing 3-13.*** Create an Action Link to Another Controller

```
<div class="col-md-12">
    <h3>3-3. Create an Action Link to another controller</h3>

    @Html.ActionLink("Action Link to another controller", "Somewhere", "Away")
</div>
```

The HTML output from this helper is as follows:

```
<a href="/Away/Somewhere">Action Link to another controller</a>
```

## How It Works

In recipe 3-2, a detailed description was provided for how the `HtmlHelper` class and `ActionLink` methods work. The only difference between what is happening behind the scenes in Listing 3-13 is how passing in the controller name affects the URL generation process.

You can find the logic used for link generation in the `UrlHelper` class. You can find the source code for this class at `http://bit.ly/UrlHelper`.

In the example shown in recipe 3-2, because the name of the controller was not supplied, `ActionLink` needs to discover the name of the current controller by inspecting the route value dictionary. When passing in the name of the controller like in Listing 3-13, this step is not required.

# 3-4. Creating an Action Link to Another Area

## Problem

You are taking advantage of the areas feature of ASP.NET Core MVC to subdivide your solution. You are creating a navigation bar in a partial view. On the navigation bar you want to use the `ActionLink` HTML Helper to create a link to an action in a controller inside an area. Looking at the possible overloads for `ActionLink`, you do not see an argument for specifying the area. You are confused on how to create the link.

## Solution

Two steps are required for link generation to an area to work. First, you need to make sure you have added a route definition that includes area as a route parameter either in an attribute route or in the `UseMvc` method in the `Startup` class of your application. Second, you need to include the area route parameter in your call to `ActionLink`. Listing 3-14 shows how to create a route that includes an area. Note that this syntax is new to ASP.NET Core. In ASP.NET MVC 5 and earlier, each area had an `AreaRegistration` class that registered area routes using the `AreaRegistrationContext` in its `RegisterArea` method. Area registration does not exist in ASP.NET MVC Core.

***Listing 3-14.*** Adding a Route That Includes an Area Route Parameter

```
app.UseMvc(routes =>
{
    routes.MapRoute(
        name: "areaRoute",
        template: "{area:exists}/{controller=Home}/{action=Index}");
    routes.MapRoute(
        name: "default",
        template: "{controller=Home}/{action=Index}/{id?}");
});
```

Once the route has been added, you can create your action link by including the `area` property in the route values argument, as shown in Listing 3-15. If this syntax seems strange, try to think of it as a terse syntax for creating a name-value collection.

*Listing 3-15.* Creating an Action Link That Includes an Area

```
<div class="col-md-12">
    <h3>3-4. Create an Action Link to another controller</h3>

    @Html.ActionLink("Link to Area",
        "InHappyLand",
        "ControllerInArea",
        new { Area = "FarFarAway" })
</div>
```

The HTML generated from the `ActionLink` shown in 3-15 is as follows:

```
<a href="/FarFarAway/ControllerInArea/InHappyLand">Link to Area</a>
```

## How It Works

The `ActionLink` method call shown in Listing 3-15 takes four parameters, which include the link text, the action name, the controller name, and then an object that represents a collection of route values.

As explained in the "How It Works" section in recipe 3-2, the `ActionLink` depends on the `Action` method of the `UrlHelper` class to resolve the URL using a combination of the data you are passing into the `ActionLink` method, information from the `HttpContext` including information regarding what controller action method had instantiated the view, and the application's route collection. It should be noted that the `HttpContext` object discussed here is a new type introduced in ASP.NET Core. It has no relation to `System.Web.HttpContext` or `HttpContext.Current` from ASP.NET MVC 5.

The route data that you pass into the `ActionLink` can be interpreted as either route parameters or query string parameters. The routing engine determines which is which by using information from the matching route template. In the `areaRoute` route created in Listing 3-14, the route template is defined as `{area:exists}/{controller=Home}/{action=Index}`. Each of the names surrounded by the curly braces is a route parameter. The construct `{area:exists}` tells the routing engine to consider the area name when resolving the route but only if it exists. You can use the `:exists` clause with any route parameter.

During the link generation process, the `UrlHelper` searches the route collection for a matching template. It will then fill the placeholders created by the template's route parameters with matching data from the route value dictionary. In the case of Listing 3-15, it will replace `{action}` with `InHappyLand`, `{controller}` with `ControllerInArea`, and `{area}` with `FarFarAway`. Any other value found in the route value dictionary would be treated as a query string parameter. In fact, if you removed the `areaRoute` route, the URL rendered by the code in Listing 3-15 would be `/ControllerInArea/InHappyLand/?Area=FarFarAway`.

# 3-5. Creating an Action Link with Custom HTML Attributes

## Problem

You are creating an `ActionLink` to your home page but do not want to use the default link styles. You need to have the link appear as a button. If you were hand-coding the link, you would accomplish this by adding a `class` attribute to the anchor tag. You are unsure how to do this with the `ActionLink` HTML Helper.

## Solution

The `ActionLink` helper has an overload with a fifth parameter that accepts an anonymous type that is converted to a dictionary of HTML attributes. Listing 3-16 shows two examples. The first example adds a single attribute, which in this case is a class. Because you want the link to look like a button, you add the `btn` and `btn-primary` CSS classes. These are styles defined in the bootstrap style sheet that is preinstalled in your solution when you create a web site using the standard ASP.NET Core MVC project template.

In the second example is a second HTML attribute. The `title` attribute is a standard HTML attribute that creates a small tooltip that can appear when you hover the mouse over the link.

***Listing 3-16.*** Creating Action Links with Custom HTML Attributes

```
<div class="col-md-12">
  <h3>3-5. Create an Action Link with custom HTML Attributes</h3>
  @Html.ActionLink("This link looks like a button",
        "Contact",
        "Home",
        null,
        new { @class = "btn btn-primary"})

  @Html.ActionLink("This one also has a tool tip",
        "Contact",
        "Home",
        null,
        new { @class = "btn btn-primary",
        title="Click to contact me" })
</div>
```

## How It Works

The `ActionLink` method call shown in Listing 3-16 takes five parameters: the link text, the action name, the controller name, an object that represents a collection of route values that is set to `null`, and finally an object that represents a collection of HTML attributes that should be added to the HTML anchor tab that will be generated.

It should be noted that the route values argument is required to get the correct method signature. If you do not need to add any route parameters, you need to set this to `null` as is the case in Listing 3-16. Since `class` is a C# keyword, the @ symbol must be used for the HTML class attribute to be added.

The link generation process is identical to the process described in recipe 3-2. The only difference is the additional attributes merged during the `GenerateLink` phase of the method. As described in recipe 3-2, the HTML Helper is using `TagBuilder` to generate the HTML. In the last phase of this process, it merges the list of attributes that you pass in as an argument to `ActionLink` using `TagBuilder.MergeAttributes`.

# 3-6. Creating an Action Link That Uses HTTPS

## Problem

As a best practice, you always use SSL when a user enters secure information such as login credentials. You want to use SSL for all the action links to your web site's login page but are unsure of the correct syntax.

# Solution

The `ActionLink` method from the `HtmlHelper` class allows you to specify arguments for specifying the protocol and host name. Listing 3-17 shows how you create a link to a secure contact page.

***Listing 3-17.*** ActionLink Syntax for Specifying a Protocol

```
<h3>3-6. Create an Action Link with HTTPS</h3>
@Html.ActionLink("Secure Page",
                 "Contact",
                 "Home",
                 "https",
                 "mywebsite",
                 null,
                 null,
                 null)
```

With the standard route templates, the `ActionLink` in Listing 3-17 would output the following HTML:

```
<a href="https://mywebsite/Home/Contact">Secure Page</a>
```

There is an important thing to note about Listing 3-17. All the arguments are required, and `null` values are supplied for the `routeValues` and `htmlAttributes` arguments because they are not needed in this example. An empty string or `null` is passed for the `fragment` argument in this case, as this is also not required. If you do not do pass all the augments, the wrong version of the `ActionLink` helper would be called.

# How It Works

The inner workings of the `HtmlHelper.ActionLink` helper are described in detail in the "How It Works" section in recipe 3-2.

If you find that you need to create many links with HTTPS rather than HTTP, you have a few options.

- Configure your web site to require SSL. If you are deploying to IIS, this setting can be found by setting the Require SSL option. If you have enabled a secure binding on your web site, you can do this by opening IIS Manager, expanding Sites, and then clicking your web site. You can then double-click SSL Settings to open the SSL Settings page. On the SSL Settings page, select the Require SSL check box. Once you apply your changes, your web site will reject all non-HTTPS traffic.

- Use the `RequireHttpsAttribute` on the controller actions that you want to ensure are always accessed on a secure communications channel. This will redirect end users to the HTTPS version of the URL when they attempt to access the page using HTTP. Listing 3-18 shows an example of this.

- Create your own HTML Helper. An example of how to do this is shown in recipe 3-7.

***Listing 3-18.*** Using RequireHttpsAttribute on a Controller Action

```
[RequireHttps]
public IActionResult SecurePage()
{
  return View();
}
```

# 3-7. Creating Your Own Action Link for Creating HTTPS Links

## Problem

The built-in HtmlHelp.ActionLink allows you to specify a protocol and host name for creating links to actions that require HTTPS. Unfortunately, you find that it has a few problems. The syntax is inconvenient because you are required to supply many arguments that you might not need. You want to create your own version of the ActionLink method that created links with the HTTPS protocol by default.

## Solution

Listing 3-19 shows a static class that defines two extension methods called SslActionLink. The first accepts linkText and actionName parameters. The second also includes a parameter for controllerName.

***Listing 3-19.*** Creating Custom Action Links for SSL

```
using Microsoft.AspNetCore.Html;
using Microsoft.AspNetCore.Mvc.Rendering;
using System;

namespace Recipe02to10.Infrastructure
{

    public static class MyHelperLinkExtensions
    {
        public static IHtmlContent SslActionLink(
            this IHtmlHelper helper,
            string linkText,
            string actionName)
        {
            return helper.SslActionLink(linkText, actionName, null);
        }

        public static IHtmlContent SslActionLink(
            this IHtmlHelper helper,
            string linkText,
            string actionName,
            string controllerName)
        {
            if (helper == null )
                throw new ArgumentNullException("helper");

            if(string.IsNullOrEmpty(linkText))
                throw new ArgumentNullException("linkText");

return helper.ActionLink(
                linkText,
                actionName,
                controllerName,
                protocol: "https",
                hostname: null,
```

```
            fragment: null,
            routeValues: null,
            htmlAttributes: null);
    }

  }
}
```

For both methods, the protocol is set to HTTPS. After creating the class, you can then use the new extension methods in your views, as shown in Listing 3-20.

***Listing 3-20.*** Using the SslActionLink HTML Extensions

```
@using Recipe02to10.Infrastructure

  <h3>3-6. Create an Action Link with SSL using custom helper</h3>
  @Html.SslActionLink("Secure Page using custom helper", "Contact", "Home")
```

# How It Works

Extension methods are a feature of the .NET Framework that was first introduced with .NET 3.5 in 2008. They allow you to extend the functionality of an existing type without creating a derived type or modifying the original. The magic of this welding is done by the C# compiler. The compiler does not actually add your method to the existing type, but it can create the illusion that it does.

At compilation, the C# compiler can detect methods with the this keyword preceding the first parameter. It then can automatically decorate the method with System.Runtime.CompilerServices. ExtensionAttribute. The C# language and Visual Studio can then take advantage of this attribute using APIs exposed by the compilation service to create the illusion that they have been added to the class.

For the example in Listing 3-19, I had created a new subdirectory under my web project root called Infrastructure. This is not a requirement, but it is a popular convention when you are creating HTML Helpers and other functions that are specific to a web application. Another approach would be to define your extensions in another project and then add that project as a reference to your web application. This second option would allow you to reuse your helper extensions across many web applications.

# SslActionLink

The second line of code in Listing 3-19 is the inclusion of the Microsoft.AspNetCore.Mvc.Rendering namespace. This is the namespace that contains all the HTML Helpers included with ASP.NET Core MVC.

Next the class is defined as public static class MyHelperLinkExtensions. Classes that contain extension methods must be declared as static. The actual name of the class does not matter because it is not used when you call your method, but it can be helpful to name your extension classes consistently so that it is obvious what their purpose is.

Looking at the method definition, it is like the class is static. The return type is IHtmlContent, which represents an HTML-encoded string that should not be encoded again. This is a common return type used for most HTML Helpers.

```
public static IHtmlContent SslActionLink(
        this IHtmlHelper helper,
        string linkText,
        string actionName)
    {
```

The first parameter is this IHtmlHelper helper. The this keyword is what tells the compiler that the method is an extension method and that it should be attached to all classes that implement the IHtmlHelper interface. The IHtmlHelper interface is new to ASP.NET Core MVC, and you must use it rather than the implementation HtmlHelper as you might have done in older versions of MVC. If you use the HtmlHelper rather than IHtmlHelper, you will be able to build your project but will get a runtime error when trying to use your helper in a view. This is because the view engine is also referencing the interface rather than an implementation of IHtmlHelper.

In the body of the method, the code simply calls HtmlHelper's ActionLink, filling in default values for hostname, fragment, routeValues, and htmlAttributes.

# 3-8. Creating an Action Link with an Anchor Target

## Problem

You have a page on your web site that allows users to edit their profiles. You are using Bootstrap's tabs component to break up the profile form into smaller subpages. You want to be able to have external links that open a specific tab. As part of this solution, you want to use hash symbols in your external links for each section of the profile form. For example, you want to have a link such as /Members/EditProfile/#Email to link to the e-mail preferences tab. You want to use an ActionLink but are not sure about the syntax.

## Solution

The solution for creating the action links requires providing a value to the HtmlHelper.ActionLink fragment parameter, as shown in Listing 3-21.

*Listing 3-21.* Creating a Link That Includes a Fragment

```
<h3>3-8. Create an Action Link with a fragment</h3>
 @Html.ActionLink("Edit email settings", "Profile", "Home", "", "", "Email", null, null)
```

The action link in Listing 3-21 will generate the following HTML:

```
<a href=" /Home/Profile#Email"> Edit email settings </a>
```

## How It Works

The HtmlHelper.ActionLink uses the UrlHelper class to generate the URLs used in the HTML markup that it generates. When UrlHelper generates the link, it checks to see whether a fragment argument has been supplied a non-null value. If it has, then it will append a hash and the string supplied in the argument to the end of the URL.

Since the beginning of HTML, a hyperlink that contained a hash symbol would allow a user to navigate to an HTML fragment on the page specified in the href attribute. Inside the page, the fragments are identified using the name attribute of the anchor tag. For example, if you had a long HTML page, you could add tags such as <a name="section1"/> to mark a section and then link to that fragment using <a href="#section1">Section 1</a>. The primary purpose of the fragment parameter of HtmlHelper. ActionLink is for that use case but is by no means the only way it can be used.

Another use for the hash symbol in front-end development is as a CSS selector that matches HTML elements with a matching id attribute. For example, if you wanted to apply a style to a paragraph tag with an ID of foo <p id="foo"/>, you can create a style such as this:

```
#foo{background-color:black;}
```

The popular JavaScript library jQuery that follows the CSS selector syntax for finding matching Document Object Model (DOM) elements also makes use of the hash symbol. This is exploited by many UI components, including Bootstrap's tabs, to enable single-page web applications that can use the browser's Back button.

Listing 3-22 demonstrates how to use Bootstrap's tabs in your view, and then Listing 3-23 shows how to enable external links to certain tabs with a few lines of JavaScript.

***Listing 3-22.*** Using Bootstrap to Create Tabs

```
@{
    Layout = "/Views/Shared/_Layout.cshtml";
    ViewBag.Title = "Edit your profile";
}
<div class="tabbable tabs-left" id="tabMenu">
    <ul class="nav nav-tabs">
        <li class="active">
            <a href="#BasicInfo"
                data-toggle="tab"
                data-tab-history="true"
                data-tab-history-update-url="true"
                data-tab-history-changer="push">Personal Info</a>
        </li>
        <li>
            <a href="#Avatar"
                data-toggle="tab"
                data-tab-history="true"
                data-tab-history-update-url="true"
                data-tab-history-changer="push">Your Avatar</a>
        </li>
        <li>
            <a href="#Bio" data-toggle="tab"
                data-tab-history="true"
                data-tab-history-update-url="true"
                data-tab-history-changer="push">Your Bio &amp; Influences</a>
        </li>
        <li>
            <a href="#Talents" data-toggle="tab"
                data-tab-history="true"
                data-tab-history-update-url="true"
                data-tab-history-changer="push">Your Talents</a>
        </li>
        <li>
            <a href="#Contact"
                data-toggle="tab"
                data-tab-history="true"
                data-tab-history-update-url="true"
                data-tab-history-changer="push">Contact Info</a>
        </li>
        <li>
            <a href="#Privacy"
                data-toggle="tab"
                data-tab-history="true"
```

```
                    data-tab-history-update-url="true"
                    data-tab-history-changer="push">Privacy Settings</a>
        </li>
        <li>
            <a href="#Email"
                data-toggle="tab"
                data-tab-history="true"
                data-tab-history-update-url="true"
                data-tab-history-changer="push">Email Settings</a>
        </li>
    </ul>
    <div class="tab-content">
        <div class="tab-pane active" id="BasicInfo">
            <h3>Basic Info</h3>
        </div>
        <div class="tab-pane" id="Avatar">
            <h3>Avatar</h3>
        </div>
        <div class="tab-pane" id="Bio">
            <h3>Your bio</h3>
        </div>
        <div class="tab-pane" id="Talents">
            <h3>Your amazing talents</h3>
        </div>
        <div class="tab-pane" id="Contact">
            <h3>Contact Info</h3>
        </div>
        <div class="tab-pane" id="Privacy">
            <h3>Privacy Settings</h3>
        </div>
        <div class="tab-pane" id="Email">
            <h3>Email Settings</h3>
        </div>
    </div>
</div>

@section scripts{
<script src="/scripts/home/editprofile.js"></script>
<script src="~/lib/bootstrap-tab-history/vendor/assets/javascripts/bootstrap-tab-
history.js"></script>
}
```

As shown in Listing 3-22, Bootstrap uses unobtrusive JavaScript so that there is a clean separation of markup and presentation logic. All the presentation logic for the tabs is in the Bootstrap.js file, leaving only clean, natural HTML. It also allows you to navigate between tabs by simply clicking hyperlinks such as `<a href="#Avatar" data-toggle="tab">Your Avatar</a>`. The only indicator that something is special about the link is the data-toggle attribute that is used by Bootstrap's script to identify what anchor elements to apply the tab behavior to. To enable Back button support, a JavaScript library named bootstrap-tab-history.js was downloaded from the Bower repository. Additional attributes with the prefix data-tab-history are added to each link. The tab content is contained inside a div tag marked with class="tab-content". Nested inside this div tag are a set of other div elements that each contain the content of a tab. Each of the inner div tags is marked with class="tab-pane" and has a unique id attribute that corresponds to each of the hyperlinks' fragments defined in the first section. The default tab is marked with an additional CSS class that marks it as the default active tab.

The Bootstrap script works by using a jQuery selector to assign an onclick event to all the anchor elements that include the data-toggle="tab" attribute. It does not consider any hash tags present in the URL. For this to work, you need to add a custom script that runs after the DOM loads that checks the current location to see whether it ends with a fragment, as shown in Listing 3-23. It should be noted that the code shown in Listing 3-23 runs only once when the page loads.

***Listing 3-23.*** JavaScript to Enable URL to Navigate to Tab

```
$(function () {

    navToTab();

    /**
     * check to see if URL contains a hash and if so try and navigate to the correct tab
     */
    function navToTab()
    {
        var tab = $(location).attr('href');
        var re = new RegExp('#+[a-z]+', 'i');
        var m = re.exec(tab);
        if (m) {
            $("#tabMenu a[href='" + m + "']").tab('show');
        }
    }

    /**
     * if someone changes fragment in address bar
     */
    $(window).bind('hashchange', function () {
        navToTab();
    });
});
```

The script shown in Listing 3-23 uses jQuery to execute a function once the DOM is ready. It then gets the URL of the current location and puts it into a variable called tab. Next it defines a regular expression that will attempt to extract the fragment part of the URL and write it to the variable m. If m is a truthy value, then the script will evoke the Bootstrap tab function to navigate to the proper tab. The code also registers an event handler for the hashchange event that fires when changes are made to the URL fragment.

---

■ **Note**  In JavaScript, all values can be evaluated as either true or false when used in a control flow expression such as if(m) shown in Listing 3-22. Values that evaluate as true are known as *truthy*, and values that evaluate as false are called *falsy*. Falsy values include false, 0, empty strings, null, undefined, and NaN. All other values are considered truthy.

---

# 3-9. Creating an Image Link

## Problem

You want to create an `ActionLink` but rather than having plain text, you want to have custom HTML including an image. You have tried to inject HTML into the `linkText` property only to find that it has been HTML-encoded.

## Solution

`HtmlHelper.ActionLink` is a useful helper, but it is not the only way to generate a link using the routing engine. For scenarios where you need more control over the HTML markup, `ActionLink` might not be the best fit. The alternative is to hand-code the HTML markup but use the `UrlHelper.Action` method to generate the URL, as shown in Listing 3-24. In fact, this is what `HtmlHelper` does internally. Please refer to the "How It Works" section in recipe 3-2.

*Listing 3-24.* Creating an Image Link Using @Url.Action

```
<h3>3-9. Create an Action Link that includes an image</h3>
<a href="@Url.Action("Contact", "Home")">
    <img src="~/images/3legdog.jpg" />
</a>
```

## How It Works

The `UrlHelper` class contains several methods that are useful for creating action links when you need full control over the HTML. `UrlHelper` follows a similar pattern as `HtmlHelper` with the core implementation logic existing inside the class but all the overloads provided via extension methods defined in another class. In the case of `UrlHelper`, the extensions are defined in the class `Microsoft.AspNetCore.Mvc.UrlHelperExtensions`. The extension class provides seven versions of the `Action` method that are like the overloads for `ActionLink` except for the ability to supply HTML attributes.

# 3-10. Creating an Image Link Using a Bootstrap Glyphicon

## Problem

You want to create a toolbar that uses the icon set provided by Bootstrap and want each toolbar link to be generated by the ASP.NET routing engine.

## Solution

The solution is to use the `UrlHelper.Action` method to generate the URL using the routing engine. Inside each, include SPAN tags with the appropriate glyphicon CSS classes. The group of links is wrapped in two outer DIV tags with the `btn-toolbar` class and `btn-group` class, creating a tight grouping of buttons that resemble a toolbar. You then add the `class="btn btn-default"` classes to each hyperlink to enable a button-like look to each link, as shown in Listing 3-25.

*Listing 3-25.* Creating a Toolbar with Icons Using Bootstrap

```
<div class="btn-toolbar" role="toolbar">
   <div class="btn-group">
     <a href="@Url.Action("Storage", "Home")" class="btn btn-default">
        <span class="glyphicon glyphicon-cloud"></span>
     </a>
     <a href="@Url.Action("Alerts", "Home")" class="btn btn-default">
        <span class="glyphicon glyphicon-bell"></span>
     </a>
     <a href="@Url.Action("Cart", "Home")" class="btn btn-default">
        <span class="glyphicon glyphicon-shopping-cart"></span>
     </a>
   </div>
</div>
```

## How It Works

The Bootstrap UI library is the default UI library that comes with the Visual Studio ASP.NET Core MVC templates. Although you do not need to use this library, it does have many useful features that make it easy to create a web application with a modern professional design. The Bootstrap library consists of three main components: a CSS style sheet, a JavaScript library, and an icon set called Glyphicons, which is based on a web font.

Using a web font for an icon set has many advantages over traditional sprite-based approaches. In a sprite-based approach, you would need to have a single large image that contained all your icons and then use CSS background positioning to display the desired icon. With the web font, you simply display the character that corresponds to the icon. Some other advantages of a web font approach are as follows:

- It is a small download, which makes your page load faster.

- You can change the icon color using standard CSS styles.

- You can change the icon size using standard CSS styles.

If you were using a sprite, you would need a separate image for each color and size. This can be a tedious exercise if you are the person creating the icons. The downside of using a web font is that you are limited to using a single color for your icons. Now that Skeuomorphism is no longer in vogue, the monotone look of the Bootstrap Glyphicon matches the look of many modern OSs including iOS, Windows 8, and Android.

To use a Glyphicon, you include an empty SPAN tag and then add a `class` attribute that includes the Glyphicon class along with the name of the Glyphicon icon class. A full list of icons is available on the GetBootstrap web site at `http://getbootstrap.com/components/`.

# 3-11. Using HTML Helpers to Create HTML Form Elements

## Problem

You are new to ASP.NET Core MVC and are looking for a general overview on how to use the HTML Helpers for creating forms.

# Solution

ASP.NET Core MVC comes with a set of HTML Helpers that help you to create forms. They are especially helpful for creating forms that are bound to server-side models. There are two main categories of HTML Helpers that can be used to create forms. The first set can generate the HTML elements required to create form elements but are not bound to model data. The second set consists of helpers that are strongly typed and can be bound to model data. The strongly typed variants in addition to the normal HTML needed to render the form also contain additional attributes that can be used with some of the JavaScript libraries that come with the Visual Studio ASP.NET templates. Listing 3-26 shows a simple example of a form created using the HTML Helpers. Strongly typed HTML Helpers are discussed in detail in recipe 3-12.

***Listing 3-26.*** Login Form Created Using HTML Helpers

```
@using (Html.BeginForm())
{

  <div class="form-group">
      @Html.Label("exampleInputEmail", "Email address")
      @Html.TextBox("exampleInputEmail","",
         new { placeholder = "Enter email", @class="form-control", type = "email" })
  </div>
  <div class="form-group">
      @Html.Label("exampleInputPassword", "Password")
      @Html.Password("exampleInputPassword","",
         new { placeholder = "Password", @class="form-control" })
  </div>
  <div class="checkbox">
    <label>
        @Html.CheckBox("RememberMe", false)
        Remember Me
    </label>
  </div>
<button type="submit" class="btn btn-default">Submit</button>

}
```

# How It Works

The Razor snippet shown in Listing 3-26 creates a simple login screen that allows the end user to enter an e-mail address and a password and optionally select a check box to remember them the next time. Figure 3-1 shows how the form appears in Internet Explorer 11.

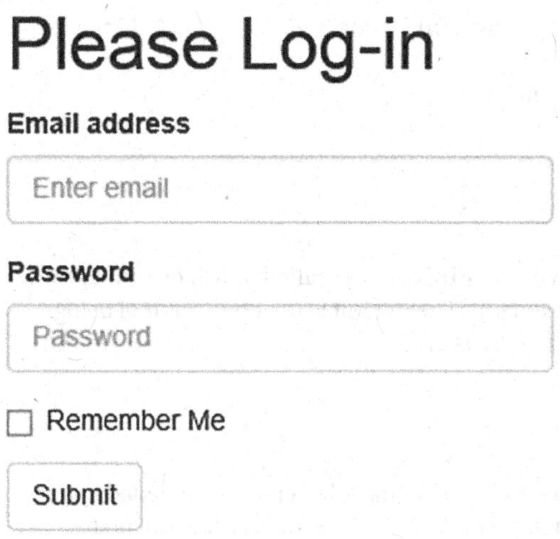

# Please Log-in

**Email address**

Enter email

**Password**

Password

☐ Remember Me

Submit

*Figure 3-1.* *How form shown in Listing 3-26 appears in Internet Explorer 11*

In the following sections, I will walk you through each part of the Razor snippet and explain how it works.

## BeginForm and the @using Statement

The BeginForm HTML Helper behaves somewhat differently than most of the other HTML Helpers. It is invoked as an argument to call a using statement. In Razor, as in C#, the using keyword has two meanings. First, and most common, it is used to include namespaces into a class (or Razor view). The second use is as a wrapper that allows you to declare and instantiate a class that implements the IDisposable interface and ensures that the Dispose method is called even if an exception occurs.

If you look at the method signature of BeginForm, you will see that it returns an MvcForm object that implements the IDisposible interface. The following describes a general sequence of what happens inside BeginForm:

1. The extension method to HtmlHelper will call HtmlHelper.BeginForm, passing in arguments supplied by the developer along with several default values. The extension methods are defined in the Microsoft.AspNetCore.Mvc.Rendering. HtmlHelperFormExtensions class.

2. HtmlHelper.BeginForm generates the opening form tag and adds the essential attributes such as action, method, enctype, and any others assigned by the developer. The action attribute specifies what URL will process the form. The method attribute describes the HTTP method that will be used when the form is submitted and could be either GET or POST.

3. HtmlHelper.BeginForm uses ViewContext.Writer to write the opening form tag to the output stream.

4. An instance of MvcForm is created and returned by HtmlHelper.BeginForm.

5. The Razor view then executes the code inside the curly braces of the using statement.

6. MvcForm's Dispose method is called when the using statement is closed. Inside MvcForm.Dispose, the Form end tag is generated and written to the output stream.

Listing 3-27 shows the HTML output of the BeginForm statement in Listing 3-26.

***Listing 3-27.*** HTML Generated by BeginForm Helper in Listing 3-26

```
<form action="/Home/SomeForm" method="post">
... other statements here
</form>
```

Because the actionName parameter was not supplied when BeginForm was called, it will default to the URL of the current page. It also will use the post method by default. The default is the equivalent of using Html.BeginForm("StandardHtmlHelpers","Home" FormMethod.Post).

## HtmlHelper.Label

The HtmlHelper.Label method will generate an HTML label tag. For the first label created, I needed to supply the for attribute to bind the label with the related input field. This is specified using the first argument.

```
@Html.Label("exampleInputEmail ", "Email Address")
```

The call to the label generated the following HTML:

```
<label for="exampleInputEmail">Email address</label>
```

## HtmlHelper.TextBox

The HtmlHelper.TextBox method generates an HTML input tag. In Listing 3-26 a custom type attribute is added that sets the input as an e-mail address field. The e-mail type is a new form field type that supplies built-in e-mail address format validation.

```
@Html.TextBox("exampleInputEmail","",
              new { placeholder = "Enter email", @class="form-control", type = "email" })
```

In the first argument, a string to be used as both the id and name attributes is supplied. In the second argument, an empty string is supplied for the value. For the final argument, an anonymous class with three members is declared. Each member of the anonymous class adds an HTML attribute. The first adds a placeholder attribute. This attribute is a new HTML 5 feature that allows you to supply a value that will be displayed in an empty form field. When a user clicks inside the field, the value disappears. The class attribute, like the for attribute in the previous example, needs to be escaped with an @ symbol because class is a C# keyword.

The following HTML is generated when the @Html.TextBox method is executed:

```
<input class="form-control" id="exampleInputEmail" name="exampleInputEmail"
placeholder="Enter email" type="email" value="" />
```

The Password and CheckBox HTML Helpers work in a similar manner as TextBox. The main difference is that the type attribute of rendered tag is set to password for Html.Password and checkbox for Html.CheckBox.

# 3-12. Using Strongly Typed HTML Helpers

## Problem

You want to create a form that is bound to a model but want to limit the amount of HTML markup that needs to be hand-coded.

## Solution

Strongly typed HTML Helpers allow you to generate HTML using model data. The model data is used in several ways. First, and probably most important, it provides the proper name and id attributes to your HTML form elements that will allow it to work with the MVC model binder. The model binder is a component that knows how to map your HTML form data to the CLR type you are using as a model. Second, the strongly typed HTML Helpers are also able to take advantage of data attributes applied to your model and can use them to add additional attributes to the generated HTML that can be used for form validation. Listing 3-28 shows a fragment of a Razor view that uses strongly typed HTML Helpers.

***Listing 3-28.*** Razor View Using Strongly Typed HTML Helpers

```
@model Recipe12.Model.LoginViewModel

@using (Html.BeginForm())
{

    <div class="form-group">
        @Html.LabelFor(m=> m.EmailAddress)
        @Html.TextBoxFor(m=> m.EmailAddress,
          new { placeholder = "Enter email", @class = "form-control", type = "email" })
    </div>
    <div class="form-group">
        @Html.LabelFor(m => m.Password)
        @Html.PasswordFor(m=> m.Password,
          new { placeholder = "Password", @class = "form-control" })
    </div>
    <div class="checkbox">
        <label>
            @Html.CheckBoxFor(m=> m.RememberMe)
            Remember Me
        </label>
    </div>
    <button type="submit" class="btn btn-default">Submit</button>

}
```

# How It Works

The strongly typed HTML Helpers take a lambda expression as the first argument. Typically you will use the form m => m.Property, where m represents the instance of the model class passed to the view. In the example shown in Listing 3-28, the LabelFor helper is used to create the markup for the HTML Label tags used in the form. In this example, the most simplistic version of the method is used. It uses data from the model to fill in all the attributes that needed to be coded manually in the example shown in recipe 3-11 (Listing 3-26).

```
@Html.LabelFor(m=> m.EmailAddress)
```

Listing 3-29 shows the model used in this example. It defines properties that align with each of the fields in the login form. It also includes data annotations that mark the EmailAddress and Password properties.

***Listing 3-29.*** Model Used with the Form in Listing 3-28

```
public class LoginViewModel
{
    [Required]
    [Display(Name ="Email Address")]
    public string EmailAddress { get; set; }

    [Required]
    public string Password { get; set; }

    public bool RememberMe { get; set; }
}
```

The true utility of the HTML Helpers can be seen when you look at the HTML rendered by the TextBoxFor method call.

```
@Html.TextBoxFor(m=> m.EmailAddress,
        new { placeholder = "Enter email", @class = "form-control", type = "email" })
```

The generated HTML, shown in Listing 3-30, demonstrates how the HTML Helper can utilize a combination of the HTML attributes passed in the method's arguments and the information from the model class to generate much of the HTML that would otherwise be tedious to hand-code.

***Listing 3-30.*** HTML Output of TextBoxFor Using Metadata from the EmailAddress Property

```
<input class="form-control"
       data-val="true"
       data-val-required="The Email Address field is required."
       id="EmailAddress"
       name="EmailAddress"
       placeholder="Enter email"
       type="email"
       value="" />
```

If you look at the HTML code in Listing 3-30, you can see the placeholder and type attributes injected from the anonymous class passed into the HTML Helper shown in Listing 3-29. The id and name values are derived from the property names of the LoginViewModel class. Two additional attributes have been added that can be used by the jQuery Validation and Microsoft Unobtrusive JavaScript libraries to enable client-side validation for the form. Because the attribute RequiredAttribute was applied to EmailAddress, the HTML Helper added the data-val attribute and the corresponding data-val-required attribute. It also used the value specified in DisplayAttribute when it generated the error message in the data-val-required attribute.

# 3-13. Using Templated HTML Helpers

## Problem

You have used Visual Studio's scaffolding feature to generate a few views and noticed that rather than using TextBoxFor or CheckBoxFor helpers, Visual Studio is using a generic EditorFor HTML Helper. You are wondering how you can use the EditorFor helper in your handcrafted views. You also want to get a better idea of how they work and what templates are included with the MVC framework.

## Solution

The EditorFor and DisplayFor HTML Helpers are special types of HTML Helpers that, rather than having the rendering logic written inside a class library, use a template file associated with a CLR type. This design is especially helpful when designing a composite helper such as a data grid where you are potentially working with many different types that you will not be able to solve for at design time.

You can also create your own templates for your own types or override the default templates. Listing 3-31 demonstrates how this technique can be used with the LoginViewModel shown in Listing 3-29.

*Listing 3-31.* Using Templated HTML Helpers

```
@using (Html.BeginForm())
{
    <div class="form-group">
        @Html.LabelFor(m => m.EmailAddress)
        @Html.EditorFor(m => m.EmailAddress, "EmailAddress",
            new { htmlAttributes =
                new { placeholder = "Enter email", @class = "form-control" } })
    </div>
    <div class="form-group">
        @Html.LabelFor(m => m.Password)
        @Html.EditorFor(m => m.Password, "Password",
            new { htmlAttributes =
                new { placeholder = "Enter password", @class = "form-control" } })
    </div>
    <div class="checkbox">
        <label>
            @Html.LabelFor(m => m.RememberMe)
            Remember Me
        </label>
    </div>
    <button type="submit" class="btn btn-default">Submit</button>

}
```

# How It Works

In the example shown in Listing 3-31, all the fields are generated using the `EditorFor` HTML Helper. The second argument used in each specifies the name of the template to use. The third argument is for additional view data. Starting with MVC 5.1, you are also able to pass in HTML attributes by passing in a nested anonymous type named `htmlAttributes`.

```
new { htmlAttributes =
                new { placeholder = "Enter password", @class = "form-control" }
```

For the `RememberMe` field, no template needs to be specified because there is a default template assigned to Booleans. For the other two fields, you need to explicitly provide the template name; otherwise, MVC would use the `String` template.

The MVC framework includes 17 built-in templates defined in the class `Microsoft.AspNetCore.Mvc.ViewFeatures.Internal.DefaultEditorTemplates`. The built-in templates include the following:

- `Boolean`: This template generates either a check box or a drop-down list, depending on whether the view data is a nullable value type. In the case of a nullable value type, a drop-down list is used because the possibility of a `null` value could allow for three possible states: `true`, `false`, or `null`. To represent the `null` value, the following option is generated: `<option selected="selected" value="">Not Set</option>`.

- `Collection`: This template renders an appropriate template for each item in the collection based on its type.

- `Decimal`: This template renders a text box using an HTML `input` tag.

- `HiddenInput`: This template renders a hidden field using the HTML `input` tag with the `type` attribute set to `hidden`.

- `Multiline`: This template creates a text area.

- `Object`: This template uses the model metadata to determine how to best render. In most cases, it will render a field that consists of both a label and an input field wrapped in a containing `div` element.

- `Password`: This template renders a password input box.

- `String`: This template renders a text box.

- `PhoneNumberInput`: This template renders a text box using the HTML `input` tag with the `type` attribute set to `"tel"`.

- `UrlInput`: This template renders a text box using the HTML `input` tag with the `type` attribute set to `"url"`.

- `EmailAddressInput`: This template renders a text box using the HTML `input` tag with the `type` attribute set to `"email"`.

- `DateTimeInput`: This template renders a text box using the HTML `input` tag with the `type` attribute set to `"datetime"`.

- `DateTimeLocalInput`: This template renders a text box using the HTML `input` tag with the `type` attribute set to `"datetime-local"`.

- `DateInput`: This template renders a text box using the HTML `input` tag with the `type` attribute set to `"date"`. It also applies RFC 3339 Date Formatting to the value if needed.

- TimeInput: This template renders a text box using the HTML input tag with the type attribute set to "time". It also applies RFC 3339 Date Formatting to the value if needed.

- NumberInput: This template renders a text box using the HTML input tag with the type attribute set to "number".

- FileInput: This template renders a file upload button using the HTML input tag with the type attribute set to "file".

- FileCollectionInput: This template renders a file upload button that allows multiple files to be selected using the HTML input tag with the type attribute set to "file" along with the multiple attribute, which allows for more than one file to be selected.

# 3-14. Creating an Inline Function in a Razor View

## Problem

You are creating a new view and have found that you need to repeat some markup repeatedly. Because this markup is applicable only to your current view, you do not want to create a custom HTML Helper or partial view. You need a way to define an HTML Helper inline.

## Solution

Razor allows you to define inline helpers, which are essentially C# functions defined inside the view. Listing 3-32 shows an example.

*Listing 3-32.* Creating Inline HTML Helpers for Showing Alert Boxes

```
@using Microsoft.AspNetCore.Html
<h1>Recipe 3-14 Creating an inline function in a Razor view</h1>
@functions
{
    IHtmlContent warning(string message)
    {
        return Html.Raw(string.Format(@"<p class=""alert alert-warning"">{0}</p>", message));
    }
}

@Html.Label("", "Enter your disposition below")
@warning("Anything you type can and will be used against you in a court of law")
@Html.TextArea("Disposition", new { @class = "form-control" })

<br />
@Html.Label("", "Enter your plea below")
@warning("If you plead guilty you will be taken to a high security prison!")
@Html.TextArea("Plea", new { @class = "form-control" })
```

## How It Works

The code in Listing 3-32 defines a new inline helper called warning. It takes a string as a parameter and uses the Bootstrap CSS styles to create an alert box with the string specified.

Functions need to be defined inside the @functions directive. Note that the function returns the type IHtmlContent and not a string. If a string was returned, then the HTML would be encoded. Past versions of ASP.NET MVC supported the creation of inline functions using the @helper directive. Unfortunately, this functionality does not exist in ASP.NET Core MVC. If you are migrating an application from an ASP MVC 5 application, you would need to refactor your view to use custom HTML Helpers.

# CHAPTER 4

# Using Tag Helpers

Tag Helpers are probably the most significant new feature in ASP.NET Core MVC. In this chapter, I will first provide some background on this new feature and discuss how Tag Helpers compare to HTML Helpers. I will then explain how to use each of the built-in Tag Helpers and then show you how to create custom tab helpers.

You can download the examples in this chapter from GitHub and view them in your web browser at the following URL:

```
https://github.com/johnciliberti/AspNetCoreRecipes/tree/master/Chapter04/Recipes01to09
```

The solutions also make use of a shared database library created for the book. You can download the library via NuGet at the book's MyGet feed. You can find detailed instructions on the setup for the database in the appendix of the book.

## 4-1. Understanding Tag Helpers

### Problem

You have heard about Tag Helpers but are confused on how they compare to HTML Helpers and when and if you should use them. You also want to understand how they work at a deeper level and how they perform in relation to HTML Helpers.

### Solution

HTML Helpers and Tag Helpers offer similar features with significant functional overlap. Tag Helpers are a new feature of the Razor view engine. You can think of them as an alternative to HTML Helpers rather than a replacement. In many cases, which programming model you choose can be based on your personal preference.

Tag Helpers take an HTML-centric approach as opposed to the C#-centric approach of HTML Helpers. Tag Helpers can be implemented as custom HTML tags or as HTML attributes applied to a standard HTML tag.

If you are porting an existing project to ASP.NET Core MVC and have a substantial investment in views built using HTML Helpers, you do not need to migrate them all to Tag Helpers. HTML Helpers are still supported, and there is no indication from Microsoft that they will go away. HTML Helpers will likely be preferred by many developers.

If you are starting a new project or adding new views to an existing project, you should consider using Tag Helpers. Tag Helpers offer an easy-to-understand syntax and give you precision control over the HTML. They do not require the use of lambda expressions to access your model data, and you do not need to define anonymous objects to customize the properties on the generated HTML as you do with HTML Helpers.

Listing 4-1 shows an example of an HTML Helper and then the equivalent Tag Helper for creating an action link to the Index action in the Home controller.

***Listing 4-1.*** Comparing HTML Helpers to Tag Helpers for Creating Action Links

```
<!-- Html Helper creates a link to the Index action on the home controller -->
@Html.ActionLink("Go to home page", "Index", "Home", null, new { @class = "h4" })

<!-- Tag Helper creates a link to the Index action on the home controller -->
<a asp-controller="Home" asp-action="Index" class="h4">Go to home page</a>
```

In both cases, a CSS class named H4 is applied to the link. In the case of the HTML Helper, except for the @ symbol (which tells the Razor parser that you are beginning a code block), the call is pure C# with no HTML mixed in. In cases where you do not need to add styles to a link, the HTML Helper can be very concise. Unfortunately, in cases where you do need to customize the HTML output, the syntax of the HTML Helper begins to become less intuitive and even confusing. In this example, you need to pass a null value for the third argument of ActionLink before constructing an anonymous class containing the name-value pairs for the desired HTML attributes. To make this even less attractive, since the HTML attribute class clashes with the C# keyword with the same name, you need to prepend the class attribute with an @ symbol.

The Tag Helper version of the action link is pure HTML with no C#. The action link consists of an HTML anchor tag with two custom HTML attributes, asp-action and asp-controller. The attributes tell the Razor parser to process the tag as a Tag Helper, and attribute values are passed to the Tag Helper as arguments. Additional HTML attributes such as class are added as usual. The Tag Helper is arguably somewhat more intuitive to write and easier to understand.

In Listing 4-2, a simple form is constructed based on a model class called Contact, which contains a single property called Name. In both the Tag Helper and HTML Helper examples, the form is constructed for posting to the Index action of the Home controller. Both versions also add an AntiForgeryToken token for an added level of security. The form consists of a single input element and a label bound to the Name property of the model.

***Listing 4-2.*** Comparing HTML Helpers to Tag Helpers for Creating Forms

```
@model Chapter04.Models.Recipe01.Contact
<!-- Simple Form Created using HTML Helpers -->
@using (Html.BeginForm("Index", "Home"))
{
    @Html.AntiForgeryToken()
    @Html.LabelFor(model => model.Name)
    @Html.TextBoxFor(model => model.Name,
    new { placeholder = "Enter your Name", @class = "form-control" })
}

<!-- Simple Form Created using Tag Helpers -->
<form asp-action="Index" asp-controller="Home" asp-anti-forgery="true">
    <label asp-for="Name"></label>
    <input asp-for="Name" class="form-control" placeholder="Enter your name" />
</form>
```

As with the action link, the HTML Helper version is pure C# except for the @ symbols. It uses lambda expressions to pass the model properties to the LabelFor and TextBoxFor helpers. Additional HTML attributes for the text box are set using an anonymous class passed as a second argument.

In the Tag Helper version, a standard HTML form tag is used with three custom attributes. The first two tell the Tag Helper where the form should be posted. A third adds the AntiForgeryToken token. The label and input tags also use plain HTML label and input elements. The asp-for attribute is used to pass the model property. No lambda expression is required.

## How It Works

In this section, you will take a deep dive into how Tag Helpers work. The code for Tag Helpers, as with the rest of ASP.NET Core MVC, is available at http://GitHub.com/aspnet. The code for Tag Helpers is split across two main areas of the code base. First is the core runtime, which is responsible for discovering Tag Helpers in Razor markup and then adding the logic dictated by the Tag Helpers in the C# classes generated by the parsing process. You can find this code in the following section of the Razor repo:

https://github.com/aspnet/Razor/tree/dev/src/Microsoft.AspNetCore.Razor.Runtime/TagHelpers

The second body of code consists of the Tag Helpers developed by the ASP.NET Core MVC team. This functionality is bundled with the main Microsoft.AspNetCore.Mvc package and included in all the project templates. At the time of this writing, 18 Tag Helpers are included in this library. You can find the code for the MVC Tag Helpers in the following section of the ASP.NET MVC repo:

https://github.com/aspnet/Mvc/tree/dev/src/Microsoft.AspNetCore.Mvc.TagHelpers

## The Life Cycle of a Tag Helper

The first time you access a Razor view, it is compiled into C# code. It does this by first locating all of the Razor view files that need to be included, parsing the content of your views, and evaluating the expressions. It determines what parts of the view are static content and what needs to be evaluated at runtime. It then generates a C# class that can execute this as efficiently as possible.

During the parsing process, Razor uses a specialized interface called ITagHelperDescriptorResolver to identify any parts of the view's static markup that contain Tag Helpers. It does this using an IEnumerable interface of TagHelperDescriptor. You can find the source code for iTagHelperDescriptorResolver on GitHub under https://github.com/aspnet/Razor/tree/dev/src/Microsoft.AspNetCore.Razor/Compilation/TagHelpers. This includes the descriptors for all Tag Helpers imported into the namespace of the executing view by the developer. Tag Helpers are added to a view using the @addTagHelper directive, as shown in Listing 4-3. This can be done in individual views or for all views by placing the directive in the _ViewImports.cshtml file. _ViewImports.cshtml is a new feature of ASP.NET Core MVC that allows you to specify directives that apply to all views in a given area.

*Listing 4-3.* Adding All Tag Helpers in the Microsoft.AspNet.Mvc.TagHelpers Namespace

```
@addTagHelper "*, Microsoft.AspNet.Mvc.TagHelpers"
```

In Listing 4-3, all 18 of the MVC Tag Helpers will now be considered by the parser as it walks the syntax tree of the view. The code in Listing 4-3 is included in the _ViewImports.cshtml file that is part of all ASP.NET Core Web Application templates. The _ViewImports.cshtml file is a new feature of ASP.NET Core that allows you to add namespaces globally to all views in your project. It should be noted that adding many Tag Helpers to a page will adversely impact parsing time. This performance overhead is limited to the parsing stage. It does not impact page performance once a page has been parsed.

In addition to using the Tag Helpers provided by Microsoft, it is easy to create your own custom Tag Helpers. Tag Helpers are defined by classes that extend the TagHelper base class. They use a set of attributes that include HtmlAttributeNameAttribute and TargetElementAttribute to determine what HTML elements and attributes need to be processed on the server by the Razor view engine. The attribute HtmlAttributeNameAttribute can be used to create a Tag Helper that can be applied to any HTML element if the HTML attribute name defined by HtmlAttributeNameAttribute is present. The attribute TargetElementAttribute will associate your Tag Helper with the specified HTML tags. In addition, you can specify a combination of HTML tags and attributes so that your Tag Helpers are processed only when specified HTML attributes are present in the HTML elements you want to target. Listing 4-4 shows a segment of the source code of the FormTagHelper class. It uses the attribute TargetElementAttribute to create a Tag Helper descriptor for HTML form elements with any of the HTML attribute names defined in the class.

***Listing 4-4.*** FormTagHelper

```
[TargetElement("form", Attributes = ActionAttributeName)]
[TargetElement("form", Attributes = AntiForgeryAttributeName)]
[TargetElement("form", Attributes = ControllerAttributeName)]
[TargetElement("form", Attributes = RouteAttributeName)]
[TargetElement("form", Attributes = RouteValuesDictionaryName)]
[TargetElement("form", Attributes = RouteValuesPrefix + "*")]
public class FormTagHelper : TagHelper
{
    private const string ActionAttributeName = "asp-action";
    private const string AntiForgeryAttributeName = "asp-anti-forgery";
    private const string ControllerAttributeName = "asp-controller";
    private const string RouteAttributeName = "asp-route";
    private const string RouteValuesDictionaryName = "asp-all-route-data";
    private const string RouteValuesPrefix = "asp-route-";
    private const string HtmlActionAttributeName = "action";
// to see full source please visit
// https://github.com/aspnet/Mvc/blob/dev/src/Microsoft.AspNetCore.Mvc.TagHelpers/
FormTagHelper.cs
```

# 4-2. Creating Hyperlinks with the Anchor Tag Helper

## Problem

You are new to ASP.NET Core MVC and want to understand the features of the Anchor Tag Helper.

## Solution

The Anchor Tag Helper allows you to add server-generated content to standard HTML anchor tags. It offers similar functionality to the ActionLink HTML Helper. The Anchor Tag Helper has seven bounded attributes, which are described in Table 4-1.

*Table 4-1.* *Anchor Tag Helper Attributes*

| Attribute Name | Markup | Description |
|---|---|---|
| ActionAttributeName | asp-action | This allows you to specify the action name you want to create a link to. When targeting an action in the same controller, this is the only attribute required for generating the link. |
| ControllerAttributeName | asp-controller | This allows you to specify a controller name. This is required only when creating a link to an action in another controller. |
| FragmentAttributeName | asp-fragment | This is used to create a link to a specific section of a page generated because of an action. The content included in the attribute is appended to the URL following a hash delimiter. For example, if the attribute FragmentAttributeName contained about, the URL of the A tag would be rendered as /someurl#about. |
| HostAttributeName | asp-host | By default, action links are generated as relative URLs. If you need to override this to specify a specific host name, you can do so by adding asp-host="hostname" to the anchor tag. |
| ProtocolAttributeName | asp-protocol | This allows you to specify a protocol such as HTTPS in your action link. It should be noted that when this attribute is included, an absolute URL will be generated. |
| RouteAttributeName | asp-route | This allows you to specify a specific route name. |
| RouteValuesDictionaryName | asp-all-route-data | This allows you to provide additional route parameters. |
| RouteValuesPrefix | asp-route- | This works in conjunction with RouteValuesDictionaryName to provide values for additional route parameters. |

## How It Works

In this section, the various options of the Anchor Tag Helper will be demonstrated in a series of examples.

## Creating a Link to an Action in the Same Controller

When creating a link to an action in the same controller, you can use the asp-action attribute. No other attributes are required. When the asp-controller attribute is omitted, the current controller is used by default. Listing 4-5 shows two links to actions in the same controller with a comment showing the HTML output following each. Notice that for the link to the Index action, the URL / is rendered rather than the full path. This is because in the route template defined in Startup, ("{area:exists}/{controller=Home}/{action=Index}") has defined default values for both the Home controller and Index action.

*Listing 4-5.* Creating a Link to an Action in the Same Controller

```
<a asp-action="Index">Link to other action in same controller</a>
@*<a href="/">Link to default route same controller</a>*@

<a asp-action="Recipe03">Link to other action in same controller</a>
@*<a href="/Home/Recipe03">Link to other action in same controller</a>*@
```

## Creating a Link to an Action in Another Controller

When creating a link to an action in another controller, you need to specify both the action and controller names by using the asp-action and asp-controller attributes. Listing 4-6 shows how to create a link to an action named Somewhere in a controller named Away.

*Listing 4-6.* Creating a Link to an Action in Another Controller

```
<a asp-action="Somewhere" asp-controller="Away">Action Link to another controller</a>
```

## Creating a Link to an Action That Includes a Route Parameter

To support route parameters, the Anchor Tag Helper has defined a wildcard-bound attribute defined as asp-route-*. This allows the hyphen in the attribute name to be followed by any name. This functionality is implemented as a collection, which allows you to pass as many route parameters as you need. Listing 4-7 shows two action links. The first passes a route parameter called Id to the Somewhere action. The second link shown in Listing 4-7 shows a link that could be used as a pager in a grid. It specifies two route parameters for page and sort.

*Listing 4-7.* Passing Route Paramaters

```
<a asp-action="Somewhere"
    asp-controller="Away" asp-route-id="12">Link to item 12</a>

<a asp-action="Somedatagrid" asp-controller="Data"
    asp-route-page="2" asp-route-sort="foo">Page 2</a>
```

## Creating a Link to an Action in an Area

As with the ActionLink HTML Helpers discussed in recipe 3-4, the Anchor Tag Helper treats area as a route parameter. If you have defined a route template for your area like the one shown in Listing 4-8, a link to an area can be created as shown in Listing 4-9.

*Listing 4-8.* Adding a Route Template That Includes an Area to Startup.cs

```
routes.MapRoute(
    name: "areaRoute",
    template: "{area:exists}/{controller=Home}/{action=Index}");
```

*Listing 4-9.* Creating a Link to an Area with the Anchor Tag Helper

```
<a asp-action="InHappyLand"
    asp-controller="ControllerInArea"
    asp-route-area="FarFarAway">Action Link to another area</a>
```

### Creating an Action Link with SSL

If only certain parts of your web site, such as the login page, require SSL, you can use the asp-protocol attribute to specify that a link should use HTTPS, as shown in Listing 4-10. Note that using asp-protocol will cause the link to be rendered as an absolute URL. If no host is given using the asp-host attribute, the host URL will be determined from the host name in the browser's address bar.

*Listing 4-10.* Creating an Action Link That Uses HTTPS

```
<a asp-action="Home" asp-controller="Home" asp-protocol="https">This link uses SSL</a>
```

### Creating an Action Link with an Anchor Target

As discussed in recipe 3-8, there may be times where you want to be able to link directly to a specific section of a page. This can be a certain section of a long document or a deep link in a single-page web application. Listing 4-11 shows an example of how this is done with the Anchor Tag Helper.

*Listing 4-11.* An Action Link with a Fragment

```
<a asp-action="Profile" asp-controller="Home" asp-fragment="Email">Link with a fragment</a>
```

# 4-3. Building a Form Using the Form, Label, and Input Tag Helpers

## Problem

You are starting a new project with ASP.NET Core MVC and want to use Tag Helpers for your new form. You want to understand what is available in the Form Tag Helper and how to use it.

## Solution

The ASP.NET Core MVC Tag Helpers library has several Tag Helpers that can be used in conjunction to create an HTML form. The ones that you will probably end up using the most are the Form, Label, and Input Tag Helpers. The Form Tag Helper creates the opening form tag. It also sets the HTML attributes for the Form tag's Action and Method attributes. The Action attribute dictates the URL the form should be submitted to. The Method attribute sets the HTTP verb that should be used.

The Label and Input helpers can create HTML labels and form fields in a similar manner as the LabelFor and TextBoxFor HTML Helpers—just like the HTML Helper counterparts that can use data from your model when using a strongly typed view.

## How It Works

To demonstrate how to use Tag Helpers, I will walk you through creating a simple contact form that will collect a person's name, e-mail address, favorite color, and whether they want to be contacted for special offers.

## The Model

The form will use a model class called Contact. To create this class, inside an ASP.NET Core MVC Web Application project, create a Models folder if one does not exist. Right-click the Models folder, select Add New Item, and then select Class from the list. Name the new class file Contact.cs.

Modify the contents of the file to match Listing 4-12.

***Listing 4-12.*** Contact.cs

```
using System.ComponentModel.DataAnnotations;

namespace Chapter04.Models.Recipe03
{
    public class Contact
    {
        public string Name { get; set; }

        public string Email { get; set; }

        public string Phone { get; set; }

        public bool AllowContactAboutOffers { get; set; }

        [Display(Name="Favorite Color?")]
        public string FavoriteColor { get; set; }
    }
}
```

The Contact class shown in Listing 4-12 is simple. It exposes several string properties and a bool property for tracking whether the user wants to be contacted about offers. The model includes a data annotation that sets a display name. As with HTML Helpers, Tag Helpers can use this information when rendering the form.

## The Controller

When you create a new ASP.NET Core MVC Web Application project in Visual Studio, it will automatically add a folder for your controllers and add a controller called HomeController. This controller contains actions for the root of the site, which includes the home page, a contacts page, and an "about us" page. An error action is also included. For this example, you will add a new action called Recipe03.

To do this, open the HomeController.cs file and create a new action. The action should include an instance of the Contact class shown in Listing 4-12. The Contact instance is created and passed as an argument to the view. Modify the AllowContactAboutOffers property of Contact so that it is set to true, as shown in Listing 4-13.

***Listing 4-13.*** Adding Model Instance to Contact Action

```
public IActionResult Recipe03()
{
    var model = new Contact { AllowContactAboutOffers = true };
    return View(model);
}
```

Next, add a new version of the Recipe03 action that takes a Contact class as an argument and decorate it with the HttpPost attribute. You should also add a ValidateAntiForgeryToken attribute to the Contact action method. The ValidateAntiForgeryToken attribute adds a security mechanism that prevents a type of attack called *cross-site request forgery*. This is an attack where another site takes advantage of the fact that a user is logged on to your web site and then tricks that user into submitting information that can expose data about that user or modify information on your web site.

Inside the body of the action, add an if statement that verifies that the ModelState.IsValid property is true. If ModelState.IsValid is true, return a view named **"Recipe03Thanks"**; otherwise, return to the Contact view. In both cases, ensure you are also passing the Contact model class. When you're done, HomeController.cs should match Listing 4-14.

---

■ **Note**    The procedure described in this section is the same as you would do if you were using HTML Helpers. Using Tag Helpers does not change how your controller logic is written.

---

*Listing 4-14.* HomeController.cs

```
using Microsoft.AspNetCore.Mvc;
using Chapter04.Models.Recipe03;

namespace Chapter04.Controllers
{
    public class HomeController : Controller
    {
        // other actions here

        public IActionResult Recipe03()
        {
            var model = new Contact { AllowContactAboutOffers = true };
            return View(model);
        }

        [HttpPost]
        [ValidateAntiForgeryToken]
        public IActionResult Recipe03(Contact model)
        {
            if (ModelState.IsValid)
            {
                return View("Recipe03Thanks", model);
            }
            return View(model);
        }
    }
}
```

## The Views

Now that you have a set of the controllers for processing the contact data, you can create the views. There are two separate views used in this example. The first is a contact form, and the second is a "thank you" page. In the Views folder, you will find a subfolder called Home that corresponds to HomeController. Add a new file named Recipe03.cshtml. Modify this file to match Listing 4-15.

*Listing 4-15.* Contact.cshtml

```
@model Chapter04.Models.Recipe03
<h2>Chapter 04 Recipe 03</h2>
<h3>
    Contact Form
</h3>

<hr />
<form asp-action=" Recipe03" asp-anti-forgery="true" method="post">
    <div class="form-group">
        <label asp-for="Name"></label>
        <input asp-for="Name" class="form-control" placeholder="Enter your name" />
    </div>
    <div class="form-group">
        <label asp-for="Email"></label>
        <input asp-for="Email" class="form-control" placeholder="Enter your Email" />
    </div>
    <div class="form-group">
        <label asp-for="Phone"></label>
        <input asp-for="Phone" class="form-control" placeholder="Enter your Phone Number" />
    </div>
    <div class="form-group">
        <label asp-for="FavoriteColor"></label>
        <input asp-for="FavoriteColor" class="form-control"
            placeholder="Select your favorite color" type="color" />
    </div>
    <div class="checkbox">
        <label asp-for="AllowContactAboutOffers">
            <input asp-for="AllowContactAboutOffers" /> Contact me about offers
        </label>
    </div>
    <input type="submit" value="Save Contact Info" class="btn btn-primary" />
</form>
```

The first thing you do in Listing 4-15 is add an @model directive that makes the view strongly typed to the Contact class. You then add a FORM tag. Inside the FORM tag you use two Tag Helper bound attributes. The first bound attribute, asp-action, will route the form submission to go to the Recipe03 action of HomeController. You do not need to add an asp-controller attribute in this case since you are posting to the same controller.

The second bound attribute is the asp-anti-forgery attribute. Including it will add a hidden form field to the view that contains the antiforgery token that was prepared for in the controller.

In addition to the bound attributes, you also add a regular HTML method attribute. This will cause the form to be submitted using an HTTP POST rather than the GET.

Since the site is using the Bootstrap UI library, when constructing the form, each pair of HTML LABEL and INPUT tags are wrapped in a DIV tag with the Bootstrap form-group CSS class applied. Each of the LABEL tags is enhanced with the Tag Helper bound attribute asp-for. This is used to pass in the name of the Model property you want to bind to each of the LABEL tags. Note that when you are typing the name of the property, Visual Studio IntelliSense is smart enough no know that this is a Tag Helper bound attribute and provides you with a list of possible property values that are bound to your model.

One exception to be aware of with LABEL tags is when you nest an input tag inside of one. When the Tag Helper detects this, it does not attempt to modify the inner HTML of the LABEL tag. For this reason, you need to manually add the text for the LABEL rather than relying on content from the data annotations. There is an open issue to address this problem in GitHub.

The INPUT tag also has an asp-for attribute like the LABEL tag. You can also add normal HTML attributes such as class and placeholder. These HTML attributes are rendered as you may expect and are not modified on the server.

For the favorite color property, the INPUT field is set to the type color. This will cause Google Chrome, Firefox, and Microsoft Edge to display a color picker for the input. In older browsers, this will display as a text box.

The last form element is a standard submit button. Clicking the button will cause the data to be posted to the server.

Listing 4-16 shows the Thanks view. Since this view was not part of the ASP.NET Core MVC Project template, it needs to be added manually by right-clicking the Views\Home folder and then selecting Add New ➤ MVC View Page. Name the file Recipe03Thanks.cshtml and click the Add button.

***Listing 4-16.*** Recipe03Thank.cshtml

```
@model Chapter04.Models.Recipe03.Contact
<h2>Thanks @Model.Name , for submitting your contact details.</h2>

@section Scripts{
    <script>
        (function () {
            var color = "@Model.FavoriteColor";
            $("body").css("background-color", color);
        })();
    </script>
}
```

In Recipe03Thanks.cshtml, add the @model directive to make it strongly typed to the Contact class and then add a thank-you message that incorporates the Name property from the model.

On the bottom of the page add a JavaScript block that uses jQuery to change the background color of the page to the color selected by the user. This code takes advantage of two features added to the _Layout.cshtml page included with the template. The Layout page includes jQuery and defines a section called scripts. This allows you to place your scripts directly after the scripts included by the layout page. Note that in Listing 4-16 the script tag omits the TYPE attribute, which is optional in HTML 5. If you are targeting Internet users or use older web browsers at your company, you should add type="text/javascript" to the script tag.

# 4-4. Data Binding a Nullable bool to an Option Tag Helper

## Problem

You have a model that includes a property with a nullable bool type. You want to use Tag Helpers for new views that you are creating but are not sure how to data bind this type of property. With HTML Helpers, you were able to use the EditorFor helper to generate a drop-down list. With Tag Helpers, you have tried using the Input Tag Helper but have found that it renders a text box rather than a drop-down list.

## Solution

Tag Helpers currently do not have a generic EditorFor or DisplayFor type of functionality that determines the template based on the data type of the model property. You can, however, re-create the same functionality in your view by adding some basic HTML code.

In the case of a nullable bool, you have three possible states: true, false, or null. The generated HTML in your view must account for all three of these values for the ASP.NET Core MVC model binder to work properly. One way to accomplish this to use an HTML SELECT element with three OPTION child elements.

## How It Works

In this section, you will create a model called Tristate and a simple form that displays a drop-down list that will be bound to it.

If you want to follow along with this example, create a new ASP.NET Core MVC project in Visual Studio using the ASP.NET Core MVC Web Application (.NET Core) template and ensure that the authentication type is set to None.

## The Model

If it does not exist, add a Models folder to the project by right-clicking the project and selecting Add ➤ Folder from the pop-up menu. Add a new class to the folder by right-clicking it and selecting Add ➤ New Item and then selecting the Class template from the Add New Item screen. Name the new class Tristate. The completed class should resemble Listing 4-17. The class consists of a single property called NullableBoolValue.

*Listing 4-17.* The Tristate Class

```
namespace Chapter04.Models.Recipe04
{
    public class Tristate
    {
        public bool? NullableBoolValue { get; set; }
    }
}
```

## The Controller

Open the Home controller and add two new version actions. Both actions should be named Recipe04, but the second Recipe04 action should have an HttpPost attribute that accepts a Tristate object as an argument named model. The Recipe04 action should consist of a single statement that returns a view with a model passed as an argument. You are not modifying the model but only passing it back to the view so you can verify that model binding occurred.

The Index action for HTTP GET should also be modified so that a new Tristate instance is passed to the view. The completed Home controller should match Listing 4-18.

*Listing 4-18.* Home Controller

```
using Microsoft.AspNetCore.Mvc;
using Chapter04.Models.Recipe04;

namespace Chapter04.Controllers
{
    public class HomeController : Controller
    {
        public IActionResult Recipe04()
        {
            Tristate model = new Tristate { NullableBoolValue = null };
            return View(model);
        }

        [HttpPost]
        public IActionResult Recipe04(Tristate model)
        {
            return View(model);
        }

        // other actions here
    }
}
```

## The View

Create a new view under the Views/Home directory and name it Recipe04.cshtml. After deleting the boilerplate content, add an @model directive to the view that makes the view strongly typed to the Tristate class. You will then need to use the Form Tag Helper to create a FORM tag. Use the asp-for bound property to set the form action to the Index action. The HTML method attribute of the FORM tag should be set to post.

Inside the form, create a SELECT element and use the asp-for bound attribute to associate the HTML element with the NullableBoolValue property of the model. You will then need to add three OPTION elements inside the SELECT element. Each of the SELECT elements should have a value attribute. The first will represent the null state and should be set to an empty string. The value of the remaining two should be set to true and false. Note that it must be set to true and false, not 1 and 0; otherwise, the model binding will not work.

To verify that the model binding did occur and the version of the model has retained its value, you can add an if statement that displays a message stating that the property contains no value if null or the value if it contains one. The completed code should look like Listing 4-19.

*Listing 4-19.* Index View with Form Demonstrating Data Binding to Tristate

```
@model Chapter04.Models.Recipe04.Tristate

<h2>Chapter 04 - Recipe 04</h2>
@if (!@Model.NullableBoolValue.HasValue)
{
    <div class="alert alert-warning">
        NullableBoolValue = No Value
    </div>
}
else
{
    <div class="alert alert-info">
        NullableBoolValue = @Model.NullableBoolValue.Value
    </div>
}
<form asp-action="Recipe04 method="post">
    <div class="form-group">
        <label asp-for="NullableBoolValue"></label>
        <select asp-for="NullableBoolValue" class="form-control">
            <option value="">None Selected</option>
            <option value="true">True</option>
            <option value="false">False</option>
        </select>
    </div>
    <input type="submit" name="save" value="Save" class="btn btn-default" />
</form>
```

# 4-5. Creating a Drop-Down List with the Select Tag Helper

## Problem

You want to display a form that would allow users to select from a list of items. The items list is data-driven and can change depending on the customer accessing your web site, so it needs to be built dynamically rather than with static HTML. You want to implement the form using Tag Helpers but are not sure how.

## Solution

The ASP.NET Core MVC Tag Helpers library comes with a Select Tag Helper. This Tag Helper implements two bounded properties. The first, asp-for, allows you to bind the HTML SELECT element to a property of your model. The second, asp-items, accepts an IEnumerable of SelectListItem objects. The SelectListItem class is defined in the Microsoft.AspNetCore.Mvc.Rendering namespace. It allows you to define the text, value, and group of each item, and it allows you to specify whether each item is selected or enabled.

The Select Tag Helper does not currently support the ability to use arbitrary collection types as a list in the current release. It would be up to you to implement an adapter to move data from your custom entity into the SelectListItem class. Another limitation is that the Select Tag Helper's asp-for element can only model bind with simple types such as integers or strings.

114

# How It Works

To demonstrate how to use a drop-down list with the Select Tag Helper, you will create a simple form that allows a user to select from a list of guitar brands and then displays which brand was selected.

## The Model

The model for this example is made up of two classes. The first class, GuitarBrand, consists of two properties, one for the ID of the brand and the other for the brand name. The second class, GuitarBrandViewModel, will be used in the strongly typed view. Listing 4-20 shows the completed models.

*Listing 4-20.* The Models

```
// GuitarBrand.cs
namespace Recipe05.Web.Models
{

    public class GuitarBrand
    {
        public int GuitarBrandId { get; set; }
        public string Name { get; set; }
    }
}

// GuitarBrandViewModel.cs
using System.Collections.Generic;
using Microsoft.AspNetCore.Mvc.Rendering;

namespace Chapter04.Models.Recipe05 {
    public class GuitarBrandViewModel
    {
        public List<SelectListItem> Brands { get; set; }
        public int SelectedBrandId { get; set; }
        public GuitarBrand SelectedBrand { get; set; }
    }
}
```

## The Controller

The controller is made up of two actions. The first action, shown in Listing 4-21, is bound to the GET HTTP verb. It sets up an instance of the GuitarBrandViewModel class and populates its Brands property with a list of SelectListItem objects. For the sake of simplicity, I have used a static list here, but you can easily create this list by creating an adapter that will build the list using values loaded from a database.

*Listing 4-21.* The Controller

```
using Chapter04.Models.Recipe05;
using Microsoft.AspNetCore.Mvc;
using Microsoft.AspNetCore.Mvc.Rendering;
using System.Collections.Generic;
using System.Linq;
```

```
namespace Chapter04.Controllers
{
    public class HomeController : Controller
    {
        private List<SelectListItem> _items = new List<SelectListItem>
        {
                new SelectListItem { Value="", Text="Please Select a Brand"},
                new SelectListItem { Value="1", Text="Gibson" },
                new SelectListItem { Value="2", Text="Charvel" },
                new SelectListItem { Value="3", Text="Ibenez" },
                new SelectListItem { Value="4", Text="Jackson"  }
        };

        public IActionResult Recipe05()
        {
            var model = new GuitarBrandViewModel { Brands = _items };
            return View(model);
        }

        // more actions here
    }
}
```

The second action, shown in Listing 4-22, is invoked for the POST verb and takes GuitarBrandViewModel as an argument. Note that the Brands property is not copied back to the server since it does not have an Input tag representation in the HTML code. You must repopulate this value to display it again on the page.

***Listing 4-22.*** Index Post Action

```
[HttpPost]
public IActionResult Recipe05(GuitarBrandViewModel model)
{
    model.Brands = _items;
    if (model.SelectedBrandId != 0)
    {
        model.SelectedBrand = (from b in model.Brands
                              where b.Value == model.SelectedBrandId.ToString()
                                select new GuitarBrand {
                                        GuitarBrandId = int.Parse(b.Value),
                                        Name = b.Text }).FirstOrDefault();

    }

    return View(model);
}
```

Since the model posted back to the server contains only the value of the selected item, not the entire item, you must use that value to query your repository if you want to display more information about the item selected. In this example I am using LINQ to Objects to select an item from the _items list defined on the page. Listing 4-23 shows the completed controller.

***Listing 4-23.*** The Controller

```
using Chapter04.Models.Recipe05;
using Microsoft.AspNetCore.Mvc;
using Microsoft.AspNetCore.Mvc.Rendering;
using System.Collections.Generic;
using System.Linq;

namespace Chapter04.Controllers
{
    public class HomeController : Controller
    {
        private List<SelectListItem> _items = new List<SelectListItem>
        {
                new SelectListItem { Value="", Text="Please Select a Brand"},
                new SelectListItem { Value="1", Text="Gibson" },
                new SelectListItem { Value="2", Text="Charvel" },
                new SelectListItem { Value="3", Text="Ibenez" },
                new SelectListItem { Value="4", Text="Jackson"  }
        };

        public IActionResult Recipe05()
        {
            var model = new GuitarBrandViewModel { Brands=_items};
            return View(model);
        }


        [HttpPost]
        public IActionResult Recipe05(GuitarBrandViewModel model)
        {
            model.Brands = _items;
            if (model.SelectedBrandId != 0)
            {
                model.SelectedBrand = (from b in model.Brands
                                       where b.Value == model.SelectedBrandId.ToString()
                                       select new GuitarBrand {
                                           GuitarBrandId = int.Parse(b.Value),
                                           Name = b.Text }).FirstOrDefault();

            }

            return View(model);
        }
    }
}
```

## The View

In addition to the form, the view consists of an `if` statement that checks whether the `SelectedBrand` property of the model has been set and, if so, displays the name of the selected item. The form is built using the `Form` Tag Helper and consists of `Label` and `Select` Tag Helpers for displaying the drop-down list and a regular HTML submit button.

Listing 4-24 shows the completed view.

***Listing 4-24.*** The View

```
@model Chapter04.Models.Recipe05.GuitarBrandViewModel
<h2>Chapter 04 - Recipe 05</h2>
@if (Model.SelectedBrand == null)
{
    <div class="alert alert-warning">
        No Brand has been selected
    </div>
}
else
{
    <div class="alert alert-success">
        @Model.SelectedBrand.Name <text>has been selected</text>
    </div>
}

<form asp-action="Recipe05" method="post">
    <div class="form-group">
        <label asp-for="SelectedBrandId"></label>
        <select asp-for="SelectedBrandId" asp-items="Model.Brands" class="form-control"></select>
    </div>
    <input type="submit" value="Save" class="btn btn-default" />
</form>
```

# 4-6. Validating Input with Tag Helpers

## Problem

To provide the best user experience for your customers, you want your web site to have clean and easy-to-understand form validation messages. You want to be able have the validation logic executed in the browser so that the user will get immediate feedback, with additional validation on the server in case the user has disabled JavaScript in the browser. You are planning on using Tag Helpers to build your form.

## Solution

Just like HTML Helpers, Tag Helpers can work in conjunction with .NET's model validation functionality and the jQuery Validation and jQuery Validation Unobtrusive jQuery plug-ins. The jQuery plug-ins take advantage of HTML attributes added dynamically to the HTML INPUT elements by the Tag Helpers to process the validation rules in the browser.

On the server, ASP.NET Core MVC exposes features of the built-in model validation functionality provided by the .NET Framework. The .NET Framework allows metadata, which includes validation rules to be applied to a class. Validation rules can be applied declaratively using data annotations or programmatically using something like the Fluent Validation library, which is available in the NuGet gallery.

To enable these features, you first need to add the metadata to your model class and then add the required JavaScript libraries and validation Tag Helpers to your view.

## How It Works

To learn how to use the validation features of the ASP.NET Core MVC Tag Helpers library, you will create a simple contact form that asks for name, e-mail address, and phone number. You will start by defining a class called Contact and then add metadata to the class using data annotations. Next, you will create a controller with actions to display the form and process the form submission. You then create a view that uses Tag Helpers to create the form.

## The Model

The model, shown in Listing 4-25, is made up of a single class called Contact that contains three properties: Name, Email, and Phone. A using statement adds the System.ComponentModel.DataAnnotations namespace to the class. System.ComponentModel.DataAnnotations contains a number of data annotation attributes that can be used by ASP.NET Core MVC's model binder to generate the appropriate validation rules. ASP. NET Core MVC applies this on the client side by using the data annotation attributes when generating the HTML form. ASP.NET Core also uses this data when it converts the data being submitted to the server into a CLR object during model binding.

The Name and Email properties have been decorated with the Required attribute. This will add a rule that will mark the property as invalid if it is Null or contains an empty string. The Email property has been decorated with an EmailAddress attribute. This attribute uses a regular expression to validate that the value of the Email property contains a value that matches the rules for a valid e-mail address. The Phone attribute on the Phone property uses the same technique to ensure that the value is a valid U.S. phone number.

*Listing 4-25.* The Model

```
using System.ComponentModel.DataAnnotations;

namespace Chapter04.Models.Recipe06
{
    public class Contact
    {
        [Required]
        public string Name { get; set; }

        [Required]
        [EmailAddress]
        public string Email { get; set; }

        [Phone]
        public string Phone { get; set; }

    }
}
```

## The Controller

The controller, shown in Listing 4-26, contains two actions. The first action simply returns the view and displays the form. The second, which is activated on an HTTP POST, checks the value of the ModelState. IsValid property. If ModelState.IsValid is true, the user will be return a view that displays a thank-you message. When the ModelState is invalid, the user is shown the Index view again so they can see the validation error messages, correct the errors, and resubmit the form.

*Listing 4-26.* The Controller

```
namespace Chapter04.Controllers
{
    public class HomeController : Controller
    {
        public IActionResult Recipe06()
        {
            return View();
        }

        [HttpPost]
        public IActionResult Recipe06(Contact model)
        {
            if (ModelState.IsValid)
            {
                return View("Recipe06Thanks");
            }
            return View();
        }
    }
}
```

## The View

In the view, shown in Listing 4-27, you make use of several Tag Helpers to make validation work.

*Listing 4-27.* The View

```
@model Chapter04.Models.Recipe06.Contact

<h2>Chapter 04 - Recipe 06</h2>

<form method="post">
<!-- NOTE: For this to work some custom styles need to be added. See wwwroot/css/site.css
for more info-->
    <div asp-validation-summary="All"
        class="validation-summary alert alert-danger alert-dismissable">
        <button type="button" class="close" data-dismiss="alert" aria-label="Close">
            <span aria-hidden="true">
                &times;
            </span>
        </button>
```

```
        <h3>We found some errors with your submission</h3>
    </div>
    <hr />
    <div class="form-group">
        <label asp-for="Name" ></label>
        <input asp-for="Name" class="form-control" />
        <span asp-validation-for="Name" class="text-danger"></span>
    </div>
    <div class="form-group">
        <label asp-for="Email"></label>
        <input asp-for="Email" class="form-control"  />
        <span asp-validation-for="Email" class="text-danger"></span>
    </div>
    <div class="form-group">
        <label asp-for="Phone"></label>
        <input asp-for="Phone" class="form-control"  />
        <span asp-validation-for="Phone" class="text-danger"></span>
    </div>
    <input type="submit" value="Save" class="btn btn-primary" />
</form>

@section scripts{
  <script src="/lib/jquery-validation/dist/jquery.validate.js"></script>
  <script src="/lib/jquery-validation-unobtrusive/jquery.validate.unobtrusive.js"></script>
}
```

The first step is to add a scripts section to the page. This is a section defined in _Layout.cshtml that will allow you to place your scripts at the end of the page. In it you reference jquery.validate.js and jquery.validate.unobtrusive.js. These libraries work together to perform client-side validation using the data attributes generated on the server side using the data annotations you added to your model. It should be noted that if these libraries are omitted, validation will still occur on the server.

Next, at the top of the form, you define a DIV tag with an asp-validation-summary attribute. The inclusion of this attribute transforms your ordinary DIV tag into a validation summary Tag Helper. You assign the asp-validation-summary attribute the value of All, which tells the summary to display all errors including property errors that are not directly related to the model. Other possible options allowed here include ModelOnly, which excludes the property errors, and None, which will not show a validation summary. You will be creating some styles (as you can see in the code comment), and I'll cover them in the next section.

Each of the properties of the model has several HTML elements associated with it. There is a DIV with a form-group class that wraps all the related elements for styling purposes. Inside the wrapping DIV is a Label Tag Helper, an Input Tag Helper, and a SPAN tag. The SPAN tag contains an asp-validation-for attribute. The asp-validation-for turns the SPAN into a validation Tag Helper and will display an error message if a validation error occurs. Figure 4-1 shows how the page will appear with the validation errors. It should be noted that if JavaScript is not available, the page must be submitted to the server before the errors will be displayed.

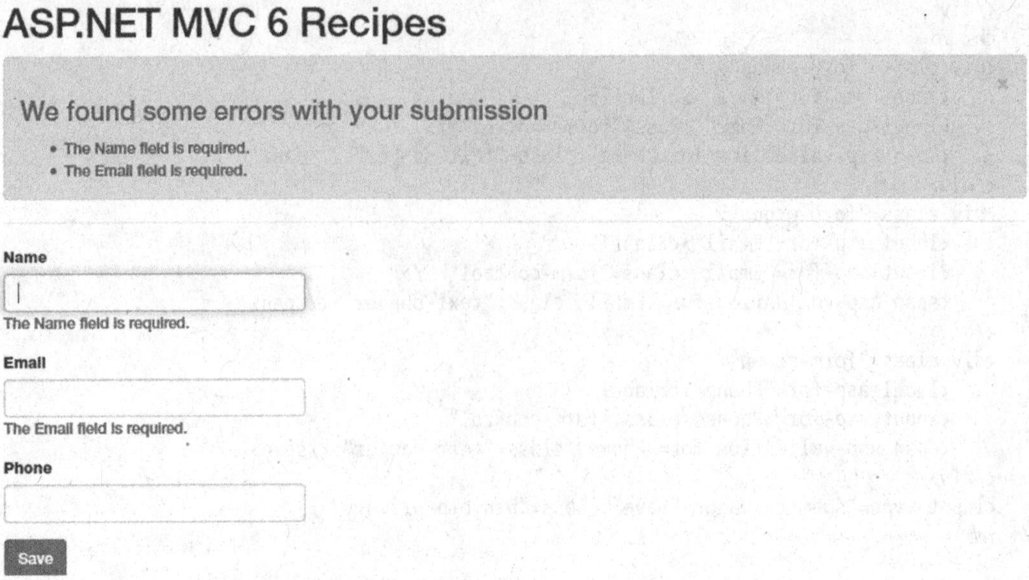

## ASP.NET MVC 6 Recipes

We found some errors with your submission

- The Name field is required.
- The Email field is required.

**Name**

The Name field is required.

**Email**

The Email field is required.

**Phone**

Save

*Figure 4-1.* *Validation errors with a validation summary*

## Enhancing the User Experience with CSS

One drawback of using the built-in Tag Helpers or HTML Helpers is that you do not have full control over the rendered HTML. For example, there is currently no mechanism with the validation Tag Helper that would allow you to specify a custom class to be applied to your form element when a validation error occurs.

A workaround for this limitation is to take advantage of some of the CSS classes added to the form fields as part of the normal functionality of the Input Tag Helper. Listing 4-28 shows the HTML rendered on the server by the Razor markup shown in Listing 4-27 when a validation error occurs. Note the addition of the input-validation-error CSS class to the INPUT elements with validation errors.

Taking advantage of some of the styling that comes out of the box with Bootstrap, the following CSS classes are added: alert alert-danger alert-dismissable. This is a custom class that you add to the site.css style sheet with a single property that sets display to none. This will hide the validation summary until it needs to be displayed.

Also in site.css is a CSS class named validation-summary-errors. This also contains a single style that sets the display property to block. This class will be injected into the class attribute automatically by unobtrusive validation if a validation error occurs and will override the validation-summary attribute causing the summary to be displayed. Listing 4-29 shows the CSS styles.

*Listing 4-28.* HTML Output by the View

```
<div class="form-group">
  <label for="Name">Name</label>
      <input name="Name" class="form-control input-validation-error"
          id="Name"
          type="text"
          value="" data-val-required="The Name field is required."
          data-val="true">
```

```
    <span class="text-danger field-validation-error"
        data-valmsg-replace="true"
        data-valmsg-for="Name"><span for="Name">The Name field is required.</span></span>
</div>
```

Since you now know that a CSS class will be added to the INPUT elements, you can use CSS to style them. In this case I am borrowing the style definition from the Bootstrap CSS library has-error CSS class and using it for the input-validation-error class, as shown in Listing 4-29. This allows the form to have styling consistent with the Bootstrap library that I am using for the rest of the site. Also shown in Listing 4-29 are the styles used to show and hide the validation summary.

*Listing 4-29.* Custom CSS for the input-validation-error Classes

```css
/* This class hides the validation summary when no errors are detected */
.validation-summary {
    display: none;
}

/* This class will be injected into the class attribute or your validation summary */
.validation-summary-errors
{
    display:block;
}

/* Puts red outline around input */
.input-validation-error {
    border-color: #b94a48;
    -webkit-box-shadow: inset 0 1px 1px rgba(0, 0, 0, 0.075);
    box-shadow: inset 0 1px 1px rgba(0, 0, 0, 0.075);
}
```

Figure 4-2 shows the result of the updated CSS. Note that input elements with validation errors now have a red border color.

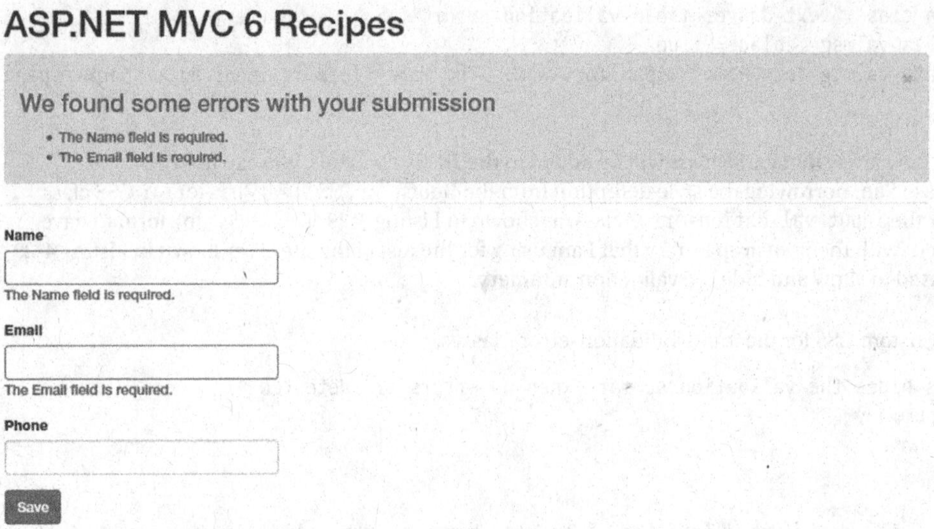

## ASP.NET MVC 6 Recipes

**We found some errors with your submission**

- The Name field is required.
- The Email field is required.

**Name**

[                    ]

The Name field is required.

**Email**

[                    ]

The Email field is required.

**Phone**

[                    ]

[Save]

*Figure 4-2.  Validation error shown with updated styles*

# 4-7. Improving Performance with the Cache Tag Helper

## Problem

You have a form with a drop-down list that requires a lookup to your database. The values used in the drop-down do not change often. You are looking for a way to optimize performance by holding a copy of the list of items for the drop-down list in memory rather than querying the database each time.

## Solution

The ASP.NET Core MVC Tag Helpers library comes with a Cache Tag Helper. The Cache Tag Helper allows you to cache sections of your view so the output for that section is retained in memory. The processing needed to create the content, which may include running queries against your data store, processing the data, and rendering content, will occur only when the cache is refreshed.

One technique that works well with the Cache Tag Helper is to use it in combination with a view component. View components are like partial views but have their own controllers and models. This allows you to separate the logic for rendering the list content from the rest of your controller logic. This pattern is especially helpful for drop-down lists.

## How It Works

To demonstrate how to improve performance with the Cache Tag Helper, you will create a view component that generates HTML OPTION elements that can be the child elements for a Select Tag Helper. You will then create a view that uses the Cache Tag Helper to cache the content generated by the view component.

## Configuring the Project to Connect to a Database

This exercise uses a SQL Server database and a data access class library for interacting with it. You can download the database with the book's source code from the Apress web site. Please refer to the appendix for instructions on how to install SQL Server to set up the database. The class library project called Shared. DataAccess contains the entity models and repository classes for accessing the database. To simplify using the library, it has been made available as a NuGet package from the book's NuGet repository on MyGet. Once you have added a reference to the Shared.DataAccess NuGet package, you will then need to add the connection string to your configuration file. You can then register the DbContext class defined in the Shared. DataAccess project in your Startup.cs file.

### Adding the Shared.DataAccess NuGet Package

If you have not configured Visual Studio to use the book's MyGet feed, please refer to the instructions to do so in the appendix. Once this is set up, you will then be able to add the book's shared libraries to your project using either the NuGet Package Manager or the Package Manager Console.

To add the package using the NuGet Package Manager Console, right-click the project name in Solution Explorer and select Manage NuGet Packages from the pop-up menu. In the NuGet window, click Browse and select AspNetCoreMVCRecipes as the package source. From the package list, select Shared.DataAccess and then click the Install button. When you're done, the Package Manager window should resemble Figure 4-3.

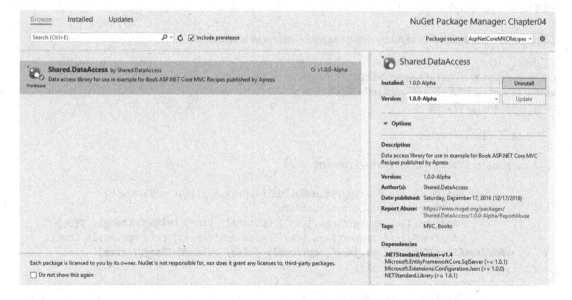

*Figure 4-3.* *Adding Shared.DataAccess to your project using NuGet Package Manager*

### Adding the ConnString.json File

For the web application to use the data access component, you need to first add a configuration file that contains the database connection string. To do this, right-click the project name in Solution Explorer and select Add New; then select the ASP.NET Configuration File template from the Add New Item window. Name the file ConnStrings.json. Listing 4-30 shows ConnStrings.json.

*Listing 4-30.* ConnStrings.json

```
{
  "ConnectionStrings": {
    "DefaultConnection": "Server=localhost;Database= AspNetCoreRecipesSharedDb;Trusted_
Connection=True;MultipleActiveResultSets=true"

}
```

In Listing 4-30, a configuration value is stored under ConnectionStrings:DefaultConnection. The connection string connects to a default instance of SQL Server 2014 running on the local machine.

## Registering Shared.DataAccess with ASP.NET Core's Dependency Injection System

Shared.DataAccess exposes an Entity Framework 7 DbContext object named MobContext. To use this component in your applications, MobContext needs to be registered with ASP.NET Core's dependency injection system. Once registered, ASP.NET Core MVC will inject an instance of MobContext into your controller class's constructor. Listing 4-31 shows how to add the new configuration file, ConnStrings.json, to the configuration builder and then use this configuration information when registering the MobContext object. The code in bold shows the modifications made from the default Startup.cs file included in the ASP.NET Core MVC template.

*Listing 4-31.* Configuration to Allow Access to MobContext in Startup.cs

```
// other using statements ...
using Microsoft.EntityFrameworkCore;
using AspNetCoreMvcRecipes.Shared.DataAccess;
namespace Recipe07.Web
{
    public class Startup
    {
        public Startup(IHostingEnvironment env)
        {
            var builder = new ConfigurationBuilder(appEnv.ApplicationBasePath)
                .SetBasePath(env.ContentRootPath)
                .AddJsonFile("appsettings.json", optional: true, reloadOnChange: true)
                .AddJsonFile($"appsettings.{env.EnvironmentName}.json", optional: true)
            .AddJsonFile("ConnStrings.json", optional: false, reloadOnChange: true)
            .AddEnvironmentVariables();

            Configuration = builder.Build();
        }

        public IConfiguration Configuration { get; set; }

        public void ConfigureServices(IServiceCollection services)
        {
            services.AddDbContext<MoBContext>(options =>
                options.UseSqlServer(Configuration.GetConnectionString("DefaultConnection")));
```

```
        // Add MVC services to the services container.
        services.AddMvc();

    }

    // Configure method goes here ...

    }
}
```

Listing 4-31 shows the Startup class constructor and the ConfigureServices method. In the constructor, the Configuration property is initialized with four configuration sources. The first three configuration sources are JSON files. The first JSON file contains basic site settings. The second is for optional environment-specific settings. The third is the new configuration you created that contains the database connection strings. The last configuration source is environment variables.

In the ConfigureServices method, you use the AddDbContext method to register MobContext with the dependency injection system. Using a lambda expression, you inject the configuration for MobContext telling it to use the SQL Server provider with the connection string you supplied in the ConnStrings.json file.

Loading configuration into an object's constructor as a set of options is known as the Options pattern. This pattern is described in the official ASP.NET documentation and can be found at the following URL:

```
http://docs.asp.net/en/latest/fundamentals/configuration.html#options-config-objects
```

## Creating the View Component

Before you can create a view component, you need to first create a new folder structure that follows the ASP. NET Core MVC convention for view components. To do this, right-click the project name and select New ➤ Folder from the context menu. Name the new folder ViewComponents. Right-click the ViewComponents folder and select Add ➤ Class. Name the class LookupListViewComponent and click the Add button.

---

■ **Note**    The name of the view component class, LookupListViewComponent, uses a convention that lets the ASP.NET Core MVC runtime know how to locate the code when it is invoked in a view. When following this convention, you can access the component using the first part, LookupList, of the class name only.

---

Modify the contents of the LookupListViewComponent class to match Listing 4-32. The LookupList ViewComponent class inherits from the ViewComponent class and implements a single method named Invoke. You can think of the ViewComponent class as a specialized controller and the Invoke method as an action. Note that since you are using the ASP.NET Core MVC dependency injection system, the instance of the database context class is passed into the ViewComponent via its constructor. This is the same technique you would use to inject a dependency into a controller.

Inside the body of the Invoke method, you will make a LINQ query against the data access code and write the results as a list of SelectListItem objects.

*Listing 4-32.* LookupListViewComponent

```
using System.Linq;
using AspNetCoreMvcRecipes.Shared.DataAccess;
using Microsoft.AspNetCore.Mvc.Rendering;
using Microsoft.AspNetCore.Mvc;
```

```
namespace Chapter04.ViewComponents
{
    public class LookupListViewComponent : ViewComponent
    {
        private readonly MoBContext _dbContext;

        public LookupListViewComponent(MoBContext dbContext)
        {
            _dbContext = dbContext;
        }

        public IViewComponentResult Invoke()
        {
            var query = from a in db.GenreLookUps
                        select new SelectListItem {
                            Text = a.GenreName,
                            Value = a.GenreLookUpId.ToString() };

            return View(query.ToList());

        }

    }

}
```

## Creating the View for the View Component

Views for view components use a standard Razor .cshtml file just like normal views. The main difference is that they must be stored in a specific directory structure, as shown in Figure 4-4.

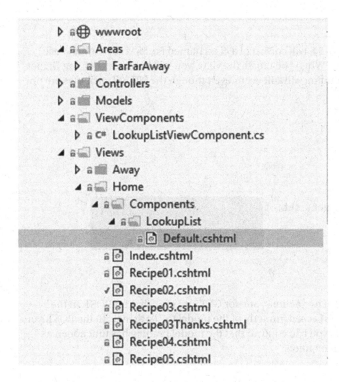

*Figure 4-4.* *Directory structure for view components*

As shown in Figure 4-4, you will need to create a directory called Components under the Views\Home directory. Under Components you can create a directory named LookupList. The name of the directory must match the name of the ViewComponent less the ViewComponent suffix. The name of the file must be Default. cshtml. If your view component needs to be shared by more than one controller, it is recommended that it be placed under Views\Shared\Components rather than under a specific controller folder such as Home.

## The ViewComponent View

As shown in Listing 4-33, the view for the view component will use a list of SelectListItems objects as the model. It will then loop through the list and add an OPTION element for each item.

*Listing 4-33.* The ViewComponent View for SelectListItems

```
@model List<SelectListItem>
@foreach(var item in Model)
{
  <option value="@item.Value">@item.Text</option>
}
```

## The Model

The model for this exercise, shown in Listing 4-34, will consist of a class named FormWithCacheViewModel and a single property named MyListIsCached. When you create the view, you will bind a Select Tag Helper to this property to demonstrate that model binding will still occur even though the OPTION attributes are not generated as part of the Tag Helper.

*Listing 4-34.* The FormWithCacheModel

```
namespace Chapter04.Models.Recipe07
{
    public class FormWithCacheModel
    {
        public string MyListIsCached { get; set; }
    }
}
```

## The Controller

The controller shown in Listing 4-35 consists of two actions, one for GET and the other for POST. In the GET action, you will manually set the MyListIsCached property of the model to "Nothing". In the POST, you will simply pass the model back to the view so you can confirm that the model binding has functioned as expected and that the selected value has been retained.

*Listing 4-35.* The Controller

```
using Chapter04.Models.Recipe07;
using Microsoft.AspNetCore.Mvc;

namespace Chapter04.Controllers
{
    public class HomeController : Controller
    {
        public IActionResult Recipe07()
        {
            var model = new FormWithCacheViewModel { MyListIsCached = "Nothing" };
            return View(model);
        }

        [HttpPost]
        public IActionResult Recipe07(FormWithCacheViewModel model)
        {
            return View(model);
        }
    }
}
```

# The View

In the view shown in Listing 4-36, you start by setting the @model directive to the FormWithCacheViewModel model. You then display the current value of the model's MyListIsCached property.

The Cache Tag Helper is nested inside the SELECT element. The Cache Tag Helper is a bit different from the other Tag Helpers you have seen so far in that Cache is an HTML element rather than just an attribute added to an element. This design allows the functionality of the Cache Tag Helper to be applied to all children of the CACHE element and not just the element itself. Inside the CACHE element, the LookupList view component is invoked asynchronously. Note that the SELECT element is model bound to the MyListIsCached property of the model using the asp-for bound attribute. The asp-for attribute adds the HTML name attribute along with any other attributes needed for validation but does not interfere with the cached set of OPTION elements generated by the ViewComponent.

*Listing 4-36.* View That Uses the Cache Tag Helper

```
@model Chapter04.Models.Recipe07.FormWithCacheViewModel

<h2>Chapter 04 - Recipe 07</h2>

Selected Value : @Model.MyListIsCached

<form method="post">
    <div class="form-group">
        <label asp-for="MyListIsCached">
        </label>
        <select asp-for="MyListIsCached" class="form-control">
            <cache>
                <!--This section is cached-->
                @await Component.InvokeAsync("LookupList")
            </cache>
        </select>
    </div>
    <input type="submit" value="Save" class="btn btn-primary" />
</form>
```

View components are asynchronous, which typically means they do not block any threads on the web server while they are waiting on I/O operations such as making a network call to a database. Instead, they relinquish the thread and give it back to the pool until the I/O operation has completed. This design increases the number of requests a web application can handle. Because view components are asynchronous, they do not return the type you expect. They instead will return a Task<T>. The Task object is a function that will be executed asynchronously at some point. Because of this, simply calling Component.InvokeAsync("LookupList") will return only a Task object but not actually execute the Invoke method implemented in Listing 4-32. To execute the code, you need to use @await Component.InvokeAsync("LookupList").

You can test that the code is executing as expected by running a tool such as SQL Server Profiler. This is a free tool that is included as part of SQL Server 2014 Express. If you start the profiler and then run the application, you should see that the query for getting the list items is run only once. You can also use Visual Studio's debugger to set a breakpoint inside your view component's Invoke method. Subsequent calls to the page should not invoke the view component to run the database the query.

In this example, the Cache Tag Helper is used with the default settings since no additional attributes were set. This will cache the lookup list until the web server needs to free memory or the process is recycled or restarted. The Cache Tag Helper has several options that allow you to specify the duration the data is held in cache and if the cached value should vary based on route, query string, logged-in user, cookie, or HTTP header.

# 4-8. Using the Environment, Script, and Link Tag Helpers for Conditionally Rendering Script and Link Tags

## Problem

You want to optimize your web site's front-end performance by utilizing a content delivery network (CDN) for some of the popular JavaScript libraries that you are using, such as jQuery and Bootstrap.

From experience, you have found that even though CDNs are relatively reliable, all of them experience occasional downtime. When using a CDN, you want to have some sort of fallback mechanism that will load a local copy of the script when the CDN version is not available.

Another issue you have run into with using a CDN is that it can sometimes make debugging more complicated. For this reason, you want to use only local copies of the libraries when in your development environment. You want to be able to have this behavior enabled or disabled automatically based on the environment.

## Solution

The ASP.NET Core MVC Tag Helpers library comes with two Tag Helpers that can aid in changing the method used to access scripts on a page. The first is the `Environment` Tag Helper, which allows you to specify blocks of code that should be evaluated only when executing in an environment with a matching environment name. You can use this feature to change the links to your CSS and script files based on the environment your code is running in.

Other useful Tag Helpers are the `Script` and `Link` helpers. They both allow you to specify two URLs for a resource such as a script file and will use the second address if a request to the primary address fails. Both the `Link` and `Script` Tag Helpers expose two bounded properties, which allow you to specify the URL for the local copy of the script, and `fallback test`, which allows you to specify a variable name that should be truthy if the script was successfully loaded from the CDN. The `Script` Tag Helper uses the bounded properties `asp-fallback-src` and `asp-fallback-test`. The `Link` Tag Helper uses a similar set of bounded properties, `asp-fallback-test-class`, `asp-fallback-test-property`, and `asp-fallback-test-value`, allowing you to test that a CSS class is present and has the expected value for a specified property.

## How It Works

You will first look at how the `Environment` Tag Helper can be used to change the CSS files included on a page based on the environment name. You will then modify the example to include a fallback test. In another example, you will use the fallback helper with a JavaScript file.

### Using the Environment Tag Helper

Listing 4-37 shows the HEAD section of an ASP.NET MVC layout page that is using the `Environment` Tag Helper. When in an environment named Development, a local copy of the Bootstrap CSS library will be used. For Staging and Production, the CDN will be used.

*Listing 4-37.* Using the Environment Tag Helper to Change the Address for a Style Sheet Based on Environment Name

```
<environment names="Development">
    <link rel="stylesheet" href="~/lib/bootstrap/dist/css/bootstrap.css" />
    <link rel="stylesheet" href="~/css/site.css" />
</environment>
<environment names="Staging,Production">
    <link rel="stylesheet"
        href="https://ajax.aspnetcdn.com/ajax/bootstrap/3.3.6/css/bootstrap.min.css"
        asp-fallback-href="~/lib/bootstrap/dist/css/bootstrap.min.css"
        asp-fallback-test-class="sr-only" asp-fallback-test-property="position"
        asp-fallback-test-value="absolute" />
    <link rel="stylesheet" href="~/css/site.min.css" asp-append-version="true" />
</environment>
```

Another useful feature of the Link Tag Helper, shown in Listing 4-37, is the `asp-append-version` attribute. When enabled, a version query string is appended to the stylesheet name. The file version will change each time the file is modified. This feature is useful for solving problems caused by end users having an old version of a CSS file in their cache.

## Using the Fallback Feature for JavaScript Files

For the JavaScript file you only need to test for the existence of a variable that should exist if the script was successfully loaded. In Listing 4-38 you will try to load the Bootstrap JavaScript file, and you will test for the existence of variables named `window.jQuery`, `window.jQuery.fn`, and `window.jQuery.fn.modal`, which should exist if Bootstrap has been loaded.

*Listing 4-38.* Fallback and Test for a JavaScript File

```
<script src="https://ajax.aspnetcdn.com/ajax/bootstrap/3.3.6/bootstrap.min.js"
            asp-fallback-src="~/lib/bootstrap/dist/js/bootstrap.min.js"
            asp-fallback-test="window.jQuery && window.jQuery.fn && window.jQuery.fn.modal">
```

The fallback test for a CSS file is like a JavaScript file but a bit more complicated. In Listing 4-39, you can test to determine whether the Bootstrap CSS file was loaded successfully by the CDN. If it loaded successfully, you should have a CSS class named `sr-only` that sets the `position` property to `absolute`. `asp-fallback-test-class` is used to check for the existence of the CSS class. `asp-fallback-test-class` and `asp-fallback-test-value` verify that the property is being set as expected.

*Listing 4-39.* Using a CSS Fallback to Load a Local Copy of a Stylesheet When the CDN Cannot Be Accessed

```
<link rel="stylesheet" href="//ajax.aspnetcdn.com/ajax/bootstrap/3.3.6/css/bootstrap.min.css"
            asp-fallback-href="~/lib/bootstrap/css/bootstrap.min.css"
            asp-fallback-test-class="sr-only"
            asp-fallback-test-property="position"
            asp-fallback-test-value="absolute"
>
```

To test how the code will work when the environment name changes on your development machine, you can edit the `ASPNETCORE_ENVIRONMENT` environmental variable. You can access this in Visual Studio by opening the project's property page by selecting [web project name] Properties from the Visual Studio Project menu. On the Debug tab of the property page, you can set the value using the "Environment variables" settings, as shown in Figure 4-5.

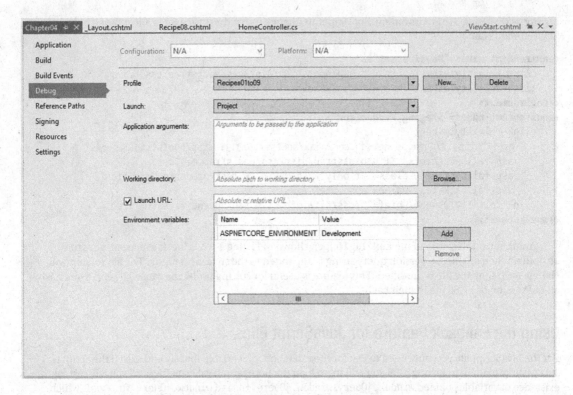

**Figure 4-5.** *Changing the ASPNET_ENV value in Visual Studio*

# 4-9. Creating a Custom Tag Helper

## Problem

You are building a new web application and want to use the Bootstrap Glyphicons for all your edit, delete, and new links. You want to encapsulate the code that creates these links using a Tag Helper.

## Solution

To create a custom Tag Helper, you need to create a class that extends the TagHelper base class, specify the tag or attribute that you want to associate with your helper, and then override the Process or ProcessAsync method to add your custom content. You should use ProcessAsync if your Tag Helper can potentially perform an expensive blocking operation, such as accessing the network or interacting with the file system.

## How It Works

To demonstrate how to create a custom Tag Helper, you will create a Tag Helper that appends a Bootstrap Glyphicon to an anchor tag. You will create a new solution with two projects. One project will be an ASP.NET Core MVC application, and the other will be a class library project that will contain the custom Tag Helper.

## Project Setup

Start Visual Studio and create a new ASP.NET Core MVC project, or if you have already created a project for the Chapter 4 examples, you can continue to use it. If creating a new project, choose the Web Site template and ensure the authentication type is set to None.

Right-click the solution in Solution Explorer and choose Add ➤ New Project. Select the Class Library (.NET Standard) template and name the project Recipe09.TagHelpers.

After the project has been created, right-click the project name and select Properties. In the Application section of the Properties window, change the target framework to .NET Standard 1.6. This is required because you will be referencing components of ASP.NET Core MVC that are not compatible with earlier versions of the .NET Standard.

## Adding Required Dependencies to the TagHelpers Project

Right-click Recipe09.TagHelpers in Solution Explorer and select Manage NuGet Packages. In the NuGet package manager, select Browse and then enter **Microsoft.AspNetCore.Mvc.Razor** in the search box. Select Microsoft.AspNetCore.Mvc.Razor in the package list and then click the Install button.

## Creating the Tag Helper

Delete the file Class1.cs from your project since it is not needed. Create a new class file and name it GlyphiconLinkTagHelper.cs. Add a using statement at the top of the file for the following namespaces if they are not present:

- Microsoft.AspNetCore.Razor.TagHelpers

- System.Threading.Tasks

Next, modify the class signature so that it is extending the TagHelper class. You will then need to decorate the class with the HtmlTargetElement attribute. This attribute is used to tell the Razor engine which tags and attributes you want to target for processing. For your Tag Helper, you will be targeting the anchor tag and will be creating a custom attribute called asp-GlyphIcon. Rather than hard-coding the string used for the Attribute argument, a constant defined in the class is used. Using constants has some minor performance benefits, but even though the benefit is small, it can make a difference for high-volume applications.

To read the value from the asp-GlyphIcon attribute, you will need to set up a property decorated with the HtmlAttributeName attribute. This will automatically take the value from the Razor markup and write it to the property.

Finally, the ProcessAsync method is overwritten. In the body of this method, you use the content provided by the developer in the asp-GlyphIcon attribute and use it to determine which Glyphicon to render. You also check to see whether any content was added into the body of the anchor tag and ensure that it is preserved. You are using the asynchronous version of the Process method since you need to access the existing content. This is done using the TagHelperContext.GetChildContentAsync method. This method does not have a synchronous equivalent. When you are done, your class should resemble Listing 4-40.

*Listing 4-40.* GlyphiconLinkTagHelper

```
using Microsoft.AspNetCore.Mvc.ViewFeatures;
using Microsoft.AspNetCore.Razor.TagHelpers;
using System;
using System.Threading.Tasks;
```

```
namespace Recipe09.TagHelpers
{
    [HtmlTargetElement("a", Attributes = GlyphIconName)]
    public class GlyphiconLinkTagHelper : TagHelper
    {
        private const string GlyphIconName = "asp-GlyphIcon";
        private const string EditIcon = "edit";
        private const string DeleteIcon = "trash";

        protected IHtmlGenerator Generator { get; }

        public GlyphiconLinkTagHelper(IHtmlGenerator generator)
        {
            Generator = generator;
        }

        [HtmlAttributeName(GlyphIconName)]
        public string IconName { get; set; }

        private string getIconName()
        {
            if(string.IsNullOrEmpty(IconName))
            {
                return string.Empty;
            }
            switch (IconName.ToLowerInvariant())
            {
                case EditIcon:
                    return EditIcon;
                case DeleteIcon:
                    return DeleteIcon;
                default:
                    return string.Empty;
            }

        }
        public override async Task ProcessAsync(TagHelperContext context,
            TagHelperOutput output)
        {
            if (context == null)
            {
                throw new ArgumentNullException(nameof(context));
            }

            if (output == null)
            {
                throw new ArgumentNullException(nameof(output));
            }
```

```
        var iconHTML =
            string.Format("<span class='glyphicon glyphicon-{0}'> </span>",
            getIconName());
        var content = await output.GetChildContentAsync();
        if (content.IsEmptyOrWhiteSpace)
        {
            output.Content.SetHtmlContent(iconHTML);
        }
        else
        {
            output.Content.SetHtmlContent(content.AppendHtml(iconHTML).GetContent());
        }
    }
}
}
```

## Adding the Custom Tag Helper to Your ASP.NET Core MVC Project

Before you can use the custom Tag Helper in your views, you will first need to add a reference to the class library project in your web application. To do this, right-click the Web Application project in Solution Explorer and then choose Add ➤ Reference. In the Reference Manager window under the Solution section, select the box next to Recipe09.TagHelpers and then click OK.

Next, to make the custom Tag Helper available for all the views, open the _ViewImports.cshtml file in the Views folder and modify it to look like Listing 4-41.

*Listing 4-41.* _ViewImports.cshtml

```
@using Recipes01to09
@addTagHelper *, Microsoft.AspNetCore.Mvc.TagHelpers
@addTagHelper *, Recipe09.TagHelpers
```

You can now use the custom Tag Helper in your views. Listing 4-42 shows a few variations on how the Tag Helper can be used. Note that you can use it in conjunction with other Tag Helpers including the built-in ones from the ASP.NET MVC Tag Helpers library.

*Listing 4-42.* Using the Custom Tag Helper

```
<h2>Chapter 04 - Recipe 09</h2>
<a href="myonlineband.com">This is a regular anchor tag</a>
<br />
<a asp-action="About">This is standard asp-action tag helper with no Glyph Icon</a>
<br />
<a asp-glyphIcon="Edit">This glyoh icon on standard anchor tag</a>
<br />
<a asp-action="About" asp-glyphIcon="Edit">This is standard asp-action tag helper with Edit
Glyph Icon</a>
<br />
<a asp-action="About" asp-glyphicon="Trash">This is standard asp-action tag helper with
Delete Glyph Icon</a>
```

# CHAPTER 5

■ ■ ■

# Getting the Most from the New Features in ASP.NET Core MVC

ASP.NET Core MVC is the biggest change in the Microsoft web development technology stack since perhaps the introduction of ASP.NET. The foundation components of ASP.NET Core MVC have been rebuilt from the ground up to be modular and cross-platform. Fortunately for ASP.NET MVC developers, most of the patterns familiar to ASP.NET MVC developers are largely unchanged. There are, however, significant changes to the ASP.NET MVC project structure. There are also many breaking changes, a new configuration system, and several new features specific to ASP.NET Core MVC.

In this chapter, you will take a deep dive into some of the new features introduced in ASP.NET Core MVC. You will start by reviewing the changes to NuGet and how NuGet fits into the ASP.NET Core MVC compilation process. You will then review the process of porting ASP.NET MVC and Web API projects to ASP.NET Core MVC. The remainder of the chapter will focus on using new features such as view components, and inject.

## 5-1. Understanding NuGet with ASP.NET Core MVC

### Problem

You have used NuGet Package Manager for managing both .NET and JavaScript libraries with your ASP.NET MVC projects. After creating a new ASP.NET Core MVC project, you have noticed that when you run NuGet Package Manager, you no longer see any JavaScript libraries listed. You may have also noticed that packages.config is no longer included in the project. You want to understand how NuGet has changed and how this impacts the way you use it for building ASP.NET Core MVC applications.

### Solution

In ASP.NET Core MVC, NuGet has been fully integrated into the ASP.NET Core project system. Information regarding NuGet packages is no longer stored in the packages.config file but is instead stored directly in the ASP.NET Core project file (.csproj).

Another major change is that NuGet is no longer used for managing client-side components such as JavaScript libraries. Visual Studio uses a dedicated JavaScript package manager called Bower for managing JavaScript and CSS libraries. In ASP.NET Core, you use NuGet for server-side components and Bower for client-side components.

© John Ciliberti 2017
J. Ciliberti, *ASP.NET Core Recipes*, DOI 10.1007/978-1-4842-0427-6_5

NuGet is also embedded into the ASP.NET Core MVC command-line interface. The command-line interface has two commands dedicated to NuGet: `restore`, which retrieves the packages referenced in the .csproj file, and pack, which can convert your .NET Standard library into a NuGet package.

## How It Works

NuGet Package Manager is an application that helps .NET developers locate, download, and use software libraries in their projects. NuGet has two major components, a repository that stores and provides access to packages and a client that allows developers to interact with the repository. For a software library to be included in a NuGet repository, it must be bundled into a NuGet package. A NuGet package consists of the compiled assemblies, resource files, and a manifest file that contains information such as the component name, version number, author, and a description. The manifest also lists all the dependencies of a component and the versions of .NET that the package is compatible with. NuGet clients use the information in the manifest to automatically locate and download the correct version of the components and include them in your project.

When an update for a NuGet package is available, the NuGet client can notify you and allow you to easily update the component to the latest version.

## NuGet Package Sources

NuGet package sources, also known as *feeds*, are collections of NuGet packages that are usually accessed over HTTP using a RESTFul API. In addition to HTTP, NuGet also supports using local folders and network shares as package sources. This flexibility makes it possible for a small team to set up a private feed on a local network without needing to install any server software. More commonly, however, developers will use a server-based solution such as NuGet.Server. Server-based package sources offer greater functionality, allowing you to do things such as browse, search, and push packages to the feed using a NuGet client. NuGet servers also support user authentication and authorization, which prevent unauthorized persons from modifying packages.

When you install Visual Studio, it will be configured by default to use Nuget.org. This is the official NuGet package source and contains all production and sanctioned prerelease versions of ASP.NET Core's components. In addition to components created by Microsoft, Nuget.org also contains thousands of packages created by the .NET developer community.

Nuget.org is not the only public NuGet package source. Thousands of public feeds are hosted using services such as MyGet.org. MyGet.org offers free hosting for public repositions. The .NET Foundation currently publishes 40 separate feeds on MyGet. These feeds contain unsanctioned prerelease versions of .NET Foundation components such as nightly builds. In addition to public package sources, MyGet allows you to create private repositories if you purchase a paid subscription.

NuGet feeds can also be hosted on your local network. Hosting your private NuGet feed on your local network can make acquiring packages substantially faster and can also be more secure. Your private NuGet feed can be as simple as a file share, or if your needs warrant it, you can invest in a commercial solution such as jFrog Artifactory. Artifactory supports other package managers in addition to NuGet including NPM, Bower, Maven, and RPM. It can also be used to host your Docker images.

Creating and publishing a NuGet package to a NuGet feed can be automated using a continuous integration (CI) server such as Visual Studio Team System or Jenkins. Using this technique, you can automatically generate packages from your latest source code and then publish the package to your NuGet feed. When you integrate your source control system with your CI server, your NuGet packages can be published automatically simply by checking in your code.

# Adding a Custom NuGet Feed to Visual Studio

You can configure NuGet Package Manager to work with multiple package sources. You can even configure individual projects to use specific feeds. This can be useful when you are collaborating with several teams and need access to specific versions of a package that are not available in the main feed.

## Using a NuGet Config File

If you want to customize a NuGet configuration for an individual project without impacting your machine-wide settings, you can add a nuget.config file to your project. The settings listed in this file will override any conflicting global configuration settings for your project. To add the configuration file using Visual Studio, follow these steps:

1. Right-click the project name in Solution Explorer and select Add ➤ New Item.

2. Select the Text File template, change the file name to nuget.config, and then click the Add button.

3. Modify nuget.config to match Listing 5-1.

*Listing 5-1.* Changing NuGet Behavior for a Project with nuget.config

```xml
<?xml version="1.0" encoding="utf-8"?>
<configuration>
  <packageRestore>
    <add key="enabled" value="true"></add>
    <add key="automatic" value="true"></add>
  </packageRestore>
  <packageSources>
    <add key="NuGet official package source"
        value=" https://api.nuget.org/v3/index.json "></add>
    <add key="ASP.NET Core MVC Recipes package source"
        value="https://www.myget.org/F/aspnetcoremvcrecipes/api/v3/index.json"></add>
  </packageSources>
</configuration>
```

The configuration file shown in Listing 5-1 contains two sections: packageRestore and packageSources. The packageRestore settings enable package restore and set it to occur automatically. This setting will ensure that if missing packages are detected, they can be downloaded automatically when the project is built. If you did not configure this behavior, the build would fail with errors related to missing packages.

The second section of settings, packageSources, consists of the package sources. The key-value pairs under packageSources add two sources: the NuGet official package source and the ASP.NET Core MVC Recipes package source.

To learn more about all the configuration options for NuGet, please refer to the following document:

```
https://docs.nuget.org/ndocs/consume-packages/configuring-nuget-behavior
```

## Changing the Global NuGet Settings from Visual Studio

If you want to change the configuration of NuGet for your entire PC, you can either directly edit the global NuGet configuration file located at %APPDATA%\NuGet\NuGet.Config or use Visual Studio's settings dialog. To add a new package source using Visual Studio settings, follow these steps:

1. Select Options from the Visual Studio Tools menu.

2. Expand NuGet Package Manager and then select Package Sources.

3. Click the plus icon to add a new source and then change the name to **ASP.NET Core MVC Recipes** and the location to https://www.myget.org/F/aspnetcoremvcrecipes/api/v3/index.json.

4. Click OK to save your settings.

You can see the changes made to the file by opening %APPDATA%\NuGet\NuGet.Config in your favorite file editor.

# Adding a NuGet Package to Your Project

You can add NuGet packages to your project in three ways: using the NuGet CLI via the Package Manager Console, using the Visual Studio NuGet Package Manager window, and manually adding package references to the .csproj file. In this section, you will first examine the .csproj file. You will use the first two methods to add packages to your project and then examine the changes made to your .csproj file.

## Examining the .csproj File

To see what the .csproj file looks like before you make any changes to the project, open the .csproj file in Visual Studio by right-clicking the project name in Solution Explorer and then selecting Edit <yourProjectName>.csproj. The project file will look like the one shown in Listing 5-2.

***Listing 5-2.*** Default .csproj File

```
<Project Sdk="Microsoft.NET.Sdk.Web">

  <PropertyGroup>
    <TargetFramework>netcoreapp1.1</TargetFramework>
  </PropertyGroup>

  <PropertyGroup>
    <PackageTargetFallback>$(PackageTargetFallback);portable-net45+win8+wp8+wpa81;
    </PackageTargetFallback>
  </PropertyGroup>
  <ItemGroup>
    <PackageReference Include="Microsoft.ApplicationInsights.AspNetCore" Version="2.0.0" />
    <PackageReference Include="Microsoft.AspNetCore" Version="1.1.0" />
    <PackageReference Include="Microsoft.AspNetCore.Mvc" Version="1.1.1" />
    <PackageReference Include="Microsoft.AspNetCore.StaticFiles" Version="1.1.0" />
    <PackageReference Include="Microsoft.Extensions.Logging.Debug" Version="1.1.0" />
  </ItemGroup>
  <ItemGroup>
```

```
<DotNetCliToolReference Include="Microsoft.VisualStudio.Web.CodeGeneration.Tools"
Version="1.0.0-msbuild3-final" />
  </ItemGroup>
```

```
</Project>
```

When you examine the file, you will see that there is an `ItemGroup` node that contains several `PackageReference` nodes. Each `PackageReference` node has two properties: `Include`, which is the name of the package you want to include in the project, and `Version`, which is the version of the package.

In Solution Explorer, if you expand Dependencies and then NuGet, the packages listed will match the contents of the `.csproj` file.

## Adding a Package Using the Package Manager Console

If you know the name and version of a package you want to install, it can be convenient to add packages using the Package Manager Console. To do this, open the Package Manager Console window if it's not already open. You can open this window from the Visual Studio menu using View ➤ Other Windows ➤ Package Manager Console. You can also access this using Tools ➤ NuGet Package Manager ➤ Package Manager Console.

In the Package Manager Console, type the following command:

```
Install-Package FluentValidation.AspNetCore -Pre
```

The command has three parts. First, `Install-Package` tells the package manager to find and then install a package. The second is the name of the package. In this case, you are looking to install the `FluentValidation.AspNetCore` package. The last argument is the `-Pre` flag, which tells the package manager to get the latest prerelease version of the package if one is available. You need to be careful about using prerelease versions of software in production since they will often contain bugs. Unfortunately, since .NET Core is so new, many essential packages are still in a prerelease state.

After tapping the Enter key, you will see the Package Manager Console display several messages about downloading and installing the package. When installation completes, you will see the following line added to your `.csproj` file. Note that the version number will likely be different. In addition to the package you selected, NuGet will download all the dependencies. Only the top-level package is stored in the `.csproj` file, however.

```
<PackageReference Include="FluentValidation.AspNetCore" Version="6.4.0-rc4" />
```

## Adding a Package Using the NuGet Package Manager UI in Visual Studio

To add a package using the NuGet Package Manager user interface, right-click Dependencies in Solution Explorer and select Manage NuGet Packages. Click the Browse tab and select ASP.NET Core MVC Recipes from the Package Sources drop-down, as shown in Figure 5-1. Select the Include Prerelease check box next to the search box. Click the Install button to install the package. In the Review Changes dialog, click OK. In the License Acceptance dialog, click I Accept.

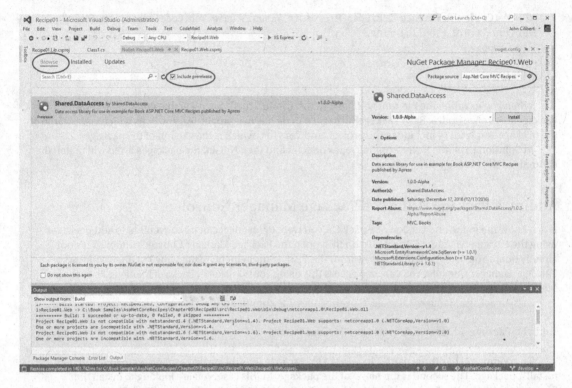

***Figure 5-1.*** *Adding a package using the NuGet Package Manager user interface*

After adding the package, the following line is added to the end of the `.csproj` file:

```
<PackageReference Include="Shared.DataAccess" Version="1.0.3-Alpha" />
```

# 5-2. Upgrading from ASP.NET MVC 5 to ASP.NET Core MVC

## Problem

You have an existing ASP.NET MVC 5 project that you want to convert to ASP.NET Core MVC. You do not see any options for automatically migrating your application. You are wondering how you can upgrade.

# Solution

ASP.NET Core MVC is a complete reimplementation of ASP.NET MVC. For this reason, there is no automatic upgrade option. Fortunately, most programming structures found in ASP.NET MVC have been ported to ASP.NET Core MVC. These similarities make it possible to manually port your controllers and views from ASP.NET MVC to ASP.NET Core MVC. The following steps describe the basic sequence of a migration. I will review each of these steps in detail in the "How It Works" section:

1. Create a new ASP.NET Core MVC project using the ASP.NET Core Web Application template.

2. On the "Select a template" page, select Web Application. Optionally you can use the Change Authentication button to add the authentication strategy that best matches the application you are porting.

3. Add the controllers, views, and other assets from your ASP.NET 5 application to the new solution.

4. Try to build the application and see what breaks. You will likely see hundreds of errors and warnings. Fortunately, it is not as bad as it looks, and many of the errors can be resolved by changing namespaces.

5. If you used NuGet to manage JavaScript libraries in your ASP.NET 5 project, replace them with the equivalent Bower packages.

6. If you used the ASP.NET Web Optimization library for bundling and minification of your script and CSS files, migrate your settings to bundleconfig.json.

# How It Works

To demonstrate the conversion procedure outlined in the recipe, you will create a new ASP.NET 5 project using Visual Studio and then manually migrate it to ASP.NET Core MVC.

## Creating the ASP.NET MVC 5 Project to Be Migrated

Open Visual Studio and select File ➤ New ➤ Project. In the New Project Window, select Web under Visual C# and then select ASP.NET Web Application (.NET Framework). Name the solution and project **Recipe02** and change the location to Chapter05\Recipe02\ASPNetMvc5\. In the Select a Template window, select MVC. Ensure the "Host in the cloud" check box is unchecked and then click OK. After the project is created, run the application to verify that it works.

## Creating the New ASP.NET Core MVC Project

Open Visual Studio and create a new ASP.NET Core Web Application project. Name the project and the solution **Recipe02** and change the location to Chapter05\Recipe02\ASPNetCoreMVC\. In the New ASP.NET Project window, select the Web Application template. Click OK to create the project.

Once the project is created, delete all controllers and views. You will be replacing them with content from the project you are porting. Do not delete the other content created by the template.

## Import Project Files from the ASP.NET MVC Project

To import project files, from Solution Explorer, right-click the Controllers folder and select Add ➤ Existing Item from the pop-up menu. Select the file Controllers\HomeController.cs from the MVC 5 project. Click OK to import the file. Repeat the same process for the Views\Home folder and import all three Razor view files from the MVC 5 project.

- Index.cshtml
- About.cshtml
- Contact.cshtml

---

■ **Tip**   You can import several files at once in the Add Existing Item window by holding down the Ctrl key and then clicking each item you want to import.

---

Once you have completed this process, try to build the solution. The build will fail, and you should see about six errors in the Error List window.

## Correcting the Errors

Even with a small project such as the one generated by the New Project template, you will have some errors to correct after the import. The good news is that correcting most of them is easy. You will start by opening HomeController.cs. Remove the using statements for System.Web.Mvc and System.Web and add a using statement for Microsoft.AspNetCore.Mvc, as shown in Listing 5-3. After making these changes, build the project again; the error count should drop to zero. Run the project to ensure it functions correctly.

*Listing 5-3.* Changes Made to the Home Controller

```
using Microsoft.AspNetCore.Mvc;

namespace Recipe02.Controllers
{
    public class HomeController : Controller
    {
        public ActionResult Index()
        {
            return View();
        }

        public ActionResult About()
        {
            ViewBag.Message = "Your application description page.";

            return View();
        }
```

```
    public ActionResult Contact()
    {
        ViewBag.Message = "Your contact page.";

        return View();
    }
  }
}
```

Since this was a basic project, the simple act of moving your controllers and views to the new template solved almost all the migration concerns.

There are many files that you did not port from the original, including the layout files and much of the front-end code. If you attempt to move these files, you will have many breaking changes. In most cases, you will be better off rebuilding the layout files from the new base.

# JavaScript and CSS Libraries

Since the Visual Studio templates for ASP.NET MVC and ASP.NET Core MVC that ship with Visual Studio 2017 contain identical content, the JavaScript libraries required are present in both projects, although the library versions are different. If you were porting a real project, this would not likely be the case. To demonstrate how ASP.NET MVC and ASP.NET MVC Core differ in handling JavaScript libraries, you will first add a library to the ASP.NET MVC project and then add the same library to the ASP.NET Core project.

## Adding Moment.js to the ASP.NET MVC Project

Moment.js is a date library for JavaScript. I will use Moment.js to demonstrate how to port your JavaScript dependencies from an ASP.NET MVC project to an ASP.NET Core MVC project. In ASP.NET MVC, JavaScript libraries are typically managed using NuGet. To add Moment.js to your ASP.NET MVC project, right-click the project name in Solution Explorer and select Manage NuGet Packages from the context menu. In the NuGet window, click Browse and then type **Moment.js** in the search box. Select Moment.js from the package list and then click the Install button. Make note of the version number. After the package has been installed, the following changes have been made to your project:

- The package.config file has been modified with a new package entry for moment.js.

- The files moment.js and moment-with-locals.js and the associated minified versions of the two files have been added to the Scripts folder.

## Adding Moment.js to the ASP.NET Core MVC Project

ASP.NET Core MVC no longer uses NuGet for managing JavaScript libraries. Bower is the recommended solution for managing JavaScript packages. Using Bower is not mandatory, but since it comes configured out of the box with the ASP.NET Core MVC project templates, it is the best option for most developers. Another benefit of using Bower is that it is the most popular JavaScript package manager used by front-end developers. Because of Bower's popularity, it has thousands of JavaScript and CSS libraries, many of which you will not find in NuGet.

To add Moment.js to your ASP.NET Core MVC project using Bower, in Solution Explorer, expand Dependencies, right-click the Bower folder, and select Manage Bower Packages from the pop-up menu. Click Browse and then type **momentjs** in the search box. Select momentjs from the package list. Ensure that the version selected in the drop-down list matches the version used in your ASP.NET MVC project and then click the Install button. After the package has been installed, the following changes will have been made to the project:

- bower.json has been updated with a new dependency listed for Moment.js.

- A folder for Moment.js has been added under wwwroot/lib.

In ASP.NET Core projects, all static files including images, CSS, and JavaScript files need to be placed under the wwwroot folder. If a file is not under wwwroot, it will not be accessible by end users.

The Bower configuration file .bowerrc specifies that packages downloaded from the Bower package store are copied to the wwwroot/lib folder.

While the default Bower configuration added to your project by Visual Studio makes it easy to get started, it has some unfortunate side effects. If you examine the moment directory created under wwwroot/lib, you will see that not only has moment.js and moment-with-locals.js been downloaded, but many other files have been too. This behavior is caused by the way Bower acquires packages. The Bower client first acquires the package metadata from the Bower package store. This metadata includes the URL to a Git repository that contains the component's source code. For the Moment.js library, the URL is https://github.com/moment/moment. The Bower client then uses a Git source control client and performs a git clone operation for the initial download and Git pulls to download updates. In the case of this example, git clone downloads the entire Git repository for the Moment.js library. This Git repository contains the entire source of Moment.js along with the change logs and readme files. You most likely do not need these files and should not deploy them to your production server. See recipe 11-2 for a detailed example of how you can correct this issue.

# 5-3. Upgrading from Web API to ASP.NET MVC 6

## Problem

Your company developed a service using ASP.NET Web API 2. You have just found out that ASP.NET Web API is no longer a separate framework, and its functionality has now been merged with ASP.NET Core MVC. You want to port your existing application to ASP.NET Core MVC.

## Solution

There is no automatic upgrade path for migrating from ASP.NET MVC Web API to ASP.NET Core MVC. ASP.NET Core MVC is a new framework and has a different project structure than ASP.NET MVC Web API. The Web API functionality has been merged with ASP.NET Core MVC, and the Web API NuGet packages, classes, and namespaces have been removed. Because of this, the Web API controller base class and configuration classes do not exist in ASP.NET Core MVC.

Since you cannot upgrade automatically, the best way to port your project is to create a new Visual Studio solution using the ASP.NET Core MVC Web API template. You can then import your code from your legacy project.

After you import your code, you will find that there are many breaking changes. Microsoft offers two paths to correcting the issues and getting your service operational.

First is the ASP.NET Web API shim. The shim is a set of classes that overlay the new ASP.NET Core MVC APIs and mimic the APIs, classes, and namespaces available with ASP.NET Web API 2. If you are porting a large project, using the shim is the fastest way to migrate your project. You can then gradually port the Web API controllers whenever major changes are required and use the new APIs for any new functionality.

Unfortunately, this option is available only for solutions targeting the .NET Framework and not for .NET Core. If you create an ASP.NET Core MVC application that targets the .NET Framework rather than .NET Core, you can only deploy your application on Windows.

The second method is to modify all your Web API controllers to use the ASP.NET Core MVC APIs. If you have a small project or do not want to deploy your application on Windows, this is the preferred method.

## How It Works

To learn how to convert an ASP.NET Web API 2 application, you will start with a simple sample application created using the Visual Studio 2017 ASP.NET Web API template.

You will then create a new Visual Studio solution using ASP.NET Core MVC (.NET Framework) and import the files from the legacy solution. Next, you will add code to the `Startup.cs` class that will activate the shim and make a few other changes.

To learn how to convert to the new ASP.NET Core MVC API, you will create a third project using the ASP.NET Core MVC (.NET Core) template and then modify the controller definitions to use the new APIs.

## Creating an ASP.NET Web API 2 Project

Use the following procedure to create a new ASP.NET Web API application.

Open Visual Studio and from the main menu select File ➤ New ➤ Project. In the New Project window, enter **Web API** in the search box and then select ASP.NET Web Application (.NET Framework). Name the project and solution **Recipe03**. In the location field, select `Chapter05\Recipe03\WebAPI2`. Ensure that "Create directory for solution" is selected and then click OK. In the New ASP.NET Web Application window, select the Web API template. Ensure that No Authentication is selected as the authentication type and the "Host in the cloud" check box is not selected. Click OK to create the project.

## Creating a New ASP.NET Core MVC (.NET Framework) Project

Open Visual Studio and create a new ASP.NET Core Web Application (.NET Framework) project. Name the project and solution **Recipe03**. In the location field, select `Chapter05\Recipe03\ASPNetCoreMVCFull`. Ensure that "Create directory for solution" is selected and then click OK. In the New ASP.NET Core Web Application window, select the Web API template. Ensure that No Authentication is selected. Click OK to create the project.

The project structure is somewhat like the structure created by the ASP.NET Core MVC Web Application template, but no views are created, and a smaller number of dependencies are added. A `wwwroot` directory is added but is empty.

Delete `ValuesController.cs` from the `Controllers` folder. You will be replacing it with the version created in the ASP.NET MVC Web API project.

### Enabling the Web API Shim

Microsoft realized that teams that have made substantial investments in Web API would struggle to migrate to ASP.NET Core because of the substantial number of changes required. To mitigate this issue, Microsoft has created a component that allows you to continue using the old Web API namespaces and classes but still target ASP.NET Core.

To enable the shim, you first need to add the component `Microsoft.AspNetCore.Mvc.WebApiCompatShim` to your project using NuGet Package Manager. To do this, right-click Dependencies in Solution Explorer and select Manage NuGet Packages. On the NuGet: Recipe03 tab, click Browse and enter **WebApiCompat**. Select `Microsoft.AspNetCore.Mvc.WebApiCompatShim` and click the Install button.

149

After you have added the Web API compatibility shim to your project, you can enable it by making a few changes to your Startup.cs class. In the ConfigureServices method, add a call to AddWebApiConventions, as shown in Listing 5-4. Calling AddWebApiConventions will enable you to use the Web API route naming conventions in your ASP.NET Core MVC controllers. If you did not do this, the MVC Core router would not know how to map action names to HTTP verbs, and you would need to add the Http[verb] attributes to each action method. With the Web API conventions added, an action named Get would be automatically be mapped to the GET HTTP verb.

Next you will need to add the default API route. As with normal ASP.NET MVC routes, the routes can be defined inside the Startup.cs Configure method. In ASP.NET Core MVC, Web APIs no longer have their own distinct route collection. Listing 5-4 shows the completed code. The required changes are shown in bold.

***Listing 5-4.*** Startup.cs with Web API Conventions and API Route

```
using Microsoft.AspNetCore.Builder;
using Microsoft.AspNetCore.Hosting;
using Microsoft.Extensions.Configuration;
using Microsoft.Extensions.DependencyInjection;
using Microsoft.Extensions.Logging;

namespace Recipe03.Service
{
    public class Startup
    {
        public Startup(IHostingEnvironment env)
        {
            var builder = new ConfigurationBuilder()
                .SetBasePath(env.ContentRootPath)
                .AddJsonFile("appsettings.json", optional: true, reloadOnChange: true)
                .AddJsonFile($"appsettings.{env.EnvironmentName}.json", optional: true)
                .AddEnvironmentVariables();
            Configuration = builder.Build();
        }

        public IConfigurationRoot Configuration { get; }

        public void ConfigureServices(IServiceCollection services)
        {
            services.AddMvc().AddWebApiConventions();
        }

        public void Configure(IApplicationBuilder app, IHostingEnvironment env,
        ILoggerFactory loggerFactory)
        {
            loggerFactory.AddConsole(Configuration.GetSection("Logging"));
            loggerFactory.AddDebug();

            // Add MVC to the request pipeline.
            app.UseMvc(routes => {
                routes.MapWebApiRoute("DefaultApi", "api/{controller}/{id?}");
            });
        }
    }
}
```

## Importing the Controller and Adding the Required using Statements

The next step is to import the controller classes from the Web API 2 project. To do this, right-click the Controllers folder in Solution Explorer and select Add ➤ Existing Item from the pop-up menu. In the Add Existing Item dialog, navigate to the controller folder and select ValuesController.cs. After importing, you will see four errors related to FromBodyAttribute. To correct this, add a using statement for Microsoft. AspNetCore.Mvc. You should also clean up the code by removing any unneeded using statements. Visual Studio will show these as grayed out. You can quickly remove them by placing the mouse cursor over one of the grayed-out using statements and clicking the light bulb icon. You can also select Remove Unnecessary Usings from the pop-up menu. Listing 5-5 shows the completed controller.

*Listing 5-5.* Imported Controller Code After Modifications

```
using System.Collections.Generic;
using System.Web.Http;
using Microsoft.AspNetCore.Mvc;

namespace Recipe03.Controllers
{
    public class ValuesController : ApiController
    {
        // GET api/values
        public IEnumerable<string> Get()
        {
            return new string[] { "value1", "value2" };
        }

        // GET api/values/5
        public string Get(int id)
        {
            return "value";
        }

        // POST api/values
        public void Post([FromBody]string value)
        {
        }

        // PUT api/values/5
        public void Put(int id, [FromBody]string value)
        {
        }

        // DELETE api/values/5
        public void Delete(int id)
        {
        }
    }
}
```

Note the inclusion of the System.Web.Http using statement in the controller. Using this namespace does not invoke the legacy System.Web assembly. System.Web.Http is defined in the shim to enable compatibility. No reference to System.Web has been added to the project.

## Using Request.CreateResponse with the Web API Compatibility Shim

In addition to the classes and namespaces used in the previous examples, the Web API compatibility shim also includes definitions for HttpResponseMessage and the Request.CreateResponse helper method. If you are importing API controllers created by using legacy versions of Visual Studio's scaffolding for Web API, the controllers will make extensive use of these classes and extension methods. Without the functionality offered by the Web API compatibility shim, porting these controllers would be labor intensive.

To learn how HttpResponseMessage and the Request.CreateResponse helper method can be used in ASP.NET Core MVC with the Web API compatibility shim, you will create a model and a controller that uses it. To create the model, create a new folder by right-clicking the Recipe03 project in Solution Explorer and selecting Add ➤ New Folder. Name the new folder Models. Add a new class to the Models folder named CellPhone.cs. Modify the class to match Listing 5-6.

***Listing 5-6.*** CellPhoneModels.cs

```
namespace Recipe03.Models
{
    public class CellPhone
    {
        public string ModelName { get; set; }
        public string Manufacturer { get; set; }
        public string OperatingSystem { get; set; }
        public double Price { get; set; }

    }
}
```

Add another class to the Models folder named CellPhoneManager and modify its content to match Listing 5-7.

***Listing 5-7.*** CellPhoneManager.cs

```
using System.Collections.Generic;

namespace Recipe03.Models
{
    public static class CellPhoneManager
    {
        public static List<CellPhone> GetPhones()
        {
            var list = new List<CellPhone>
            {
                new CellPhone
                {
                    Manufacturer = "Samsung",
                    ModelName = "Galaxy S4",
                    OperatingSystem = "Android",
                    Price = 24.98
                },
```

```
            new CellPhone
            {
                Manufacturer = "Samsung",
                ModelName = "Galaxy S5",
                OperatingSystem = "Android",
                Price = 99.99
            },

            new CellPhone
            {
                Manufacturer = "Samsung",
                ModelName = "Galaxy S6",
                OperatingSystem = "Android",
                Price = 199.98
            },

            new CellPhone
            {
                Manufacturer = "Samsung",
                ModelName = "Galaxy S6 Edge",
                OperatingSystem = "Android",
                Price = 299.98
            }
        };

        return list;
    }
  }
}
```

Next, add a new controller class to the project by right-clicking the Controllers folder and selecting Add ➤ Class from the pop-up menu. Name the class CellPhoneController and modify its content to match Listing 5-8.

***Listing 5-8.*** CellPhoneController.cs

```
using System.Net;
using System.Net.Http;
using System.Web.Http;
using Recipe03.Models;

namespace Recipe03.Controllers
{
    public class CellPhoneController : ApiController
    {
        public HttpResponseMessage GetPhones()
        {
            return Request.CreateResponse(HttpStatusCode.OK, CellPhoneManager.GetPhones());
        }
    }
}
```

Note that `System.Net`, `System.Net.Http`, and `System.Web.Http` are all imported from the Web API compatibility shim and not `System` and `System.Web` and the Web API NuGet packages as they would have been in an ASP.NET MVC project.

With the Web API compatibility shim in place, most Web API code imported from Web API 2 projects should work without alterations. If you plan on continuing to deploy your application on Windows Server, this is a good approach to quickly migrate your Web API application to ASP.NET Core MVC.

## Converting Your Web API Controller to the ASP.NET Core MVC Without the Compatibility Shim

While the ASP.NET Web API compatibility shim is helpful for porting your existing project to ASP.NET Core MVC, it is limited to projects targeting .NET Framework 4.x, which can be deployed only on Windows. The ASP.NET Web API compatibility shim solution will not work if you want to deploy your application on Linux or Mac.

You should avoid using the shim for building new functionality. While using the shim does not cause any unexpected side effects or cause significant performance degradation, it is meant to be temporary. In this section, I show how the examples shown in Listings 5-5 and 5-8 can be ported without using the Web API compatibility shim. Since you will not be using the Web API compatibility shim, you can set up the project to target .NET Core rather than the .NET Framework.

### Creating the ASP.NET Core Web Application (.NET Core)

To create the project, open Visual Studio and create a new ASP.NET Core Web Application (.NET Core) project. Name the project and solution **Recipe03**. In the location field, select `Chapter05\Recipe03\ ASPNetCoreMVCCore`. Ensure that "Create directory for solution" is selected and then click OK. In the New ASP.NET Core Web Application window, select the Web API template. Ensure that No Authentication is selected and Enable Container (Docker) Support is not selected. Click OK to create the project.

Delete `ValueController` from the `Controllers` folder and then import `ValuesController` from the Web API 2 project. After importing the controller, you will see six errors.

To correct the errors, you will need to change the class that your controller inherits from. In ASP.NET Web API 2, the controller is derived from `ApiController`. In ASP.NET Core MVC, API controllers derive from `Controller` just like regular controllers. To do this, you will need to add a `using` statement that includes `Microsoft.AspNetCore.Mvc`. The `using` statement for `System.Web.Http` should be removed since it is no longer required.

Even though you no longer see any errors, the application will not run as expected. If you run the application, the web browser will show a "page not found" message. This is because without the Web API compatibility shim, the Web API routing conventions are not present. In addition, no route has been defined in the `startup.cs` file to match `api/[controller]`. To correct these issues, you can add an attribute-based route to the controller file and `HttpGet`, `HttpPost`, `HttpPut`, and `HttpDelete` attributes to the actions. When that's completed, your code should match Listing 5-9. The code in bold are the modifications from the original class.

*Listing 5-9.* Values Controller Ported to ASP.NET Core MVC Without Using the Shim

```
using System.Collections.Generic;
using Microsoft.AspNetCore.Mvc;

namespace Recipe03.Controllers
{
    [Route("api/[controller]")]
    public class ValuesController : Controller
    {
        // GET api/values
        [HttpGet]
        public IEnumerable<string> Get()
        {
            return new string[] { "value1", "value2" };
        }

        // GET api/values/5
        [HttpGet("{id}")]
        public string Get(int id)
        {
            return "value";
        }

        // POST api/values
        [HttpPost]
        public void Post([FromBody]string value)
        {
        }

        // PUT api/values/5
        [HttpPut("{id}")]
        public void Put(int id, [FromBody]string value)
        {
        }

        // DELETE api/values/5
        [HttpDelete("{id}")]
        public void Delete(int id)
        {
        }
    }
}
```

After making the changes, your application should work as expected. If you run the application, you should see a file named values.json returned.

## Porting CellPhone Controller to ASP.NET MVC Core

The CellPhoneController program shown in Listing 5-8 will have a different set of challenges to port without the shim. To demonstrate the problems you will face and how to correct them, copy the files you created earlier to the new ASP.NET Core MVC (.NET Core) project.

You will need to create the Models folder as you did in the previous exercise and import the CellPhone.cs and CellPhoneManager.cs files shown in Listings 5-3 and 5-4 from the WebAPI2 project. Next, import the CellPhoneController.cs file from the WebAPI2 project to the Controllers folder.

After importing CellPhoneController.cs, you will see three errors. The first error states that the namespace Web does not exist in the namespace System. To correct this, remove the using statement for System.Web.Http. The second error message states that "The type or namespace name 'ApiController' could not be found." To correct this, add a using statement for Microsoft.AspNetCore.Mvc and then make the class extend Controller rather than ApiController.

The last error message states that HttpRequest does not contain a definition for CreateResponse. To correct this, you will have the action return the type IActionResult rather than an HttpResponseMessage. You will then modify the body of the method so it simply returns an OKActionResult using the Ok method of the Controller class with the results of the CellPhoneManager.GetPhones() method passed as an argument. Note that it is also possible to have your action use a return type of ICollection<CellPhone> without using the Ok method, but that approach gives you less flexibility in supporting error conditions such as Bad Requests.

While the HTTPResponseMessage class does exist in ASP.NET Core, the helper methods in an intrinsic Request object such as CreateResponse do not exist. This makes using HTTPResponseMessage more complex. In addition, as described in recipe 1-7, ASP.NET Core ships with several classes that implement IActionResult. The Controller class has built-in methods that simplify using these IActionResult classes. These helper methods, which include BadRequest, Created, File, NotFound, Ok, and others, return corresponding IActionResult types. For example, the BadResults method returns a BadRequestResult object. These new methods replace HTTPResponseMessage and should be used in place of it when creating new APIs.

Another difference shown in Listing 5-10 is that an attribute route is used rather than a template defined inside of the StartUp.cs file. Using this technique, you can customize the URLs for your API for each action. This approach makes it easy to create deep URL patterns that are sometimes necessary when defining APIs. The HttpGet attribute performs two functions. First, it binds the GetPhones action to the HTTP GET verb. Second, by accepting a route template as an argument, it allows you to customize the URL for the GetPhones action. The route template api/[controller] uses the route variable [controller] to map the CellPhone action to the URL /api/CellPhone.

Listing 5-10 shows the completed example. Code that should be removed is shown commented out, and new code is shown in bold.

***Listing 5-10.*** Refactoring an API Controller to Work Without the Compatibility Shim

```
//using System.Net;
//using System.Net.Http;
//using System.Web.Http;
using Recipe03.Models;
using Microsoft.AspNet.Mvc;
using System.Collections.Generic;

namespace Recipe03.LegacyWebApi.Controllers
{
    public class CellPhoneController : Controller //ApiController
    {
        [HttpGet("api/[controller]")]
```

```
    public IActionResult GetPhones()
    {
        //return Request.CreateResponse(HttpStatusCode.OK, GetPhoneManager.GetPhones());
        return Ok(CellPhoneManager.GetPhones());
    }
  }
}
```

You should now be able to debug the project. One major difference between the Web API template in older versions of MVC and ASP.NET Core is that no HTML content is included with the template. By default, when running the project, it will try to execute the route api/values. The values controller is a controller that is added automatically by the ASP.NET Web API template. If you delete this controller, you will see a 404 (Not Found) error when debugging your project. If you want to have the controller you are currently working on launch on debug, you can change the settings by right-clicking the project name, which in this case is Recipe03, and then selecting Properties from the pop-up menu. In the properties window, click the Debug tab and then modify the URL, as shown in Figure 5-2.

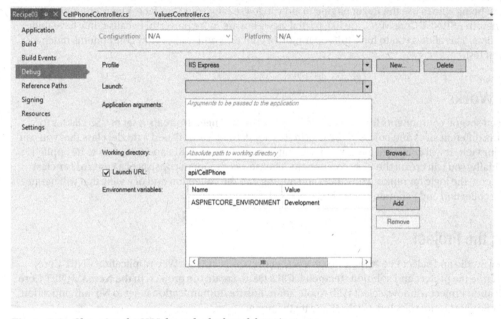

*Figure 5-2.* *Changing the URL launched when debugging*

After launching the project in the debugger, Internet Explorer will prompt you to download the JSON content produced by the server as a file.

# 5-4. Creating a Tag Cloud Using a View Component

## Problem

Your marketing department has asked you to add a tag cloud to your home page that shows a listing of all the musical genres for your web site. A *tag cloud* is a list of links that uses font size and color to show which links are most important. For example, on your web site, heavy metal is the most popular musical genre and will show as the largest link. Polka, on the other hand, is less popular and should be displayed as the smallest link.

Your marketing department has also hinted that it may want similar functionality on other pages. You are looking for a good way to encapsulate this functionality so it can be reused on several pages on your site.

## Solution

ASP.NET Core MVC supports several methods for creating reusable user interface components including custom Tag Helpers, custom HTML Helpers, partial views, and view components. Partial views and view components are less complex to create than Tag Helpers and HTML Helpers. They also provide the advantage of being able to use the Razor engine to aid you in creating your interface. View components, which are new in ASP.NET Core MVC, are like partial views but are more powerful because they have their own controllers. This allows you to have full separation of concerns and makes view components much easier to unit test.

## How It Works

You will need several components for your tag cloud. First, you will need to create a set of CSS classes to represent the different sizes and colors of the tags in the cloud. Next, you will add a model class that you can use with your view. It will consist of a list of objects that contain the text, URL, and CSS class to be applied for each. Finally, you will create the view component. The view component consists of a `Controller` class that will execute the logic for ranking the items and adding it to the collection and of a view that will iterate through the collection and generate the HTML.

## Creating the Project

Open Visual Studio and select File ➤ New Project. Select the ASP.NET Core Web Application (.NET Core) template. Name the project and solution **Recipe04**. Click OK to create the project. In the New ASP.NET Core Web Application Project window, select Web Application. Ensure Authentication is set to No authentication and Docker Support is not selected. Click OK create the project.

## Creating the CSS Classes

You will need a set of classes to represent the visual look and feel of the tag cloud. In addition to the font size and color for the links, you will also need to specify the size of the area, how to handle overflow, and the background color. Open the file `wwwroot\css\site.css` and add the CSS classes shown in Listing 5-11.

***Listing 5-11.*** CSS Styles for the Tag Cloud

```css
.tagcloud {
    z-index: 100 !important;
    background-color: #e7f5f7;
    padding: 25px;
    height: 500px;
    width: 100%;
    -webkit-border-radius: 30px;
    -moz-border-radius: 30px;
    border-radius: 30px;
    overflow: hidden;
}

    .tagcloud a {
        text-decoration: none;
        padding: 5px;
    }

.linkLevel-1 {
    font-size: 10pt;
    color: #cacaca;
}

.linkLevel-2 {
    font-size: 11pt;
    color: #a8a8a8;
}

.linkLevel-3 {
    font-size: 13pt;
    color: gray;
}

.linkLevel-4 {
    font-size: 15pt;
    color: black;
}

.linkLevel-5 {
    font-size: 18pt;
    color: black;
}

.linkLevel-6 {
    font-size: 20pt;
    color: black;
}

.linkLevel-7 {
    font-size: 22pt;
    color: black;
}
```

```
.linkLevel-8 {
    font-size: 24pt;
    color: black;
}

.linkLevel-9 {
    font-size: 26pt;
    color: black;
}
.linkLevel-10 {
    font-size: 30pt;
    font-weight: bold;
    color: #ff0000;
    text-shadow: 8px 4px 11px #800000;
}
```

This code defines a style for the CSS container that sets the background color to a light blue-green and rounds the corners using the border radius. It then defines a style that will be applied to all links defined inside the tag cloud container. Next, ten styles in the format of linkLevel-[number] are defined. The higher the number, the larger the font and the more vivid the color. For level 10, the font color is set to red, and a text shadow has been added for an additional effect.

## Creating the Tag Cloud Model

View components consist of a view component class that acts in a similar manner as a controller and one or more Razor views. The Razor views used in the view component are regular Razor view pages and can be strongly typed just like any other Razor view. To simplify the view logic and to add some additional flexibility as you evolve the design, you will create a set of model classes that will decouple the data passed to the view from the underlying data model. The model will consist of two classes. The first is TagCloud, which will define the overall structure and encapsulate some of the calculations required to generate the tag cloud. The other class, TagCloudItem, will represent the individual items in the tag cloud with properties for the display text, URL, and weight.

To create the TagCloud class, right-click Recipe04 in Solution Explorer and select Add ➤ New Folder. Name the new folder Models. Right-click the Models folder and select Add ➤ New Item. Select the Class template. Name the class TagCloud.cs and click the Add button. Modify the class to match Listing 5-12.

*Listing 5-12.* TagCloud.cs

```csharp
using System.Collections.Generic;
using System.Collections.ObjectModel;
using System.Linq;

namespace Recipe04.Models
{

    public class TagCloud
    {
        public int MaxSize { get; set; }
        public int MinSize { get; set; }
        public string BaseLinkClassName { get; set; }
        public string ContainerClassName { get; set; }
```

```
    private List<TagCloudItem> _Items { get; set; }
    private int minRank = 1;
    private int maxRank = 1;

    public ReadOnlyCollection<TagCloudItem> Items {
        get {
            if (_Items != null)
            {
                var readOnlyCollection = new ReadOnlyCollection<TagCloudItem>(_Items);
                return readOnlyCollection;
            }
            return null;
        }
    }

    public void AddItem(TagCloudItem item)
    {
        _Items.Add(item);
        minRank = _Items.Min(x => x.Weight);
        maxRank = _Items.Max(x => x.Weight);
    }

    public TagCloud()
    {
        MaxSize = 10;
        MinSize = 1;
        BaseLinkClassName = "linkLevel-";
        ContainerClassName = "tagcloud";
        _Items = new List<TagCloudItem>();
    }

    public string GetLinkItemClassName(TagCloudItem item)
    {
        int itemCount = Items.Count;
        if (maxRank == MaxSize && minRank== MinSize)
        {
            return string.Concat(BaseLinkClassName, item.Weight);
        }

        int normalizedRank = 1 + (item.Weight - minRank) *
            (MaxSize - 1) / (maxRank - minRank);

        return string.Concat(BaseLinkClassName, normalizedRank);
    }
}

}
```

In addition to defining properties that can be used by the view component to generate the lists, the class contains a method called GetLinkItemClassName. This method takes TagCloudItem as an argument and then determines what CSS class to use based on the weight of the item.

While it is possible to build a tag cloud that uses the raw data from the weight of each item to determine the font size, this design is very limiting. You may end up with many items too small to read and others so large that they would consume the entire screen. For example, imagine a blog site with 5,000 posts on ASP.NET Core MVC and 3 posts on Java. It would not be practical to use a 5,000-point font, which would be too large, and a 3-point font for Java would be too small. To get around this issue, you use a standard linear function to normalize the value to fit inside a predefined range. The TagCloud class has a MinSize property and a MaxSize property to allow a programmer to customize the range. The default values set in the constructor will limit the values to between 1 and 10.

Add a second class to the Models folder named TagCloudItem.cs and modify its contents to match Listing 5-13.

*Listing 5-13.* TagCloudItem.cs

```
namespace Recipe04.Models
{
    public class TagCloudItem
    {
        public string Url { get; set; }
        public int Weight { get; set; }
        public string DisplayText { get; set; }
    }

}
```

# Creating the Tag Cloud View Component

View components require a view component class that acts like the controller and one or more views. View component classes can be placed anywhere in the project, but to keep your project organized, you will first create a new folder called ViewComponents and then add your class to the folder. To create the folder, right-click Recipe04.Web in Solution Explorer and select Add ➤ New Folder. Name the folder ViewComponents. Right-click the ViewComponents folder and then select Add ➤ Class. Name the class TagCloudViewComponent.

Like ASP.NET Core MVC controller classes, the name of the class is important. View component class names need to either end with ViewComponent or use the ViewComponentAttribute for them to be recognized by ASP.NET Core MVC as view components. In most cases, using the naming convention will be the best choice since it will make it easier to identify view component classes in your project.

All view component classes must derive from the ViewComponent class. In addition, they must implement a method called Invoke. The Invoke method can take zero or more arguments. The arguments can be used to pass data to the component from a view. In the example shown in Listing 5-14, Invoke does not take any arguments and instead uses a hard-coded query to get the list of items for the tag cloud. If needed, the view component could be enhanced to take an argument that can be used to specify what query it should execute.

The code in the Invoke method uses LINQ to join data from two objects in the Entity Model exposed by the DBContext object. The Entity Model defines a foreign key that allows the GenreId property of the songs entity to link to a corresponding record in the genres entity. Since GenreId is an optional property, it is defined as a Nullable Int. Since you want the query to return only those songs that have a GenreId value assigned, the WHERE clause uses songs.GenreId.HasValue. The LINQ query returns an anonymously typed IQueriable that includes the values for GenreName and GenreId. A second LINQ query is then applied to the result that groups the result by GenreName. Table 5-1 shows the top 15 results of this query.

***Table 5-1.*** *Top 15 Results of the Query Shown in Listing 5-14*

| Name | Count |
|------|-------|
| Rock | 841 |
| Heavy Metal | 874 |
| Jazz | 10 |
| Blues | 40 |
| Dance & DJ | 29 |
| Experimental | 20 |
| Country | 9 |
| Hard Core | 1 |
| Pop | 15 |
| Alternative | 29 |
| Hip Hop | 34 |
| Punk | 3 |
| Christian & Gospel | 2 |
| Children's Music | 11 |

Since TagCloudViewComponent uses the database that is part of the downloadable code samples for the book, you will need to add the Shared.DataAccess NuGet package to the project. Instructions on how to install the database and custom NuGet feed are available in the appendix.

***Listing 5-14.*** TagCloudViewComponent

```
using AspNetCoreMvcRecipes.Shared.DataAccess;
using Microsoft.AspNetCore.Mvc;
using System.Collections.Generic;
using System.Linq;
using Recipe04.Models;

namespace Recipe04.ViewComponents
{
    public class TagCloudViewComponent : ViewComponent
    {
        private readonly MoBContext _context;

        public TagCloudViewComponent(MoBContext dbcontext)
        {
            _context = dbcontext;
        }
```

```
public IViewComponentResult Invoke()
{
    var items = (from songs in _context.Songs
                 join genres in _context.GenreLookUps on songs.GenreId equals
                 genres.GenreLookUpId
                 where songs.GenreId.HasValue
                 select new { genres.GenreName, songs.GenreId }).ToList();

    var grouped = items.GroupBy(s => s.GenreName).Select(
    gen => new { Name = gen.Key, Count = gen.Count() });

    var model = new TagCloud();

    foreach (var item in grouped)
    {
        var cti = new TagCloudItem {
            DisplayText = item.Name,
            Url = string.Concat("/Genres/", item.Name),
            Weight = item.Count };

        model.AddItem(cti);
    }
    return View(model);
}
}
}
```

## Adding the Component Views

The next step is to create a view that will be used to generate the HTML that makes up the tag cloud. View component views must be placed in a folder named Components. If your view component needs to be used with many controllers, it should be placed in the Views\Shared\Components folder; otherwise, it can be placed as a subfolder under the Views folder for the target controller. For this example, since the tag cloud will be used only on the home page, you will create the Components folder under Views\Home.

Inside the Components folder, a child folder needs to be created for each view component. The name of the folder needs to match the name of the component. This is a similar relationship to what you see between controllers and views. To create a folder for the TagCloud view component, right-click the Views\Home\Components folder and select Add ➤ New Folder and then name the folder TagCloud.

Next add a Razor view to the TagCloud directory and name it Default.cshtml. The view must be named Default. When you are done, Solution Explorer should resemble Figure 5-3.

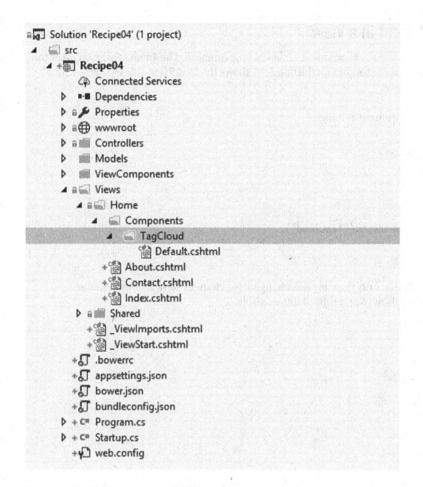

*Figure 5-3.* *View component folder structure*

In Default.cshtml, you will set the model directive to the TagCloud type you created earlier. You will then add a DIV tag to serve as the container for the tags. Inside the DIV you will use a for loop to write the links. When completed, Default.cshtml should match Listing 5-15.

*Listing 5-15.* Views/Home/Components/TagCloud/Default.cshtml

```
@model Recipe04.Models.TagCloud
<div class="tagcloud">
    @foreach (var item in Model.Items)
    {
        <a href="@item.Url" class="@Model.GetLinkItemClassName(item)">
            @item.DisplayText
        </a>
    }
</div>
```

## Using the View Component in a View

To use your view component, you use the @Component.InvokeAsync function. The Invoke function takes the name of the view component as the first argument. Listing 5-16 shows the file \Views\Home\Index.cshtml modified to use the view component.

***Listing 5-16.*** Using the View Component as a View

```
@{
    ViewBag.Title = "Home Page";
}
<h1>Tag Cloud Test</h1>
<div class="row">
    <div class="col-lg-5">
        @await Component.InvokeAsync("TagCloud");
    </div>
</div>
```

An interesting fact to note is that only the view was changed. No changes were required on the HomeController class. Figure 5-4 shows the results of this example.

***Figure 5-4.*** *Results of tag cloud view component*

# 5-5. Using the Inject Feature to Implement a Hit Counter

## Problem

You need to implement a basic hit counter. You need to add this functionality to several pages on your site. Since the hit counter does not need an elaborate user interface, you do not want to create a view component.

## Solution

The ASP.NET Core MVC inject feature is probably the simplest way to implement reusable functionality in your ASP.NET Core MVC application. The inject feature allows you to inject data into a view using any standard public C# class provided it is registered with the ASP.NET Core dependency injection system.

# How It Works

In this recipe, you will try the inject feature using a novel hit counter implementation. The feature will be implemented using a simple class and will store the hit count in a text file.

## Creating the Project

Open Visual Studio and select File ➤ New ➤ Project. Select the ASP.NET Core Web Application (.NET Core) template. Name the project and solution **Recipe05**. Click OK. In the New ASP.NET Core Web Application Project window, select Web Application and ensure Authentication is set to No authentication and Add Docker Support is not selected. Click OK to create the project.

## Creating the Hit Counter Service Class

The hit counter service will implement an interface called IHitCounterService that exposes a single method called UpdateCount. Before creating the class file, first add a new directory under the web site root named Services. You can do this by right-clicking Recipe05 in Solution Explorer and then selecting Add ➤ New Folder.

After the folder has been created, right-click it in Solution Explorer and select Add ➤ New Item. Select the Interface template and name the interface IHitCounterService. Make the interface public and define a method called UpdateCount that takes no arguments and returns an int. When done, your interface should match Listing 5-17.

***Listing 5-17.*** IHitCounterService

```
namespace Recipe05.Services
{
    public interface IHitCounterService
    {
        int UpdateCount();
    }
}
```

Next add a class that implements the IHitCounterService interface and name it HitCounterService. Since you are going to use a file to store the hit count, you will need to be able to locate the file. To do this, you will need to get the absolute base path for the application and then combine that with a relative path to the text file. Since the root path information is not available in the context of the class, you will allow this information to be passed in the class's constructor.

Once you have the path to the file, you can use the File.ReadAllText method to get the contents of the file; you can then convert the value to an integer, increment it, and then overwrite the file with the updated information. Listing 5-18 shows the completed class.

***Listing 5-18.*** HitCounterService Class

```
using System.IO;

namespace Recipe05.Web.Services
{
    public class HitCounterService : IHitCounterService
    {
        private string _rootPath;
```

```
    public HitCounterService(string rootPath)
    {
        _rootPath = rootPath;
    }

    public int UpdateCount()
    {
        var hitCountFilePath = "\\Services\\hitcount.txt";
        var fullPath = string.Concat(_rootPath, hitCountFilePath);
        var count = int.Parse(File.ReadAllText(fullPath));
        count++;
        File.WriteAllText(fullPath, count.ToString());

        return count;
    }
    }
}
```

While it would be trivial to modify your class to create the text file if it did not exist, to keep things simple, you will add the text file manually. To do so, right-click the Services folder and select Add ➤ New Item. Select the Text template and name the file hitcount.txt. In the text file, enter **0**. This will be the initial value of the hit counter. Note that since the file is not being saved under the wwwroot folder, it will not be directly accessible via a web browser. In earlier versions of ASP.NET, you would have needed to either save the file under the App_Data folder or configure the web server to not return the MIME type for the file.

## Registering the Interface with the Dependency Injection System

For the ASP.NET Core runtime to locate the HitCounterService class, you must register it in the Startup class. You will also exploit this requirement by passing some of the runtime environment information that is available in Startup into the HitCounterService class's constructor. Specifically, you need the root path, which is available in the IApplicationEnvironment instance passed into the Startup class's constructor by ASP.NET Core's dependency injection system. To access this data outside of the constructor, you will need to create a private member variable to hold the value of the application environment's ApplicationBasePath property.

Next, in the ConfigureServices method, create a ServiceDescriptor object that associates the IHitCounterService interface with a new instance of the HitCounterService class, with the local member variable containing the application base path as an argument. You can then add ServiceDescriptor to the application's IServiceCollection. Listing 5-19 shows the modified StartUp class with the changes shown in bold.

*Listing 5-19.* Startup.cs

```
using Microsoft.AspNetCore.Builder;
using Microsoft.AspNetCore.Hosting;
using Microsoft.Extensions.Configuration;
using Microsoft.Extensions.DependencyInjection;
using Microsoft.Extensions.Logging;
using Recipe05.Services;
```

```
namespace Recipe05.Web
{
    public class Startup
    {
        private string _rootPath;

        public Startup(IHostingEnvironment env)
        {
            _rootPath = env.ContentRootPath;

            var builder = new ConfigurationBuilder()
                .SetBasePath(_rootPath)
                .AddJsonFile("appsettings.json", optional: true, reloadOnChange: true)
                .AddJsonFile($"appsettings.{env.EnvironmentName}.json", optional: true)
                .AddEnvironmentVariables();
            Configuration = builder.Build();
        }

        public IConfiguration Configuration { get; set; }

        public void ConfigureServices(IServiceCollection services)
        {
            services.AddMvc();

            var descriptor = new ServiceDescriptor(typeof(IHitCounterService),
                new HitCounterService(_rootPath));
            services.Add(descriptor);
        }
        // Configure is called after ConfigureServices is called.
        public void Configure(IApplicationBuilder app,
                IHostingEnvironment env, ILoggerFactory loggerfactory)
        {
            loggerFactory.AddConsole(Configuration.GetSection("Logging"));
            loggerFactory.AddDebug();

            if (env.IsEnvironment("Development"))
            {
                app.UseDeveloperExceptionPage();
            }
            else
            {
                app.UseErrorHandler("/Home/Error");
            }
```

```
        app.UseStaticFiles();

        app.UseMvc(routes =>
        {
            routes.MapRoute(
                name: "default",
                template: "{controller=Home}/{action=Index}/{id?}");
        });
    }
  }
}
```

## Using the Class in a View

For the final part of this exercise, you will use the class inside a view. To do this, open the Index view for the Home controller and modify it so it matches Listing 5-20.

*Listing 5-20.* Index View of the Home Controller Using the HitCounterService Class

```
@inject Recipe05.Web.Services.IHitCounterService HitCounter
@{
    ViewBag.Title = "Home Page";
}

<h1>Welcome</h1>
You are the @HitCounter.UpdateCount() person to view this page.
```

The first change is the use of the @inject directive. Note that you are specifying the Interface name and not the implementation. Using the interface makes it easier to write unit tests for the view. Unit testing is covered in detail in Chapter 7. Once you set this up, you can call any public methods that may have been defined in the IHitCounterService interface.

When you run the application the first time, you should see a message stating "You are the 1 person to view this page." After refreshing the page, the message will change to reflect the number of times the page was loaded.

# CHAPTER 6

■ ■ ■

# Solution Design Using ASP.NET Core MVC

Before you can begin developing an application, you need to make several important decisions that will impact your application's performance, its ability to scale, and how easy it will be to maintain and operate. These decisions include how you structure your code; how you store and access data; how you secure your application; and what configuration, high availability, and deployment models are used.

In the first part of this chapter, several recipes are dedicated to tackling the larger design questions and exploring the common reference architectures that can be applied to an ASP.NET Core MVC application. The latter part looks at designing specific parts of your solution, including designing your data access layer, adding support for multiple languages, and more.

The source code for the examples is available on GitHub. You can find instructions for installing the sample database used in several of the recipes in the appendix.

## 6-1. Developing Reference Architectures for ASP.NET Core MVC Applications

### Problem

Your organization has decided to begin using ASP.NET Core MVC for developing web applications. You want to develop several reference architectures to guide developers who are starting new projects.

### Solution

As a developer, one of the greatest challenges you face when starting a new project is getting high-quality requirements. Requirements are often vague and incomplete and will certainly change over time. When designing your application, you will need to make many decisions based on assumptions and estimates that may turn out to be incorrect. Because of this uncertainty, all application designs require some level of flexibility. On the other hand, over-engineering an application so that it can adapt to every scenario is wasteful and often counterproductive. The design methodology that I favor is to decompose the requirements into what I call *design aspects*. I then use this information to find the correct balance between simplicity and flexibility.

Once you have a general idea of how complex an application's requirements are and the size and usage patterns of the application's users, you can use a reference architecture to accelerate your design process and ensure that it is applying proven practices. *Reference architectures* are generalized blueprints that

© John Ciliberti 2017

J. Ciliberti, *ASP.NET Core Recipes*, DOI 10.1007/978-1-4842-0427-6_6

describe how application code is structured into subcomponents, what hardware or cloud infrastructure is needed, how components are deployed on the infrastructure, and what security controls including network design and authentication and authorization schemes are applied.

Application architecture is a complex topic. Reference architectures are by no means a replacement for a skilled architect. The reference architectures shown here are intended to be starting points that highlight the breadth of solutions that can be accomplished using ASP.NET Core.

## How It Works

In this section, I first discuss the factors that impact design. Then I introduce several reference architectures and how to apply them in an ASP.NET Core MVC application.

## Application Design Factors

Scope, audience, usage patterns, scalability, reliability, and security requirements are the major factors that dictate how you design your application and what reference architecture is the best fit for your requirements. Once you select a reference architecture to start with, you can customize it to meet the unique requirements of your application.

### Scope and Schedule

*Scope* dictates the size and complexity of your project. Scope, when combined with *schedule*, determines your project's budget and how many developers need to work on it. Large projects may have multiple teams working together, which require different strategies for how you structure your code. For example, you may want to divide your project into several loosely coupled components that can each be worked on and maintained by different development teams, each with its own release cycle.

### Audience and Usage Patterns

The people who are using the application are its *audience*. The size of the audience and how often they will use your application will shape both the infrastructure architecture and how your application components are deployed across the infrastructure. Another aspect of the audience that impacts design is whether people will be accessing the application over the Internet or through a corporate intranet. This aspect will influence how your application is deployed on a network and what type of authentication and authorization model is employed by the application. For example, an Internet-facing application may want to use ASP.NET Identity and configure one or more external login providers such as Facebook. An intranet-facing application, on the other hand, would more than likely want to integrate with Active Directory or a corporate single sign-on solution.

*Usage patterns* describe how end users interact with your application. In cases where end users spend most of their workday interacting with your system, a more robust and responsive user interface may be required. Design patterns such as rich Internet applications (RIAs) or single-page web applications may be a better design for these scenarios.

### Scalability

*Scalability* is how your application can be reconfigured to accommodate increases in usage. The scalability of your application is directly related to its audience and usage patterns but also needs to account for how the audience will change over time. Scalability can be limited by several factors, such as an inability for application components to be distributed across multiple nodes, poor performance, network latency, and limitations of the application's data persistence tier.

## Reliability

*Reliability* describes the resiliency of your application. Can your application recover from a failure? Will the application still be available when a node is disabled? Can your application be partially available if one or more components are disabled? Can your application be upgraded on a regular basis without requiring significant downtime?

Reliability requirements are usually dictated by how critical an application is to its user base. For example, if an airline reservation system goes down for several hours, it can cause major travel disruptions and can cost the airline millions of dollars per hour. Other applications, such as a corporate travel portal, could inconvenience some business travelers but would be able to tolerate modest downtimes without significant adverse effects to the business.

## Security

Security impacts all aspects of your design including how you acquire and vet third-party software components, where your application is deployed, and how the network infrastructure is defined. Security also dictates how you store and transfer data. For example, if your application stores credit card information, data will need to be encrypted when it is being transmitted over a network and when it is at rest. You will also need to ensure you have access controls in place to ensure that only authorized users can access that data, and you will need logging in place to monitor who accessed the data.

# Reference Architectures

ASP.NET Core supports many deployment scenarios. ASP.NET Core applications range from small self-hosted services running on a desktop PC to massive global-scale web applications that serve billions of users. In this section, I discuss two high-level architectural blueprints that demonstrate different approaches for deploying an application.

## Small Internet-Facing Applications

The small Internet-facing application reference architecture, shown in Figure 6-1, is a low-cost design that can support up to 20,000 user sessions per day. If the expected usage is much lower than 20,000 sessions a day, this architecture can support hosting multiple web applications on a single server. If the user base expands, this architecture supports adding additional web servers and database hardware. When scaled out, this architecture can support up to 1 million user sessions per day. Of course, the actual number of user sessions that can be supported will vary based on usage patterns and the nature of the modules you are deploying to the servers. It is possible that a single poorly designed database query or a CPU-intensive .NET Core module could dramatically limit your scalability.

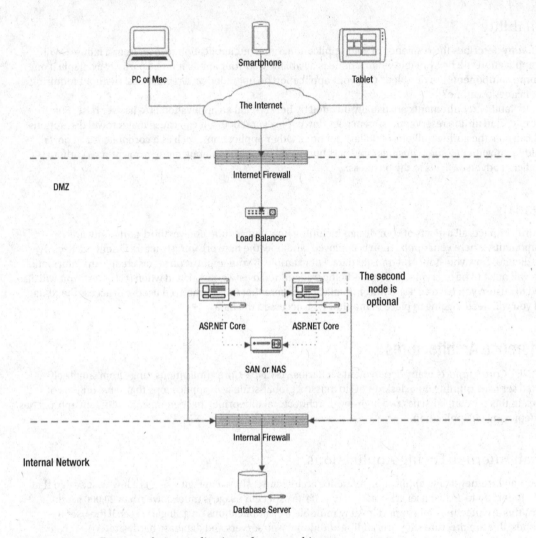

*Figure 6-1. Small Internet-facing application reference architecture*

Figure 6-1 shows the physical view of the web application reference architecture.

The architecture consists of three logical tiers: the front-end, an application tier, and the database. The separate tiers are hosted on separate nodes. If your application has a small user base, it is possible to host the database and application server on the same node, but this is not recommended for security reasons.

Even though only one web server will be deployed initially, the web server is placed behind a hardware load balancer so it can scale horizontally if required. A second benefit of using a load balancer is that most load balancers also have security features that can block certain types of attacks.

Both the web and database tiers will be virtualized, meaning they will be running inside virtual machines rather than dedicated physical hardware. For the initial deployment, the web server will be assigned a single CPU and 2GB of RAM. This might seem low, but based on the requirements, it should be more than what is needed for this application. If it is found that the application needs additional RAM, the virtual machine infrastructure allows RAM and CPU to be easily upgraded.

## Large Internet-Facing Application

Large Internet-facing applications support tens of millions of user sessions a day and thousands of transactions per second. They can scale up and down on demand, which allows them to handle peak loads while controlling costs.

Large Internet-facing applications are usually accessed globally and will have high usage 24 hours per day. This constant usage pattern makes it impractical to take the application offline for maintenance. To solve this problem, large Internet-facing applications can implement an architectural style known as *microservices*. Each microservice implements a specific role and is loosely coupled with other application components. This allows each component to be deployed and maintained independently and when properly designed will prevent the need to take the entire application offline for maintenance purposes. This design also allows each microservice to be scaled independently. They can each have their own persistent storage layer, which allows for the best technology to be selected for each service and prevents the database from becoming a bottleneck like it can with the small Internet-facing application reference architecture.

The emergence of application container technologies such as Docker and container orchestration tools such as Kubernetes allow microservices to be scaled up and down as needed, and these tools greatly simplify upgrades. Containers provide an abstraction layer that decouple an application from an individual machine. The reference architecture is using the Kubernetes orchestration engine on top of the Azure container service. Kubernetes allows you to organize your application components into services that are made up of *pods*. Pods contain a set of related containerized applications that can be deployed and scaled together.

To deal with the potentially massive number of transactions, the large Internet-facing application reference architecture employs several strategies to accelerate performance while reducing load on the microservices.

- It caches static content such as images, CSS, and script files on a content delivery network (CDN).

- It uses a distributed cache to reduce redundant SQL Server calls. The reference architecture uses the Azure Redis cache, which offers a high-performance key-value store.

- It employs a queuing mechanism to help you stay responsive during large spikes in transactions. The application uses Azure Service Bus queues.

- It uses a Binary Large Object (BLOB) storage service to handle the storage of any large objects such as documents, images, audio, and video that might be uploaded to the service. The reference architecture uses Azure BLOB storage. This design frees the developer from needing to worry about running out of disk space.

- It keeps your server software as simple as possible and pushes complex UI rendering logic to the client whenever possible. The microservices use the Web API features of ASP.NET Core MVC to provide a RESTful service interface. All the UI logic is delivered from the static content store. The architecture does not dictate a specific front-end UI framework but can be made to work with any popular framework such as ReactJS/Flux or Angular 2. All front-end assets including JavaScript, CSS, images, fonts, and HTML files will be deployed in a dedicated static content pod and will not be intermingled with the service pods.

- Microservices that require a database use SQL Server instances deployed in an elastic pool. Each microservice has its own database, which allows the individual databases to be scaled independently. Using an elastic pool makes it easier to manage the set of databases by allowing the databases to share a pool of resources.

Figure 6-2 shows a reference architecture for a large-scale web application hosted in the Microsoft Azure public cloud.

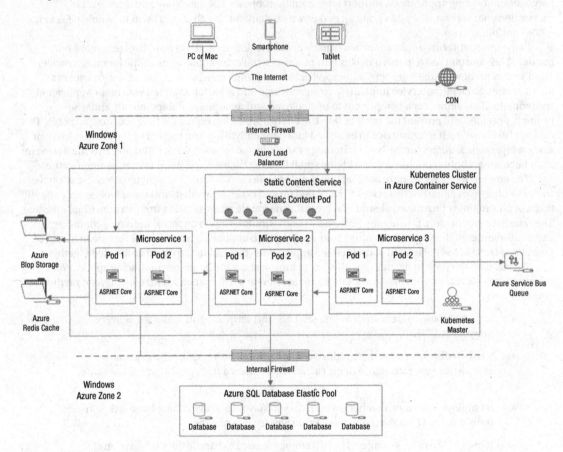

***Figure 6-2.** Large Internet-facing application reference architecture*

## Other Deployment Scenarios

The small Internet-facing application reference architecture and large Internet-facing application reference architecture show very different designs and complexity. Both designs assume that the applications will be consumed over the Internet. Once you select a reference architecture that best meets your scalability requirements, you can adjust the design to meet the unique needs of the application. For example, Figure 6-3 shows a small line-of-business application. It was derived from the small Internet-facing application, but since it is accessed only by employees inside the firewall, it has been simplified and no longer has firewalls separating the users from the application servers. The application adds Active Directory, which is used for authentication for both the application and database tiers.

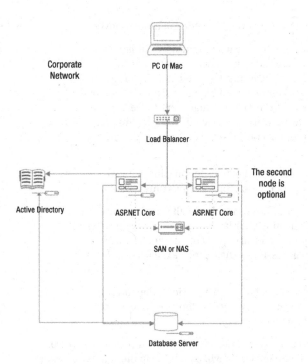

*Figure 6-3.* *Small line-of-business application*

# 6-2. Designing Your ASP.NET Core MVC Project for the Cloud

## Problem

While reviewing possible deployment scenarios with a client, you were asked if you thought the application should be deployed to the cloud. You have never built an application to run in the cloud and need guidance on how using a public cloud service changes how you design an application.

## Solution

When you are designing an application to run in your company's datacenter, there might be a few things that you take for granted. Most corporate IT departments purchase servers with multiple layers of redundancy. They have multiple fans, power supplies, hard disks, network adapters, and other features that prevent the failure of a single component from taking down an entire server. Although this does not prevent all hardware failures, it does make them relatively rare. This might not be the case in the cloud. While cloud vendors have high overall reliability, they use a variety of techniques to lower operational costs that can result in a higher rate of failure for individual nodes. When this occurs, your application may experience an intermittent outage while it is automatically moved to a new node. You need to expect that individual node failures could occur and build resiliency into your application so your application can recover automatically.

Another difference between the public cloud and traditional applications is that cloud applications are generally more distributed. For example, rather than writing files to attached storage on a server, you will be more likely to be using a BLOB storage service. It should be noted that most of the advice given here can also be applied to a microservices architecture in general and is not unique to any specific cloud vender.

Here are some general tips for making your ASP.Net Core MVC application more robust:

- Design your services to be stateless. Assume that the next request by the same user could be handled by another server. Do not rely on local server memory for maintaining state. This is also true for applications deployed in a corporate datacenter that have more than one node behind a load balancer. Even if your cloud vendor supports the use of "sticky cookies" to keep individual users pinned to a specific server, these solutions do not always work as expected and will ultimately limit your scalability and increase operational complexity. See recipe 9-6 for more information.

- Have a contingency plan that allows your application to function with reduced functionality if a service the application is dependent on becomes unreachable.

- Code defensively and test your edge cases. For example, how will your application respond if the content delivery network hosting your JavaScript libraries goes down or is performing poorly? Can you fall back to a local copy of the library? For more information on this technique, see the discussion on using the `Fallback` Tag Helper in recipe 4-8.

- Employ retry logic so your application does not fail when a service it depends on experiences an intermittent outage. For example, recipe 6-4 shows how to enable retry logic when configuring a connection to SQL Server.

Another aspect you might be taking for granted is the proximity of the servers in your architecture. For example, in most corporate deployments, your database server will usually be in the same datacenter as your application server, and you will have very low latency when running a query. This might not be the case in the cloud. You should assume a higher level of network latency when running your database queries and calling services on other nodes. You might find that the code that runs fine in your local development environment is significantly slower in production. Here are some general tips for reducing the impact of network latency:

- Be cognizant about when your code is calling remote services. When designing your APIs, use naming conventions that make it clear when network communications are required.

- Avoid designs that require many trips to the database or web service to process a single request. If you are making hundreds of separate network calls to your database to handle a single service call, consider a redesign.

- Consider using the Unit of Work pattern so you can package a set of commands and then send them over the wire as a batch. This technique is shown in recipe 6-9.

# 6-3. Deploying an ASP.NET Core MVC Application in a Docker Container

## Problem

You may have heard that using container technologies such as Docker can greatly simplify application deployment. You want to get a better understanding of what Docker is and how it can be used to deploy your ASP.NET Core application.

# Solution

Containerization platforms are a technology that allows you deploy an application and all its dependencies in a single file. This file contains a complete file system, runtime, operating system–specific libraries and tools, and anything else that would normally be installed on a server.

Containers provide the isolation benefits of a virtual machine but have much lower overhead. Containers use fewer system resources than virtual machines because they do not carry the weight of a hardware virtualization layer and an operating system. Because containers do not need to wait for an operating system to boot up, they start up in seconds.

Containers also offer benefits over installing an application on bare hardware. Since containers are self-contained, many containers can run on the same server without interfering with each other. Another benefit of the container concept is that containers are composed in layers. Each change to the base layer is stored as a new layer with the base layer never actually being changed. This allows many images to share a common base. When you download an image that uses the same base image as one you have downloaded previously, Docker will only need to download the delta. Because of this, even complex applications can be downloaded to a server and be online in less than a minute. For example, the `Microsoft/aspnetcore 1.1` image that is used as the base image for ASP.NET Core applications is made up of 11 layers. The layers include the Debian operating system, a subset of Linux utilities such as unzip and curl, ASP.NET Core Runtime for Linux, and libuv (which is the multiplatform asynchronous I/O library used by Kestrel).

Docker is the most popular container platform. Docker has millions of users and the support of many major companies including Google and Microsoft. Many software vendors and open source projects have created official containers and made them available for downloading on the public container repository Docker Hub.

## Containerizing an ASP.NET Core MVC Application

Microsoft has simplified the process of getting your application into a Docker container. Microsoft has created a Docker image that contains all the dependencies for ASP.NET Core MVC and has made it publicly available on Docker Hub. A new feature in Visual Studio has made it easy to compose a new Docker image that uses Microsoft's official ASP.NET Core MVC container as a base layer and then adds your application to it. Visual Studio even allows you to debug your application running inside the Docker container.

# How It Works

Before you can use Visual Studio's Docker support features, you must first install Docker for Windows. It is also recommended that you install the Hyper-V feature of Windows. Docker will use Hyper-V to run the Docker host. If Hyper-V is not available, Docker for Windows will install Oracle Virtual Box and create a virtualized Docker host using Virtual Box.

For instructions on installing Hyper-V please, see the following page:

```
https://docs.microsoft.com/en-us/virtualization/hyper-v-on-windows/quick-start/enable-
hyper-v
```

The Docker installer can be downloaded from `https://www.docker.com/products/overview`. Once the installer has been downloaded, double-click it to begin the installation process. Once the process has been completed, ensure that the Launch Docker check box has been selected and click the Finish button. After several minutes, you will see a Welcome window informing you that Docker is up and running.

After installing Docker, you can verify your installation by opening a PowerShell window and trying out some of the Docker commands.

- `docker --help`: This command will list all the available commands in the Docker CLI.

- `docker --version`: This command will show what version of Docker you are running.

- `docker info`: This command will give you detailed information regarding your Docker installation including how many containers are running, how many images are installed, and the kernel and operating system of the Docker host. It should be noted that the Docker host is running a custom version of Linux called Alpine Linux.

If you are using Hyper-V, you can open the Hyper-V console by entering **Hyper-V** in the Windows search box and then clicking Hyper-V Manager desktop application in the results list. In the Hyper-V Manager window, you will see a virtual machine named MobyLinuxVM, as shown in Figure 6-4. This is the Docker host that was created by the Docker for Windows installation program.

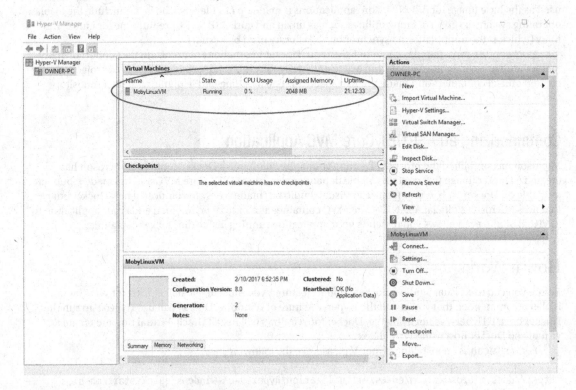

*Figure 6-4.* *The Docker host VM in Hyper-V Manager*

## Creating a Shared Drive

The Visual Studio build process requires that a volume be shared in order for it to build and run the Docker images. This should be the same volume where you will be creating the Visual Studio solution for your ASP.NET Core MVC project. To create the shared drive, right-click the Docker icon in the Windows system tray and select Settings from the pop-up menu. In the Docker settings window, click Shared Drives and then select the drive where you will be creating your solution, as shown in Figure 6-5.

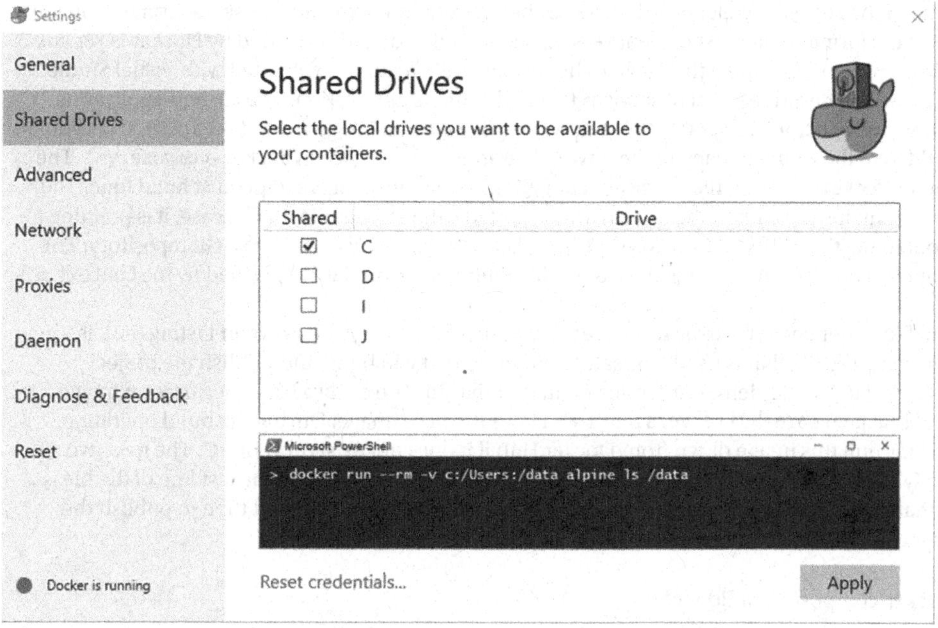

*Figure 6-5.* *Sharing a drive with Dockyer*

# Creating an ASP.NET Core MVC Project with Docker Support

To create a new ASP.NET Core MVC Web Application project with Docker support, open Visual Studio 2017 and then select New ➤ Project from the File menu. In the New Project window, search for ASP.NET Core and then select ASP.NET Core Web Application (.NET Core). Name the solution and project **Recipe03**. In the New ASP.NET Core Web Application window, select ASP.NET Core 1.1 from the drop-down list and then select Web Application from the list of available ASP.NET Core 1.1 templates.

Ensure that the Enable Docker Support check box is selected and then click OK.

After the project has been created, you will see two folders under the solution in Solution Explorer. The first folder is docker-compose, and the second is the ASP.NET Core application. docker-compose contains two files, docker-compose.ci.build.yml and docker-compose.yml. These files are used by the Compose feature of Docker that allows you to define and run an application that is composed of one or more Docker containers. The docker-compose.yml files describe the services, networks, and volumes used by the application. Listing 6-1 shows the docker-compose.yml file created by Visual Studio.

*Listing 6-1.* docker-compose.yml Created by Visual Studio

```
version: '2'

services:
  recipe03:
    image: recipe03
    build:
      context: ./Recipe03
      dockerfile: Dockerfile
```

The first line of the docker-compose.yml file describes the version of the Compose file format. You are using version 2 of the format. The most current version supported and recommended by Docker is version 3. For now, I am keeping version 2 since this is what the Visual Studio team has validated with Visual Studio.

The services section describes a list of services that make up the application. The current application contains only one service named recipe03. The recipe03 service uses an image named recipe03. If additional projects were added to the solution, each of them would be added as a service in docker-compose.yml. The build section in the docker-compose file describes configuration options that are applied at build time. The Context property contains the path to the directory that contains the Docker file. In this case, it is pointing to the directory containing the ASP.NET Core MVC project. The context can also point to a Git repository. The dockerfile property contains the name of the Docker file found in the directory specified by the Context property.

The second file under docker-compose, docker-compose.ci.build.yml (shown in Listing 6-2), is another Docker Compose file that is used to create a container that will build and publish the project. docker-compose.ci.build.yml defines a service named ci-build. The ci-build service uses an image named microsoft/aspnetcore-build version 1.0-1.1 as the base image. During the build operation, it will automatically pull this image down from Docker Hub if it does not exist on your PC. The next two properties specify the volume and directory path where the build will be created. The last line of the file is the command that will be run to restore the NuGet packages used in the project and then to publish the project to the specified path.

*Listing 6-2.* docker-compose.ci.build.yml

```
version: '2'

services:
  ci-build:
    image: microsoft/aspnetcore-build:1.0-1.1
    volumes:
      - .:/src
    working_dir: /src
    command: /bin/bash -c "dotnet restore ./Recipe03.sln && dotnet publish ./Recipe03.sln -c
Release -o ./obj/Docker/publish"
```

If you want to learn more about the Docker Compose file format, you can access the documentation online here:

```
https://docs.docker.com/compose/compose-file/compose-file-v2/#/service-configuration-reference
```

Inside the ASP.NET Core MVC project folder, Visual Studio has added two files, Dockerfile and .dockerignore. Note that the .dockerignore file is nested under Dockerfile in Solution Explorer. The .dockerignore file shown in Listing 6-3 tells the Docker CLI not to include the files specified in the listed glob patterns when it sends the context to the Docker daemon. This prevents large or sensitive files from being added to an image. Glob patterns are Unix-style pathname pattern expansions. Glob patterns allow you to use wildcards to include or exclude groups of files. For example, * matches any string, ? matches any single character, and [...] can be used to match a set of enclosed characters. The ! character, as you may suspect, tells Docker to ignore all but the pattern listed. The result of the file shown in Listing 6-3 is that Docker will ignore all files except for the obj/Docker/empty folder and the obj/Docker/publish folder and all its contents.

***Listing 6-3.*** .dockerignore

```
*
!obj/Docker/publish/*
!obj/Docker/empty/
```

Listing 6-4 shows the Docker file.

***Listing 6-4.*** Dockerfile

```
FROM microsoft/aspnetcore:1.1
ARG source
WORKDIR /app
EXPOSE 80
COPY ${source:-obj/Docker/publish} .
ENTRYPOINT ["dotnet", "Recipe03.dll"]
```

The first line of Dockerfile uses the FROM command to set the base image to Microsoft/ aspnetcore:1.1. If this image does not exist on your PC, Docker will automatically download it from Docker Hub. The aspnetcore image contains .NET Core and native images for all ASP.NET Core libraries. Including native images of the core libraries results in significantly faster cold start times since it will not be necessary to JIT compile the .NET libraries before the application loads.

If you want to learn more about what is in the aspnetcore image, you can view its page on Docker Hub here:

```
https://hub.docker.com/r/microsoft/aspnetcore/
```

In the next line, the ARG command is used to define a variable named source whose value can be passed in at build time. The WORKDIR command sets the working directory that will be used by the COPY and ENTRYPOINT commands. The specified directory will be created automatically if it does not exist. The EXPOSE command tells Docker that the container will listen on port 80 at runtime. It should be noted that EXPOSE does not expose port 80 to the host. To expose the port to the host, you need to use the -p flag when executing the Docker run command.

The COPY command copies the objects specified in the source variable to the file system on the container. The last command in the file ENTRYPOINT allows the container to run as an executable. It tells Docker to execute the dotnet executable with the parameter Recipe03.dll. This causes the ASP.NET Core MVC application to launch when the container is launched with the docker run command.

## Running and Debugging the Application in the Container

After adding Docker support to the project, you should see Docker as the only item in the toolbar, as shown in Figure 6-6.

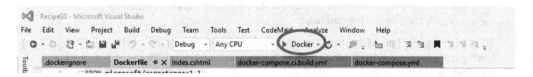

***Figure 6-6.*** *Docker as an option in the run toolbar*

Clicking the Run button or pressing the F5 key on your keyboard will launch the application inside the Docker container. You will be able to debug the application just like you can if the application was run in IIS or the command line. While the application is running, you can inspect it using some of the Docker command-line tools.

# 6-4. Creating a Data Access Layer Using Entity Framework Core Code First

## Problem

You have just started a new project but have not created your database. You like to work with plain old C# objects (POCO), but you do not want to hand-code all your data access code. You would like to take advantage of the Code First features of Entity Framework Core to generate the database code.

## Solution

Like ASP.NET Core, Entity Framework Core is new and was written from the ground up over the past few years. It shares many of the same patterns with Entity Framework 6.x but is a new code base with new tooling. As with Entity Framework 6, Entity Framework Core supports the concept of *migrations*. Migrations track changes in an object model and can be used to automatically generate the SQL code required to create or modify a database.

Unlike Entity Framework 6.x, the current version of Visual Studio does not offer any graphical tools for creating migrations and applying them to the database. This functionality is available only in the dotnet command-line interface.

There are seven basic steps required to set up Entity Framework Core in your project and run migration on a database:

1. Create the object model using plain old C# classes. These classes can be optionally decorated with data annotations to designate which fields are required as well as the length of the strings.

2. Add the Entity Framework Core NuGet packages to the project.

3. Create a class that extends Entity Framework Core DbContext and includes DbSet collections for all the top-level classes in the object model you created in step 1. Optionally, you can add validation rules and customize how object relationships will be generated in the database in the DbContext OnModelCreating method. This technique can be used as an alternative to using data annotations in your model.

4. Create a configuration file that contains the connection string to the database server.

5. Modify the Startup.cs class's ConfigureServices method in the web application so the DbContext class is added and configured. This is required for the web application to use the database.

6. Add a Startup.cs class to the class library project and then modify the ConfigureServices method so DbContext is added and configured. This is required for step 7 to work.

7. Use the dotnet ef migration command to create migrations.

8. Use the dotnet ef database command to commit migrations to the database or generate the SQL scripts.

# How It Works

For this example, you start by creating an empty solution and then add two projects to it. The first project is an ASP.NET Core class library that will contain your data access library, and the second will contain your ASP.NET Core MVC web application. Although you can create your classes directly inside your ASP.NET Core MVC project, in most cases it is best to define this in a separate class library. Using a separate class library allows you to reuse the model in other projects and aids in team development scenarios. For example, you may have a team member who focuses on the data model, while other developers concentrate on the service layer and user interface.

## Creating the Solution

Open Visual Studio to start creating the solution. On the Get Started page, under New Project you should see ASP.NET Core Web Application (.NET Core) under Recent Project Templates. Click ASP.NET Core Web Application (.NET Core) to open the New Project window. Name the project **Recipe04.Web** and the solution **Recipe04**. Ensure that "Create directory for solution" is selected. You can then click OK.

In the New ASP.NET Core Web Application window, ensure that ASP.NET Core 1.1 is selected from the drop-down list, Web Application is selected under ASP.NET Core 1.1 Templates, and Authentication type is set to No Authentication. Ensure that Enable Docker Support is not selected and then click OK. After the solution has been created, right-click the Solution node in Solution Explorer and then select Add ➤ New Project. Select the Class Library (.NET Core) template from the template list and name the project **Recipe04.DataAccess**.

After the project has been created, in Solution Explorer, right-click `Class1.cs` and select Delete. Click OK when prompted.

## Adding Entity Framework Core NuGet Packages

To use Entity Framework Core in the Recipe04.DataAccess library, you need to add references to several NuGet packages. There are several ways you can add NuGet packages to a project. You can use the NuGet Package Manager GUI, you can install them using the Package Manager Console, or you can manually add package references by editing the project's `.csproj` file. Editing the `.csproj` file is the fastest way when you need to add several packages at the same time. To edit the `.csproj` file, right-click the Recipe04.DataAccess project in Solution Explorer and select Edit Recipe04.DataAccess.csproj. The completed project file should match Listing 6-5.

***Listing 6-5.*** Recipe04.DataAccess.csproj

```
<Project Sdk="Microsoft.NET.Sdk">

  <PropertyGroup>
    <TargetFramework>netcoreapp1.1</TargetFramework>
  </PropertyGroup>

  <ItemGroup>
    <PackageReference Include="Microsoft.AspNetCore" Version="1.1.1" />
    <PackageReference Include="Microsoft.EntityFrameworkCore.SqlServer" Version="1.0.2" />
    <PackageReference Include="Microsoft.EntityFrameworkCore.Design" Version="1.0.2" />
  </ItemGroup>
```

```
  <ItemGroup>
    <DotNetCliToolReference Include="Microsoft.EntityFrameworkCore.Tools.DotNet"
Version="1.0.0 " />
  </ItemGroup>
</Project>
```

Note that by adding `Microsoft.EntityFrameworkCore.SqlServer` you are also adding its dependencies to your project. You can explore this by expanding the References node in Visual Studio's Solution Explorer. You will see under Dependencies ➤ NuGet ➤ Microsoft.EntityFrameworkCore.SqlServer that `Microsoft.EntityFrameworkCore.Relational` has also been added.

The reference to `Microsoft.EntityFrameworkCore.Tools.DotNet` is required in order for you to use the Entity Framework Core command-line tools with the dotnet CLI. `Microsoft.EntityFrameworkCore.Tools.DotNet` is a DotNetCliToolReference item. It adds the `dotnet ef` command in the CLI. Note at the time of this writing, a bug in NuGet Package Manager prevents you from adding DotNetCliToolReference items using the GUI. The only way to add `Microsoft.EntityFrameworkCore.Tools.DotNet` is to manually modify the `.csproj` file, as you have done in this example.

Next, you will add the NuGet packages to the web project. Since you need to add only a single package, it is fastest to do it via the Package Manager Console. To show the Package Manager Console, select View ➤ Other Windows ➤ Package Manager Console from Visual Studio's main menu. In the Package Manager Console window, change the Default project in the Package Manager Console to Recipe04.Web and then run the following command:

```
Install-Package Microsoft.EntityFrameworkCore.SqlServer
```

Even though you will be maintaining a separation of concerns in your code by not doing any explicit manipulation of database objects, the web project still needs a reference to `Microsoft.EntityFrameworkCore.SqlServer` in order for you to configure the connection string for your DbContext in the web application's startup file.

## Creating the Model Classes

For this example, the model will consist of two classes: `Artist` and `ArtistSkill`. The first class will represent a recording artist, and the second class will represent skills possessed by that artist. The classes themselves will be plain C# classes. There will be no Entity Framework–specific code required.

1. Add a new folder under the Recipe04.DataAccess project and name it `Entities`.

2. Right-click this folder and select Add ➤ Class.

3. In the Add New Item window, name your file `Artist.cs` and then click Add.

4. Repeat this process for the second class, naming the file `ArtistSkill.cs`.

Modify the files to match Listing 6-6 and Listing 6-7.

***Listing 6-6.*** Artist.cs

```
using System;
using System.Collections.Generic;

namespace Recipe04.DataAccess.Entities
{
    public class Artist
```

```
    {
        public int ArtistId { get; set; }
        public string UserName { get; set; }
        public string Country { get; set; }
        public string Provence { get; set; }
        public string City { get; set; }
        public string WebSite { get; set; }
        public DateTime CreateDate { get; set; }

        public virtual IList<ArtistSkill> ArtistSkills { get; set; }
    }
}
```

The Artist class is a plain old CLR object (POCO). It contains seven properties. Even though there is nothing in this code specific to the Entity Framework, two of the properties have been specifically designed to follow conventions that can be leveraged by Entity Framework Code First. The first is the ArtistId field. By convention, Entity Framework will create the database table for a class: it looks to see if it has a property named either Id or Id prefixed with the name of the class, as in ArtistId. In the examples in this book, I use the latter style.

The second property of interest is the ArtistSkills collection. This property holds a collection of ArtistSkill objects and is marked as virtual. This signature is a convention that Entity Framework Code First will use to create a navigation property that represents a relationship between the two entities.

*Listing 6-7.* ArtistSkill.cs

```
namespace Recipe04.DataAccess.Entities
{
    public class ArtistSkill
    {
        public int ArtistSkillId { get; set; }
        public string TalentName { get; set; }
        public int SkillLevel { get; set; }
        public string Details { get; set; }
        public string Styles { get; set; }

        public virtual Artist Artist { get; set; }
    }
}
```

Like the code in Listing 6-6, Listing 6-7 uses the ID convention to create a property that will represent a primary key. It also has a property named Artist marked as virtual. This is the other side of the navigation property defined in Listing 6-5. Both navigation properties are required for you to write LINQ queries that extract data from both tables. The Artist property of ArtistSkill allows reverse navigation to the parent Artist object.

## Creating the DbContext

The Artist and ArtistSkill classes are normal C# classes. These classes by themselves do not have any knowledge of any database and have no way of persisting their values. To enable this functionality, you need to create a class that extends the DbContext class and then have that class reference your entity classes.

To add a DbContext to the project, follow these steps:

1.  Create a new folder at the root of your project and name it Context.

2.  Right-click the folder and select Add ➤ New Class. Name the class ArtistContext.cs.

Modify the class to match Listing 6-8.

*Listing 6-8.* The ArtistContext Class

```
using Microsoft.EntityFrameworkCore;
using Recipe04.DataAccess.Entities;

namespace Recipe04.DataAccess.Context
{
    public class ArtistContext : DbContext
    {
        public ArtistContext(DbContextOptions<ArtistContext> options) : base(options)
        {
        }

        public DbSet<Artist> Artists { get; set; }
        public DbSet<ArtistSkill> ArtistSkill { get; set; }
    }
}
```

The ArtistContext class shown in Listing 6-8 extends Microsoft.EntityFrameworkCore.DbContext. By doing this, you have transformed this simple class into a proxy to your back-end data store and made it implement both the Repository and Unit of Work patterns.

Inside the body of ArtistContext are two public properties that expose a DbSet collection of Artist and ArtistSkill. A DbSet class represents a collection of entities of a given type within the context. It allows data to be queried, updated, and deleted from the back-end database.

From the perspective of the developer, you have just made a persistent-ignorant pair of C# classes into an almost fully functional data access layer.

Your DbContext class is the proxy that your code uses to communicate with its persistence store. The back-end store that DbContext uses is determined by one of two things: a connection string that you explicitly provide in your code or configuration or, if nothing is provided, a dynamically generated connection string based on its class name and namespace.

Later in this recipe, you will pass configuration information to the ArtistContext class when you load it in StartUp.cs. The DbContext base class implements the Options pattern, which allows the database provider type and connection string to be injected into the DbContext class. For dependency injection to work, a public constructor that accepts a DbContextOptions<ArtistContext> object as an argument must be added to ArtistContext.

## Using the Fluent API to Specify Database Mapping Details

Entity Framework offers a feature known as *migrations* to help you keep your code and database in sync. The migrations feature creates an initial snapshot of your entity model and then compares changes in the model to the snapshot and generates a set of scripts to implement the delta between the code and the stored snapshot.

The migration feature uses a combination of Code First conventions, data annotations, and the Fluent API to determine how the POCOs should be mapped to database tables.

Code First conventions are standard naming conventions that allow the migration feature to infer things such as primary keys and relationships based on property names and data types.

Data annotations are a set of attributes that allow you to annotate classes and properties with attributes that can specify whether properties are required, the max length, and whether a property is a key.

The Fluent API is a code-based method for specifying similar information data annotations, but it is somewhat more flexible and allows you to keep your entity classes clean and free of database-specific concerns. While it is possible to use both data annotations and Fluent API together, it is usually best to use one or the other. Mixing the two techniques can lead to duplicate or contradictory settings that can be difficult to debug. For this example, you will be using the Fluent API.

In Listing 6-9 you override the OnModelCreating method and use the Fluent API to specify the maximum length of all the properties with string data types. This is important because otherwise all properties with the string data type would be mapped to varchar(max) fields in the database, which can have detrimental performance impacts. For the Artist.UserName and ArtistSkill.TalentName properties, the Fluid API's IsRequired property is set to true. In Entity Framework Core, all nullable typed properties are optional by default. Since strings can be assigned null values, you need to explicitly set the property to true if you want to make the database field required when the database table is generated.

*Listing 6-9.* OnModelCreating Method Added to ArtistContext

```
protected override void OnModelCreating(ModelBuilder builder)
{
        // Artist
        builder.Entity<Artist>().Property(x => x.City).HasMaxLength(50);
        builder.Entity<Artist>().Property(x => x.Country).HasMaxLength(50);
        builder.Entity<Artist>().Property(x => x.Provence).HasMaxLength(50);
        builder.Entity<Artist>().Property(x => x.UserName).IsRequired(true).
        HasMaxLength(50);
        builder.Entity<Artist>().Property(x => x.WebSite).HasMaxLength(255);

        // ArtistSkill
        builder.Entity<ArtistSkill>().Property(x => x.Details).HasMaxLength(255);
        builder.Entity<ArtistSkill>().Property(x => x.TalentName).IsRequired(true).
        HasMaxLength(50);
        builder.Entity<ArtistSkill>().Property(x => x.Styles).HasMaxLength(255);
}
```

# Setting the Connection String Using a Configuration File

It is a best practice to avoid hard-coding database connection strings into your source code since database connection strings will vary depending on where the application is deployed. Ideally, you would store this information in a file that can be easily modified without the need to recompile code. In older versions of ASP.NET, you would have stored the connection string in the web.config file. ASP.NET Core uses a new configuration system that allows you to use many configuration files and different file formats. In this example, you will create a new ASP.NET configuration file in the JSON format. To do this, select the Recipe04.Web project in Solution Explorer and then press Ctrl+Shift+A to open the Add New Item window. Enter **json** into the search box and then select the ASP.NET Configuration File template. Name the new file dbconfig.json; then click the Add button in the Recipe04.Web project and modify it to match Listing 6-10. When done, repeat this step on the Recipe04.DataAccess project.

*Listing 6-10.* dbconfig.json

```
{
  "ConnectionStrings": {
        "DefaultConnection":
      "Server=.;Database=Chapter06Recipe04;Trusted_Connection=True;MultipleActiveResult
Sets=true"
    }
}
```

The configuration shown in Listing 6-10 is a JSON-formatted data structure. The configuration file has no set schema, which leaves developers with total freedom of how they want to structure the configuration file. In this case, I have created a two-level hierarchy. This format could potentially allow you to store configuration information for several DbContext classes, each with their own set of properties.

The connection string has several properties that should be noted. First is the Server property that points to a default instance of SQL Server running on the local machine. This assumes you have a SQL Server Express or Developer edition running locally and configured as a default instance. Note that if you set up SQL Express with the default settings, it would have created a named instance accessed using .\SQLEXPRESS.

The connection string uses the shorthand format that allows you to use a period rather than type out the local machine name. The appendix of this book provides instructions on how to install SQL Server Express. While it is possible to use LocalDB, which comes with Visual Studio, I have found inconsistent behavior depending on how you launch your application.

Next is the Database property, which allows you to specify the name of the database, Chapter06Recipe04.

The Trusted_Connction property is next. When Trusted_Connction is set to true, ASP.NET will use the login credentials of the current system process to connect to the database. When the application is running in IIS Express, it will log on to SQL Server using your credentials. Because of this, you need to make sure that your account has administrative access to the database.

The last property of the connection string, MultipleActiveResultSets, activates a feature of SQL Server known as MARS, which allows the execution of multiple SQL Server batches on a single connection.

## Adding a Reference to the Data Access Project to the Web Project

Before you can access any of the types defined in the data access layer from your web application, you must first add a reference. To do this, right-click Dependencies in Solution Explorer under the Recipe04.Web project and select Add Reference from the pop-up menu. In the Reference Manager window, select Solution under the Projects node in the left panel and then check the box next to Recipe04.DataAccess. Click the OK button. If you expand the Dependencies node in Solution Explorer, you should now see a Projects node that contains a link to the Recipe04.DataAccess project.

## Adding a Startup Class to the Recipe04.DataAccess Project

For the dotnet CLI to create the migrations, it needs a Startup class to be added so that database provider and connection string information can be loaded into ArtistContext. The ArtistContext class's constructor shown in Listing 6-8 takes a DbContextOptions object as an argument. By registering the DbContext object in the Startup class, you are instructing the dependency injection system to inject the DBContextOptions object into the ArtistContext class each time one is created. Listing 6-11 shows the Startup class.

*Listing 6-11.* Startup Class in Recipe04.DataAccess

```
using Microsoft.AspNetCore.Hosting;
using Microsoft.EntityFrameworkCore;
using Microsoft.Extensions.Configuration;
using Microsoft.Extensions.DependencyInjection;
using Recipe04.DataAccess.Context;

namespace Recipe04.DataAccess
{
    public class Startup
    {
        public Startup(IHostingEnvironment env)
        {
            var builder = new ConfigurationBuilder()
                .SetBasePath(env.ContentRootPath)
                .AddJsonFile("dbconfig.json", optional: false);
            Configuration = builder.Build();
        }
        public IConfigurationRoot Configuration { get; }

        public void ConfigureServices(IServiceCollection services)
        {
            var connString = Configuration.GetConnectionString("DefaultConnection");
            services.AddDbContext<ArtistContext>(
                options => options.UseSqlServer(connString)
                );
        }
    }
}
```

# Database Migrations

In older versions of Entity Framework, the database migrations feature was implemented as a set of PowerShell cmdlets that were typically run using the NuGet console. In Entity Framework Core, this functionality has been moved to the framework commands, which are invoked using the dotnet command-line interface. Commands are a new concept for ASP.NET Core that moves many features that were previously available only in Visual Studio to a set of command-line utilities that can be run in any environment supported by .NET Core.

## Creating Your First Migration

To create a database migration, open the Visual Studio command prompt. This is a special version of the command prompt that contains all the environment variables needed for working with .NET. Once the command window is open, you will need to navigate to the directory. You can do this using the cd command. Here's an example:

```
cd "\MvcRecipes\Chapter06\Recipe04\src\Recipe04.DataAccess"
```

After navigating to the directory, enter the following command to create the initial migration named `Initial`:

```
dotnet ef migrations add Initial
```

This command launches the .NET Runtime Engine, which will run your `Startup` class loading the configuration information. It then executes the `ef migrations add` command.

After running the command, you should see a new directory added to the Recipe04.DataAccess project called `Migrations` with three files. The first file, `ArtistContextModelSnapshot`, is a class that describes a snapshot of the current state of your model. This will be updated each time you add a new migration. It is used by the Entity Framework migration command to determine what changed in your model since the last migration. The second two files shown in Listing 6-12 are named using the date and time the migration was generated in the format `{ YYYYMMDDHHMMSS }_initial.cs` and `{ YYYYMMDDHHMMSS }_initial.Designer.cs`. For example, if the file was created on March 18, 2017, the files would be named `20170318063117_Initial.cs` and `20170318063117_Initial.Designer.cs`.

`Initial` and `Initial.Designer` are partial classes that contain the scaffolding for the migration. `Initial` has two methods, `Up` and `Down`. The `Up` method contains code that will implement the required changes on the database. The `Down` method will revert the changes. The `Initial.Designer` file contains a single method called `BuildTargetModel`. The `BuildTargetModel` method is generated based on a combination of Fluent API calls from the `DBContext OnModelCreating` method, data annotations on the model, and Code First conventions. It is generally a good idea to review this code before committing changes to the database. If you made a mistake in the class design or Fluent API calls, you should be able to find it by reviewing the code.

***Listing 6-12.*** Migration File Generated by Entity Framework Migration Command

```
/// 20170318063117_Initial.cs
using System;
using System.Collections.Generic;
using Microsoft.EntityFrameworkCore.Migrations;
using Microsoft.EntityFrameworkCore.Metadata;

namespace Recipe04.DataAccess.Migrations
{
    public partial class initial : Migration
    {
        protected override void Up(MigrationBuilder migrationBuilder)
        {
            migrationBuilder.CreateTable(
                name: "Artists",
                columns: table => new
                {
                    ArtistId = table.Column<int>(nullable: false)
                        .Annotation("SqlServer:ValueGenerationStrategy",
                        SqlServerValueGenerationStrategy.IdentityColumn),
                    City = table.Column<string>(maxLength: 50, nullable: true),
                    Country = table.Column<string>(maxLength: 50, nullable: true),
                    CreateDate = table.Column<DateTime>(nullable: false),
                    Provence = table.Column<string>(maxLength: 50, nullable: true),
                    UserName = table.Column<string>(maxLength: 50, nullable: false),
                    WebSite = table.Column<string>(maxLength: 255, nullable: true)
                },
```

```
            constraints: table =>
            {
                table.PrimaryKey("PK_Artists", x => x.ArtistId);
            });

        migrationBuilder.CreateTable(
            name: "ArtistSkill",
            columns: table => new
            {
                ArtistSkillId = table.Column<int>(nullable: false)
                    .Annotation("SqlServer:ValueGenerationStrategy",
                    SqlServerValueGenerationStrategy.IdentityColumn),
                ArtistId = table.Column<int>(nullable: true),
                Details = table.Column<string>(maxLength: 255, nullable: true),
                SkillLevel = table.Column<int>(nullable: false),
                Styles = table.Column<string>(maxLength: 255, nullable: true),
                TalentName = table.Column<string>(maxLength: 50, nullable: false)
            },
            constraints: table =>
            {
                table.PrimaryKey("PK_ArtistSkill", x => x.ArtistSkillId);
                table.ForeignKey(
                    name: "FK_ArtistSkill_Artists_ArtistId",
                    column: x => x.ArtistId,
                    principalTable: "Artists",
                    principalColumn: "ArtistId",
                    onDelete: ReferentialAction.Restrict);
            });

        migrationBuilder.CreateIndex(
            name: "IX_ArtistSkill_ArtistId",
            table: "ArtistSkill",
            column: "ArtistId");
    }

    protected override void Down(MigrationBuilder migrationBuilder)
    {
        migrationBuilder.DropTable(
            name: "ArtistSkill");

        migrationBuilder.DropTable(
            name: "Artists");
    }
}
}

/// 20170318063117_Initial.Designer.cs
using System;
using Microsoft.EntityFrameworkCore;
using Microsoft.EntityFrameworkCore.Infrastructure;
using Microsoft.EntityFrameworkCore.Metadata;
using Microsoft.EntityFrameworkCore.Migrations;
using Recipe04.DataAccess.Context;
```

```
namespace Recipe04.DataAccess.Migrations
{
    [DbContext(typeof(ArtistContext))]
    [Migration("20170319063117_Initial")]
    partial class Initial
    {
        protected override void BuildTargetModel(ModelBuilder modelBuilder)
        {
            modelBuilder
                .HasAnnotation("ProductVersion", "1.0.2")
                .HasAnnotation("SqlServer:ValueGenerationStrategy",
                SqlServerValueGenerationStrategy.IdentityColumn);
            modelBuilder.Entity("Recipe04.DataAccess.Entities.Artist", b =>
                {
                    b.Property<int>("ArtistId")
                        .ValueGeneratedOnAdd();

                    b.Property<string>("City")
                        .HasMaxLength(50);

                    b.Property<string>("Country")
                        .HasMaxLength(50);

                    b.Property<DateTime>("CreateDate");

                    b.Property<string>("Provence")
                        .HasMaxLength(50);

                    b.Property<string>("UserName")
                        .IsRequired()
                        .HasMaxLength(50);

                    b.Property<string>("WebSite")
                        .HasMaxLength(255);

                    b.HasKey("ArtistId");

                    b.ToTable("Artists");
                });

            modelBuilder.Entity("Recipe04.DataAccess.Entities.ArtistSkill", b =>
                {
                    b.Property<int>("ArtistSkillId")
                        .ValueGeneratedOnAdd();

                    b.Property<int?>("ArtistId");
```

```
                b.Property<string>("Details")
                    .HasMaxLength(255);

                b.Property<int>("SkillLevel");

                b.Property<string>("Styles")
                    .HasMaxLength(255);

                b.Property<string>("TalentName")
                    .IsRequired()
                    .HasMaxLength(50);

                b.HasKey("ArtistSkillId");

                b.HasIndex("ArtistId");

                b.ToTable("ArtistSkill");
            });
        modelBuilder.Entity("Recipe04.DataAccess.Entities.ArtistSkill", b =>
            {
                b.HasOne("Recipe04.DataAccess.Entities.Artist", "Artist")
                    .WithMany("ArtistSkills")
                    .HasForeignKey("ArtistId");
            });
        }
    }
}
```

---

■ **Tip** Always review your migration code. Even though the Entity Framework team did a good job with the code generator, it is not perfect. There are times when you might need to tweak the code so it creates the database objects you need.

---

At this point, even though the scaffolding has been generated, it has not been executed. If you notice that you are missing something and need to make changes to your model, you can make the changes, run the following command to remove the migration, and then run the add command again to regenerate the code.

```
dotnet ef migrations remove
```

## Running the Migration

To run the migration, you can use the following:

```
dotnet  ef database update
```

The migration will now use the connection string specified in your ArtistContext constructor. If the connection is successful, it will verify that the database exists. In this case, because you have not created the database, the migration will create the database for you automatically using the server's default settings for new databases. Once the database is created, dotnet ef will use the code in the migration's Up method to generate the DDL code required to create the database objects.

## Backing Out a Migration

If you want to revert to a previous migration, you can call the following:

```
dotnet  ef database update Initial
```

Here, Initial is the name of the migration you want to revert to. If you want to back out all migrations and start over, you can pass in 0 for the name.

```
dotnet ef database update 0
```

## Promoting the Changes to Production

In most organizations, developers do not have direct access to production. There is usually some sort of change control process in place by which the developers create a change ticket and then attach a script that includes the needed changes.

To accommodate this need, the Code First migration commands include a script command. When the following script command is used, a SQL script will be created, and no actions will be taken against the database:

```
dotnet ef migrations script -o initial.sql
```

This command generates a script for all your migrations, including the script to create the _MigrationHistory table and insert the data for each migration. The –o command option allows you to specify the name of the output file.

If you do not want to include all the migrations, you can specify the start and end migrations as the first two arguments to the script command. A full list of arguments and options for the script command can be displayed using the following:

```
dotnet ef migrations script --help
```

## Modifying the Startup So the Web Application Can Use Your DbContext

Before you can use ArtistContext in your controllers, you will need to add the ArtistContext configuration information to the Startup class. Modify the Startup class in the Recipe04.Web project to match Listing 6-13. The changes to the class are shown in bold.

*Listing 6-13.* Adding an OnConfiguring Method to ArtistContext

```
using Microsoft.AspNetCore.Builder;
using Microsoft.AspNetCore.Hosting;
using Microsoft.Extensions.Configuration;
using Microsoft.Extensions.DependencyInjection;
using Microsoft.Extensions.Logging;
using Microsoft.EntityFrameworkCore;
using Recipe04.DataAccess.Context;

namespace Recipe04.Web
{
    public class Startup
```

```
{
    public Startup(IHostingEnvironment env)
    {
        var builder = new ConfigurationBuilder()
            .SetBasePath(env.ContentRootPath)
            .AddJsonFile("appsettings.json", optional: false, reloadOnChange: true)
            .AddJsonFile($"appsettings.{env.EnvironmentName}.json", optional: true)
            .AddJsonFile("dbconfig.json", optional: false, reloadOnChange: true)
            .AddEnvironmentVariables();
        Configuration = builder.Build();
    }

    public IConfigurationRoot Configuration { get; }

    public void ConfigureServices(IServiceCollection services)
    {
        services.AddDbContext<ArtistContext>(
            options => options.UseSqlServer(Configuration.GetConnectionString
            ("DefaultConnection"))
            );
        services.AddMvc();
    }
    public void Configure(IApplicationBuilder app, IHostingEnvironment env,
    ILoggerFactory loggerFactory)
    {
        loggerFactory.AddConsole(Configuration.GetSection("Logging"));
        loggerFactory.AddDebug();

        if (env.IsDevelopment())
        {
            app.UseDeveloperExceptionPage();
        }
        else
        {
            app.UseExceptionHandler("/Home/Error");
        }

        app.UseStaticFiles();

        app.UseMvc(routes =>
        {
            routes.MapRoute(
                name: "default",
                template: "{controller=Home}/{action=Index}/{id?}");
        });
    }
}
}
```

In the `Startup` class's constructor, you initialize the `Configuration` property by adding the JSON file you had created earlier and then calling the build method to create a single configuration object that contains the values from all the configuration files.

In the `ConfigureServices` method, you use the extension method `AddDbContext`, which is included in the `Microsoft.EntityFrameworkCore` namespace. The `AddDbContext` method adds the `ArtistContext` class to the ASP.NET Core dependency injection system and allows it to be injected into the controller classes. The dependency injection system is also used by the command-line tools when generating the migrations and updating the database. `AddDbContext` accepts an `options` parameter called `UseSqlServer` that allows you to configure the context to use SQL Server. The connection string that was defined in the `dbconfig.json` file shown in Listing 6-10 is passed as an argument to `UseSqlServer`.

# 6-5. Creating a Data Access Layer Using Entity Framework Core Code First from an Existing Database

## Problem

You want to create a data access layer based on an existing SQL Server database using Entity Framework Core. You want to generate POCO classes based on your database tables and then use migrations for all future enhancements to your application.

## Solution

Entity Framework Core has a scaffolding feature that will generate C# classes based on the structure of an existing database. The tool will also generate a `DbContext` class. To use this feature, you can create a new ASP.NET Core project and add the required NuGet dependencies.

You can the run the scaffolding commands from the command prompt, which will add the generated classes to your project.

## How It Works

As with the examples in recipe 6-4 and later in recipe 6-6, you create the data access layer in a separate class library.

## Creating the Solution

Open Visual Studio. On the Start Page, click New Project. In the left pane that lists the template categories, expand Visual C# and then the .NET Core Web node, and then click ASP.NET Core Web Application (.NET Core). Name the project **Recipe05.Web** and the solution **Recipe05**.

In the New ASP.NET Core Web Application window, ensure that ASP.NET Core 1.1 is selected in the drop-down list and then select Web Application under ASP.NET Core 1.1 Templates. Ensure that the authentication type is set to No Authentication and that Enable Docker Support is not selected. You can then click OK to create the solution. After the solution has been created, right-click the Solution node in Solution Explorer and then select Add ➤ New Project. Select the Class Library (.NET Core) template from the template list and name the project **Recipe05.DataAccess**.

After the project has been created, in Solution Explorer, right-click `Class1.cs` and select Delete. Click OK when prompted.

## Creating the Sample Database

This example requires that you have a SQL Server database installed on your PC. If you have not set this up, please follow the instructions in the book's appendix.

To create the sample database used for this recipe, you can use the script provided in the book's code samples available on GitHub. If you cloned the repository, you will find the file under AspNetCoreRecipes\ Chapter06\ Recipe05_Database.sql. You can also download the script from GitHub here:

https://github.com/johnciliberti/AspNetCoreRecipes/blob/develop/Chapter06/Recipe05_Database.sql

Once you have the script file, first verify that the paths to the .mdf and .ldf files in the SQL script make sense for your system and adjust as required. You can then create the database by running the following at the command prompt:

```
sqlcmd -i Recipe05_Database.sql
```

Note that the command will run under your user context. If you have a sysadmin role on the database, it will be created without any further action. If you do not have sysadmin or SQL Server has not been set up to allow Windows authentication, you will be prompted for a username and password.

## Reverse Engineering Your Database

The first step in reverse engineering a database is to add the Entity Framework Core command-line tools to your project. To do this, right-click the Recipe05.DataAccess project in Solution Explorer and click Edit Recipe05.DataAccess.csproj. Modify the solution to match Listing 6-14.

***Listing 6-14.*** Modifying Recipe05.DataAccess.csproj to Add Entity Framework Command-Line Tools

```
<Project Sdk="Microsoft.NET.Sdk">

  <PropertyGroup>
    <TargetFramework>netcoreapp1.1</TargetFramework>
  </PropertyGroup>

  <ItemGroup>
    <PackageReference Include="Microsoft.AspNetCore" Version="1.1.1" />
    <PackageReference Include="Microsoft.EntityFrameworkCore.Design" Version="1.0.2" />
    <PackageReference Include="Microsoft.EntityFrameworkCore.SqlServer" Version="1.0.2" />
    <PackageReference Include="Microsoft.EntityFrameworkCore.SqlServer.Design"
    Version="1.0.2" />
  </ItemGroup>
  <ItemGroup>
    <DotNetCliToolReference Include="Microsoft.EntityFrameworkCore.Tools.DotNet"
    Version="1.0.0" />
  </ItemGroup>
  <ItemGroup>
    <Folder Include="Entities\" />
  </ItemGroup>

</Project>
```

Now that you have the required dependencies, open the Visual Studio command prompt and use the cd command to navigate to the directory of the data access project that contains the project file. You will now use the Entity Framework dotnet ef dbcontext scaffold command to create a Code First entity data model from the database you created earlier. The dotnet ef dbcontext scaffold command requires two arguments: a connection string and the name of the provider. It also accepts several optional arguments that allow you to customize how the code is generated. Listing 6-15 shows an example of the command syntax and the output generated by running the command.

*Listing 6-15.* Reverse Engineer Command and Output

```
dotnet ef dbcontext scaffold "Server=.;Database=Chapter06Recipe05;Trusted_Connection=True;
MultipleActiveResultSets=true" Microsoft.EntityFrameworkCore.SqlServer -o "Entities"
```

Inside Solution Explorer you will now see that a new folder named Entities has been added and a C# class has been created for each of the tables in the database and that a DbContext class named Chapter06Recipe05Context has been created. Inside the DbContext class, OnModelCreating has been overridden, and Fluent API commands have been added to enforce the constraints and relationships defined in the database.

Now that your code has been generated, you may want to refactor the code and modify it as shown in recipe 6-4 (Listings 6-10 and 6-11) so it will work with the ASP.NET configuration system. This should include adding a constructor to the Chaper06Recipe05Context class that will allow a DbContextOptions object to be injected and removing the hard-coded connection string from the OnConfiguring method.

# 6-6. Using the Repository and Unit of Work Patterns in Your Data Access Layer

## Problem

You are building a data access layer using Entity Framework Core Code First but have several concerns. First, because Entity Framework Core is new, it will likely go through a significant change over the next few years. These changes could result in breaking changes in your application. You want to isolate the breaking changes as much as you can. Second, not everyone on your team is an expert in creating LINQ queries against Entity Framework. You want to encapsulate some of the more complex queries into simple methods. At the same time, you want to preserve the flexibility offered by Entity Framework and avoid duplicate redundant code as much as possible.

## Solution

In many real-world application scenarios, object relation mapping software such as Entity Framework might not be enough to constitute the entire data access layer of your application. Applying a light layer of abstraction can help protect the other components of your application from breaking changes in Entity Framework. If done properly, this layer could even allow you to replace Entity Framework with another technology without breaking downstream components. In addition to decoupling the web application from Entity Framework, you also have an opportunity to hide some of the complexity of your data access code and consolidate other data access concerns that might be otherwise spread around your application.

A common design pattern for building a data access layer is to use a combination of the Unit of Work and Repository patterns.

The Unit of Work pattern maintains a list of domain objects and coordinates, persisting them to a storage medium. This often includes tracking changes, managing concurrency, and optimizing database access. When using Entity Framework, the DbContext class performs most of this heavy lifting.

In the Repository pattern, a layer of abstraction brokers the relationship between domain entities and the mechanism in which they are stored. A consumer of the repository can have zero knowledge of the storage mechanism. Entity Framework also provides this capability by allowing you to work with plain C# classes that in and of themselves are ignorant of how they are persisted. Entity Framework can even allow you to swap out one database technology such as Microsoft SQL Server with another database such as Oracle.

Just as Entity Framework abstracts the mechanisms of your relational database of choice, the data access layer shown in this recipe will abstract away Entity Framework. When other components of your application consume your data access layer, they do so using only standard C# mechanisms and should have no knowledge that you are using Entity Framework under the covers.

## How It Works

The example data access library shown in this section is reused in many other examples in this book. You can easily access the full source code for this module in your web browser on GitHub here:

https://github.com/johnciliberti/AspNetCoreRecipes/tree/develop/Shared/DataAccess.

Figure 6-7 shows a layer diagram describing the components that make up the data access layer. The design of the library purposely segregates all the concerns into separate namespaces and ensures that each class has a specific job.

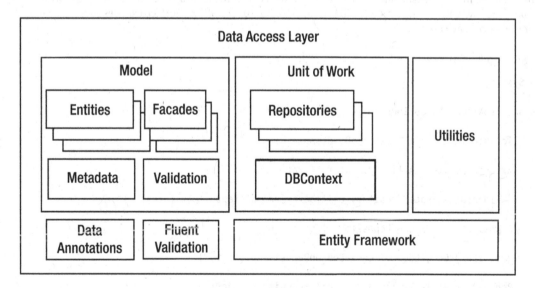

*Figure 6-7.* *High-level design of data access layer that uses the Unit of Work and Repository patterns*

Exposed via the data access layer are several entity classes, metadata classes, façades, and validation classes. The entity classes are simple, clean C# classes that describe objects in the business domain.

The metadata classes contain companion classes to the entities. Inside each metadata class, data annotations are applied to the properties that correspond to the properties in each companion entity and provide information such as localized display names, descriptions, and help text. This information can be used by the ASP.NET Core MVC model to aid in rendering forms. It is also possible to consume this data outside ASP.NET Core MVC if needed.

The validation classes contain validation rules for each of the entities. The rules are built using the Fluent Validation library. This is a third-party library that allows you to create validation rules in a similar syntactical style as the Fluent API used by Entity Framework to specify how the entities map to the relational database.

Façade classes are used in cases where you might need to return a custom view of the data that does not correspond to an entity. But be careful when creating façade classes in this layer because you must ensure that they are general-use and are not specific to any view in a consuming application.

The Unit of Work container provides a wrapper to the DbContext but does not expose it directly to the consumer. Rather than creating an instance of the DbContext as shown in recipe 6-4, components that consume your data access library instead create an instance of the Unit of Work container. Exposed through the Unit of Work pattern is a set of repository classes. You have one repository class for each of the entities you want to expose.

## The IUnitOfWork Interface

To allow components that consume your data access layer to be tested independently, it is essential to define an interface. Using an interface also allows you to take advantage of the ASP.NET Core dependency injection system. In theory, using an interface even allows a consumer to swap out your Entity Framework implementation with their own. As shown in Listing 6-16, the IUnitOfWork interface exposes several repositories and a Save method.

*Listing 6-16.* IUnitOfWork

```
using System;

namespace AspNetCoreMvcRecipes.Shared.DataAccess
{
    public interface IUnitOfWork : IDisposable
    {
        ArtistRepository ArtistRepository { get;  }

        CollaborationSpaceRepository CollaborationSpaceRepository { get;  }

        Repository<Band> BandRepository { get; }

        Repository<GenreLookUp> GenreLookUpRepository { get; }

        Repository<ArtistSkill> ArtistSkillRepository { get; }

        void Save();
    }
}
```

# The Generic Repository

To reduce the duplication of code, you will create a generic class to be used as the repository. Generic classes allow you to apply a common set of functionality to many types without losing the benefit of compilation-time type checking or duplicating code for each class.

The generic repository class exposes a set of methods that allow create, read, update, and delete (CRUD) operations to be performed for any of the entities in your model. For entities that have commonly used or complex queries, a custom repository class that is derived from the generic repository can be used.

Like IUnitOfWork, you must first define an interface and then have the generic repository implement this interface. Listing 6-17 shows the IRepository interface. Listing 6-18 shows the generic repository implementation.

***Listing 6-17.*** IRepository Interface

```
using System;
using System.Collections.Generic;
using System.Linq;
using System.Linq.Expressions;

namespace AspNetCoreMvcRecipes.Shared.DataAccess
{
    public interface IRepository<TEntity> where TEntity : class
    {
        void Delete(TEntity entityToDelete);
        TEntity GetEntityByKey(object key);
        void Insert(TEntity entity);
        IEnumerable<TEntity> Query(Expression<Func<TEntity, bool>> filter = null,
                    Func<IQueryable<TEntity>,
                    IOrderedQueryable<TEntity>> orderBy = null,
                    int page = 1,
                    int pageSize = 0,
                    params Expression<Func<TEntity, object>>[] includedProperties);

        void Update(TEntity entityToUpdate);
    }
}
```

***Listing 6-18.*** Generic Repository

```
using Microsoft.EntityFrameworkCore;
using System;
using System.Collections.Generic;
using System.Linq;
using System.Linq.Expressions;

namespace AspNetCoreMvcRecipes.Shared.DataAccess
{
    public class Repository<TEntity> IRepository<TEntity> where TEntity : class
    {
        // variables hold the database context and entity set
        // for the entity type that the instance of the repo
        internal MoBContext _context;
        internal DbSet<TEntity> _dbSet;
```

```csharp
public Repository(MoBContext context)
{
    _context = context;
    _dbSet = context.Set<TEntity>();
}

/// <summary>
/// Allows you to query an entity
/// </summary>
/// <param name="filter">Lambda expression for filtering rows</param>
/// <param name="orderBy">Lambda expression for sorting</param>
/// <param name=" includedProperties">Add an argument for each
///   property that should be eager loaded</param>
/// <param name="page">When pageSize is greater than 0 then will return
///    a particular data page</param>
/// <param name="pageSize">Number of items per page.
///    0 will return all data without pages</param>
/// <returns>An IEnumerable of the type or null if no data is found</returns>
public virtual IEnumerable<TEntity> Query(
    Expression<Func<TEntity, bool>> filter = null,
    Func<IQueryable<TEntity>, IOrderedQueryable<TEntity>> orderBy = null,
    int page = 1,
    int pageSize = 0,
    params Expression<Func<TEntity, object>>[] includedProperties)
{
    IQueryable<TEntity> query = _dbSet;

    if (filter != null)
    {
        query = query.Where(filter);
    }
    foreach (var includeProperty in includedProperties)
    {
        query.Include(includeProperty);
    }

    if (pageSize > 0)
    {
        query = query.Take(pageSize).Skip((page-1) * pageSize);
    }

    if (orderBy != null)
    {
        return orderBy(query).ToList();
    }
    else
    {
        return query.ToList();
    }
}
```

```
        /// <summary>
        /// Gets the first entity an object as key
        /// </summary>
        /// <param name="key">The key of the object you are looking for</param>
        /// <returns>An instance of the entity or null</returns>
        public virtual TEntity GetEntityByKey(object key)
        {
            return _dbSet.Find(key);
        }

        /// <summary>
        /// Insert a new entity
        /// </summary>
        /// <param name="entity">Entity you would like to add</param>
        public virtual void Insert(TEntity entity)
        {
            _dbSet.Add(entity);
        }

        /// <summary>
        /// Update entity
        /// </summary>
        /// <param name="entityToUpdate">Entity that you would like to update</param>
        public virtual void Update(TEntity entityToUpdate)
        {
            _dbSet.Attach(entityToUpdate);
            _context.Entry(entityToUpdate).State = EntityState.Modified;
        }

        /// <summary>
        /// Delete the entity
        /// </summary>
        /// <param name="entityToDelete">Entity that you wish to delete</param>
        public virtual void Delete(TEntity entityToDelete)
        {
            _context.Remove(entityToDelete);
        }
    }
}
```

The Insert, Update, Delete, and GetEntityByKey methods are straightforward. They provide a thin layer over the equivalent mechanisms in the Entity Framework. They have been marked as virtual so that derived classes may override the implementation and provide repository-specific logic.

The Query method is the most complex. It takes several lambda expressions as parameters and supports filtering, paging, and sorting of data.

## Creating Repository Classes That Derive from the Generic Repository

In some cases, you might need to add some additional functionality specific to an individual entity to a repository class. For instance, let's say you discovered that your application has many queries for the top 20 new artists. Rather than having the code for that query repeated in several places, you can create an Artist repository class that exposes a "canned" get new artist query in addition to the standard functions offered by the generic repository. To maintain testability in the design, first an interface will be created and then a class will implement that interface. Listing 6-19 and Listing 6-20 show an example of this technique.

*Listing 6-19.* ArtistRepositoryClass

```
using System.Collections.Generic;

namespace AspNetCoreMvcRecipes.Shared.DataAccess
{
    public interface IArtistRepository
    {
        IList<Artist> GetNewArtists(int page = 1);
    }
}
```

*Listing 6-20.* ArtistRepositoryClass

```
using System.Collections.Generic;
using System.Linq;

namespace AspNetCoreMvcRecipes.Shared.DataAccess
{
    public class ArtistRepository : Repository<Artist> , IArtistRepository
    {
        public ArtistRepository(MoBContext context) : base(context)
        {
        }

        /// <summary>
        /// Gets a list of artists
        /// </summary>
        /// <param name="page">Allows you to move between pages</param>
        /// <returns>List of artists</returns>
        public IList<Artist> GetNewArtists(int page=1)
        {
            var pageSize = 20;
            return Query(null, (qry) => qry.OrderByDescending(a => a.CreateDate), page,
            pageSize).ToList();
        }
    }
}
```

## The UnitOfWork Implementation

Earlier in this section you created an interface called IUnitOfWork. Listing 6-21 shows the implementation of this interface. Note that because IUnitWork inherits from IDisposable, both interfaces need to be implemented in this class. In addition, you create a constructor that allows a connection string to be injected. You will later use this constructor to allow a connection string to be specified in a consuming application's Startup class. Another feature of the UnitOfWork class is that the repositories are exposed as properties but are lazy loaded. By using the Lazy Loading pattern, the repositories are created only when needed, which reduces the overhead of using the UnitOfWork class. The UnitOfWork class also exposes two constructors. The first allows a connection string to be passed in. The second constructor takes a MoBContext as a parameter, which allows it to be injected by dependency injection system such as the one included with ASP.NET Core.

***Listing 6-21.*** Implementing the IUnitOfWork Interface

```
using System;

namespace AspNetCoreMvcRecipies.Shared.DataAccess
{
    public class UnitOfWork : IUnitOfWork
    {
        private MoBContext _context;
        private IArtistRepository _ArtistRepository;
        private IRepository<Band> _BandRepository;
        private ICollaborationSpaceRepository _CollaborationSpaceRepository;
        private IRepository<GenreLookUp> _GenreLookUpRepository;
        private IRepository<ArtistSkill> _ArtistSkillRepository;

        public UnitOfWork(string connectionString)
        {
            _context = new MoBContext(connectionString);
        }

        /// <summary>
        /// Allows class to be created using DBContext injected by application
        /// </summary>
        /// <param name="context"></param>
        public UnitOfWork(MoBContext context)
        {
            _context = context;
        }
        public IRepository<ArtistSkill> ArtistSkillRepository
        {
            get
            {
                if (_ArtistSkillRepository == null)
                {
                    _ArtistSkillRepository = new Repository<ArtistSkill>(_context);
                }
                return _ArtistSkillRepository;
            }
        }

        public IRepository<GenreLookUp> GenreLookUpRepository
        {
            get
            {
                if (_GenreLookUpRepository == null)
                {
                    _GenreLookUpRepository = new Repository<GenreLookUp>(_context);
                }
```

```
                return _GenreLookUpRepository;
        }
}

public IArtistRepository ArtistRepository
{
    get
    {
        if (_ArtistRepository == null)
        {
            _ArtistRepository = new ArtistRepository(_context);
        }
        return _ArtistRepository;
    }
}

public ICollaborationSpaceRepository CollaborationSpaceRepository
{
    get
    {
        if (_CollaborationSpaceRepository == null)
        {
            _CollaborationSpaceRepository = new CollaborationSpaceRepository(_context);
        }
        return _CollaborationSpaceRepository;
    }
}
public IRepository<Band> BandRepository
{
    get
    {
        if (_BandRepository == null)
        {
            _BandRepository = new Repository<Band>(_context);
        }
        return _BandRepository;
    }
}

public void Save()
{
    _context.SaveChanges();
}

private bool disposed = false;

protected virtual void Dispose(bool disposing)
{
    if (!this.disposed)
    {
        if (disposing)
```

```
            {
                _context.Dispose();
            }
        }
        this.disposed = true;
    }

    public void Dispose()
    {
        Dispose(true);
        GC.SuppressFinalize(this);
    }
  }
}
```

# Passing a Connection String to MoBContext and Using It to Initialize the Database Connection

MoBContext supports two initialization scenarios. In the first and probably most common scenario, MoBContext will be created by the ASP.NET dependency injection system. In this scenario, a DbContextOptions instance that includes the connection string will be passed to the DbContext base class.

In the second scenario, MoBContext is created manually. In this case, MoBContext requires a connection string for it to connect to a SQL Server database to be passed into its constructor. UnitOfWork can then inject the connection string into the MoBContext class via its constructor. Shown in Listing 6-22, the database provider is initialized using the connection string passed from the constructor and stored in a private member variable. In the OnConfiguring method, the provider is initialized with the connection sting by calling the UseSqlServer method.

*Listing 6-22.* Adding a Constructor That Takes a String to DbContext

```
public sealed class MoBContext : DbContext
{
        private string _connectionString = null;
        public MoBContext(string connectionString)
        {
            _connectionString = connectionString;
        }

        public MoBContext(DbContextOptions<MoBContext> options)
            : base(options) { }

        protected override void OnConfiguring(DbContextOptionsBuilder options)
        {
            If (_connectionString==null)
            {
                base.OnConfiguring(options);
            }
```

```
        else
        {
            options.UseSqlServer(_connectionString);
        }
    }
}
```

## Consuming the UnitOfWork Class in an ASP.NET MVC Core Application

To follow a test-first programming style, it is best practice to use the Dependency Injection pattern. In this pattern, the controllers will not be coupled to any implementation of the data access layer, which allows a mock implementation of the data access layer to be substituted when the controller is executed in a unit test.

ASP.NET Core ships with a simple dependency injection container. You can use it to register what concrete class should be used for a given interface. Listing 6-23 shows the UnitOfWork class being registered for the IUnitOfWork interface inside a StartUp class in an ASP.NET Core application. There are two methods that can be used to register the UnitOfWork class. The first is to manually create a service descriptor for the IUnitOfWork interface and then create a new instance passing the connection string into the constructor. The second method is to register the MoBContext with the ASP.NET dependency injection system using the AddDbContext method and then use the AddScoped method to register IUnitOfWork. The second method is described in detail in recipe 7-5.

*Listing 6-23.* Registering the IUnitOfWork Interface

```
using Microsoft.EntityFrameworkCore;
using Microsoft.AspNetCore.Builder;
using Microsoft.AspNetCore.Hosting;
using Microsoft.Extensions.Configuration;
using Microsoft.Extensions.DependencyInjection;
using Microsoft.Extensions.Logging;
using AspNetCoreMvcRecipes.Shared.DataAccess;
namespace Recipe06.Web
{
    public class Startup
    {
        public Startup(IHostingEnvironment env , IApplicationEnvironment appEnv)
        {
            // Set up configuration sources.
            var builder = new ConfigurationBuilder(appEnv.ApplicationBasePath)
                .AddJsonFile("config.json");

            Configuration = builder.Build();
        }

        public IConfiguration Configuration { get; set; }

        // This method gets called by the runtime.
        public void ConfigureServices(IServiceCollection services)
        {
            // Add MVC services to the services container.
            services.AddMvc();
            var d = new ServiceDescriptor(typeof(IUnitOfWork),
```

```
        new UnitOfWork(Configuration.GetConnectionString("DefaultConnection")));
        services.Add(d);
    }

    /// other methods not shown here


    }
  }
}
```

# 6-7. Using the Options Pattern to Simplify Configuration of Your ASP.NET Core MVC Application

## Problem

Your application is complex, and you have many configuration options. You find it difficult to remember all the names of the configuration options and often run into errors caused by configuration property names being mistyped. This is especially problematic when the value you are looking for is deep in a configuration hierarchy. You are looking for a better way to structure your application configuration so you can use Visual Studio's IntelliSense feature to ensure you are entering the correct value. In addition, you want to have default values when the properties are missing from the configuration.

## Solution

A pattern commonly used to simplify configuration is the Options pattern. With the Options pattern an object containing all the required configuration for a component is passed to the object via its constructor when it is created. Inside the constructor, the options object is inspected, and missing values are substituted with defaults. Many ASP.NET Core components use this pattern. For example, in recipe 6-4 the Options pattern is used with the DbContext object.

## How It Works

In this example, you will use the Options pattern to configure an e-mail service that will be used by an ASP.NET Core MVC application. The example will start with the web application template and with Individual User Accounts authentication enabled. This template will create shells for services for sending e-mail and SMS messages. You will implement the mail service using a NuGet package called MailKit. The configuration for the e-mail service will be passed to the e-mail service using constructor injection when the application starts.

## Creating the Project

Open Visual Studio and from the Start Page select ASP.NET Core Web Application (.NET Core) under "New project." Name the application and solution **Recipe07** and then click OK.

In the New ASP.NET Core Web Application window, ensure that ASP.NET Core 1.1 is selected from the drop-down list and then click Web Application under ASP.NET Core 1.1 Templates to select it. Next, click the Change Authentication button. In the Change Authentication window, select Individual User Accounts and then click OK.

Ensure that Enable Docker Support is not selected and then click the OK button.

## Installing MailKit from Nuget

MailKit is an advanced open source e-mail library for .NET Core. MailKit supports all the standards for sending e-mail securely including SASL authentication, OpenPGP, and DKIM signature support and can cancel e-mails that have been sent but not yet delivered.

To install MailKit, open the Package Manager Console if it is not open and then type the following command:

```
Install-Package MailKit
```

MailKit and several dependencies will be added to your project.

## Creating the EmailSenderOptions Class

The EmailSenderOptions class is the class that will provide all the configurable properties and default values that you may want to pass to the e-mail service. The class will use inner classes to allow for a hierarchy of configuration options. To create the class, right-click the Services folder in Solution Explorer and select Add ➤ Class. Name the class EmailSenderOptions and then click OK. Modify the class to match Listing 6-24.

*Listing 6-24.* EmailSenderOptions

```
namespace Recipe07.Services
{
    public class EmailSenderOptions
    {
        public EmailSenderOptions()
        {
            EmailServerPort = 25;
            FromMailBoxName = "Gavel Shreds";
            FromMailBoxAddress = "noreply@gavelshreds.com";
        }

        public class AuthenticationSettings
        {
            public string EmailPassword { get; set; }
            public string EmailUserName { get; set; }
        }

        public EmailSenderOptions.AuthenticationSettings Authentication { get; set; }

        public string LocalDomain { get; set; }
        public string EmailServer { get; set; }
        public int EmailServerPort { get; set; }
        public string FromMailBoxName { get; set; }
        public string FromMailBoxAddress { get; set; }
    }
}
```

The EmailSenderOptions class provides default values for the EmailServerPort, FromMailBoxName, and FromMailBoxAddress properties in its constructor. These default values can be overwritten via configuration.

# Modifying MessageService to Use EmailSenderOptions

The ASP.NET Core web application created a folder called Services that contains two interfaces, IEmailSender and ISmsSender. These interfaces work with the authentication system to send registration e-mails and SMS messages when the two-factor authentication feature is enabled. Both interfaces are implemented by the class MessageService. The ASP.NET Core template did not provide only an empty implementation of this class.

Listing 6-25 shows a fully implemented version of the MessageService class using the MailKit component.

*Listing 6-25.* MessageService.cs

```
using System.Threading.Tasks;
using MailKit.Net.Smtp;
using MimeKit;
using MailKit.Security;
using Microsoft.Extensions.Options;

namespace Recipe07.Services
{
    public class AuthMessageSender : IEmailSender, ISmsSender
    {
        private EmailSenderOptions _Options;

        public AuthMessageSender(IOptions<EmailSenderOptions> options)
        {
            _Options = options.Value;
        }

        public async Task SendEmailAsync(string email, string subject, string message)
        {
            var emailMessage = new MimeMessage();
            emailMessage.From.Add(new MailboxAddress(_Options.FromMailBoxName, _Options.
            FromMailBoxAddress));
            emailMessage.To.Add(new MailboxAddress("", email));
            emailMessage.Subject = subject;
            emailMessage.Body = new TextPart("plain") { Text = message };

            using (var client = new SmtpClient())
            {
                client.LocalDomain = _Options.LocalDomain;
                await client.ConnectAsync(_Options.EmailServer, _Options.EmailServerPort,
SecureSocketOptions.StartTls).ConfigureAwait(false);
                await client.AuthenticateAsync(_Options.Authentication.EmailUserName,
                _Options.Authentication.EmailPassword);
                await client.SendAsync(emailMessage).ConfigureAwait(false);
                await client.DisconnectAsync(true).ConfigureAwait(false);
            }
        }
```

```
        public Task SendSmsAsync(string number, string message)
        {
            // Plug in your SMS service here to send a text message.
            return Task.FromResult(0);
        }
    }
}
```

The configuration is passed into the class using a constructor. All the values used by MailKit are supplied from the EmailSenderOptions class. No configurable values are hard-coded.

## Setting Up the Configuration

Most of the configuration used by the MessageService class will be placed in a configuration file named emailSettings.json, as shown in Listing 6-26.

*Listing 6-26.* emailSettings.json

```
{
  "LocalDomain": "gavelshreds.com",
  "EmailServer": "email-smtp.us-east-1.amazonaws.com",
  "EmailServerPort": 25,
  "FromMailBoxName": "Gavel Shreds",
  "FromMailBoxAddress": "noreply@gavelshreds.com"
}
```

emailSettings.json contains the following settings:

- LocalDomain: The Internet domain name that e-mails will be originating from.

- EmailServer: The server that will be relaying the SMTP e-mail messages. In this case, the server being used is the SMS service offered by Amazon Web Services.

- EmailServerPort: The port used for sending SMTP messages. This is set to port 25, which is the standard SMTP port.

- FromMailBoxName: The name that will appear in the From field.

- FromMailBoxAddress: The e-mail address that will be used as the From address in the e-mail sent from the site.

The e-mail server's username and password are not stored in emailSettings.json. The username and password will be kept in the user secret store on the development machine and inside environment variables on the production server.

> ■ **Caution**   You should avoid placing secrets such as login credentials and SSH keys in configuration files. These files may be checked into the source control system, which would expose the secrets to anyone who has access to the source control system. This problem is endemic in public source control systems such as GitHub and Bitbucket but can also be a problem in corporate source control systems. Many high-profile data breaches have been tied to passwords in public source control repositories such as GitHub. For example, a study found that many companies had leaked their Slack access tokens because they were embedded in code posted to GitHub. For more information, see the following article from Cio.com:
>
> www.cio.com/article/3062566/security/developers-leak-slack-access-tokens-on-github-putting-sensitive-business-data-at-risk.html

## Adding Settings to User Secrets

The user secrets feature consists of three primary components: a command-line utility that allows you to store and view secrets added to your secret store, a component of the ASP.NET Core configuration system that allows the configuration system to load values from the user secret store, and a feature of Visual Studio that allows you to edit the user secrets for a project in JSON format. You can access this by right-clicking the Project node in Solution Explorer and then selecting Manage User Secrets.

User secrets are stored in a local user profile and are not encrypted, which is why user secrets are recommended for nonproduction use only.

To add the e-mail username and password to the user secret store, open a command prompt, navigate to the Recipe07 project directory, and enter the commands shown in Listing 6-27. Note that the ASP.NET Core Web Application template includes the NuGet packages required for using this feature. If the NuGet package was not included in the project, you will see the error message "No executable found matching command 'dotnet-user-secrets'" when you run the command.

***Listing 6-27.***  Adding Items to the User Secret Score

```
dotnet user-secrets set Authentication:EmailUserName AAABBBBSOMENAME
dotnet user-secrets set Authentication:EmailPassword thisisapasswordforAwS_Not
```

Note the use of a colon to separate the category Authentication from the setting named EmailUserName in Listing 6-27. This is the same format that you can use with the ASP.NET Core configuration system when retrieving the value.

## Loading the Configuration in Startup.cs

Before your application can access the values from your custom configuration, you must change Startup.cs so it adds the emailSettings.json configuration file and registers the EmailSenderOptions class with the configuration system. To do this, modify the Startup.cs file as shown in Listing 6-28.

***Listing 6-28.***  Registering Options Class with the ASP.NET Configuration System

```
using Microsoft.AspNetCore.Builder;
using Microsoft.AspNetCore.Hosting;
using Microsoft.AspNetCore.Identity.EntityFrameworkCore;
using Microsoft.EntityFrameworkCore;
```

```
using Microsoft.Extensions.Configuration;
using Microsoft.Extensions.DependencyInjection;
using Microsoft.Extensions.Logging;
using Recipe07.Data;
using Recipe07.Models;
using Recipe07.Services;

namespace Recipe07
{
    public class Startup
    {
        public Startup(IHostingEnvironment env)
        {
            var builder = new ConfigurationBuilder()
                .SetBasePath(env.ContentRootPath)
                .AddJsonFile("appsettings.json", optional: false, reloadOnChange: true)
                .AddJsonFile($"appsettings.{env.EnvironmentName}.json", optional: true)
                .AddJsonFile("emailSettings.json", optional: false); // add custom config

            if (env.IsDevelopment())
            {
                // For more details on using the user secret store see
                http://go.microsoft.com/fwlink/?LinkID=532709
                builder.AddUserSecrets<Startup>(); // use user secrets in development
            }

            builder.AddEnvironmentVariables(); // use environment variables in production
            Configuration = builder.Build();
        }

        public IConfigurationRoot Configuration { get; }

        public void ConfigureServices(IServiceCollection services)
        {
            services.AddDbContext<ApplicationDbContext>(options =>
options.UseSqlServer(Configuration.GetConnectionString("DefaultConnection")));

            services.AddIdentity<ApplicationUser, IdentityRole>()
                .AddEntityFrameworkStores<ApplicationDbContext>()
                .AddDefaultTokenProviders();

            services.AddMvc();

            services.Configure<EmailSenderOptions>(Configuration); // Registers the
            EmailSenderOptions class

            services.AddTransient<IEmailSender, AuthMessageSender>();
            services.AddTransient<ISmsSender, AuthMessageSender>();
        }
```

```
public void Configure(IApplicationBuilder app, IHostingEnvironment env,
ILoggerFactory loggerFactory)
{
        // This section was omitted for brevity
}
    }
}
```

The first change made to `Startup.cs` was to use the `AddJsonFile` method to add `emailSettings.json` to the configuration. The other required configuration sources, user secrets and environment variables, are part of the default template. With the default template, user secrets are added only if the hosting environment is Development. Inside the `ConfigureServices` method, you used `services.Configure<Email SenderOptions>(Configuration)` to register the option `EmailSenderOptions` with the configuration system. The ASP.NET Core Configuration system will use reflection to inspect the properties exposed by the `EmailSenderOptions` class and will automatically create an instance of the class and populate it with the matching configuration values when `EmailSenderOptions` is injected, as shown in Listing 6-25.

## Using Environment Variables in Production

Since user secrets are not recommended in production and would not be available to a production process such as an app pool identity used by Internet Information Services, the e-mail server username and password will be placed in environment variables. This can be done on the production system using standard user interfaces such as the Advanced System Settings screen on Windows Server or via the command line using the `setx` command. The name of the environment variable will be the same as the user secret name, as shown in Listing 6-27.

Here are a few things to note about environment variables:

- Environment variables are not encrypted. Anyone who has access to the server will be able to see them.

- When an ASP.NET Core application is hosted in Internet Information Services, it will not see changes in environment variables until IIS is reset. Starting and stopping the web site is not enough; you need to do a full IIS reset, which will restart Windows Activation Services. If you are running your app in a shared server, all sites running on that server will be disrupted.

# 6-8. Using Areas to Organize a Large ASP.MVC Project

## Problem

You are designing a somewhat sophisticated ASP.NET Core MVC application that consists of several subsystems. You want to have a Home controller for each of the main subsystems. Because it is not possible to have two controllers with the same name, you have been creating controllers with names such as `ArtistHomeController`, `AdminHomeController`, `MusicHomeController`, and more. You have created new routing rules to maintain your URL structure, but you are finding this process cumbersome as your project grows. You are looking for a better way to organize your project.

## Solution

ASP.NET Core MVC has a concept known as *areas*, which allow you to define separate MVC folder structures for each subsystem. You can easily create a new area in Visual Studio by right-clicking your application's Project node and selecting Add ➤ Area.

## How It Works

Areas help you organize your site by separating subdivisions of your site into functionally independent sections. In this example, you will see a musicians' collaboration community web site that has divided its functionality into areas for collaboration, music, and administration. Each area will have its own Home controller as well as controllers specific to each area. The normal controllers and views defined outside areas still exist and are used for the root of the web site.

## Creating the Project

Open Visual Studio. On the Start Page, click the New ASP.NET Core Web Application (.NET Core) Project link. If you have not used this template before, you can use the search box in the upper-right section of the window to find it. Name the project and solution **Recipe08** and select a location.

On the New ASP.NET Core Web Application (.NET Core) Project screen, under ASP.NET Core 1.1 Templates, select the Web Application template. Ensure Authentication is set to No Authentication and Enable Docker Support is not selected.

Click OK to create the project.

## Creating a New Area

To create a new area, right-click the Project node of your ASP.NET Core MVC project in Solution Explorer and select Add ➤ Folder. Name the folder Areas. Right-click the Area folder and select Add ➤ Folder. Name the new folder Administration. Under the Administration folder, create the folders for Controllers, Models, and Views. Repeat this process and create additional areas for collaboration and music. If required, a models folder can also be added at the root level of the application.

When you are done, your project should look like Figure 6-8.

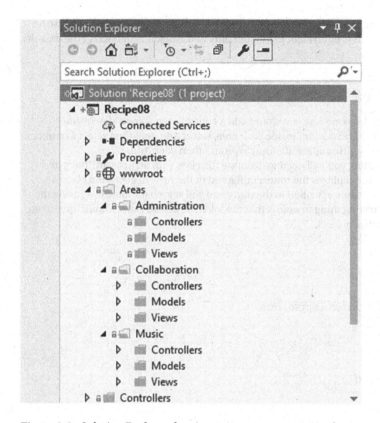

**Figure 6-8.** *Solution Explorer showing a site structure organized using areas*

Inside each of your Areas folders, you have a similar structure—as in the root of the web site—with folders for Controllers, Models, and Views. Just like in the root of your site, the Views folder can have a subfolder named Shared. Unlike the root, the Areas\<your area name>\Views\Shared folder is empty. The Views folder is also missing _Layout.cshtml and does not contain a _ViewStart.cshtml file.

In earlier versions of ASP.NET MVC, each area contained an area registration class. This was required to register routes specific to your area. In ASP.NET Core this is no longer required. You can now add area routes in the same manner as other routes, as shown in Listing 6-29.

**Listing 6-29.** Adding an Area Route in Startup.cs

```
// Add MVC to the request pipeline
app.UseMvc(routes =>
{

    routes.MapRoute(
                name: "areaRoute",
                template: "{area:exists}/{controller=Home}/{action=Index}");

    routes.MapRoute(
                name: "default",
                template: "{controller}/{action}/{id?}",
                defaults: new { controller = "Home", action = "Index" });

});
```

In the first route, a route constraint will restrict matches to only URLs that contain an area. It is also using the inline route default syntax. This is equivalent in functionality to the defaults defined in the default and API routes.

## Adding Controllers to an Area

You can add a controller to an area in the same way you would add a controller to a main site. Inside Solution Explorer, right-click the Controllers folder inside your area, select Add, and then select Controller. In the Add Scaffold window, select the appropriate scaffolding type and then click Add.

Once the controller has been created, you will need to decorate the class with an Area attribute, as shown in Listing 6-30. The Area attribute replaces the route configured in the Area Registration classes used in ASP.NET MVC. It adds the area name specified to the route and will search for the views inside the folder area's folder structure. An interesting thing to note is that the folder structure is not mandatory, so the controller can be placed anywhere in the project.

*Listing 6-30.* A Controller Inside an Area

```
using Microsoft.AspNetCore.Mvc;

namespace Recipe08.Areas.Administration.Controllers
{
    [Area("Administration")]
    public class Home : Controller
    {
        public IActionResult Index()
        {
            return View();
        }
    }
}
```

## CHAPTER 7

■ ■ ■

# Test-Driven Development with ASP.NET Core MVC

The cost of bugs that make their way into production code is difficult to measure. This is especially true if a bug (or a combination of them) results in lost customers and decreased sales. While it may not be possible to prevent all defects from reaching production, you can significantly improve the quality of your application by implementing a comprehensive quality control strategy. This strategy should consist of unit tests, static code analysis, peer code reviews, integration tests, and performance tests, topped off with manual testing and a customer feedback program.

Unit tests are the area of quality control that is owned by the development team. As a developer, it is your responsibility to ensure that your code is testable and that a suite of automated tests covers most of your application. In this chapter, you will learn about the testing features of ASP.NET Core and how to create tests for the different parts of your application.

## 7-1. Adding an xUnit Test Project to an ASP.NET Core Web Application Solution

### Problem

You want to create a test project for your ASP.NET Core MVC application. In past versions of ASP.NET Core, Visual Studio would automatically create a test project when you selected the Create Unit Tests check box when creating a project. This check box does not exist for ASP.NET Core projects in Visual Studio 2017. You want to understand how to create unit test projects for ASP.NET Core using Visual Studio. You want to see how it can be done from the command line using the dotnet CLI.

### Solution

Although .NET Core has been released to production for more than a year, the tooling is still somewhat immature. Many of the features you are used to with ASP.NET MVC have not yet made their way into Visual Studio 2017 for .NET Core. It is expected that these features will come soon. Each update of the .NET Core tooling expands the capabilities. In the meantime, you can use the dotnet command-line interface (CLI) to make up for the missing features in Visual Studio.

© John Ciliberti 2017
J. Ciliberti, *ASP.NET Core Recipes*, DOI 10.1007/978-1-4842-0427-6_7

## How It Works

In this section, you will create the solution and web application using Visual Studio. You will then add an xUnit project using Visual Studio and finally create the test project using the dotnet CLI.

## Creating the Solution and Web Application Project

All the exercises in this chapter will be in one solution. To create this solution, open Visual Studio 2017 and then select New ➤ Project. Select the ASP.NET Core Web Application (.NET Core) template. Name the project **Chapter07.Web** and name the solution **Chapter07**. Ensure "Create directory for solution" is selected and then click OK. In the New ASP.NET Core Web Application (.NET Core) window, ensure ASP.NET Core 1.1 is selected and then select the Web Application template. Ensure that No Authentication is selected and Enable Docker Support is not selected. Click OK to create the project.

## Creating the Test Project from Visual Studio

To create a new xUnit test project to the solution using Visual Studio, right-click the solution Recipe01 in Solution Explorer and select Add ➤ New Project. In the Add New Project window, click .NET Core in the left navigation pane to filter the list of templates. Select the xUnit Test Project (.NET Core) template. Name the project **Recipe01.TestVS**.

## Creating the Test Project from the Command Line

The .NET Core SDK that is installed with Visual Studio 2017 comes with a command-line tool called dotnet. The dotnet CLI allows you to do many of the things that you normally would do in Visual Studio, such as creating new projects, restoring NuGet packages, building your application, executing tests, and running the application. To learn about the capabilities of the dotnet command-line tool, you will use it to create a new xUnit test project and then add that xUnit test project to the solution you created using Visual Studio.

The dotnet new command is used to create new projects from the command line. The dotnet new command allows you to choose from several templates including the xUnit unit test project and MSTest-based unit test project templates. The xUnit test project creates a project using the xUnit test framework. xUnit is a free open source testing framework that has been designed with test-driven development (TDD) in mind. xUnit was used by the ASP.NET Core team for testing ASP.NET Core. You can find more information about xUnit at https://xunit.github.io/.

The Unit Test Project template uses Microsoft's MSTest framework. MSTest is a closed-source proprietary framework that comes with Visual Studio. Both unit test frameworks offer rich functionality, but the xUnit framework is better suited for test-first development because it offers significantly better test runner performance, is more extensible, and is community focused. MSTest, on the other hand, would be a better fit for someone who is porting a project from ASP.NET MVC and wants to migrate existing unit tests created using MSTest. All the test examples in this book will use xUnit.

To create the unit test project, open a command window and navigate to the directory that contains the solution file. Once in the directory, enter the following command:

```
dotnet new xunit -n Chapter07.Test
```

A new directory will be created named Chapter07.Test. The directory will contain two files, Chapter07.Test.csproj and UnitTest1.cs. Listing 7-1 shows the contents of Chapter07.Test.csproj.

*Listing 7-1.* Chapter07.Test.csproj

```
<Project Sdk="Microsoft.NET.Sdk">

  <PropertyGroup>
    <OutputType>Exe</OutputType>
    <TargetFramework>netcoreapp1.1</TargetFramework>
  </PropertyGroup>

  <ItemGroup>
    <PackageReference Include="Microsoft.NET.Test.Sdk" Version="15.0.0" />
    <PackageReference Include="xunit" Version="2.2.0 " />
    <PackageReference Include="xunit.runner.visualstudio" Version="2.2.0 " />
  </ItemGroup>

</Project>
```

The new project file targets .NET Core 1.1 and contains three references. The first is the `Microsoft.NET.Test.Sdk` component. This is the Visual Studio test platform, which includes a test runner and engine. This component is used by both Visual Studio and the dotnet CLI to run tests and collect test results. In Visual Studio, it is also used to power Test Explorer and `vstest.console`. You can find the source code for it in the GitHub repository here:

```
https://github.com/Microsoft/vstest
```

The second package is the xUnit Test Framework for .NET Core. The source code for this project is also located on GitHub. The source is located at `https://github.com/xunit/xunit`, and you can find the documentation at `https://xunit.github.io/docs/getting-started-dotnet-core.html`.

# Running the Test Project for the First Time

To run the test project, in navigate to the test project the command window by using the following:

```
cd Recipe07.Test
```

Next, run the following command:

```
dotnet restore
```

This will pull all the required packages from the NuGet repository.
To run the test, use the following command:

```
dotnet test
```

The results of the test will resemble Listing 7-2. It shows a single test was run and passed.

*Listing 7-2.* Test Results

```
Build started, please wait...
Build completed.

Test run for C:\ AspNetCoreRecipes\Chapter07\Chapter07.Test\bin\Debug\netcoreapp1.1\
Chapter07.Test.dll(.NETCoreApp,Version=v1.1)
Microsoft (R) Test Execution Command Line Tool Version 15.0.0.0
Copyright (c) Microsoft Corporation.  All rights reserved.

Starting test execution, please wait...
[xUnit.net 00:00:00.6346515]   Discovering: Chapter07.Test
[xUnit.net 00:00:00.7318149]   Discovered:  Chapter07.Test
[xUnit.net 00:00:00.7725945]   Starting:    Chapter07.Test
[xUnit.net 00:00:00.9003922]   Finished:    Chapter07.Test

Total tests: 1. Passed: 1. Failed: 0. Skipped: 0.
Test Run Successful.
Test execution time: 2.5384 Seconds
```

## Exploring the Test Project

The test project created by the dotnet CLI added a test class called UnitTest1. UnitTest1 contains a single method called Test1, as shown in Listing 7-3. Test1 is a public method with a void return type decorated with the xUnit Fact attribute. The Fact attribute tells the test runner that Test1 is a test.

xUnit supports two test types.

- *Facts*: Traditional unit tests that should always assert true. Facts do not support parameters.

- *Theories*: Parameterized unit tests. Theories assert true for certain data but false for others. Parameters can be passed to a theory using the InlineData attribute.

*Listing 7-3.* UnitTest1 Class Generated by the dotnet CLI

```csharp
using System;
using Xunit;

namespace Recipe07.Test
{
    public class UnitTest1
    {
        [Fact]
        public void Test1()
        {

        }
    }
}
```

## Adding the Test Project to the Solution

Now that the test project has been created, you will add it to the Visual Studio solution created earlier. There are two ways to do this. You can right-click the solution in Visual Studio and select Add ➤ Existing Project. You then browse to the location of the project file.

The second method is to use the dotnet CLI. To do this, use the following command in the command window to navigate backward to the solution directory:

```
cd ..
```

Next, run the following:

```
dotnet sln add Chapter07.Test\Chapter07.Test.csproj
```

To confirm that the solution was added, run the following:

```
dotnet sln list
```

Listing 7-4 shows the command output.

***Listing 7-4.*** Output of the dotnet sln list Command

```
Project reference(s)
--------------------
Chapter07.Web\Chapter07.Web.csproj
Chapter07.Test\Chapter07.Test.csproj
```

Visual Studio will display a message stating the following: "The solution 'Chapter07' has been modified outside the environment." Click the Reload button. The Recipe07.Test project should now appear in Solution Explorer.

You should now also be able to see the tests in your solution in Test Explorer. To open Test Explorer, select Test ➤ Windows ➤ Test Explorer. If you click the Run All link in Test Explorer, the text will run, and after several seconds, you will see a green check mark icon next to the `Chapter07.Test.UnitTest1.Test1` test.

## Adding Chapter07.Web as a Reference to Chapter07.Test

Before you can use the xUnit unit test project to begin testing `HomeController`, you must add a reference to Chapter07.Web to Chapter07.Test. To do this, right-click the Chapter07.Test project in Solution Explorer and select Add ➤ Reference. In the Reference Manager window, select Projects and then select the Chapter07. Web box. Click OK to add the reference.

Now that you have all the references and framework dependencies squared away, you can start writing your tests.

# 7-2. Creating Unit Tests for a Controller

## Problem

You are new to unit testing and are not sure how to go about getting started. You want to get a basic idea of how you can create unit tests for a simple ASP.NET Core MVC controller such as the HomeController controller that comes with the web application template.

## Solution

ASP.NET Core MVC was designed to make writing automated unit tests easy. Controllers are not coupled with the web server or other ASP.NET Core Framework components such as routing and can be instantiated and run independently.

You write unit tests with the help of a test framework. The test framework helps you to create classes and methods that can be automatically discovered by a test runner. The test runner can then execute your tests and then display the test results.

This solution builds on recipe 7-1 where a solution, an ASP.NET Core Application project, and an xUnit unit test project were created. To demonstrate the basic mechanics of creating unit tests for ASP.NET Core controllers, you will create a class in the Recipe07.Test project for each controller in Chapter07.Web. Each test class will have several test methods for each action in your controller class. Ideally, you will have at least one test for each branch of code in your action so that every line of code is covered by a test.

To keep this example as simple as possible, you will write tests to cover the actions in HomeController. You should test to ensure the following:

- That the controller is returning the correct view

- That the contents of the data passed to the view are as expected

## How It Works

To create the web application and test project, please see recipe 7-1.

## Modifying HomeController for Testability

When writing unit tests, you need to ensure that you are testing only the desired code and not components that the code under test depends on or the infrastructure it runs on top of. The first step in writing a good unit test is to analyze the code and determine whether it is possible to test the code without invoking dependencies and infrastructure. To demonstrate how to do this, you will analyze the HomeController class and make a few changes to it to maximize testability.

The HomeController class was added to the Chapter07.Web project by the Web Application template. It contains four actions: Index, About, Contact, and Error. The functionality of the Index and Error actions are limited to returning an ActionResult instance by calling the View() method. The About and Contact actions modify the contents of ViewData and then return an ActionResult instance by calling View().

These actions are not ideal for testing. The Home controller has the following problems that will need to be corrected before you can begin writing tests:

- The actions are currently relying on the ASP.NET Core infrastructure to dynamically determine the name of the view page by using reflection to inspect the name of the action. During the unit test, the controller will be executed in the test runner and will not be able to use the ASP.NET Core infrastructure. Because of this, the view page name will never be resolved, and the tests will not be able to determine the view page name.

- Hard-coded strings are used. To test that the values written to ViewData have been set correctly, you will need to hard-code the values in both HomeController and the test class. This will make your tests fragile and more difficult to manage.

To correct the problem caused by the hard-coded strings, you can store the string values as constants inside a static class. To create the static class, first create a new folder under the Chapter07.Web project named Strings. Inside the folder, create a static class named HomeStrings. Modify HomeStrings to match Listing 7-5.

***Listing 7-5.*** HomeStrings.cs

```
namespace Chapter07.Web.Strings
{
    public static class HomeStrings
    {
        public const string ViewDataMessageKey = "Message";
        public const string AboutMessage = "Your application description page.";
        public const string ContactMessage = "Your contact page.";

        public const string IndexView = "Index";
        public const string AboutView = "About";
        public const string ErrorView = "Error";
        public const string ContactView = "Contact";
    }
}
```

Next, modify HomeController so that the hard-coded strings are replaced by the constants, as shown in Listing 7-6.

To correct the second issue, modify each of the actions so you pass the name of the view page to the View method. For example, the call to View() in the Index action will be replaced with View("Index"). Listing 7-6 shows the updated HomeController class.

***Listing 7-6.*** HomeController Modified for Testability

```
using Microsoft.AspNetCore.Mvc;
using Chapter07.Web.Strings;

namespace Chapter07.Web.Controllers
{
    public class HomeController : Controller
    {
        public IActionResult Index()
```

```
    {
        return View(HomeStrings.IndexView );
    }

    public IActionResult About()
    {
        ViewData[HomeStrings.ViewDataMessage] = HomeStrings.AboutMessage;

        return View(HomeStrings.AboutView );
    }

    public IActionResult Contact()
    {
        ViewData[HomeStrings.ViewDataMessage] = HomeStrings.ContactMessage;

        return View(HomeStrings.ContactView );
    }

    public IActionResult Error()
    {
        return View(HomeStrings.ErrorView );
    }
    }
}
```

## Creating Tests for HomeController

To keep your test project organized, you will create a folder structure in the test project that matches the web project. The names of the test classes will also match the class names under test but will have the suffix Test. To update the test project to match this format, follow these steps:

1. Add a new folder named Controllers to the test project. To create the Controllers folder in the test project, right-click its project node in Solution Explorer and select Add ➤ New Folder. Name the folder Controllers.

2. Move UnitTest1 into the Controller folder by clicking and dragging it into the folder in Solution Explorer.

3. Right-click the UnitTest1.cs file in Solution Explorer and then select Rename. Change the name to HomeControllerTests. When prompted, confirm that you want to rename the class as well.

4. Update the namespace so it includes Controllers to match the folder structure.

5. Add using statements for Microsoft.AspNetCore.Mvc, Chapter07.Web.Strings, and Chapter07.Web.Controllers.

For the first test, you will verify that HomeController.Index will return a view named Index. To do this, you will need to create an instance of HomeController, call the Index method, and then assert that the ViewName value is equal to Index.

To write the test, rename UnitTest1 to IndexAction_ReturnsIndexView. Note that the name of the test method is very verbose. The name should make it clear what is being tested and the expected results.

The code in the test will be structured following the Arrange, Act, and Assert pattern. This pattern promotes readability and helps keep test code simple and uniform.

- *Arrange*: Sets up the objects that you will use in your test and the variables that contain the expected result

- *Act*: Performs the action being tested

- *Assert*: Verifies the results

In the Arrange section, the code under test is initialized, and the expected results are stored in a variable named expected. In the Act portion, the method under test is executed, and the results are written to a variable named actual. In the Assert portion, the expected condition is verified against the actual result. This is done using one of the methods of the xUnit Assert object. In this case, since you are testing for equality, the Assert.Equal method is used.

To apply this pattern to HomeController for the Arrange stage of the test, create an instance of HomeController. Next, create a variable named expected that will hold the expected value of the ViewName property. For the Act portion of the test, you will execute the controller's Index method and write the ViewResult class of the action to a local variable named result. Note that calling Index returns an IActionResult and not a ViewResult. Because of this, it is necessary to cast the result using the following:

```
var result = controller.Index() as ViewResult;
```

By using the as keyword to perform the cast, the result value would be null if the type returned by Index was not a ViewResult. Since it is possible for result to be null, you need to use a null conditional operator to first verify result is not null before inspecting the ViewName property.

Finally, in the Assert section, you will compare the view name in the action result to the expected value. You will use the Assert.Equal method to verify a match.

Listing 7-7 shows the completed IndexAction_ReturnsIndexView test.

**Listing 7-7.** Completed IndexAction_ReturnsIndexView Test

```
[Fact]
public void IndexAction_ReturnsIndexView()
{
    // Arrange
    var controller = new HomeController();
    var expected = HomeStrings.IndexView;

    // Act
    var result = controller.Index() as ViewResult;
    var actual = result.ViewName;

    // Assert
    Assert.Equal(expected, actual);
}
```

In the next test, you will verify that ViewData has been set with the expected values. This test will follow the same format as the one shown in Listing 7-5, but rather than testing the ViewName property of ViewResult, you will check the Message value of ViewResult's ViewBag property. Create a new test named AboutAction_ReturnsExpectedMessageInViewBag. The completed test should match Listing 7-8.

*Listing 7-8.* Completed AboutAction_ReturnsExpectedMessageInViewBag Test

```
[Fact]
public void AboutAction_ReturnsExpectedMessageInViewBag()
{
    // Arrange
    var controller = new HomeController();
    var expected = HomeStrings.AboutMessage;

    // Act
    var result = controller.About() as ViewResult;
    var actual = result?.ViewData[HomeStrings.ViewDataMessageKey];

    // Assert
    Assert.Equal(expected, actual);
}
```

■ **Note**    Note the use of the null conditional operator in the Act portion of Listing 7-8. Null conditional operators are a feature introduced with C# 6 that simplifies checking for null conditions. Before C# 6, you would have needed to write a conditional statement to verify that the value of result was not null before accessing the ViewData property to avoid possible null pointer exceptions. With C# 6 and later, you can use the syntax result?.ViewData.

Following the pattern established with the tests shown in Listing 7-7 and Listing 7-8, you can complete the rest of the tests for HomeController. The tests should include AboutAction_ReturnsAboutView, ContactAction_ReturnsContactView, ContactAction_ReturnsExpectedMessageInViewBag, and ErrorAction_ReturnsErrorView. The completed test class should match Listing 7-9.

*Listing 7-9.* Completed HomeControllerTests Class

```
using Xunit;
using Microsoft.AspNetCore.Mvc;
using Chapter07.Web.Strings;
using Chapter07.Web.Controllers;

namespace Recipe07.Test.Controllers
{
    public class HomeControllerTests
    {
        [Fact]
        public void IndexAction_ReturnsIndexView()
        {
            // Arrange
            var controller = new HomeController();
            var expected = HomeStrings.IndexView;

            // Act
            var result = controller.Index() as ViewResult;
            var actual = result?.ViewName;
```

```csharp
        // Assert
        Assert.Equal(expected, actual);
    }

    [Fact]
    public void AboutAction_ReturnsExpectedMessageInViewBag()
    {
        // Arrange
        var controller = new HomeController();
        var expected = HomeStrings.AboutMessage;

        // Act
        var result = controller.About() as ViewResult;
        var actual = result?.ViewData[HomeStrings.ViewDataMessage];

        // Assert
        Assert.Equal(expected, actual);
    }

[Fact]
 public void AboutAction_ReturnsAboutView()
    {
        // Arrange
        var controller = new HomeController();
        var expected = HomeStrings.AboutView;

        // Act
        var result = controller.About() as ViewResult;
        var actual = result?.ViewName;

        // Assert
        Assert.Equal(expected, actual);
    }
    [Fact]
    public void ContactAction_ReturnsContactView()
    {
        // Arrange
        var controller = new HomeController();
        var expected = HomeStrings.ContactView;

        // Act
        var result = controller.Contact() as ViewResult;
        var actual = result?.ViewName;

        // Assert
        Assert.Equal(expected, actual);
    }
```

```
[Fact]
public void ContactAction_ReturnsExpectedMessageInViewBag()
{
    // Arrange
    var controller = new HomeController();
    var expected = HomeStrings.ContactMessage;

    // Act
    var result = controller.Contact() as ViewResult;
    var actual = result?.ViewData[HomeStrings.ViewDataMessageKey];

    // Assert
    Assert.Equal(expected, actual);
}

[Fact]
public void ErrorAction_ReturnsErrorView()
{
    // Arrange
    var controller = new HomeController();
    var expected = HomeStrings.ErrorView;

    // Act
    var result = controller.Error() as ViewResult;
    var actual = result?.ViewName;
    // Assert
    Assert.Equal(expected, actual);
}
    }
}
```

## Running the Tests for HomeController

Visual Studio has several features that allow you to view available tests for a given project, execute the tests, and then examine the results. To see how these features work, you will build the solution and then execute the tests, as follows:

1. If Test Explorer is not visible, open it by selecting Test ➤ Windows ➤ Test Explorer. Since the project has not been built yet, no tests are shown.

2. From the Visual Studio Build menu, select Build Solution. After the build completes, Test Explorer will show the six tests categorized under Not Run Tests. Each of the tests will have a blue icon that denotes that it has not yet run.

3. To run the tests, click the Run All link on the top left of the Test Explorer pane. It should be noted that running all the tests will also build the project.

All tests should pass. You should see green check mark icons next to each test name, as shown in Figure 7-1.

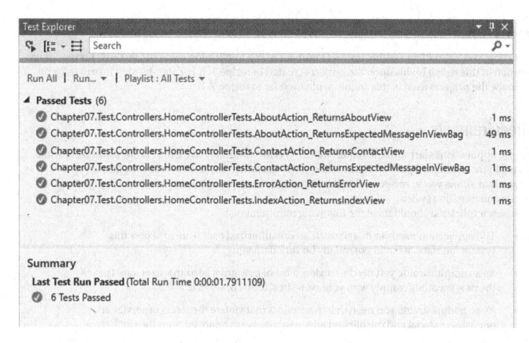

*Figure 7-1.* *Test Explorer showing all tests passing*

# 7-3. Understanding Test-Driven Development Strategies

## Problem

You have heard a lot about test-first and test-driven development but are not sure if this approach will work for you. You want to understand what these strategies are about and how they can be applied to ASP.NET Core MVC development.

## Solution

In most development methodologies, developers write a lot of code, and then if they have time, they maybe write a few unit tests. Testing is part of the development process, but it is usually focused on integration testing and occurs toward the end of the development life cycle.

*Test-driven development* (TDD), on the other hand, is a completely different way of thinking about code. Rather than tests being an afterthought, they are front and center in the design process. In TDD, you always create tests for your code. If you find it difficult to test your code in isolation, you refactor it. The design of your project changes to make it easier to test. Tests drive your application design and development cycles. You do not check your code into source control until all your unit tests pass.

In the *test-first development* (TFD) methodology, this concept is taken a step further. Tests are written before you write your production code. While this practice may occur in TDD, it is not always the case. In TFD, the first code you create in your solution consists of your unit tests. You will first write just enough stub code to allow the program to compile. You then run your tests, which will fail. Next, you implement your production code. Once all your tests pass, you can refactor to improve the readability and maintainability of both your production code and your tests.

## How It Works

In this section, you will add an administrative feature for a web application using the test-first methodology. The solution in this recipe builds upon the projects created in recipe 7-1. For step-by-step instructions on how to create the projects used in this solution, please refer to recipe 7-1.

## The Requirements

All software applications start with the requirements. It is important to have a firm understanding of what is expected in the completed project. For the sake of this example, you need to create an administrative application that allows you to review and edit information about recording artists who have registered in your music collaboration system.

This new application should meet the following requirements:

- The application needs to be secure. If an unauthorized user were to access this system interface, it could potentially be very damaging.

- As an administrator, you need to review a list of new artist accounts to ensure that all the new accounts comply with your web sites' terms of service.

- As an administrator, you need delete accounts that violate the terms of service so offensive material and unsolicited advertisements are removed from the site.

- As an administrator, you need to be able to confirm that you really want to delete a selected account so you do not delete valid accounts by accident.

- As an administrator, you should be shown a confirmation screen that confirms the deletion was successful so you can act in cases where the deletion fails.

## Creating the Design

Based on the requirements, your first priority is security. Security researchers have found that the most effective designs follow a layered approach with many levels of controls. This application will use Windows authentication and will be locked down via access control lists (ACLs) as part of the deployment. In production, the site will also use SSL to protect data in transit and to verify to users that they are connected to a valid server.

Using Windows authentication and ACLs frees the developer from most of the responsibility of writing code to handle authentication or authorization.

The next set of requirements roughly describes the screens that will list the new artists, view the details of each, and then allow the administrator to delete the artist record and confirm that the deletion was successful. To meet this set of requirements, you create a controller named ArtistAdminController. This controller will have five actions.

- List: Displays the list of new artists.

- Review: Displays detailed information on the artist and contains buttons that allow the administrator to either delete the artist or return to the list.

- DeleteConfirm: Displays the delete confirmation message and allows the administrator to either confirm or cancel the deletion.

- DeleteCompleted: Displays a view that shows a delete confirmation message.

- DeleteFailed: Displays a view showing a failure message, including the error details that can be used by the administrator to help solve the problem.

## Adding the Test Class

Since you are using the test-first methodology, you first need to create your unit tests. If you have never done this style of development, it may seem bizarre to create a test when you have yet to create the code to be tested.

Since you have not yet written code, you need to refer to your design to decide which tests to write. Per the design, you will have a controller named ArtistAdminController. Because you will create the controllers inside the Controllers folder in your web project, you will echo that structure in your test project, as discussed in recipe 7-2. This will help keep your test classes organized and easy to maintain.

To add a new test to your project, follow these steps:

1. Right-click the Controllers folder and select Add ➤ New Class. Name the class **ArtistAdminControllerTests**. Click OK to create the class.

2. Make the class public. Test runners will only be able to discover public classes.

3. Add using statements for the following

   a. Xunit

   b. Microsoft.AspNetCore.Mvc

4. Create an empty region for each of the items listed in the design.

5. Inside each region create a unit test skeleton for every scenario you can think of. For example, for the List action, create test skeletons for the success paths, such as the following:

   a. The correct view is returned.

   b. The model passed to the view is not null.

   c. The model passed to the view is of the correct type.

   d. The model passed to the view shows the correct number of rows.

You may also want to create skeletons for some of the failure paths, such as the following:

   a. The controller cannot connect to the back end.

   b. The list is null.

   c. The user is not authorized.

Listing 7-10 shows the skeletons for the List action.

***Listing 7-10.*** New Test Class with Test Skeletons for List Action

```
using Xunit;
using Microsoft.AspNetCore.Mvc;

namespace Recipe07.Test.Controllers
{
    public class ArtistAdminControllerTests
```

```
{
    #region List

    [Fact]
    public void ListAction_ReturnsListView()
    {
        // Arrange

        // Act

        // Assert
        Assert.True(false);
    }

    [Fact]
    public void ListAction_ReturnsNewArtistList_ToListView()
    {
        // Arrange

        // Act

        // Assert
        Assert.True(false);
    }
    [Fact]
    public void ListAction_ReturnsEmptyNewArtistList_ToListView()
    {
        // Arrange

        // Act

        // Assert
        Assert.True(false);
    }

    [Fact]
    public void ListAction_PassesArtistListViewModel_ToListView_HasCorrectRowCount()
    {
        // Arrange

        // Act

        // Assert
        Assert.True(false);
    }

    [Fact]
    ListAction_RedirectToErrorAction_WhenItCannotConnectToBackend()
    {
        // Arrange
```

```
        // Act

        // Assert
        Assert.True(false);
    }

    [Fact]
    public void ListAction_UnAuthorizedUserCannotAccess()
    {
        // Arrange

        // Act

        // Assert
        Assert.True(false);
    }

    #endregion
    #region Review
    #endregion

    #region DeleteConfirm
    #endregion

    #region DeleteCompleted
    #endregion

    #region DeleteFailed
    #endregion
    }
}
```

Notice each of the skeleton methods contains the code Assert.True(false). This ensures that all the incomplete tests will fail. It is important that you do this to avoid missing incomplete tests.

At this point, click the Run All button in Test Explorer. Your project will build, and the tests will be executed. All the tests will fail. If you click a failed test result, the details of why the test failed are displayed, as shown in Figure 7-2.

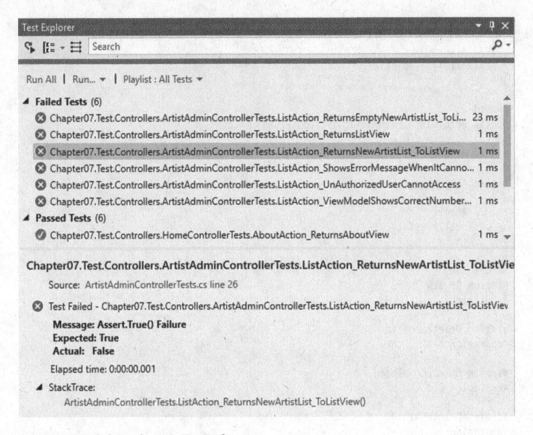

*Figure 7-2.* *Failed tests shown in Test Explorer*

## Creating the Controller

Now that the test has been created, the next step is to create the controller that will be tested. To create the controller, right-click the Controllers folder in the Chapter07.Web project and select New ➤ Class. Name the class **ArtistAdminController**.

To turn this class into a controller, add a using statement for Microsoft.ASpNetCore.Mvc to the start of the file, change the class signature to be public, and make it inherit from the Controller base class.

The next step is to stub out the controller actions per the design. The stubbed-out controller should match Listing 7-11.

*Listing 7-11.* Stubbed-Out ArtistAdminController

```
using Microsoft.AspNetCore.Mvc;

namespace Chapter07.Web.Controllers
{
    public class ArtistAdminController : Controller
    {
        public IActionResult List()
        {
```

```
            return View("List");
        }

        public IActionResult Review()
        {
            return View("Review");
        }

        public IActionResult DeleteConfirm()
        {
            return View("DeleteConfirm");
        }

        public IActionResult DeleteCompleted()
        {
            return View("DeleteCompleted");
        }

        public IActionResult DeleteFailed()
        {
            return View("DeleteFailed");
        }
    }
}
```

# Implementing the First Test

Now that ArtistAdminController has been created, you can begin implementing the tests.

The first test you will implement is ListAction_ReturnsListView. This test will verify that the List action in ArtistAdminController returns a ViewResult with the ViewName property of List.

When completed, ListAction_ReturnsListView should match Listing 7-12.

*Listing 7-12.* Completed ListAction_ReturnsListView

```
[Fact]
public void ListAction_ReturnsListView()
{
    // Arrange
    var controller = new ArtistAdminController();
    var expected = "List";

    // Act
    var result = controller.List() as ViewResult;
    var actual = result?.ViewName;

    // Assert
    Assert.Equal(expected, actual);
}
```

After completing this step, click the Run All button in Test Explorer. You should see one test pass and five fail.

One thing you should be aware of is even though your test proves that the controller will return the correct view, it does not mean that the application will work. In this case, since you did not create the view page, the application will throw an error if the action is executed. Beware of writing unit tests that attempt to load the view or check for its existence on the file system. In both cases, you will be breaking the isolation rule of unit testing by invoking external dependencies. For testing view pages, you should consider using an integration testing tool such as Selenium.

In recipes 7-4 through 7-5, you will continue to build upon the example started in this recipe and will complete the implementation of ArtistAdminController and the associated tests.

# 7-4. Simulating Calls to External Dependencies Using Moq

## Problem

You are developing an ASP.NET Core application using the test-driven development methodology. You need to implement a controller that will use a data access component to get data from a database. You need a way to test this controller without invoking the data access component so your test can maintain isolation so that only the controller's logic is tested. If the data access component was invoked by the unit tests, it would create several challenges, including the following:

- The test cannot control the state of the database. Data may be modified by the test or other outside actor. Changed or inconsistent data may cause the test to fail or in some cases appear to pass when it should not.

- Issues with the data access component may cause the tests to fail. It would be difficult to know the difference between tests failing because of your code and tests failing because of defects or back-end issues with the data access layer.

- Since the data access component calls a back-end database, it is much slower than typical unit tests that are self-contained. As the application grows and the test suit expands to thousands of tests, the additional latency will make the time it takes to run the tests unacceptable.

## Solution

Isolating your code from its dependencies is perhaps the single greatest challenge you face when writing unit tests. Doing this requires a combination of several techniques that work best when used together. These techniques include separating the interface from the implementation, mocking, and inversion of control and dependency injection.

### Separating the Interface from Implementation

Before implementing a class containing application logic, separating the interface from the implementation requires that you first define the public methods and properties required in an interface. Your class will then implement this interface. Separating the interface from the implementation allows you to create alternate implementations that can be used for testing.

## Mocking

While it is possible to hand-code a mock implementation of an interface for use in unit testing, in most cases it would be labor intensive and impractical. To get around this problem, you can use mocking frameworks to generate an instance of a class, which then allows you to implement a method or methods that can be used by the code you are testing.

## Inversion of Control and Dependency Injection

Using interfaces provides a raw language–level ability to provide loose coupling between components. However, that independence is lost when you hardwire an implementation to a component by using the new keyword to create an instance of an implementation. To get around this issue, you need to use an inversion of control (IoC) container to inject an implementation of an interface. I will discuss this technique in detail in recipe 7-5.

## How It Works

To learn how to use a mocking framework in a unit test, you will complete the implementation of the tests for the `List` action of `ArtistAdminController` started in recipe 7-3. The first step in this process will be to add a reference to the Shared Data Access library that is distributed with the book's source code. Next, you will modify `ArtistAdminController` so the dependencies it requires can be injected via the constructor. In the last step, you will add the Moq mocking framework to the test project and use it to simulate calls to the data access layer.

## Adding a Reference to the Data Access Library

To follow along with this step, you will need to follow the instructions in the appendix for setting up the SQL Server database. You will also need to configure Visual Studio so that the book's NuGet feed has been added to the NuGet configuration. You can find detailed instructions for doing this in the appendix. To install the shared library in the Chapter07.Web project, run the following command in the Package Manager window:

```
Install-Package Shared.DataAccess
```

Since you need to use the interfaces defined in the Shared.DataAccess package in the test project, you will also need to install Shared.DataAccess in Chapter07.Test. To do this, in the Package Manager Console, change the Default project to Recipe07.Test and then run the command again.

## Modifying ArtistAdminController

In the `ArtistAdminController` class, add a using statement for `AspNetCoreMvcRecipes.Shared.DataAccess`. Next, in the body of the class, create a private member variable of the type `IUnitOfWork` named `_DataAccessLayer`. Add a constructor to the controller that accepts an argument of the type `IUnitOfWork` and assigns it to the member variable. Listing 7-13 shows the updated controller.

*Listing 7-13.* ArtistAdminController Modified to Allow IUnitOfWork to Be Injected

```
public class ArtistAdminController : Controller
{
        private IUnitOfWork _DataAccessLayer;

        public ArtistAdminController(IUnitOfWork dataAccessLayer)
        {
            _DataAccessLayer = dataAccessLayer;
        }

        public IActionResult List()
        {
            return View("List");
        }

        // other actions here...
}
```

## Adding Moq to the Test Project

Moq is the most popular mocking framework for .NET. Moq's popularity is driven by its ease of use and its support for LINQ queries against Moq objects. Moq supports mocking abstract classes and interfaces.

Before Moq can be used in the Chapter07.Test project, it needs to be added to the project from NuGet. To do this, in the Package Manager Console, make sure the Default project is set to Recipe07.Test and then use the following command to add Moq to the project:

```
Install-Package Moq
```

## Updating ListAction_ReturnsListView to Use Moq

Now that Moq has been added to the project, you can use it to create a Moq object from the IUnitOfWork interface and then pass the Moq object as a constructor to ArtistAdminController. Listing 7-14 shows the ListAction_ReturnsListView test modified with the Moq object passed to the constructor.

*Listing 7-14.* Creating an Moq of IUnitOfWork

```
[Fact]
public void ListAction_ReturnsListView()
{
    // Arrange
    var controller = new ArtistAdminController(Mock.Of<IUnitOfWork>());
    var expected = "List";

    // Act
    var result = controller.List() as ViewResult;
    var actual = result?.ViewName;

    // Assert
    Assert.Equal(expected, actual);
}
```

At this point, you can run the tests again. `ListAction_ReturnsListView` should pass, but the other tests should still fail.

## Verifying the Model Is the Correct Type

For the next test, you need to verify that the `ViewResult` class returned from the `List` action contains a model of the type `ArtistAdminViewModel`. The `ArtistViewModel` class will contain the list of artists that you want to display, the number of total items found, and a message that will indicate whether any items are found. Using the view model allows you to write automatic unit tests that verify the state of the view without testing the view directly. Testing the view itself requires an integration test that verifies the HTML was properly rendered.

To verify the model is the correct type, you will need to implement a unit test that contains two asserts. The first assert will ensure that the model is not `null`. This is done using xUnit's `Assert.NotNull` method. The second assert uses `Assert.IsType` to check the type of model class. The null check prevents an error from occurring when running the test in cases that the model is never set in the controller. When errors occur, the test still fails, but it will be more time-consuming to troubleshoot. Listing 7-15 shows the completed test.

An additional feature of the xUnit framework being introduced here is the use of the `DisplayName` property of the `Fact` attribute. This allows you to specify a friendlier name to appear in the test runner.

*Listing 7-15.* Testing That the Correct Model Type Has Been Returned

```
[Fact(DisplayName = "List Action ActionResult Model is of type ArtistListViewModel")]
public void ListAction_PassesArtistListViewModel_ToListView_IsNotNull()
{
    // Arrange
    var controller = new ArtistAdminController(Mock.Of<IUnitOfWork>());

    // Act
    var result = controller.List() as ViewResult;

    // Assert
    Assert.NotNull(result.Model);
    Assert.IsType(typeof(ArtistListViewModel), result.Model);
}
```

Note that since the class `ArtistListViewModel` has not been created yet, you will not be able to build and run the test.

## Using Moq to Simulate Data Returned from the Data Access Layer

In the next test, Moq will be used to simulate the data access component returning data. To do this, the `Mock` object will be created using the `Mock<T>` constructor rather than `Mock.Of` as it was in the past tests. Next, the `Mock.SetUp` function will be used to provide an implementation to methods needed for the test. In this test method, implementations will be provided for the `IUnitOfWork.ArtistRepository.GetNewArtist` method. The mock will simulate a single item being returned. It should be noted that Moq cannot use default method parameters and requires that a value be passed for each, even if a default value is present.

Inside the setup method, a lambda is used to tell the setup method which method you want to set up. The `Returns` method is used to then provide the mock implementation of that method. In this case, a new list is created, and a single object is added to the list. An instance of the controller is then created with the mock object. The rest of the test attempts to get the value from the model and verifies that the RecordsFound property contains the correct value of 1. Listing 7-16 shows the code for this test.

***Listing 7-16.*** Simulating Call to Data Access Layer

```
[Fact(DisplayName ="List Action Artist List View has correct row count")]
public void ListAction_PassesArtistListViewModel_ToListView_HasCorrectRowCount()
{
    // Arrange
    var unitOfWorkMock = new Mock<IUnitOfWork>();
    unitOfWorkMock.Setup(m => m.ArtistRepository.GetNewArtists(1))
            .Returns(new List<Artist> {
                new Artist{ CreateDate= new DateTime(2017,2,26),
                            UserName="TestUser1",
                            EmailAddress = "TestUser1@myonlineband.com",
                            ArtistId = 1,
                            WebSite = "http://foxnews.com"
                }
    });

    var controller = new ArtistAdminController(unitOfWorkMock.Object);
    var expected = 1;

    // Act
    var result = controller.List() as ViewResult;
    var viewModel = result?.Model as ArtistListViewModel;
    var actual = viewModel?.RecordsFound;

    // Assert
    Assert.NotNull(viewModel?.Artists);
    Assert.Equal(expected, actual);
}
```

It should be noted that the test project will not compile now since the ArtistListViewModel class does not exist. You can create this class now by creating a folder under the Chapter07.Web project called ViewModels and then creating a new class called ArtistListViewModel. The class should match Listing 7-17. Note I am making a distinction here that the class is a view model rather than a model since it contains several properties specific to the view that are not persisted to the database. While this technique is not required by ASP.NET Core, it can help developers distinguish view-related models to entity models.

***Listing 7-17.*** ArtistListViewModel

```
using AspNetCoreMvcRecipes.Shared.DataAccess;
using System.Collections.Generic;

namespace Chapter07.Web.ViewModels
{
    public class ArtistListViewModel
    {
        public IList<Artist> Artists { get; set; }
        public int RecordsFound { get; set; }
        public Artist SelectedArtist { get; set; }
```

```
            public bool DeletedSuccessfully { get; set; }
            public string Message { get; set; }
        }
    }
```

You should now be able to compile the project and run the tests. The `ListAction_PassesArtist` `ListViewModel_ToListView_HasCorrectRowCount` test will fail since the code under test did not complete this business logic.

## Testing for a Condition When No Data Is Found

A common scenario when creating a page that displays data from a database is no data being returned from a query. For the Artist Admin page, the requirements dictate that a message appears stating that no data was found. The view model shown in Listing 7-17 provides a `Message` property where you expect your controller will write the message.

As you did in recipe 7-2, hard-coded strings will be factored out into a static class to avoid error-prone copying and pasting of strings between files. To set this up, add a new class to the `Strings` folder in the Chapter07.Web project and name it `ArtistAdminStrings`. Listing 7-18 shows the `ArtistAdminStrings` class.

*Listing 7-18.* ArtistAdminStrings

```
namespace Chapter07.Web.Strings
{
    public static class ArtistAdminStrings
    {
        public const string NoDataFound = "No data was found matching your request.";
    }
}
```

To test the no data scenario, the `Mock` object will be set up in a similar fashion as with the test shown in Listing 7-16. The difference is, in this case, the artist list is empty, and the assert is verifying that the `Message` property is set to a string defined in a constant defined in `ArtistAdminStrings.NoDataFound`. Listing 7-19 shows the completed test.

*Listing 7-19.* Testing the No Data Found Scenario

```
[Fact(DisplayName = "List Action Artist List View Model Shows No Data message when empty")]
public void ListAction_ReturnsEmptyNewArtistList_ToListView()
{
    // Arrange
    var unitOfWorkMock = new Mock<IUnitOfWork>();
    unitOfWorkMock.Setup(m => m.ArtistRepository.GetNewArtists(1))
            .Returns(new List<Artist> { });

    var controller = new ArtistAdminController(unitOfWorkMock.Object);
    var expected = ArtistAdminStrings.NoDataFound;

    // Act
    var result = controller.List() as ViewResult;
    Assert.NotNull(result.Model);
```

```
    var viewModel = result?.Model as ArtistListViewModel;
    var actual = viewModel?.Message;

    // Assert
    Assert.Empty(viewModel?.Artists);
    Assert.Equal(expected, actual);
}
```

## Using Moq to Test for a Back-End Database Failure

It is important to understand how your application will respond when it cannot communicate with one or more subcomponents. Subcomponents such as web services, databases, and even file systems can fail, and your application needs to plan for these failures and should have tests to cover these scenarios.

The data access component used in the book uses Entity Framework Core to communicate to a SQL Server database. Entity Framework does not wrap database connectivity errors but instead allows the underlying database driver error to bubble up from the SQL Client driver. This creates a problem from a unit testing perspective since no interface for SqlException is available and no public constructor for SqlException exists. Because of this, you cannot use Moq to create a mock of SqlException. You can, however, mock DbException. Because DbException is an abstract class, Moq can mock it even though it does not provide an interface and has no public constructor. DbException is the base type for many database exceptions including SqlException, OdbcException, and OracleException. A catch clause for DbException also will catch exceptions from derived types. Using DbException also has the advantage of decoupling the test suite from a specific implementation of the data access class.

For this test, you will verify that when calling IUnitOfWork.ArtistRepository.GetNewArtists results in a DbException object, the Error view page will be displayed. The first step is to use Moq to create a mock of a DbException object. Next, inside the setup for IUnitOfWork.ArtistRepository.GetNewArtists, the Throws method is used rather than Returns as with the past tests. The exception mock is used as the exception type passed to the Throws method. Listing 7-20 shows the completed test.

***Listing 7-20.*** Testing for Back-End Failure Scenarios

```
[Fact(DisplayName = "List Action Redirect To Error Action When Back-end down")]
public void ListAction_RedirectToErrorAction_WhenItCannotConnectToBackend()
{
    var exception = new Mock<System.Data.Common.DbException>();
    // Arrange
    var unitOfWorkMock = new Mock<IUnitOfWork>();
    unitOfWorkMock.Setup(m => m.ArtistRepository.GetNewArtists(1))
                .Throws(exception.Object);
    var controller = new ArtistAdminController(unitOfWorkMock.Object);
    var expected = "Error";

    // Act
    var result = controller.List() as ViewResult;
    var actual = result?.ViewName;

    // Assert
    Assert.Equal(expected, actual);
}
```

You should now be able to build the project and run the tests. All the tests will still fail since the functionality has not yet been implemented. In recipe 7-5, the ASP.NET Core IoC container will be used to inject the data access component to the controller, which will allow you to complete the functionality.

# 7-5. Using the Inversion of Control and Constructor Injection Patterns with ASP.NET Core MVC

## Problem

You are implementing a controller that uses a database access component but do not want to execute database commands during your unit tests. You need a way to automatically inject the correct component at runtime as well as manage the lifetime of the components and ensure they are disposed of when no longer needed.

## Solution

Support for test-first development and dependency injection is central to the design of ASP.NET Core. ASP.NET Core comes with a built-in IoC container that contains essential functionality. ASP.NET Core also supports the use of third-party IoC containers, such as Autofac, that contain more robust features. Whether you use the built-in IoC container or a third-party container, configuration is done in the Startup.cs class.

The IoC container configuration in Startup.cs is used to load not only your custom components but also components of ASP.NET Core including the Static File module, logging middleware, and MVC. Startup.cs has two methods used for loading and configuring components: ConfigureServices and Configure. The ConfigureServices method allows you to add components to the ISevicesCollection of the application but does not wire them up to the request pipeline. Adding components to the IServicesCollection makes them available to be used via dependency injection. It is in ConfigureServices that interfaces are paired to implementations. ConfigureServices is also used when applying advanced configuration using the Options pattern as described in recipe 6-7.

The Configure method in Startup.cs adds components to the request pipeline. If you added a custom middleware component to the IoC container during ConfigureServices, you would need to add it to the request pipeline in Configure.

## How It Works

Tightly coupled components make your application difficult to maintain and nearly impossible to test. If you are creating instances of a class in your code using the new operator, you are hard-linking your code to the class and creating coupling. Using the new operator is not always bad. In some cases, it can't be avoided such as when you are creating instances of strings and arrays. On the other hand, if it is possible to avoid hard linking a dependency, you should consider it.

Dependency injection is an important technique to help you write loosely coupled and testable code. With dependency injection, instances of a class are provided at runtime. Objects can be injected either by being passed as a parameter to the consuming class's constructor, known as the Constructor Injection pattern, or by setting the values of properties, known as the Setter Injection pattern. The Setter Injection pattern was popularized with the Java Spring framework, but many had found it to be error-prone because of its reliance on default values when a property was not set. With the Constructor Injection pattern, all dependencies are injected when the consuming class is created, and no default values are used. Constructor Injection is the recommended pattern and the only one supported by the ASP.NET Core IoC container.

## Using Constructor Injection

There are three steps for using the Constructor Injection pattern.

1. Set up your class so it has a member variable for each of the dependencies you want to inject.

2. Add a constructor that accepts parameters for each dependency and then assigns them to the member variables. An example of this was shown in recipe 7-4 (see Listing 7-6).

3. The final step is to configure the IoC container so that it knows what implementation classes should be used for each interface and what the lifetime of each class should be. Once this has been set up, then the IOC container in combination with ASP.NET Core can automatically create instances of the classes, inject them at runtime, and then dispose of them when they are no longer required.

Once your class has been set up to accept the required dependencies, the next problem is configuring your application so it can locate the correct implementations for your interfaces and then inject them into your consuming classes as needed. This is where the IoC container becomes useful. The IoC container allows you to register interfaces with a matching implementation. It can then respond to a request for an interface type with an associated instance. The IoC container also manages the life cycle of the instance and will dispose of it when required.

## Registering Types with the ASP.NET Core IoC Container

As mentioned previously, the Startup class's ConfigureService method is used to register types with the ASP.NET Core IoC container. The IServiceCollection class contains many methods that simplify the task of registering a type with the IoC container and specifying how the instance should be managed.

The ArtistAdminController class that was first introduced in recipe 7-3 depends on a data access component that is an instance of a class that implements IUnitOfWork. The UnitOfWork class, which was discussed in detail in Chapter 6 (see recipe 6-6), depends on an Entity Framework Core DBContext class called MoBContext. UnitOfWork uses constructor injection to get an instance of the MoBContext object just as ArtistAdminController requires that an IUnitOfWork instance be injected. This type of dependency chaining is common. Listing 7-21 shows how both classes are registered in the Startup.cs class.

***Listing 7-21.*** Registering Multiple Dependencies in the ASP.NET Core IoC

```
public void ConfigureServices(IServiceCollection services)
{
    // Add framework services.
    services.AddMvc();

    // Register the DBContext that is required by UnitOfWork
    services.AddDbContext<MoBContext>(
            options => options.UseSqlServer(Configuration.GetConnectionString("Default
            Connection")));

    // Register UnitOfWork as Scoped so it will have one instance per request
    services.AddScoped<IUnitOfWork, UnitOfWork>();

}
```

The UnitOfWork class and the MoBContext class are both registered with a scoped lifetime, which means they are created once for each request. The scoped lifetime is the default setting when calling AddDbContext and is the recommended scope for database-connected services. The ASP.NET Core IoC container allows three types of service lifetime scopes.

- *Singleton*: One instance is created per application. It is created the first time it is needed. You need to be careful with this approach since the state of the instance can be changed by multiple requests.

- *Scoped*: One instance is created for each request.

- *Transient*: This is created each time it is requested. This works best for lightweight stateless components.

## Implementing the ArtistAdminController List Action

Now that the tests have been written (recipes 7-3 and 7-4) and the dependencies have been configured, the next step is to implement the code for the List action. Shown in Listing 7-22, the action starts off by creating an instance of the view model class ArtistListViewModel. Next a try/catch block is created to catch possible database faults. A DbException is caught by the block rather than a SqlException. This allows the code flow to be tested in the unit test and does not couple the controller to a specific database driver. Inside the try block, the model.Artists property is populated with a call to IUnitOfWork. The null conditional operator is used to help verify that none of the objects is null before calling the next in the chain. Not only is this a good general best practice, but it is required because of the way your tests have been written. For the first two tests that used only a simple Mock object, the ArtistRepository property of the IUnitWork instance will be null since it was not explicitly created when the mock was set up.

Next, the RecordsFound property is populated. Finally, the Message property is set, which meets the needs of the last test, which expected the NoDataFound message to be used when the collection was empty.

*Listing 7-22.* Completed List Action

```
public IActionResult List()
{
    var model = new ArtistListViewModel();
    try
    {
        model.Artists = _DataAccessLayer?.ArtistRepository?.GetNewArtists(1);
        var nInt = model?.Artists?.Count;
        model.RecordsFound = nInt ?? 0;
        if(model.RecordsFound>0)
        {
            model.Message = string.Format("{0} Records found", model.RecordsFound);
        }
        else
        {
            model.Message = ArtistAdminStrings.NoDataFound;
        }

    }
```

```
        catch(DbException dbE)
        {
            model.Message = dbE.Message;
            return View("Error", model);
        }
    return View("List", model);
}
```

You should now be able to run your unit tests, and they should all pass.

The last step is to create the view pages. To do this, first create a new folder under Views in the Chapter07.Web project named ArtistAdmin. Next add a new view page named List.cshtml. Modify List.cshtml to match Listing 7-23.

***Listing 7-23.*** List.cshtml

```
@model Chapter07.Web.ViewModels.ArtistListViewModel

<h2>Artists</h2>
@Model.Message
<table class="table table-striped">
    @foreach (var item in Model.Artists)
    {
        <tr>
            <td>
                @item.UserName
            </td>
            <td>
                @item.Country
            </td>
            <td>
                @item.CreateDate.ToString("d")
            </td>
        </tr>
    }
</table>
```

You should now be able to run your application and navigate to the page.

# CHAPTER 8

■ ■ ■

# Moving from Web Forms to ASP. NET Core MVC

Many people who have been working with Microsoft web technologies have built up years of experience using ASP.NET Web Forms. The recipes in this chapter attempt to bridge the gap between ASP.NET Web Forms and ASP.NET Core MVC by discussing common programing tasks performed using Web Forms and then showing the equivalent technique using ASP.NET Core MVC and the Razor view engine.

## 8-1. Deciding Between Staying with Web Forms, a Full Rewrite, or Gradual Migration

### Problem

You're a veteran ASP.NET Web Forms developer, and you are assigned to a new project that is wrapping up requirements gathering and are about to begin your design. You need help deciding whether to stick with ASP.NET Web Forms or dive into ASP.NET Core MVC. If ASP.NET Core MVC is not yet a standard development framework in your organization, you may need to justify this design decision to management or an enterprise architecture team.

### Solution

ASP.NET Web Forms is Microsoft's most popular web application framework and has been used to create hundreds of thousands of applications since its introduction in January 2002. While it has been continually updated and improved, its overall architecture is outdated. While its design made it easy for Visual Basic 6 developers to adapt to the Web, its layers of abstraction create challenges when attempting to create fresh user experiences that require more precise control of HTML.

For most situations, ASP.NET Core MVC will be your best choice for new projects. ASP.NET Core MVC offers many benefits over ASP.NET Web Forms, including the following:

- ASP.NET Core's lightweight modular architecture and streamlined hosting models make ASP.NET Core faster and more scalable then ASP.NET Web Forms.

- ASP.NET Core MVC has built-in features for creating RESTful web services. While ASP.NET Web Forms has basic functionality for creating SOAP-based web services, in most cases you would need to use WCF to build out a service layer if you stayed with Web Forms.

- ASP.NET Core allows more control of the HTML and does not attempt to abstract HTML away as Web Forms does. This makes ASP.NET Core much easier to integrate with modern front-end frameworks such as ReactJS and Angular.

- ASP.NET Core has built-in support for dependency injection, which greatly simplifies following test-driven development practices. ASP.NET Web Forms, on the other hand, is difficult to test because it is tightly coupled with many system components.

## Deciding Between a Gradual Migration and a Full Rewrite

The choice between a gradual migration and a full rewrite depends on the size and complexity of the application and the overall business value your customer will receive from the rewrite. For example, if the business case for your existing application has changed and most of the application will need to be updated anyway regardless of technology choice, a total rewrite in ASP.NET Core MVC may be well worth the extra investment. On the other hand, if you rewrite the entire application but the result as perceived by your customer does not provide additional business value, your customer may be unhappy. In this case, you may be better off sticking with ASP.NET Web Forms or performing a gradual migration.

### Gradual Migration from ASP.NET Web Forms to ASP.NET Core

ASP.NET Core MVC does not support Web Forms. Because of this, you cannot have both Web Forms and ASP.NET Core running side by side in the same web application. This makes a gradual migration challenging and requires that components built using ASP.NET Core be placed in a separate web application.

There are several strategies for integrating multiple web applications so that they appear as a single application to the end user. In cases where the entire application is deployed to a single web server, virtual directories in IIS can be used. Virtual directories allow you to host many applications under a single web site, with each web site appearing as a separate subdirectory. If you choose this path, however, you may find it difficult to maintain consistency in your presentation layer and will have to address problems such as maintaining state when a user navigates between pages in the separate web application.

An alternative to the method of using virtual directories is to consider migrating business logic and data access code to .NET Standard–compatible libraries and then exposing the functionality to the legacy Web Forms application via a RESTful API created using ASP.NET Core. The Web Forms UI pages can then be gradually replaced by static pages that consume the API using a modern front-end framework such as ReactJS. This method would still require creating a new web application to host the ASP.NET Core APIs but would not be mixing UI components from the two web applications. The drawback of this approach is that you will not be able to take advantage of the productivity offered by the Razor view engine and will face a steep learning curve with ReactJS. For more information on how to use ReactJS with ASP.NET Core, see Chapter 11.

# 8-2. Converting a Web Forms Page to MVC

## Problem

You have decided to migrate your Web Forms application to ASP.NET Core MVC. Since the programming model in ASP.NET Core MVC is so different from Web Forms, you are not sure where to start.

## Solution

Each Web Forms page has two parts: an ASPX page or web form that contains a mix of HTML markup server-side controls and a code-behind page that is a .NET class that contains server-side event handlers and other helper code. In a well-factored Web Forms application, things such as data access code will typically be factored out into a class library in a separate assembly. In less complex applications, the data access code may be directly in the code-behind page.

To convert a Web Forms page to MVC, you can perform the following actions:

1. Identify an existing MVC controller or create a new one to host the page's control logic.

2. Add a new action to the controller with an IActionResult return type.

3. If the Web Forms page was in a subfolder that had access restricted by role, decorate the action with an AuthorizeAttribute attribute and pass in the required security parameters as necessary.

4. In the models folder, create a new model class that abstracts the types of data you are working with in your Web Forms page. I will go over what this means in detail in the "How It Works" section of this recipe.

5. Create a new view that corresponds with the action in the Controller's View folder. This can be done inside Visual Studio by right-clicking the action name in the controller class and then selecting Add View from the context menu. You will then be prompted to confirm the view name and select a scaffolding template for the view.

6. Add logic to your Action method to take the data from the model and pass it to your view.

## How It Works

To illustrate the procedure described in the solution, you will take a web form called MyWorkspaces.aspx and convert it to ASP.NET Core MVC. MyWorkspaces.aspx was designed to be used only by authenticated users who were members of the Artists security group and was placed in a subdirectory called Members with a web.config file that contained an Authorization section, as shown in Listing 8-1.

*Listing 8-1.* Web Forms Access Control in web.config

```xml
<?xml version="1.0"?>
<configuration>
    <system.web>
        <authorization>
            <allow roles="Artist"/>
            <deny users="*"/>
        </authorization>
    </system.web>
</configuration>
```

MyWorkspaces.aspx displays a list of collaboration spaces that a user has either created or contributed to. The data is displayed on the page using a DataList control. The DataList control uses data binding expressions to display the data. It also encapsulates the looping logic and provides sections where the developer can supply templates for the header, footer, and items that will be displayed. In addition to the Repeater, a PlaceHolder control is used to display content that should be displayed only when no data is found. Listing 8-2 shows MyWorkspaces.aspx.

***Listing 8-2.*** Markup and Data Binding Code for MyWorkspaces.aspx

```
<%@ Page Language="C#" AutoEventWireup="true" CodeBehind="MyWorkspaces.aspx.cs"
Inherits="Recipe02.WebForms.Members.MyWorkspaces" MasterPageFile="~/Site.Master" %>
<asp:Content ID="Content4"
    ContentPlaceHolderID="MainContent"
    runat="server">
<h1>My Song Workspaces</h1>
<div class="tab-content" id="flowtabsPanes">
    <div class="tab-pane active" id="MyWorkspaces">
        <asp:PlaceHolder
          Text="You have not created any song workspaces."
          runat="server"
          Visible="false"
          ID="noWorkspaces" />
        <asp:Repeater ID="ProjectsRepeater" runat="server">
          <HeaderTemplate>
              <table class="table table-striped">
                  <thead>
                      <tr>
                          <th>
                              <asp:Label ID="ProjectNameHdrLabel"
                                  runat="server"
                                  Text="Project Name">
                              </asp:Label>
                          </th>
                          <th>
                              <asp:Label ID="ProjectDetailsHdrLabel"
                                  runat="server"
                                  Text="Status">
                              </asp:Label>
                          </th>
                          <th>
                              <asp:Label ID="ProjectStatusHdrLabel"
                                  runat="server"
                                  Text="Created">
                              </asp:Label>
                          </th>
                          <th>
                              <asp:Label ID="ProjectDateModHdrLabel"
                                  runat="server"
                                  Text="Modified">
                              </asp:Label>
                          </th>
                      </tr>
                  </thead>
              </HeaderTemplate>

              <ItemTemplate>
                  <tr>
                      <td>
                          <asp:Label ID="ProjectNameLabel"
```

```
                              runat="server">
                    <a title="Go to the project workspace." href="#">
                        <%# Eval("Title") %></a></asp:Label>
                </td>
                <td>
                    <asp:Label ID="ProjectDetailsLabel"
                        runat="server"><%# Eval("Status") %>
                    </asp:Label>
                </td>
                <td>
                    <asp:Label ID="ProjectStatusLabel"
                        runat="server">
                        <%# Eval("CreateDate")%>
                    </asp:Label>
                </td>
                <td>
                    <asp:Label ID="ProjectDateModLabel"
                        runat="server"><%# Eval("ModifiedDate")%>
                    </asp:Label>
                </td>
            </tr>
        </ItemTemplate>

        <FooterTemplate>
            </table>
        </FooterTemplate>
    </asp:Repeater>
    </div>
    </div>
</asp:Content>
```

The web form markup page does not contain any logic. All the code is for calling the data access layer and for determining what parts of the content should be visible in the code-behind page. In this example, the code-behind page handles a single server-side event that fires when the page loads. Inside the event handler, shown in Listing 8-3, the code first verifies that this is the initial page load and not a subsequent request caused by a user interacting with another page control such as a button. This is done by checking the IsPostBack property. Next the code in the event handler creates an instance of the repository and gets a list of collaboration spaces. If data is found, it is bound to the Repeater control; otherwise, the noWorkspaces placeholder is displayed.

*Listing 8-3.* Code-Behind Page for MyWorkspaces.aspx

```
using System;
using AspNetCoreRecipes.Shared.DataAccess.Repository;

namespace Recipe02.WebForms.Members0
{
    public partial class MyWorkspaces : System.Web.UI.Page
    {
        protected void Page_Load(object sender, EventArgs e)
        {
            if (IsPostBack) return;
```

```
            // in order to simplify this example we are hard coding a user name
            var id = 1784;
            using (var unitOfWork = new UnitOfWork())
            {
                var list = unitOfWork.CollaborationSpaceRepository.GetCollaborationSpaces
                ForArtist(id);

                if (list.Count > 0)
                {
                    ProjectsRepeater.DataSource = list;
                    ProjectsRepeater.DataBind();
                }
                else
                {
                    noWorkspaces.Visible = true;
                }
            }
        }
    }
}
```

## Moving to ASP.NET Core MVC

For this example, you will add a new controller named MembersController to an existing ASP.NET Core MVC project.

To add the new controller, inside Visual Studio, right-click the Controllers folder and select Add ➤ New Item. In the Add New Item dialog, select MVC Controller Class. Change the name of the new class file to MembersController.cs and then click the Add button.

To meet the security requirement implemented by the Web Forms project of restricting access to authorized users who are members of the security group Artist, you will add an AuthorizeAttribute attribute to the class. You are adding the attribute at the class level in this case since all the actions in this controller are meant only for members of the Artist role. The AuthorizeAttribute attribute provides similar functionality as the authorization settings configured in the web.config file of the Web Forms project.

Next, you will add an action method that will contain the control logic for the My Collaboration Spaces page. Add a new public method to the MembersController class with a return type of IActionResult named MyCollaborationSpaces.

In the Web Forms page, calls to the UnitOfWork data access layer class were wrapped inside a using block to ensure that all resources were disposed of. In ASP.NET Core, the life cycle of the UnitOfWork object is managed by the ASP.NET Core IoC container. For details on using the IoC container and registering the UnitOfWork class in Startup.cs, please refer to Chapter 6 (see recipe 6-6). Also, since you are using dependency injection, you always access the data access layer using the interface IUnitOfWork rather than using a specific implementation of it.

To allow the IoC container to inject an instance of the IUnitOfWork instance into the controller, first you will add a private member variable named _unitOfWork to the page to hold it. You then create a constructor that takes an IUnitOfWork object as an argument and assigns it to _unitOfWork.

Finally, you can add the logic to your action method that will use the IUnitOfWork class to pull the data from your repository and then pass the result as the model to the view. Listing 8-4 shows the completed MembersController class.

*Listing 8-4.* The MembersController Class

```
using Microsoft.AspNetCore.Mvc;
using Microsoft.AspNetCore.Authorization;
using AspNetCoreMvcRecipes.Shared.DataAccess;

namespace Recipe03.Core.Web.Controllers
{
    [Authorize(Roles = "Artist")]
    public class MembersController : Controller
    {
        private IUnitOfWork _unitOfWork;
        public MembersController(IUnitOfWork unitOfWork)
        {
            _unitOfWork = unitOfWork;
        }

        public IActionResult MyCollaborationSpaces()
        {
            // in order to simplify this example we are hard coding a user name
            var id = 1784;
            var model = _unitOfWork.CollaborationSpaceRepository.GetCollaborationSpacesFor
            Artist(id);

            return View("MyCollaborationSpaces", model);
        }
    }
}
```

The last step is to create the view. Create a new subfolder under the Views folder called Members and then add a new view page named MyCollaborationSpaces.cshtml.

Inside MyCollaborationSpaces.cshtml, the first thing you need to do is add a model directive that tells the view what CLR type you want to use for the model.

Next, you will add some presentation logic that will show a message if no data is found. In the Web Forms example, this was done in the code-behind page by toggling the Visible property of the noWorkSpaces ASP Placeholder control. In the Razor page, this is accomplished using an If block that checks that Model is not null and contains at least one item.

In the case in which you have data, the view will display the data in an HTML table. In the Web Forms version, the looping logic for creating this table was encapsulated inside the Repeater control. In the Razor view, this is accomplished with a foreach block. Listing 8-5 shows the completed example.

*Listing 8-5.* MyCollaborationSpaces.cshtml

```
@model IList<AspNetCoreMvcRecipes.Shared.DataAccess.CollaborationSpace>
@{
    ViewBag.Title = "My Collaboration  Spaces";
}
<h2>@ViewBag.Title.</h2>
@if (Model == null || Model.Count < 1)
{
    <div>
        Sorry no data found!
    </div>
}
```

```
else
{
    <table class="table table-striped">
        <tr>
            <th>
                Project Name
            </th>
            <th>
                Status
            </th>
            <th>
                Created
            </th>
            <th>
                Modified
            </th>
        </tr>
        @foreach (var item in Model)
        {
            <tr>
                <td><a href="#">@item.Title</a></td>
                <td>@item.Status</td>
                <td>@item.CreateDate</td>
                <td>@item.ModifiedDate</td>
            </tr>
        }
    </table>
}
```

# 8-3. Creating a Custom Tag Helper That Mimics the ASP.NET Data List Control

## Problem

You are building a new application using ASP.NET Core MVC. You have requirements to display a list of items in a four-column format. As a veteran ASP.NET Web Forms developer, you would normally accomplish this using a DataList control. You want to know how to do the same thing using ASP.NET Core MVC with the Razor view engine. You want to reuse existing code where possible and are required to support legacy browsers including Internet Explorer 7.

## Solution

This problem has a few possible solutions. One is to build an HTML table like you did in recipe 8-2, which was shown in Listing 8-5. This is simple and will probably work in most cases but does not provide much in the way of reuse and can potentially become tedious if you need to create many similar pages.

Another approach is to use a foreach loop in your view to output your template as a series of list items in an HTML unordered list (<ul>). An added benefit of this approach is rather than hard-coding four columns, you can then use CSS media queries to dynamically adjust the number of columns displayed based on the resolution of the user's display. The only problem with this approach is that it does not support all legacy browsers. It is possible to add this capability for older browsers using a type of JavaScript library known as a *polyfill*. A popular library for providing media query support to Internet Explorer 6-8 is Respond. js. The Respond.js library can be easily added to your project using Bower.

The third approach, shown in this example, is to create a Tag Helper that lets you specify the number of columns that you need to create and then lets you specify the template for each column defined in a partial view.

## How It Works

From a straight productivity standpoint, it is hard to argue with the simplicity of being able to drag a DataList control to a web form, specify the direction and number of columns required, and then bind the list to a data source. For this reason, ASP.NET Web Forms continues to be popular, especially in corporate environments where the deadline is typically the first documented requirement.

It is possible to create a similar level of efficiency with ASP.NET Core MVC once you learn the correct techniques and build up a library of custom Tag Helpers that aid you in your design. In addition to having a highly productive developer experience, you can reap the advantages of clean HTML and increased testability.

## Creating a Tag Helper to Mimic the Web Forms DataList Control

As stated in the "Solution" section, you will create a custom Tag Helper that will allow you to be more productive when implementing views with a multiple-column requirement. The Tag Helper will take the number of columns to generate, the model expression to use as a data source, and the name of a view component as parameters. You can then use the Tag Helper, as shown in Listing 8-6.

***Listing 8-6.*** Desired Syntax for the ColumnList Tag Helper

```
<column-list asp-number-of-columns="2"
             asp-for="@Model"
             asp-view-component="ArtistCard"></columnlist>
```

Using a view component adds complexity but has two key advantages. First, it allows your view to be kept very simple with most of the view markup moved into the view component. Another advantage of using a view component is that additional transformation logic can be applied to the data before displaying it.

### Creating the ColumnList Tag Helper

Create a new folder named TagHelpers under the Recipe03.Web project. Add a class to the folder named ColumnListTagHelper. Add a using statement for Microsoft.AspNetCore.Razor.TagHelpers and then make the class extend TagHelper. Inside the body of the class, override the ProcessAsync method, as shown in Listing 8-7.

***Listing 8-7.*** Tag Helper Starting Point

```
using Microsoft.AspNetCore.Razor.TagHelpers;
using System.Threading.Tasks;

namespace Recipe03.Web.TagHelpers
{
```

```
    public class ColumnListTagHelper : TagHelper
    {

        public override async Task ProcessAsync(TagHelperContext context, TagHelperOutput output)
        {

        }

    }
}
```

## Adding Properties to the Tag Helper

ColumnListTagHelper is now a Tag Helper that can be included in a view. However, since no functionality has been implemented, the markup added to the view will not be modified at all by the Tag Helper. The Tag Helper syntax shown in Listing 8-6 had a tag named column-list with three attributes: asp-number-of-columns, asp-for, and asp-view-component. To add the attributes to the Tag Helper, add three new public properties to the class that are named NumberOfColumns, For, and ViewComponent. Decorate each of the properties with an HtmlAttributeName attribute. This is required to use asp-prefix. By convention, Razor will automatically convert Pascal-cased property names into lowercase HTML property names. For example, ViewComponent would be converted to a view component. Using the asp- prefix is not required but can make it easier to distinguish normal HTML properties from Tag Helper properties. The updated Tag Helper will match Listing 8-8.

***Listing 8-8.*** Adding Properties to the Tag Helper

```
using Microsoft.AspNetCore.Mvc.ViewFeatures;
using Microsoft.AspNetCore.Razor.TagHelpers;
using System.Threading.Tasks;

namespace Recipe04.Web.TagHelpers
{

    public class ColumnListTagHelper : TagHelper
    {
        public const string NumberOfColumnsAttributeName = "asp-number-of-columns";
        private const string ForAttributeName = "asp-for";
        private const string ViewComponentAttributeName = "asp-view-component";

        [HtmlAttributeName(NumberOfColumnsAttributeName)]
        public int NumberOfColumns { get; set; }

        [HtmlAttributeName(ForAttributeName)]
        public ModelExpression For { get; set; }

        [HtmlAttributeName(ViewComponentAttributeName)]
        public string ViewComponentName { get; set; }
```

```
        public override async Task ProcessAsync(TagHelperContext context, TagHelperOutput output)
        {

        }

    }
}
```

## Validating the Properties of the Tag Helper

In the next step, you can add some validation logic to throw exceptions if the arguments supplied do not
match your expectations. Throwing exceptions will aid developers who are consuming the Tag Helper to
spot issues. If exceptions are not explicitly thrown, Razor will suppress unexpected errors and not render
any content, making programming errors difficult to solve. The revised version of the ProcessAsync method
shown in Listing 8-9 validates that TagHelperContext and TagHelperOutput have been properly set by the
runtime or test class. Next, you validate that the NumberOfColumns property has been set between 1 and 12.
Finally, you inspect the model expression. If it is null, the processing is halted, and the output is suppressed.
A null model expression may be a legitimate value. In this case, you do not want to return an error but
return nothing at all. In the final check, you verify that the model expression is an ICollection.

***Listing 8-9.*** Validation Logic in the Tag Helper

```
public override async Task ProcessAsync(TagHelperContext context, TagHelperOutput output)
{
        if (context == null)
        {
            throw new ArgumentNullException(nameof(context));
        }

        if (output == null)
        {
            throw new ArgumentNullException(nameof(output));
        }

        if (NumberOfColumns < 1 || NumberOfColumns > 12)
        {
            throw new ArgumentOutOfRangeException("NumberOfColumns",
                    "The number of columns must be at least 1 and at most 12.");
        }

        if (For == null)
        {
            output.SuppressOutput();
            return;
        }
        var collection = For.Model as ICollection;
        if (collection == null)
        {
            throw new ArgumentOutOfRangeException("For", "The Model Expression need to
            be a collection.");
        }
}
```

## Setting Up the Tag Helper to Execute View Components

Before you can go any further, some additional work needs to be done to allow the Tag Helper to execute a view component. When Razor executes a view component, it uses an instance of an IViewComponentHelper. This instance is passed to Razor using dependency injection. For the Tag Helper to execute the view component, it will also need to have an instance of IViewComponentHelper passed to it. In addition, you will also need to get a copy of the view context and use it to contextualize the IViewComponentHelper instance. The first step in this process is to add a private read-only member variable to hold the IViewComponentHelper instance. Next, create a constructor that accepts an IViewComponentHelper parameter and writes it to the instance variable. This setup will allow the ASP.NET Core dependency injection system to automatically inject the IViewComponentHelper.

The second step is to create a public property called ViewContext. This property needs to be decorated with the ViewContext attribute to allow ASP.NET Core to inject the ViewContext property into the Tag Helper. This is necessary since the ViewContext property is created later in the request life cycle after the Tag Helper has been initialized. The ViewContext property should also have an HtmlAttributeNotBound attribute. This will prevent the property from appearing as an option to developers from Visual Studio IntelliSense. Listing 8-10 shows the new constructor and ViewContext property.

***Listing 8-10.*** Setting Up the Tag Helper to Call a View Component

```
private readonly IViewComponentHelper _viewComponentHelper;
public ColumnListTagHelper(IViewComponentHelper viewComponentHelper)
{
    _viewComponentHelper = viewComponentHelper;
}

/// <summary>
/// The context of the current view
/// </summary>
[HtmlAttributeNotBound] // do not show in VS as something for users to add
[ViewContext]
public ViewContext ViewContext { get; set; } // set View Context property once constructed
```

## Adding the Rending Logic

Now that the Tag Helper has been set up to get all the data it needs from the view, you can add the logic for implementing the dynamic column layouts. Unlike the ASP.NET Web Forms DataList control, which uses HTML tables for layout, the ColumnList Tag Helper will use the Bootstrap grid system. Bootstrap is the UX library that is added with the ASP.NET Core template. Bootstrap uses a 12-column grid system that uses CSS to create a column structure that can adapt based on the size of the screen. Columns in Bootstrap are defined using CSS classes in the format col-[screen-size]-[column-span]. For example, if you want a column that spans three columns for extra-small screens, you can add a class named col-xs-3 to the HTML element. You can find a full description of the Bootstrap grid here:

http://getbootstrap.com/css/#grid-options

To use the grid system to dynamically create columns, you will create a helper function that calculates the required column span based on the value of the NumberOfColumns property. Listing 8-11 shows the method.

***Listing 8-11.*** Creating Columns Using the Bootstrap Grid System

```
private string GetColumnDivTag()
{
    var colSpan = (int)Math.Round((double)(12 / NumberOfColumns));
    return string.Format(@"<div class=""col-xs-{0} col-sm-{0} col-md-{0} col-lg-{0}"">",
    colSpan);
}
```

Finally, the logic to loop through the items in the collection passed via the model expression is added to the `ProcessAsync` method. This starts by setting the outer HTML tag rendered by the Tag Helper to a DIV using `output.TagName = "div"`. You can then add the Bootstrap `container-fluid` class to the DIV using `output.Attributes.SetAttribute("class", "container-fluid")`. Next, you need to initialize several variables used to monitor the progress of the loop. In the body of the loop, a new row is created when the loop is started and each time you reach the maximum number of items in a column. Inside each row, columns are added for each item. The view component is executed for each of the items in the collection, and the output of the view component is appended to the output. At the end of the loop, if there is not enough data to fill all the columns in the last row, empty columns are created. Listing 8-12 shows the full `ProcessAsync` method.

***Listing 8-12.*** Completed ProcessAsync Method

```
public override async Task ProcessAsync(TagHelperContext context, TagHelperOutput output)
{
        if (context == null)
        {
            throw new ArgumentNullException(nameof(context));
        }

        if (output == null)
        {
            throw new ArgumentNullException(nameof(output));
        }

        if (NumberOfColumns < 1 || NumberOfColumns > 12)
        {
            throw new ArgumentOutOfRangeException("NumberOfColumns", "The number of
            columns must be at least 1 and at most 12.");
        }
        if (For == null)
        {
            output.SuppressOutput();
            return;
        }
        var collection = For.Model as ICollection;
        if (collection == null)
        {
            throw new ArgumentOutOfRangeException("For", "The Model Expression need to
            be a collection.");
        }
```

```
        //add the view context of the current view to the view component, enable to invoke
        ((IViewContextAware)_viewComponentHelper).Contextualize(ViewContext);

        output.TagName = "div";
        output.Attributes.SetAttribute("class", "container-fluid");

        var columnsInRow = 1;
        var rowsDone = 0;
        var numberOfItemsDone = 0;
        var numberOfExtraColumnsInLastRow = 0;

        //calculate the needed table structure
        int numberOfRows = collection.Count / NumberOfColumns;

        foreach (var item in collection)
        {
            if (columnsInRow == 1)
            {
                output.Content.AppendHtml(@"<div class=""row"">");
            }

            output.Content.AppendHtml(GetColumnDivTag());

          var viewContent = await _viewComponentHelper.InvokeAsync(ViewComponentName, item);
            output.Content.AppendHtml(viewContent);
            output.Content.AppendHtml("</div>");

            bool isLastItem = (collection.Count == numberOfItemsDone + 1);

            if ((columnsInRow == NumberOfColumns) || isLastItem)
            {
                if (isLastItem)
                {
                    numberOfExtraColumnsInLastRow = NumberOfColumns - columnsInRow;

                    output.Content.AppendHtml((RenderExtraColumns(numberOfExtraColumns
                    InLastRow)));
                }
                output.Content.AppendHtml("</div>");
                columnsInRow = 1;
                rowsDone++;
            }
            else
            {
                columnsInRow++;
            }

            numberOfItemsDone++;
        }
    }
}
```

```csharp
private string RenderExtraColumns(int numberOfExtraColumnsInLastRow)
{
            if (numberOfExtraColumnsInLastRow > 0)
            {
                var builder = new StringBuilder();
                for (int i = 0; i < numberOfExtraColumnsInLastRow; i++)
                {
                    builder.Append(GetColumnDivTag());
                    builder.Append("</div>");
                }
                return builder.ToString();
            }
            return string.Empty;
}
```

# Using the ColumnsList Tag Helper

In the last part of this exercise, you will add the Tag Helper to the Home controller and corresponding view that will display a list of new artists who have recently joined your music collaboration community web site. The view will use the ColumnsList helper to display a template for each artist.

## Creating the ArtistCard View Component

The ColumnList Tag Helper requires that you use a view component to render the template displayed in each block in the grid. This design provides additional flexibility allowing you to intercept and transform the data before passing it to the view.

In the Web Forms way of doing things, you need to rely on event handlers such as ItemDataBound to perform data transformation logic. The ItemDataBound event handlers allow you to access the model data indirectly by pulling it out of child controls exposed via DataListItemEventArgs, but this was somewhat cumbersome and often resulted in brittle and hard-to-read code.

In the view component model employed here, you have full control over the data and can transform it into a view model if needed.

The other advantage of this design is that you have full control over the HTML on the page. You can also take advantage of the full feature set of the Razor view engine.

To create the view component, first create a new folder in the root of the web application named ViewComponents. Add a new class to that folder named ArtistCardViewComponent. Modify the class to match Listing 8-13.

*Listing 8-13.* ArtistCardViewComponent

```csharp
using AspNetCoreMvcRecipes.Shared.DataAccess;
using Microsoft.AspNetCore.Mvc;
using System.Threading.Tasks;

namespace Recipe04.Web.ViewComponents
{
    public class ArtistCardViewComponent : ViewComponent
    {
        public async Task<IViewComponentResult> InvokeAsync(Artist artist)
        {
```

```
            return View(artist);
        }
    }
}
```

Next, you need to add a view that will display the information for each artist. To do this, first create a new folder under Views\Shared named Components. In the Components folder, create a new folder called ArtistCard. In the ArtistCard folder, create a new view page named Default.cshtml. Modify the view to match Listing 8-14.

*Listing 8-14.* ArtistCard View Page

```
@model AspNetCoreMvcRecipes.Shared.DataAccess.Artist
<div class="panel panel-default">
    <div class="panel-heading">
        <h4>@Model.UserName</h4>
    </div>
    <div class="panel-body">
        <div class="col-lg-4 col-md-4">
            <img src="@Model.AvatarUrlSample"
                class="img-circle img-responsive"
                alt="Click Image to view full profile" />

        </div>
        <div class="col-lg-8 col-md-8">
            <p>Country: @Model.Country</p>
            <p>Joined: @Model.CreateDate.ToString("MM/dd/yyyy")</p>
            <p>Views: @Model.ProfileViews</p>
        </div>
    </div>
</div>
```

The ArtistCard view page shown in Listing 8-14 also takes advantage of the Bootstrap library. The CSS classes panel, panel-default, panel-heading, and panel-body create a clean layout for the artist card. The name of the artist is displayed in the header. The body of the panel is split, with the image on the left taking up one-third of the area and stats about the artists displayed in the other two-thirds of the card. The Bootstrap panel feature is described in detail here:

http://getbootstrap.com/components/#panels

## Making the Custom Tag Helpers Visible to the Views

To use your custom Tag Helper in views for the project, the Tag Helpers need to be registered in the _ViewImports.cshtml file using the @addTagHelper directive, as shown in Listing 8-15. This will make all Tag Helpers defined in the assembly available to all views in the web application.

*Listing 8-15.* _ViewImports.cshtml

```
@using Recipe04.Web
@addTagHelper *, Microsoft.AspNetCore.Mvc.TagHelpers
@addTagHelper *, Recipe04.Web
```

## Adding the Controller Logic

The controller logic in this example is simple. In this case, it has been refactored for testability with all the LINQ queries to the data context being factored into a repository class in the data access layer. The controller class has a private member variable that holds the repository, which is passed into the constructor by ASP.NET Core's dependency injection system. For more information on the Repository and Unit of Work patterns used in this example, please refer to recipe 6-7. Listing 8-16 shows the code for the controller.

*Listing 8-16.* HomeController

```
using Microsoft.AspNetCore.Mvc;
using AspNetCoreMvcRecipes.Shared.DataAccess;

namespace Recipe03.Web.Controllers
{
    public class HomeController : Controller
    {
        IUnitOfWork _UnitOfWork;
        public HomeController(IUnitOfWork unitOfWork)
        {
            _UnitOfWork = unitOfWork;
        }

        public IActionResult Index()
        {
            var model = _UnitOfWork.ArtistRepository.GetNewArtists();
            return View("Index", model);
        }

        public IActionResult Error()
        {
            return View();
        }
    }
}
```

## Using the ColumnList Tag Helper in a View

You can now use the ColumnList Tag Helper in your views. To do this, modify the Home/Index.cshtml file to match Listing 8-17. In this case, you are creating a three-row grid. You can experiment with the Tag Helper by changing the value of the asp-number-of-columns attribute.

*Listing 8-17.* Index.cshtml Using the ColumnList Tag Helper

```
@model IList<AspNetCoreMvcRecipes.Shared.DataAccess.Artist>
@{
    ViewData["Title"] = "Home Page";
}

<h1>Chapter 08 - Recipe 03</h1>
<p>Below is an example of the Column List tag helper working in conjunction with the
ArtistCard View Component</p>
<hr />
```

```
<column-list asp-number-of-columns="3"
             asp-for="@Model"
             asp-view-component="ArtistCard"></column-list>
```

Figure 8-1 shows the results of the view.

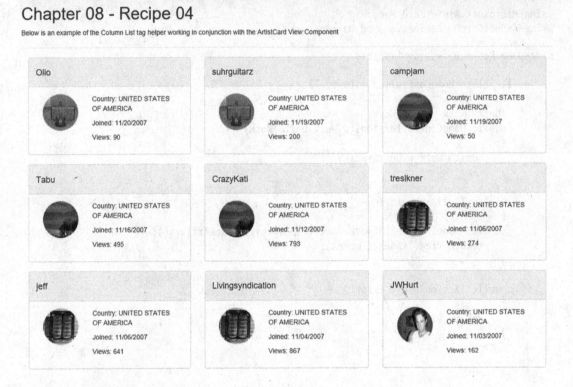

***Figure 8-1.*** *The output of the ColumnList Tag Helper*

Even though it took some effort to create the custom helper, the fact that you will be able to reuse this in many places in your project, and possibly in future projects, makes it worth it.

# 8-4. Creating a Data Grid with Paging, Sorting, and Filtering Support

## Problem

It can be said that the ASP.NET Web Forms DataView control is the bread and butter of most .NET-centric development shops using Web Forms. Many applications have pages that require paging, sorting, and filtering support. In Web Forms, this was as simple as dragging a DataView control from your toolbox to your design canvas and then adding some declarative data binding statements.

You finally convinced your boss to allow you to do your next project using ASP.NET Core MVC with Razor only to discover that there is no DataView control to drag. You need to figure out how to do this and get a prototype working before your next status meeting.

## Solution

Data grids are a well-defined pattern. There are hundreds of commercial and open source products that can get the job done. In fact, in modern web browsers, the performance of these solutions can be as smooth and interactive as that of native client applications. Some nice examples are at the following web sites:

- Kendo UI (http://bit.ly/1CWPWHL)

- jQx Grid (http://bit.ly/1cDJCzM)

If you do not want to invest in a commercial product or if you find that the products offer much more than you need, you can implement some rudimentary, grid-like functionality in ASP.NET Core MVC using a combination of view logic, Tag Helpers, and action filters.

In the view, you will create an HTML table for displaying your data. You will create Tag Helpers to provide navigation between pages of data in the grid and an action filter to encapsulate controller logic that will be shared across multiple grid pages.

## How It Works

I will start by discussing the features and drawbacks of the Web Forms GridView control. Next, I will show you how to create similar behavior using the ASP.NET Core MVC framework while avoiding some of the problems that can exist with the Web Forms GridView control.

### Features of the Web Forms GridView Control

The Web Forms GridView is packed with functionality including sorting results, paging results, selecting rows, editing rows in place, and more. The default functionality allows the data in the grid to be sorted by clicking the column header and offers page numbers on the bottom of the grid to allow you to move between pages of result sets.

The GridView control offered a default layout that created HTML table columns for each of the columns in your record set. If the default template did not meet your needs, you could customize it by passing in a custom template.

The state of the GridView, including the data it displays, the current page number, and whether a row is selected, is tracked using ViewState. ViewState is an encoded representation of the GridView object that is passed back and forth between the server and the web browser on every request by way of a hidden form field.

The GridView is a great productivity feature for Web Forms developers, but it has some drawbacks including the following:

- The ViewState mechanism is required for most functionality. For a large data set, the ViewState mechanism can often be large, which can degrade performance because of all the additional data that needs to be passed between the browser and the server.

- As with most Web Forms controls, displaying changes in the UI required a round-trip to the server where server-side events are processed and the HTML is rendered and sent back to the browser.

- GridView controls are not search engine friendly. Moving between pages of data is done via server-side event processing with state maintained by the ViewState mechanism. It does not offer a unique URL for each page that is easy for a search engine to index.

- Advanced customization is possible but can get very complex.

## Features of the ASP.NET Core MVC Grid View

One of the major benefits of ASP.NET Core MVC over Web Forms is clean HTML without the need to use mechanisms such as ViewState to maintain state. You also have full control of the URLs and can design a URL scheme that is friendly to search engines and intuitive to end users. It is also relatively straightforward to design a grid that does not require full-page refreshes when navigating pages of data. This is demonstrated in recipe 11-4, which shows how to create an Ajax-based data grid.

For this example, you will focus on a more traditional navigation structure designed to be optimal for end users and search engines. It will contain the following features:

- Each page in the result set should have a specific URL.

- You will also include route parameters for sort order and for filters.

- In addition to the grid, you will offer a set of search facets on the side of the page that will allow the user to filter the results by clicking links.

- Clicking the column header will change the sort of the result set.

- A pager on the bottom of the grid will allow navigation between pages of data.

## Performance Considerations for Working with Large Data Sets

A common mistake made by web developers is retrieving a large result set from the database, then filtering and sorting the data at the application layer, and finally sending only a small portion of that result set to the browser. This process is less than optimal for a few reasons. First, this adds a significant unnecessary load on your network. It also adds extra stress on both your database server and application servers that will need to retrieve and process all this data. It is always much better to perform all the sorting and filtering at the database when possible. Databases such as SQL Server have been optimized to perform these types of operations.

Starting with SQL Server 2012, Microsoft simplified the process of writing queries to allow you to select a specific window of data with the introduction of the Offset and Fetch keywords. Listing 8-18 shows a SQL Server query that would return the second page of data from a sorted result.

***Listing 8-18.*** Fetching a Page of Data from a Sorted Result in SQL Server

```
select title, [description] from CollaborationSpace
order by CreateDate
offset 10 rows fetch next 10 rows only
```

On older versions of SQL Server, a similar but slightly more complex query could be constructed using the SQL Server ROW_NUMBER() function. Listing 8-19 shows an example of this technique.

***Listing 8-19.*** Fetching a Page of Data Using the ROW_NUMBER Function in SQL Server

```
WITH CollaborationSpaceList AS
(
SELECT ROW_NUMBER() OVER( Order by CreateDate) as rownumber, title, [description] from
CollaborationSpace
)
SELECT * FROM CollaborationSpaceList
WHERE rownumber between 11 and 20
```

If you are using Entity Framework Core, its query generator will generate the query for you automatically when you use the Skip and Take expressions. Even though Entity Framework hides these details from you, understanding the queries Entity Framework generates can help you troubleshoot issues in your application.

Another important performance consideration is to make sure you are returning only the columns that you require for your page. This is especially important if the tables you are querying have many columns or if they contain data types such as varchar(max) or varbinary(max). For example, if you are querying a table that contains a list of documents to display the title and a link to a details page but are pulling down the entire row including the document itself, this would be extremely wasteful.

Entity Framework Core can help you here as well by allowing you to specify only a subset of columns in your query and then writing the results to an anonymous class that contains only a subset of the fields required. There are a few drawbacks to using anonymous types, however.

- You cannot use an anonymous type in a strongly typed Razor view because the Razor views do not have visibility in the definition of the anonymous type at runtime and will throw a parsing error if you attempt to reference the properties of that type in your view.

- If the anonymous type was defined in a different assembly, such as your data access assembly, it would not be visible to your web application. This is because anonymous classes are defined as Internal.

A workaround for both problems is to define an explicit type and to use it as the return type of the LINQ expression. In the Shared Data Access library used by many examples in this book, there is a subfolder called facade that contains a number of classes to be used in situations where only a small subset of records is required.

## The Data Access Code

For this recipe, the query logic needed to support the grid has been factored out into the data access layer. The design of the data access layer allows the ASP.NET Core MVC developer to access entities via a set of repository classes exposed by a class called UnitOfWork. This allows for access for more than one repository while using a single instance of the DbContext object. In addition to a set of generic repository functions, the data access layer also contains several static query methods that encapsulate some of the commonly

271

used and complex queries. Listing 8-20 shows the GetActiveCollaborationSpaces method from the CollaborationSpaceRepository class in the data access layer.

***Listing 8-20.*** The GetActiveCollaborationSpaces Method of the CollaborationSpaceRepository Class

```
public List<CollaborationSpaceSearchResult> GetActiveCollaborationSpaces(CollaborationSpace
SearchParams filter, out int resultsFound)
{
    if (filter == null)
        throw new ArgumentNullException("filter");

    var collabSpacesQuery = from a in _context.CollaborationSpaces
        join o in _context.CollaborationSpaceGenres
        on a.CollaborationSpaceId equals o.CollaborationSpaceId
        join p in _context.ArtistCollaborationSpaces
        on a.CollaborationSpaceId equals p.CollaborationSpaceId
        join artist in _context.Artists
        on p.ArtistId equals artist.ArtistId
        where a.Status != ProjectStatus.Canceled &&
            a.Status != ProjectStatus.OnHold &&
            a.Status != ProjectStatus.Published &&
            a.AllowPublicView == true &&
            p.IsCreator == true
        select new CollaborationSpaceSearchResult()
        {
            CollaborationSpaceId = a.CollaborationSpaceId,
            CreateDate = a.CreateDate,
            Description = a.Description,
            LastPostDate = a.LastPostDate,
            ModifiedDate = a.ModifiedDate,
            NumberComments = a.NumberComments,
            NumberViews = a.NumberViews,
            RestrictContributorsToBand =.RestrictContributorsToBand,
            Status = a.Status,
            Title = a.Title,
            GenreLookUpId = o.GenreLookUpId,
            UserName = artist.UserName,
            WebSite = artist.WebSite,
            AvatarURL = artist.AvatarUrl
        };

    if (filter.GenreFilter != null)
    {
        // using a custom utility to build OR clause
        // allows filtering based on more than one item
        collabSpacesQuery = collabSpacesQuery.Where(
            LinqUtilities.BuildOrExpression<CollaborationSpaceSearchResult,
            int>(p => p.GenreLookUpId, filter.GenreFilter));
    }
```

```
        // First round trip to the database that runs a query to
        // get the count
        resultsFound = collabSpacesQuery==null ? 0 : collabSpacesQuery.Count();
        int skip = getSkip(filter.CurrentPageNumber, filter.ItemsPerPage);

        // using a custom extension method to simplify sorting
        collabSpacesQuery =
                collabSpacesQuery.OrderByText(filter.SortExpression).Skip(skip).Take(filter.
                ItemsPerPage);

        // second round trip to the database retrieves (count) 10 records
        return collabSpacesQuery == null ?  null : collabSpacesQuery.ToList();

}

private int getSkip(int page, int count)
{
    if (page < 2)
    {
      return 0;
    }
      else
    {
      return page * count;
    }
}
```

There are few details to note about the LINQ queries in Listing 8-20.

- The query is taking advantage of Entity Framework's support for enums.
  This simplifies the life of the programmer and increases readability.

- Rather than using an anonymous type, an explicit type named
  CollaborationSpaceSearchResult was created in a separate class file.

- A custom extension method named OrderByText is used that allows you to pass a
  string (rather than an expression) as the order by clause. This dramatically reduces
  the amount of code that needs to be maintained for this class. It also increases your
  flexibility, making it easy to add additional sort options at the view level without
  needing to make additional changes in either the controller or the repository. The
  downside is that it increases the likelihood of a typo in a property name, resulting in
  a runtime error.

- Most important, you have added the Skip and Take modifiers to the query. This
  allows LINQ to create database queries that will only return the number of rows
  needed to render a page.

- Since the query is not pulling back the entire record set, an additional query is
  required to get the count by calling collabSpacesQuery.Count().

- Another helper function, LinqUtilities.BuildOrExpression, is used to implement
  the filtering by genres. In this example, you will allow the user to filter by a variable
  list of genres. The utility function simplifies your LINQ query by allowing an
  IEnumerable object to be passed in.

You can find the code for custom LINQ extensions in the Util folder of the Shared.DataAccess access project.

---

■ **Tip** It may not always be obvious which LINQ statements trigger calls to the database. If you are not sure what LINQ to Entities is doing, it is a good practice to use a tool such as SQL Monitor, which is included as part of the SQL Server tools. SQL Monitor allows you to see what queries are being run against your database. If you notice that more queries are being run than you expect, you may need to adjust your code.

---

## Creating the Model

Now you will create a new class in the web application to act as the model. The model consists of several classes. The first, CollaborationSpaceSearchResult, is defined in the data access layer and represents each row of data in your grid. It is used in Listing 8-14 in place of an anonymous type. The second class, CollaborationSpaceSearchResultModel, contains a list of CollaborationSpaceSearchResult objects and a list of GenreLookUp objects. The GenreLookUp type is an Entity class defined in the data access layer assembly.

The remaining items in the model represent the state of the page, including the number of search results found, the current page number, the filter expression, and the sort expression used. Listing 8-21 shows both classes.

***Listing 8-21.*** Models Used with the Data Grid

```
using AspNetCoreMvcRecipes.Shared.DataAccess;
using AspNetCoreMvcRecipes.Shared.DataAccess.Facade;
using System.Collections.Generic;

namespace Recipe05.Models
{
    public class CollaborationSpaceSearchResultModel
    {
        public IList<CollaborationSpaceSearchResult>
                CollaborationSpaceSearchResults
        { get; set; }
        public IList<GenreLookUp> GenreLookUpList { get; set; }
        public int NumberOfResults { get; set; }
        public string ResultsDescription { get; set; }
        public int ItemsPerPage { get; set; }
        public int CurrentPage { get; set; }
        public string SortExpression { get; set; }
        public int GenreLookUpId { get; set; }
        public int TotalPages
        {
            get
            {
                if (ItemsPerPage != 0)
                {
                    return NumberOfResults / ItemsPerPage;
                }
```

```
                return 0;
            }
        }
    }
}
```

# Creating the Controller

With most of the heavy lifting moved out to the repository class, the controller logic is somewhat simplistic. One thing to notice is that all the primitive types passed as parameters to the controller are set as nullable (int?). This is required so that the MVC data binder can assign null values to properties that are bound to empty fields. If you do not make your primitive types nullable, a runtime error will occur if the parameters are missing.

The first few lines of code in the method body check whether the nullable types have values and, if not, assign a default value. You then create an instance of your CollaborationSpaceSearchResultModel model class. After creating the instance of the model, you then make the calls to the repository. The results of the queries are then used to populate the model. Listing 8-22 shows the controller action.

***Listing 8-22.*** Controller Logic for Data Grid

```
using System.Collections.Generic;
using Microsoft.AspNetCore.Mvc;
using AspNetCoreMvcRecipes.Shared.DataAccess;
using Recipe05.Models;
using AspNetCoreMvcRecipes.Shared.DataAccess.Facade;

namespace Recipe05.Controllers
{
    public class HomeController : Controller
    {
        private IUnitOfWork _UnitOfWork;
        public HomeController(IUnitOfWork unitOfWork)
        {
            _UnitOfWork = unitOfWork;
        }

        public IActionResult Index(int? Page,
                                   string SortExpression,
                                   bool? Acsending,
                                   List<int> Genres)
        {
            // set default values for all optional  parameters
            var safePage = Page ?? 1;
            var safeSortExpression =
                string.IsNullOrEmpty(SortExpression) ? "CreateDate" : SortExpression;
            bool useDefaultSort = Acsending.HasValue ? Acsending.Value : true;

            var resultsFound = 0;
            var model = new CollaborationSpaceSearchResultModel();
            var search =
              new CollaborationSpaceSearchParams
```

```
        {
            SortExpression = safeSortExpression,
            CurrentPageNumber = safePage,
            ItemsPerPage = 10,
            GenreFilter = Genres
        };

    model.CollaborationSpaceSearchResults =
    _UnitOfWork.CollaborationSpaceRepository.GetActiveCollaborationSpaces(search,
                                out resultsFound);
    model.NumberOfResults = resultsFound;
    model.GenreLookUpList =
        (IList<GenreLookUp>)_UnitOfWork.GenreLookUpRepository.Query();
    model.CurrentPage = safePage;
    model.ItemsPerPage = 10;
    model.SortExpression = safeSortExpression;

    // if a filter has been selected add to the model
    // so we can show what filter is selected in the view
    if (Genres != null && Genres.Count > 0)
    {
        model.GenreLookUpId = Genres[0];
    }

    model.ResultsDescription =
    string.Format("Displaying records {0} - {1} of {2} sorted by {3}",
        (safePage * 10),
        (safePage * 10) + 10,
        resultsFound,
        safeSortExpression);
    return View("Index", model);
}

public IActionResult Error()
{
    return View();
}
    }
}
```

## Creating the View

The view is divided into two sections. On the left side of the screen is a list of musical genres. Clicking the genre name will filter the items in the grid. The rest of the page consists of the grid itself.

The view is strongly typed with the type Recipe05.Models.CollaborationSpaceSearchResultModel, which was shown in Listing 8-21.

The layout of the view is built around the Bootstrap CSS grid system. Bootstrap is a CSS and JavaScript library created by Twitter. It is included by default in the Visual Studio web application template. Its responsive grid system allows you to divide a page into 12 columns. For your view, you will split the page in two with a two-column-wide section used to display the search facets and a ten-column-wide section to display the data grid.

To do this, you first define a parent DIV element and assign it the class row. You then add a child DIV element that uses the Bootstrap col-lg-2 and col-md-2 classes. You can apply multiple CSS classes to an element by using the HTML class attribute, with each class name separated by a space. Doing this adds both sets of styles to the target element. By using the col-lg-2 and col-md-2 classes, you are telling the Bootstrap grid system that for large- and medium-sized screens display this section as a separate column but for smaller displays stack it vertically. For more information on the Bootstrap grid system, please see http://getbootstrap.com/css/#grid.

Inside the DIV element, you then create an unordered list and use a foreach loop to display a list of links. Inside the loop, you check the GenreLookUpId of each item to see whether it matches the GenreLookUpId value of the model. If it matches, you display a selected check box icon; otherwise, you display an unselected one. Here again you are taking advantage of functionality in the Bootstrap framework. In this case, you are using the glyph icons. Glyph icons are a set of icons implemented as a font. When you apply the Bootstrap glyphicon classes to a SPAN element, the icon selected will be displayed. For example, <span class="glyphicon glyphicon-check"></span> displays a check mark icon. Figure 8-2 shows the results of using the glyph icons after the Heavy Metal genre has been selected.

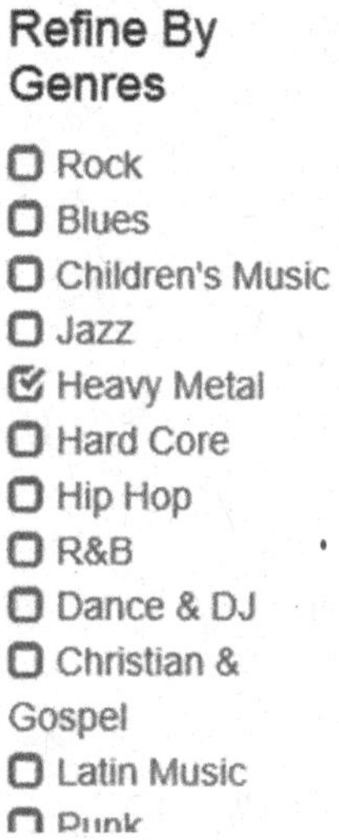

## Refine By
## Genres

- ☐ Rock
- ☐ Blues
- ☐ Children's Music
- ☐ Jazz
- ☑ Heavy Metal
- ☐ Hard Core
- ☐ Hip Hop
- ☐ R&B
- ☐ Dance & DJ
- ☐ Christian & Gospel
- ☐ Latin Music
- ☐ Punk

*Figure 8-2.* *Displaying the check box icon using Bootstrap glyph icons*

Inside the second column you will place the data grid. As you may expect, the grid is defined as an HTML table. You will style the table using the Bootstrap table and table-striped CSS classes. The table class defines the padding and spacing of the HTML table's rows and columns. The table-striped class will apply alternate coloring for each table row, making it easier to see the boundaries for each record displayed in the table.

Inside the table, the first thing defined is the headers. Each header uses the action link Tag Helper to create a link to the Index action but with different sort parameters. It also ensures that the current filter is preserved. Additionally, the Page route parameter is hard-coded to the value 1 to ensure that the first data page will be displayed after a sort occurs.

```
<a asp-action="Index"
                asp-route-Genres="@Model.GenreLookUpId"
                asp-route-Page="1"
                asp-route-SortExpression="Title">Collaboration Space</a>
```

After the table header, a foreach statement iterates through the record set, rendering each item in a table row. Listing 8-23 shows the view.

***Listing 8-23.*** View Containing Data Grid That Supports Filtering and Sorting

```
@model Recipe05.Models.CollaborationSpaceSearchResultModel
@{
    ViewData["Title"] = "ASP.NET Core MVC Recipes Data Grid";
}
<h1>Data Grid Example</h1>
<p>
    This example shows how you could replace the GridView control when used as a read only
    list that supports filtering and
    paging and sorting.
</p>

<h3>@Model.ResultsDescription</h3>
<div class="row">
    <div class="col-lg-2 col-md-2">
        <h4>Refine By Genres</h4>
        <ul class="list list-unstyled">
            @foreach (var item in Model.GenreLookUpList)
            {
                <li>
                    <a href="@Url.Action("Index",
                    new { Genres = item.GenreLookUpId , Page = 1,
                    SortExpression = Model.SortExpression })">
                        @if (Model.GenreLookUpId == item.GenreLookUpId)
                        {
                            <span class="glyphicon glyphicon-check"></span>
                        }
                        else
                        {
                            <span class="glyphicon glyphicon-unchecked"></span>
                        }
                        @item.GenreName
                    </a>
                </li>
            }
        </ul>
    </div>
    <div class="col-lg-10 col-md-10">
        <table class="table table-striped">
            <tr>
                <th>
                    <a asp-action="Index"
                    asp-route-Genres="@Model.GenreLookUpId"
                    asp-route-Page="1"
                    asp-route-SortExpression="Title">Collaboration Space</a>
                </th>
```

```
        <th>
            <a asp-action="Index"
                asp-route-Genres="@Model.GenreLookUpId"
                asp-route-Page="1"
                asp-route-SortExpression="UserName">Artist</a>
        </th>
        <th>
            <a asp-action="Index"
                asp-route-Genres="@Model.GenreLookUpId"
                asp-route-Page="1"
                asp-route-SortExpression="CreateDate">Created</a>
        </th>
        <th>
            <a asp-action="Index"
                asp-route-Genres="@Model.GenreLookUpId"
                asp-route-Page="1"
                asp-route-SortExpression="ModifiedDate">Modified</a>
        </th>
        <th>
            <a asp-action="Index"
                asp-route-Genres="@Model.GenreLookUpId"
                asp-route-Page="1"
                asp-route-SortExpression="NumberViews">Stats</a>
        </th>
    </tr>
    @foreach (var item in Model.CollaborationSpaceSearchResults)
    {
        <tr>
            <td>@item.Title</td>
            <td>@item.UserName</td>
            <td>@item.CreateDate.ToString("MM/dd/yyyy")</td>
            <td>@item.ModifiedDate.ToString("MM/dd/yyyy")</td>
            <td>
                <ul class="ItemList">
                    <li>
                        Hits: @item.NumberViews
                    </li>
                    <li>
                        Posts: @item.NumberComments
                    </li>
                    <li>
                        Status: @item.Status
                    </li>
                </ul>

            </td>
        </tr>
    }
</table>
```

```
            <nav>
                <grid-pager asp-total-number-of-results="@Model.NumberOfResults"
                            asp-items-per-page="@Model.ItemsPerPage"
                            asp-current-page="@Model.CurrentPage"></grid-pager>
            </nav>
        </div>
</div>
```

## Creating the Numeric Pager

To facilitate paging on the data grid, you need to have a way for the user to navigate between the pages. The GridPager Tag Helper creates a pager that will display a maximum of 20 links at once. In addition, it displays links to the first and last pages of the page list. The tricky part is displaying the appropriate links, depending on what page in the list the user is viewing. For example, if you are on page 1, you would need to see the links for pages 1 through 20. If you are on page 15, you may want to see links for pages 6 through 26.

You may want to hide the pager if only a single page of results is displayed. If fewer than 20 pages of results are shown, you may want to hide the first and last page links.

The problem of hiding the pager is easy to solve. You can compare the total number of results to the number of items on a page. If the items per page is less than or equal to the number of pages, then you will return an empty string.

The next interesting bit of logic is determining the first and last pages that need to be displayed. This code has been factored out into the helper methods getStartPage and getEndPage, as shown in Listing 8-24. Once you have these values, you can use a loop to create the list of links, which outputs as an unordered list. The links themselves are created by using another helper method called buildActionLink. buildActionLink takes advantage of the HTML generator that is built into ASP.NET Core. To get an instance of the HTML generator, a constructor is added to GridPagerTagHelper that allows the ASP.NET Core dependency injection system to inject an instance of IHtmlGenerator. Listing 8-24 shows GridPagerTagHelper.

*Listing 8-24.* GridPagerTagHelper

```
using Microsoft.AspNetCore.Mvc.Rendering;
using Microsoft.AspNetCore.Mvc.ViewFeatures;
using Microsoft.AspNetCore.Razor.TagHelpers;
using Microsoft.AspNetCore.WebUtilities;
using Microsoft.Extensions.Primitives;
using System.Threading.Tasks;

namespace Recipe05.TagHelpers
{
    public class GridPagerTagHelper : TagHelper
    {
        public GridPagerTagHelper(IHtmlGenerator generator)
        {
            Generator = generator;
        }
        protected IHtmlGenerator Generator { get; }

        [HtmlAttributeName("asp-total-number-of-results")]
        public int TotalNumberOfResults { get; set; }
```

```
[HtmlAttributeName("asp-items-per-page")]
public int ItemsPerPage { get; set; } = 20;

[HtmlAttributeName("asp-current-page")]
public int CurrentPage { get; set; } = 1;

[HtmlAttributeName("asp-pager-css-class")]
public string PagerCssClass { get; set; } = "pagination";

[HtmlAttributeName("asp-active-css-class")]
public string ActiveCssClass { get; set; } = "active";

[HtmlAttributeNotBound]
[ViewContext]
public ViewContext ViewContext { get; set; }

public override async Task ProcessAsync(TagHelperContext context, TagHelperOutput output)
{
    if(TotalNumberOfResults <= ItemsPerPage)
    {
        // pager is not required so return nothing
        output.SuppressOutput();
        return;
    }
    if (ItemsPerPage == 0) throw new InvalidOperationException("ItemsPerPage must be
    greater than 0");

    int numberOfPages = TotalNumberOfResults / ItemsPerPage;
    var maxNumberOfPagesShown = 20;

    bool showFirstAndLast = numberOfPages > maxNumberOfPagesShown;
    int startPage = getStartPage(numberOfPages, CurrentPage);
    int endPage = getEndPage(numberOfPages, CurrentPage, startPage);

    output.TagName = "div";

    output.Content.AppendHtml(string.Format("<ul class={0}>", PagerCssClass));
    if (showFirstAndLast && startPage > 1)
    {
        output.Content.AppendHtml("<li>");
        output.Content.AppendHtml(buildActionLink("...", 1));
        output.Content.AppendHtml("</li>");
    }
    for (int i = startPage; i <= endPage; i++)
    {
        string PageLinkText = i.ToString();

        if (i != CurrentPage)
        {
            output.Content.AppendHtml("<li>");
            output.Content.AppendHtml(buildActionLink(PageLinkText, i));
        }
```

281

```
            else
            {
                output.Content.AppendHtml(string.Format(@"<li class=""{0}"">",
                        ActiveCssClass));
                output.Content.AppendHtml(string.Format(@"<a href=""#"">{0}</a>", i));
            }
            output.Content.AppendHtml(" </li>");

        }
        if (showFirstAndLast && (endPage != numberOfPages))
        {
            output.Content.AppendHtml("<li>");
            output.Content.AppendHtml(buildActionLink("...", numberOfPages));
            output.Content.AppendHtml("</li>");
        }
        output.Content.AppendHtml("</ul>");
    }
  }
}
```

Listing 8-25 shows the getStartPage and getEndPage methods. In the getStartPage method, you first check the current page. If it is greater than ten, you will place the current page near the middle of the list by making the start page nine less than the current page. If you are nearing the end of the list, you need to make sure that the start page stays 20 pages behind the end page. This prevents you from creating links to pages that do not exist. Lastly, if you are on one of the first ten pages, you will always start your counter on page 1.

The calculation for the end page is less complicated. You might be tempted to think that you can just add 20 to the start page, and then you are done. Unfortunately, this will not work because if you have only 16 pages of results and you started on page 1, you would end up creating four extra links to pages that do not exist. The getEndPage method solves this problem by checking to see whether your calculated last page is greater than the total number of pages. If so, it will subtract the overage.

A final check in the getEndPage method determines whether you are on one of the last ten pages. In this case, you need to always show all the remaining pages.

***Listing 8-25.*** Getting the First and Last Pages

```
private int getStartPage(int numberOfPages, int currentPage)
{
    int minToDisplay = 1;
    if (currentPage > 10)
    {
        minToDisplay = currentPage - 9;
    }
    if (currentPage > (numberOfPages - 10) && (numberOfPages > 20))
    {
        minToDisplay = numberOfPages - 20;
    }
    return minToDisplay;
}

private int getEndPage(int numberOfPages, int currentPage, int startPage)
{
    int maxToDisplay = startPage + 19;
```

```
    if (maxToDisplay > numberOfPages)
    {
        maxToDisplay = maxToDisplay - (maxToDisplay - numberOfPages);
    }
    if ((currentPage > numberOfPages - 10) && (startPage != 1))
    {
        maxToDisplay = numberOfPages;
    }
    return maxToDisplay;
}
```

The last bit of logic needed for the grid is the method used to create the action links. Since you are inside a Tag Helper extension method, you do not know what controller action you need to link to. Luckily, you can derive this information by inspecting the RouteData collection of the ViewContext property. Calling ViewContext.RouteData.Values["action"] gives you the name of the current action. Similarly, ViewContext.RouteData.Values["controller"] will give you the current controller. You can then use that value to construct the action link.

Also, since you are using the query string to preserve the state of your grid, you will need to copy existing query string values to each link you build. To do this, you first check to see whether there are values in the query string by using the HasValue method. This method returns true if values are found. You then use the existing query string values to build the query string for the links. Listing 8-26 shows the buildActionLink method.

*Listing 8-26.* The buildActionLink HTML Helper

```
private TagBuilder buildActionLink(string linkText, int page)
{
        if(ViewContext.HttpContext.Request.QueryString.HasValue)
        {
            var queryString = QueryHelpers.ParseQuery(ViewContext.HttpContext.Request.Query
            String.Value);
            StringValues sort, categoryId;
            queryString.TryGetValue("SortExpression", out sort);
            queryString.TryGetValue("Genres", out categoryId);
            return Generator.GenerateActionLink(
                ViewContext,
                linkText: linkText,
                actionName: ViewContext.RouteData.Values["action"].ToString(),
                controllerName: ViewContext.RouteData.Values["controller"].ToString(),
                protocol: null,
                hostname: null,
                fragment: null,
                routeValues: new
                {
                    SortExpression = sort,
                    Genres = categoryId,
                    Page = page
                },
                htmlAttributes: null);
        }
```

```
        return Generator.GenerateActionLink(
                ViewContext,
                linkText: linkText,
                actionName: ViewContext.RouteData.Values["action"].ToString(),
                controllerName: ViewContext.RouteData.Values["controller"].ToString(),
                protocol: null,
                hostname: null,
                fragment: null,
                routeValues: new
                {
                    Page = page
                },
                htmlAttributes: null);
}
```

Now that you have built a Tag Helper that creates a pager for the data grid, you can add it to the view. For this to work, you will first need to register the Tag Helper in the ViewImports.cshtml file using the @addTagHelper directive.

```
@addTagHelper *, Recipe05
```

Next you will need to add a call to GridPagerTagHelper, as shown in Listing 8-27, to display the pager below the data grid.

**Listing 8-27.** Adding the Numeric Pager Below the Data Grid

```
<nav>
        <grid-pager asp-total-number-of-results="@Model.NumberOfResults"
                    asp-items-per-page="@Model.ItemsPerPage"
                    asp-current-page="@Model.CurrentPage"></grid-pager>
</nav>
```

You may have noted from Listing 8-24 that the Tag Helper had default values for several properties including PagerCssClass, which allows you to specify CSS classes for the pager. The default values for these arguments are the class names that are part of the Bootstrap CSS framework. Leaving the default values will leverage the Bootstrap styles and will render the counter, as shown in Figure 8-3.

| | | | | |
|---|---|---|---|---|
| | | | | • Posts: 195<br>• Status: Active |
| Drum Recording | Henkjan | 11/25/2008 | 8/28/2012 | • Hits: 2878<br>• Posts: 195<br>• Status: Active |
| Drum Recording | Henkjan | 11/25/2008 | 8/28/2012 | • Hits: 2878<br>• Posts: 195<br>• Status: Active |
| Drum Recording | Henkjan | 11/25/2008 | 8/28/2012 | • Hits: 2878<br>• Posts: 195<br>• Status: Active |
| Drum Recording | Henkjan | 11/25/2008 | 8/28/2012 | • Hits: 2878<br>• Posts: 195<br>• Status: Active |

```
...  5  6  7  8  9  10  11  12  13  14  15  16  17  18  19  20  21  22  23  24  ...
```

*Figure 8-3.* *Numeric pager styled using Bootstrap*

## Making Friendly URLs for Paging and Sorting

As mentioned earlier in this section, one of the goals of your data grid would be to have clean URLs that both humans and search engines can easily understand. In the current implementation, since you have not changed any of the routing configuration, the route parameters Page, Genres, and SortExpression that you defined on the Index controller action in Listing 8-16 will be exposed as query string arguments, such as the following:

```
http://localhost:3243/?Genres=40&Page=1&SortExpression=CreateDate
```

To create the clean URL, you can use ASP.NET Core MVC's attribute routing system to specify a new URL pattern. To do this, modify the Index action in the Home controller, as shown in Listing 8-28.

*Listing 8-28.* Adding Attribute Routes to Home Controller

```
[Route("/{Page?}/{SortExpression?}/{Genres?}")]
public IActionResult Index(int? Page,
                           string SortExpression,
                           bool? Acsending,
                           string Genres
)
```

Note the question marks in the route template after each of the route arguments in Listing 8-28. They tell the routing engine that these are optional arguments. If you omitted the question marks, the default route would no longer match your index routes, and the URLs ~/, ~/Home, and ~/Home/Index would result in a "page not found" error.

# 8-5. Creating a Data Grid That Allows Inline Editing

## Problem

Coming from a Web Forms background, you normally use a `GridView` control for implementing grids that allow inline editing of rows. You want to understand how to do this using ASP.NET Core MVC.

## Solution

Since the ASP.NET Core MVC framework does not use server controls such as the `GridView` control, you will need to create this functionality. Luckily, with the help of a few HTML Helpers, it is a relatively straightforward implementation that requires the following steps:

1. Create a model that represents the data that you want to view and edit in your grid view. Alternatively, you can use a class or entity defined in an external library.

2. Create an HTML Helper that will encapsulate the substitution of read-only rows with editable rows when a row is selected for editing.

3. Create the view that will display the editable grid.

As another option, you can combine the techniques shown in this recipe with recipe 8-5 to create a full data grid solution that supports editing, filtering, sorting, and paging. Note that it is also possible to do this using a custom Tag Helper, but the implementation is somewhat more complex.

## How It Works

In addition to allowing you to have a read-only data grid with paging and sorting capabilities, the ASP.NET Web Forms `GridView` control also allowed you to select a row for editing, make changes to the data in the row, and then save the changes. To replicate this functionality in ASP.NET Core MVC, you will need to create a model that not only represents the data needed to display but also allows you to specify which row is selected. You also need to track the changes in the model so that you can make changes to the rows that have changed.

You should also create some reusable components that can be used on several pages. This will simplify your views by removing the need for some conditional logic while increasing your productivity and increasing maintainability for the application.

For this example, you will create several HTML Helper extensions that will check to see whether a row is selected and, if selected, replace the display with the appropriate editor for the field's data type.

## The HTML Helpers

The logic for the in-place editing helpers is simple. You will create an HTML Helper to match the out-of-the-box xxxFor Tag Helper. For example, for the `EditorFor` method, you will create a `DataGridEditorFor` method. Each of the helpers will take two parameters: a `bool` value that indicates whether the item is selected and an expression that represents the field you want to display or edit.

If you want to follow along with this example, open the code example from the code samples downloaded from the book's web site. If you prefer, you can also access this code sample from GitHub at the following URL:

```
https://github.com/johnciliberti/AspNetCoreRecipes/tree/master/Chapter08/Recipe06
```

After opening the project, create a folder named HtmlHelpers. Right-click the new folder and select Add a Class. Name the class EditInPlaceHelpers. Since this class will contain extension methods, it must be declared as public static class. Each method must also be declared as public and static and will return an IHtmlContent. For you to follow the pattern used by the built-in HTML Helper extensions, your method signatures need to follow this format:

```
xxxxFor<TModel, TProperty>(this IHtmlHelper<TModel> helper,
            Expression<Func<TModel, TProperty>> expression) where TModel : class
```

This ugly signature is the magic that allows HTML Helpers to be strongly typed. TModel represents the type you are passing to the helper, and TProperty is the property of the class that you are evaluating. The inclusion of this IHtmlHelper<TModel> helper in each helper tells the compiler which class to add the extension to. The expression parameter is what allows a lambda expression to be passed in rather than a static property. This adds the additional flexibility.

In the body of the helper method, first check the value of the isSelected parameter. If it is set to true, call EditorFor, one of the built-in HTML Helpers. This helper will render the appropriate HTML input type for the property passed in the expression property. If isSelected is false, then the built-in DisplayFor helper is used to render the property as text.

Listing 8-29 shows the completed class.

*Listing 8-29.* The EditInPlace Helpers

```
using Microsoft.AspNetCore.Html;
using Microsoft.AspNetCore.Mvc.Rendering;
using System;
using System.Linq.Expressions;

namespace Recipe05.HtmlHelpers
{
    public static class EditInPlaceHelpers
    {
        // returns the default editor for the property    when isSelected
        // is true
        public static IHtmlContent DataGridEditorFor<TModel, TProperty>
                        (this IHtmlHelper<TModel> helper,
                         bool isSelected,
                         Expression<Func<TModel, TProperty>> expression)
                         where TModel : class
        {
            if (isSelected)
            {
                return helper.EditorFor(expression);
            }
            else
            {
                return helper.DisplayFor(expression);
            }
        }
```

```
        // returns a text box for the property when isSelected
        // is true
        public static IHtmlContent DataGridTextBoxFor<TModel, TProperty>
                            (this IHtmlHelper<TModel> helper,
                            bool isSelected,
                            Expression<Func<TModel, TProperty>> expression)
                            where TModel : class
    {
        if (isSelected)
        {
            return helper.TextBoxFor(expression);
        }
        else
        {
            return helper.DisplayFor(expression);
        }
    }

        // returns the default editor for the property when isSelected
        // is true
        public static IHtmlContent DataGridTextAreaFor<TModel, TProperty>
                            (this IHtmlHelper<TModel> helper,
                            bool isSelected,
                            Expression<Func<TModel, TProperty>> expression)
                            where TModel : class
    {
        if (isSelected)
        {
            return helper.TextAreaFor(expression);
        }
        else
        {
            return helper.DisplayFor(expression);
        }
    }
    }
}
```

# The Model

The model for the solution contains a list of ArtistSkill objects that are defined by the entity data model from a library used by the project. It also keeps track of which item is selected and includes a helper method that allows a test to see whether the current item is selected. This was necessary to simplify the view logic. To create the model, right-click the Models folder in the Recipe06 project and select Add a Class. Name the class InlineEditingArtistSkillListModel. Listing 8-30 shows the completed model.

***Listing 8-30.*** Inline Editing Model

```
using AspNetCoreMvcRecipes.Shared.DataAccess;
using System.Collections.Generic;

namespace Recipe05.Models
{
    public class InlineEditingArtistSkillListModel
    {
        public int SelectedRow { get; set; }
        public IEnumerable<ArtistSkill> ArtistSkillList { get; set; }
        public bool IsSelected(ArtistSkill item)
        {
            if (item == null)
                return false;
            return item.ArtistTalentId == SelectedRow;
        }
    }
}
```

# The Controller

The controller requires two actions to support the display and processing of the edited results. The first action supports HTTP GET and contains an optional parameter named Selected, which needs to be optional since no item will be selected when the page is first loaded.

The example uses a repository that is in the Models folder. The repository exposes two methods relevant to this recipe. The first, GetArtistSkill, returns a list of ArtistSkill objects for a given artist specified by the Id parameter. It also contains a method to update a skill, which takes an ArtistSkill object as a parameter. To keep the example a little less complex, the GET action is using a hard-coded Id parameter.

The HTTP POST version of the action, shown in Listing 8-31, takes a FormCollection as a parameter. Unfortunately, this method is not able to take advantage of the model binding since there will not be an exact match between the property names in the model and the names of the form fields being returned from the view. Because of this, you need to perform additional work in mapping the input fields to the property names.

***Listing 8-31.*** GridViewReplacementWithInplaceEditing Controller Actions

```
using System;
using Microsoft.AspNetCore.Mvc;
using AspNetCoreMvcRecipes.Shared.DataAccess;
using Recipe06.Models;
using Microsoft.AspNetCore.Http;

namespace Recipe06.Controllers
{
    public class HomeController : Controller
    {
        // make sure you add the service descriptor to StartUp.cs
        // ConfigureServices for this to work
        private IUnitOfWork _UnitOfWork;
        public HomeController(IUnitOfWork unitOfWork)
```

```
    {
        _UnitOfWork = unitOfWork;
    }

    public IActionResult Index()
    {
        return View();
    }

    public IActionResult GridViewReplacementWithInplaceEditing(int? Selected)
    {
        // hard code artistId for this example
        var skills = _UnitOfWork.ArtistSkillRepository.Query(a => a.ArtistId == 2);
        var model = new InlineEditingArtistSkillListModel()
        {
            ArtistSkillList = skills
        };
        if (Selected.HasValue)
        {
            model.SelectedRow = Selected.Value;
        }
        return View("GridViewReplacementWithInplaceEditing", model);
    }

    [HttpPost]
    public IActionResult GridViewReplacementWithInplaceEditing(FormCollection collection)
    {
        ArtistSkill skill = new ArtistSkill();
        skill.ArtistId = Int32.Parse(collection["item.ArtistId"]);
        skill.ArtistTalentId = Int32.Parse(collection["item.ArtistTalentID"]);
        skill.TalentName = collection["item.TalentName"];
        skill.SkillLevel = Int32.Parse(collection["item.SkillLevel"]);
        skill.Details = collection["item.Details"];
        skill.Styles = collection["item.Styles"];
        _UnitOfWork.ArtistSkillRepository.Update(skill);
        return RedirectToAction("GridViewReplacementWithInplaceEditing");
    }

    public IActionResult Error()
    {
        return View();
    }
    }
}
```

## The View

The view is strongly bound to the Recipe06.Models.InlineEditingArtistSkillListModel type. It includes the standard @using(Html.BeginForm()) and @Html.ValidationSummary(), which wrap the grid table in an HTML form and provide an area for validation errors to be displayed.

Inside the grid, a foreach statement loops through each record in the model's `ArtistSkillList` property. The HTML Helper extensions are used to create your fields.

For the first column in your grid, you use a conditional statement to decide whether you should show a link for saving the form or a link to update the view's selected property. For the Edit link, you use a standard `ActionLink` specifying the talent that you want to edit, but for the Save link, you create an anchor tag that will submit the form when clicked. For the Save link use case, you also include several hidden fields so that you have the rest of the data required to update the field.

At the end of the view is a call to `@Scripts.Render("~/bundles/jqueryval")`, which provides the validation logic for the form. Listing 8-32 shows the view.

***Listing 8-32.*** GridViewReplacementWithInplaceEditing View

```
@model Recipe06.Models.InlineEditingArtistSkillListModel
@{
 ViewBag.Title = "Grid View Replacement With In place Editing";
}


<h1>@ViewBag.Title</h1>
Click the edit link to edit the row.
@using (Html.BeginForm())
{
    @Html.ValidationSummary()
    <table class="table table-striped">
        <tr>
            <th>

            </th>
            <th>
                Talent
            </th>
            <th>
                Level
            </th>
            <th>
                Details
            </th>
            <th>
                Musical Styles
            </th>
        </tr>

        @foreach (var item in Model.ArtistSkillList)
        {
            <tr>
                <td>
                    @if (Model.IsSelected(item))
                    {
                        <a href="#" onclick="document.forms[0].submit()">Save</a>
                        @Html.HiddenFor(modelItem => item.ArtistId)
                        @Html.HiddenFor(modelItem => item.ArtistTalentId)
                    }
```

```
                    else
                    {
                        @Html.ActionLink("Edit", "GridViewReplacementWithInplaceEditing",
                        new { Selected = item.ArtistTalentId })
                    }
                </td>
                <td>
                    @Html.DataGridTextBoxFor(Model.IsSelected(item), modelItem => item.TalentName)
                </td>
                <td>
                    @Html.DataGridEditorFor(Model.IsSelected(item), modelItem => item.SkillLevel)
                </td>
                <td>
                    @Html.DataGridTextAreaFor(Model.IsSelected(item), modelItem => item.Details)
                </td>
                <td>
                    @Html.DataGridEditorFor(Model.IsSelected(item), modelItem => item.Styles)
                </td>
            </tr>
        }

    </table>
}

@section Scripts {
    <script src="~/lib/jquery-validation/jquery.validate.js"></script>
}
```

The last bit of detail is the style sheet information needed to style the form and tables. While the table is using the built-in styles from the Bootstrap framework, some customization was required for the text area to be displayed properly. To add the custom style, modify the style sheet wwwroot/css/site.css. Listing 8-33 shows the CSS selectors added specifically for this example. The style targets only textarea and text input types inside table columns for tables assigned to the CSS class grid. It makes the form field stretch to fill the entire horizontal space of the table row and outlines the fields with a thin blue border.

*Listing 8-33.* Adding CSS to Customize Look or Text Area

```
.table td textarea {
        width:98%;
        border: 2px solid lightblue;
        height: 3em;
}
.table td input[type="text"], .grid td input[type="number"] {
        border: 2px solid lightblue;
        width: 98%;
        height: 2em;
}
```

Figure 8-4 shows the result of this work. Here you see a total of five rows, with the fourth row selected. Notice how the Level column is rendered as the new HTML5 number type. Clicking the up and down arrows will change the value of the number.

# Grid View Replacement With In place Editing

Click the edit link to edit the row.

| | Talent | Level | Details | Musical Styles |
|---|---|---|---|---|
| Edit | Guitar | 1 | I do the metal stuff the best but can play blues, funk, and other types of music pretty well. Guitar is my primary intrument. | Alternative,Blues,Metal,Rock, |
| Save | Bass Guitar | 2 | I can play basic bass parts and have gear for when needed. | Alternative,Blues,Metal,Rock |
| Edit | Songwriter | 2 | Not sure how to qualify my song writing abilties. Some people like the stuff I come up with, some don't. | Alternative,Blues,Metal,Rock, |
| Edit | Sound Designer | 2 | Create cool sounds on my My | Electronica, |
| Edit | Lyricist | 2 | I have been known to write some interesting lyrics (he he) | Alternative,Metal,Rock, |

**Figure 8-4.** *Data grid with in-place editing*

# CHAPTER 9

# Data Validation Using ASP.NET Core MVC

Almost all applications require some sort of validation. For web applications, validation may appear in several tiers, including within an HTML form, in controllers on the server, and even at the data tier implemented as constraints. One of the challenges you will face in designing your application is deciding on where validation should occur and how to reduce the duplication of efforts when you need to perform validation on multiple tiers. This chapter focuses on the different options for performing data validation with ASP.NET Core MVC. I will begin by covering the built-in validation features of Razor and the ASP.NET Core MVC model binder. I will then show how you can extend these features to meet the individual needs of your application.

## 9-1. Validating Form Data Using Data Annotations

### Problem

You are building a new application that allows people to sell T-shirts in your online store. The application will have a form to capture information about the T-shirts including the start and end dates of the sale, a T-shirt name, a description, and the price. You want to make sure that the information sellers provide is complete and in the expected format. You also want to make sure that the information is still validated when client-side scripting has been disabled. You want to avoid writing duplicate code across tiers when possible.

### Solution

ASP.NET Core has built-in features that allow simple validation rules to be applied to a model declaratively using attributes defined in the System.ComonentModel.DataAnnotations namespace. When the model class is used in a strongly typed view, HTML Helpers and Tag Helpers, which were discussed in Chapters 3 and 4, will generate HTML code that will work in conjunction with the jQuery Validation and jQuery Unobtrusive Validation libraries to provide client-side validation. ASP.NET Core MVC's model binding feature can also be used to validate the model on the server. This allows you to verify that the model state is valid in the controller. It is a best practice to always validate input on the server to protect against cases where JavaScript is disabled or a form is being submitted by an automated process such as a bot.

© John Ciliberti 2017
J. Ciliberti, *ASP.NET Core Recipes*, DOI 10.1007/978-1-4842-0427-6_9

# How It Works

In this section, you will learn at how to use data annotations and Razor Tag Helpers to create a form that has validation enforced on both the client and the server. The exercise will also expose some of the limitations of the data annotations approach. This solution will use the code generation tools in Visual Studio to generate much of your code.

## Create the Visual Studio Project

Create a new ASP.NET Core Web Application project (.NET Core 1.1) using the Web Application template with no authentication and no Docker support. Name the project and solution **Recipe01**. After the project has been created, right-click the Controllers folder in Solution Explorer and select Add ➤ Controller. You will be promoted to add the MVC dependencies. Click the Add button to enable the scaffolding features to your project. You can delete the ScaffoldingReadMe.txt file that was added to your project since all the suggestions in that document were already added to your project when you created it. Another thing to note is that a new controller has not been added to the project.

---

■ **Note** At the time of this writing, the Visual Studio tooling for ASP.NET MVC Core is still a work in progress. Much of the scaffolding functionality does not work as expected. You can think of the features that do work as a preview of what is to come in future releases.

---

## Creating the View Model

Create a new folder named ViewModels under the project root. Add a new class to the ViewModels folder named TShirtViewModel. Add properties to the class as described in Table 9-1. Use data annotations to implement the validation rules. You can also use the display attribute to customize the form.

**Table 9-1.** *Validation Requirements*

| Property Name | Data Type | Validation Rules |
|---|---|---|
| TShirtId | int | Autogenerated; do not display on the form. |
| SalesStartDate | DateTime | Needs to be a valid date in the format yyyy-MM-dd and should be before the SaleEndDate value. This field is required. |
| SaleEndDate | DateTime | Needs to be a valid date in the format yyyy-MM-dd and should be after the SaleEndDate value. This field is required. |
| Title | String | Required; must be at least 6 but no more than 30 characters long. Can contain only uppercase and lowercase letters. |
| Description | String | Must be at least 6 but no more than 255 characters long. |
| Price | decimal | Must be numeric with a value between 5 and 100. |
| SellerEmailAddress | String | Must be an e-mail address with a length of no more than 50 characters. |
| ConfirmSellerEmailAddress | String | Must be an e-mail address with a length of no more than 50 and must match the value of SellerEmailAddress. |
| AgreeToTermsAndConditions | bool | The check box must be selected. |

Listing 9-1 shows the completed view model. Note that not all of the requirements listed in Table 9-1 have been met.

***Listing 9-1.*** TShirtViewModel Implemented Using Data Attributes

```csharp
using System;
using System.ComponentModel.DataAnnotations;

namespace Recipe01.ViewModels
{
    public class TShirtViewModel
    {
        const string EmailAddressRegEx = @"^\w+([-+.']\w+)*@\w+([-.]\w+)*\.\w+([-.]\w+)*$";
        const string LettersOnlyRegEx = @"^[A-Z]+[a-zA-Z''-'\s]*$";

        [ScaffoldColumn(false)]
        public int TShirtId { get; set; }

        [Display(Name ="Start selling this item on:", Order = 3)]
        [DisplayFormat(DataFormatString = "{0:yyyy-MM-dd}", ApplyFormatInEditMode = true)]
        [Required]
        [DataType(DataType.Date)]
        public DateTime SaleStartDate { get; set; } = DateTime.Now;

        [Display(Name = "Stop selling this item on:", Order = 4)]
        [DisplayFormat(DataFormatString = "{0:yyyy-MM-dd}", ApplyFormatInEditMode = true)]
        [Required]
        [DataType(DataType.Date)]
        public DateTime SaleEndDate { get; set; } = DateTime.Now.AddDays(7);

        [Required]
        [Display(Name ="T-Shirt Name", Order = 1)]
        [StringLength(30, MinimumLength = 6,
                            ErrorMessage ="T-Shirt Name must have at least 6
                            characters but no more then 30." )]
        [RegularExpression(LettersOnlyRegEx , ErrorMessage = "The T-Shirt name can only
        contain letters")]
        public string Title { get; set; }

        [Required]
        [Display(Name = "T-Shirt Description", Order = 2)]
        [DataType(DataType.MultilineText)]
        [StringLength(255, MinimumLength = 6,
                            ErrorMessage = "Description must have at least 6 characters
                            but no more then 255.")]
        public string Description { get; set; }

        [Required]
        [Range(5,100)]
        [DataType(DataType.Currency)]
        public decimal Price { get; set; } = 5;
```

```
    [StringLength(50)]
    [DataType(DataType.EmailAddress)]
    [RegularExpression(EmailAddressRegEx, ErrorMessage ="Invalid email address.")]
    public string SellerEmailAddress { get; set; }

    [StringLength(50)]
    [DataType(DataType.EmailAddress)]
    [Compare("SellerEmailAddress")]
    public string ConfirmEmailAddress { get; set; }

    [Required]
    [Display(Name ="Accept to the terms and conditions.")]
    public bool AgreeToTermsAndConditions { get; set; } ;
    }
}
```

The following validation attributes have been used in Listing 9-1:

- Required: Makes the specified property required.

- Display: Allows you to change the default display name that will be generated by the Tag Helpers and HTML Helpers. This also allows you to specify the order that a property will be displayed on a form when the form is generated using scaffolding.

- DisplayFormat: Allows a format string to be specified. In Listing 9-1, the DisplayFormat attribute is used with the SaleStartDate and SaleEndDate properties to ensure that the dates are displayed in the yyyy-MM-dd format.

- Range: When used with numeric properties, allows you to specify the minimum and maximum values.

- StringLength: Allows you to specify the minimum and maximum lengths for a string property.

- DataType: Specifies the data type of property. If the data type has an associated template, Tag Helpers and HTML Helpers will use that template when generating the HTML for the property. For example, the SalesEndDate property uses the DataType.Date data type, which the Input Tag Helper uses to generate an INPUT element with the type attribute set to date.

- Compare: Ensures that the property being validated contains the same value as the property specified in the argument. In Listing 9-1, Compare is used to ensure that the ConfirmEmailAddress property matches the SellerEmailAddress property.

- RegularExpression: Validates that the property matches the specified regular expression.

Note that two of the requirements cannot be met using the built-in data annotations. First, you are not able to compare the two date fields to verify that SaleStartDate is before SaleEndDate. Recipe 9-3 shows how this issue can be corrected by having the model implement the IValidadableObject interface. The second requirement you are not able to meet is the ability to verify that AgreeToTermsAndConditions has been set to true. Recipe 9-2 demonstrates how the requirements can be met using a custom validation attribute.

# Scaffolding the Controller

Visual Studio has a set of built-in code generation tools that can automatically create controllers and views based on the properties of a class. Although most of the code generation functionality is designed to work with Entity Framework, you can also build forms based on Plain Old C# Objects (POCOs). To create a controller using the code generation features, right-click the Controllers folder and select Add ➤ Controller. Select the MVC Controller with the read/write actions template and then click Add. In the Add Controller window, name the controller TShirtController and then click Add.

After a few seconds, the autogenerated controller will appear in the code editor window. It contains actions for Index, Details, Create, Edit, and Delete. For Create, Edit, and Delete, actions are generated for both HTTP GET and HTTP POST. The HTTP GET version of each action is used to display the form, and the HTTP POST action is used to process the form data.

The HTTP POST actions are decorated with ValidateAntiforgeryToken attributes. The ValidateAntiforgeryToken attribute is designed to prevent cross-site request forgery (CSRF) attacks. In a CSRF attack, the attacker tricks the user into submitting a malicious request often by having an authenticated user click a link from an e-mail or social media post. The ValidateAntiforgeryToken attribute works by ensuring that the CSRF token included in the request is the expected value. The CSRF token is added to the request by using a hidden form field that contains a large random value generated using a cryptographically secure random number generator that is unique to each user session. To learn more about CSRF, see the following URL:

```
https://www.owasp.org/index.php/Cross-Site_Request_Forgery_(CSRF)_Prevention_Cheat_Sheet
```

While the generated code is a helpful starting point, it is not complete. For some reason, most likely for backward compatibility, the generated code uses ActionResult as the return type rather than IActionResult. Since this could compromise the ability of containers and test harnesses to inject different IActionResult implementations, you will change all the return types to IActionResult.

For now, you will only be implementing the Create action; you will also add a new action named CreateSuccess. Using this technique allows the success page to have a unique URL and protects against repeat submissions by users clicking the Refresh button.

The next change you need to make is that rather than having the HTTP POST methods accept IFormCollection as a model, you will use TShirtViewModel. When the form is submitted, the ASP.NET Core model binder will automatically pair the form data with the properties of the TShirtViewModel class. The model binder will also check the values of the properties against the validation rules applied to the model. If validation errors are found, they will be added to ModelErrorCollection, and the controller's ModelState. IsValid property will be set to false.

The model binder minimizes the code developers are required to write to implement server-side validation. In the HTTP POST version of the Create action, the only validation-specific code that you need to write is to check the value of the ModelState.IsValid property. Listing 9-2 shows the completed code.

*Listing 9-2.* TShirtController Create Actions

```
using Microsoft.AspNetCore.Mvc;
using Recipe01.ViewModels;

namespace Recipe01.Controllers
{
    public class TShirtController : Controller
    {
```

```
        // GET: TShirt/Create
        public ActionResult Create()
        {
            return View();
        }

        // POST: TShirt/Create
        [HttpPost]
        [ValidateAntiForgeryToken]
        public ActionResult Create(TShirtViewModel viewModel)
        {
            if(ModelState.IsValid)
            {
                return RedirectToAction("CreateSuccess", viewModel);
            }

            return View("Create", viewModel);
        }

        public IActionResult CreateSuccess(TShirtViewModel viewModel)
        {
            return View("CreateSuccess", viewModel);
        }
    }
}
```

## Scaffolding the View

Next, you create the views. For the Create view, you can take advantage of the Visual Studio code generation features to generate most of the code for you. To do this, follow these steps:

1.  Create a new folder under Views named TShirt.

2.  Right-click the TShirt folder and then select Add ➤ View.

3.  In the Add View window, change the view name to Create and select the Create template. For the Model class, select TShirtViewModel.

4.  Click Add to create the form.

After the code generator completes, you will see your new view in the code editor. Notice it used Tag Helpers to generate the form fields and has applied the layout conventions and CSS classes as required by the Bootstrap library. While the code generator created a good starting point and saved you a great deal of typing, it did not do everything you want. For example, the Description field was rendered as a standard input box rather than a text area. This is because no HTML template has been defined by the ASP.NET team that specifies that a TextArea tag be generated for the DataType.MultilineText data type. In fact, the scaffolding used the asp-for Tag Helper for all the properties. In some cases, asp-for will add the appropriate markup, but in other cases, such as the date fields, the generated HTML will contain an input element type attribute of date. Since each browser has implemented the date control differently, this setting will cause the date properties to be rendered differently in each browser leading to an inconsistent user experience. In most cases, you would want to replace the asp-for Tag Helpers with a specialized Tag Helper or front-end date picker widget. For simplicity here, you will keep the default.

After you correct the Description field, your form should match Listing 9-3.

*Listing 9-3.* TShirt Create View

```
@model Recipe01.ViewModels.TShirtViewModel

@{
    ViewData["Title"] = "Add New T-Shirt";
}

<h2>Add New T-Shirt</h2>

<form asp-action="Create">
    <div class="form-horizontal">
        <hr />
        <div asp-validation-summary="ModelOnly" class="text-danger"></div>
        <div class="form-group">
            <label asp-for="SaleStartDate" class="col-md-2 control-label"></label>
            <div class="col-md-10">
                <input asp-for="SaleStartDate" class="form-control" />
                <span asp-validation-for="SaleStartDate" class="text-danger"></span>
            </div>
        </div>
        <div class="form-group">
            <label asp-for="SaleEndDate" class="col-md-2 control-label"></label>
            <div class="col-md-10">
                <input asp-for="SaleEndDate" class="form-control" />
                <span asp-validation-for="SaleEndDate" class="text-danger"></span>
            </div>
        </div>
        <div class="form-group">
            <label asp-for="Title" class="col-md-2 control-label"></label>
            <div class="col-md-10">
                <input asp-for="Title" class="form-control" />
                <span asp-validation-for="Title" class="text-danger"></span>
            </div>
        </div>
        <div class="form-group">
            <label asp-for="Description" class="col-md-2 control-label"></label>
            <div class="col-md-10">
                <textarea asp-for="Description" class="form-control" rows="5"></textarea>
                <span asp-validation-for="Description" class="text-danger"></span>
            </div>
        </div>
        <div class="form-group">
            <label asp-for="Price" class="col-md-2 control-label"></label>
            <div class="col-md-10">
                <input asp-for="Price" class="form-control" />
                <span asp-validation-for="Price" class="text-danger"></span>
            </div>
        </div>
```

```
        <div class="form-group">
            <label asp-for="SellerEmailAddress" class="col-md-2 control-label"></label>
            <div class="col-md-10">
                <input asp-for="SellerEmailAddress" class="form-control" />
                <span asp-validation-for="SellerEmailAddress" class="text-danger"></span>
            </div>
        </div>
        <div class="form-group">
            <label asp-for="ConfirmEmailAddress" class="col-md-2 control-label"></label>
            <div class="col-md-10">
                <input asp-for="ConfirmEmailAddress" class="form-control" />
                <span asp-validation-for="ConfirmEmailAddress" class="text-danger"></span>
            </div>
        </div>
        <div class="form-group">
            <div class="col-md-offset-2 col-md-10">
                <div class="checkbox">
                    <input asp-for="AgreeToTermsAndConditions" />
                    <label asp-for="AgreeToTermsAndConditions"></label>
                </div>
            </div>
        </div>
        <div class="form-group">
            <div class="col-md-offset-2 col-md-10">
                <input type="submit" value="Create" class="btn btn-default" />
            </div>
        </div>
    </div>
</form>

<div>
    <a asp-action="Index">Back to List</a>
</div>

@section Scripts {
    @{await Html.RenderPartialAsync("_ValidationScriptsPartial");}
}
```

Note that the scaffolding has added a Scripts section to the page and used RenderPartialAsync to include the script references required for the validation scripts.

When you run the application and navigate to http://localhost:63079/TShirt/Create, you will see that all the validation rules are functioning as expected. The Date fields will use the browser's built-in data selector, and an error will be displayed if you attempt to add an invalid date. If you try to disable JavaScript, you will see that the rules are processed on the server.

# 9-2. Creating a Custom Validation Attribute

## Problem

You are creating a web application for the legal department of a software company that displays software license agreement forms. The form also has a check box that confirms that the user has accepted the licensing agreement. You want to use data annotations on the model to implement these rules but have found the required functionality is not available. You want the validation checks to occur during model validation along with the other validation rules.

## Solution

When the built-in data annotation validators do not meet your requirements, you can create custom validation attributes by creating a class that is derived from the abstract class `ValidationAttribute`. You can then override the `IsValid` method to implement the required validation logic.

Validation attributes are validated only on the server. If you want to also have client-side validation working in conjunction with your custom `ValidationAttribute`, the custom validation attribute class must also implement the `IClientModelValidator` interface and implement the `AddValidation` method. This solution also requires that you create a JavaScript function that extends the functionality of the jQuery Unobtrusive Validation library.

## How It Works

In this section, you will build a custom validation attribute and apply it to the model. Start by creating a new ASP.NET Core Web Application (.NET Core 1.1) project using the Web Application template with both the solution and the project named **Recipe02**. Ensure that no authentication is used and that Docker support is not enabled.

## Creating the Model

The model used in this recipe will represent a software licensing agreement. The model class will have four properties: `SoftwareProductName`, `LicenseAgreementText`, `LicenseeName`, and `AgreementAccepted`. To create the model, first create a new folder under the root of the Recipe02 project named `Models`. Add a class named `SoftwareLicenseAgreement` to the folder. Use some of the built-in data annotation attributes to customize the display of the model and to ensure that `LicenseAgreementText`, `SoftwareProductName`, and `LicenseeName` are required and have sensible string length limitations. The completed model should match Listing 9-4.

*Listing 9-4.* The SoftwareLicenseAgreement Model

```
using System.ComponentModel.DataAnnotations;

namespace Recipe02.Models
{
    public class SoftwareLicenseAgreementModel
    {
        [Required]
        public string AgreementText { get; set; } = @"Lorem ipsum dolor sit amet,
        consectetur adipiscing elit...";
```

```
        [Required]
        [StringLength(50)]
        public string SoftwareProductName { get; set; }

        [Required]
        [StringLength(50)]
        [Display(Name = "Licensee Name")]
        public string LicenseeName { get; set; }

        [Display(Name = "Agreement Accepted")]
        public bool AgreementAccepted { get; set; }
    }
}
```

# Creating the Custom Validation Attribute

To create the custom validation attribute, first add a folder to the project named Attributes under the root of the Recipe02 project. Next, add a new class to the folder named ConfirmValueAttribute. By convention all attribute classes should be named with the suffix attribute. When using the attribute to decorate a property on a model, that suffix can be omitted.

Inside the ConfirmValueAttribute class, add a using statement for System.ComponentModel. DataAnnotations and then change the class signature so that it derives from ValidationAttribute.

To maximize the usefulness of this validator, rather than simply checking that the value of the property you are validating is true, you will allow the developer to specify the value he or she is expecting. This will allow the validation attribute to be used in many scenarios and not be limited to the check box use case. To do this, add a constructor to the class that takes an argument called expectedValue of the type object. Inside the constructor, the expectedValue argument will be written to a backing field named _expectedValue.

## Overriding IsValid

In the next step, you will override the IsValid method. The IsValid method takes two arguments, value and validationContext. The value argument contains the value of the property that is being validated. The validationContext property contains the current instance of the model class that is being validated and exposes it through the ValidationContext.ObjectInstance property. In addition, validationContext also contains metadata about the model class including the type, display name of the property being validated, and member name of the property being validated.

Inside the IsValid method, you first validate that the value argument is not null. When value is null, an ArgumentNullException is thrown. Next, you compare value to _expectedValue using the Object.Equals method. You must use Object.Equals rather than the == operator in this case because when the == operator is used with an expression of the type Object, the == operator will resolve to Object.ReferenceEquals. The Object.ReferenceEquals object will always return false when used with a value type such as a bool even if the values are the same since the value types will be boxed into separate object instances.

If value and _expectedValue match, then you return ValidationResult.Success; otherwise, you return a new ValidationResult instance with the ErrorMessage property passed as a constructor argument. Listing 9-5 shows the completed code.

***Listing 9-5.*** Creating a Custom Validation Attribute

```
using System;
using System.ComponentModel.DataAnnotations;

namespace Recipe02.Validation
{
    [AttributeUsage(AttributeTargets.Property)]
    public class ConfirmValueAttribute : ValidationAttribute
    {
        private object _expectedValue;
        public ConfirmValueAttribute(object expectedValue)
        {
            _expectedValue = expectedValue;
        }

        public override bool IsValid(object value)
        {
            if (value == null)
            {
                throw new ArgumentNullException("value");
            }

            return Equals(value, _expectedValue);
        }

    }
}
```

Now that you have created the attribute, you can apply it to the model, as shown in Listing 9-6.

***Listing 9-6.*** SoftwareLicenseAgreement Model Updated with ConfirmSelectionAttribute

```
using Recipe02.Validation;
using System.ComponentModel.DataAnnotations;

namespace Recipe02.Models
{
    public class SoftwareLicenseAgreement
    {
        // other properties ....

        [ConfirmValue(true, ErrorMessage = "Please accept the licensing agreement.")]
        [Display(Name = "Agreement Accepted")]
        public bool AgreementAccepted { get; set; }
    }
}
```

## Updating the Home Controller

To test the custom validator, modify the Home controller so that the Index action will use the SoftwareLicenseAgreement class as a model. You will also need to add an HttpPost version of the action that accepts SoftwareLicenseAgreement as an argument. In the body of the HttpPost version of the Index action, add a check for ModelState.IsValid. When the model is valid, redirect to an action named Download; otherwise, return the Index view. Listing 9-7 shows the updated Home controller. Note that in a real-life application you would need to implement logic that would prevent users from bypassing the license agreement page and going directly to the download page.

***Listing 9-7.*** Home Controller Modified to Use the SoftwareLicenseAgreement Class

```
using Microsoft.AspNetCore.Mvc;
using Recipe02.Models;

namespace Recipe02.Controllers
{
    public class HomeController : Controller
    {
        public IActionResult Index()
        {
            var model = new SoftwareLicenseAgreement() { SoftwareProductName = "Some really
            Great Software"};
            return View("Index", model);
        }

        [HttpPost]
        public IActionResult Index(SoftwareLicenseAgreement model)
        {
            if(ModelState.IsValid)
            {
                return RedirectToAction("Download");
            }
            return View("Index", model);
        }

        public IActionResult Download()
        {
            return View("Download");
        }

        public IActionResult Error()
        {
            return View();
        }
    }
}
```

## Updating the Index View

In the Index view, Delete the boilerplate code that comes with the template and replace it with a form that will display the text of the software agreement and allow the licensee to enter their name and select the Agreement Accepted check box. Remember to add _ValidationScriptsPartial to the bottom of the page so that client-side validation will work. _ValidationScriptsPartial adds the JavaScript required for the client-side validation. Listing 9-8 shows the completed Index view.

Note that in Listing 9-8 I am showing both a validation summary using the validation-summary Tag Helper in addition to the validation-for Tag Helper. Both Tag Helpers show the same error messages. In most cases, you want to use only one of the Tag Helpers. The validation-for helper is useful since it shows the error message next to the HTML element that contains the error, making it easy for the user to see the mistake. On the other hand, validation-summary can show errors not associated with a specific field such as when a business rule is broken because of input entered in several fields.

***Listing 9-8.*** Index View with Software License Acceptance Form

```
@model Recipe02.Models.SoftwareLicenseAgreement
@{
    ViewData["Title"] = "Home Page";
}

<h1>Chapter 09 - Recipe 02</h1>
<hr />
<h2>License Agreement for @Model.SoftwareProductName</h2>
<p>
    @Model.AgreementText
</p>
<form asp-action="Index">
    <div asp-validation-summary="All"></div>
    <div class="form-group">
        <label asp-for="LicenseeName"></label>
        <input asp-for="LicenseeName" class="form-control" />
        <span asp-validation-for="LicenseeName" class="text-danger"></span>
    </div>
    <div class="checkbox">
        <label>
            <input asp-for="AgreementAccepted" /> Tick the box to accept the agreement
            <span asp-validation-for="AgreementAccepted" class="text-danger"></span>
        </label>
    </div>
    <button type="submit" class="btn btn-default">Submit</button>
</form>

@section scripts{
    @Html.Partial("_ValidationScriptsPartial")
}
```

Next, add a view that corresponds to the Download action. The Download view does not need to have any specific content.

You should now be able to run the application and verify the functionality of the custom validator. Notice that validation will occur only when the form is submitted to the server.

# Adding Client-Side Validation

Adding client-side validation requires two steps. First, you must modify the ConfirmValueAttribute class so that it implements the IClientModelValidator interface. Second, you must add JavaScript to the page to extend the functionality of the JQuery Unobtrusive Validation library.

The IClientModelValidator interface defines a single method named AddValidation that takes a single argument of the type ClientModelValidationContext. AddValidation allows you to modify the HTML generated by the Tag Helper or HTML Helper. The ClientModelValidationContext instance that is passed to the method allows you to access the attributes of the generated HTML tag. It also allows you to access the ModelMetadata property, which contains metadata such as the Description and DisplayName properties.

Three attributes will need to be added to the HTML for the client-side script to work with the JQuery Unobtrusive Validation library. First you need to add the data-val attribute. This will tell the JQuery Unobtrusive Validation library to consider the field when running validation. Next you need to add custom attributes that correspond to the ConfirmValue class. First add an attribute named data-val-confirmvalue and pass it the value of the ErrorMessage property. The JQuery Unobtrusive Validation library will use the data-val-confirmvalue value to display the correct error message if the validator method named confirmvalue returns false. Note that the attribute contains the class name but in all lowercase with the Attribute suffix removed. Finally, you need to add an attribute to hold the expected value so that it can be compared to the current value or the HTML form field. Listing 9-9 shows the completed AddValidation method.

***Listing 9-9.*** Changes to the ConfirmValueAttribute Class

```
public void AddValidation(ClientModelValidationContext context)
{
    if (context == null)
    {
        throw new ArgumentNullException("context");
    }

    context.Attributes.Add("data-val", "true");
    context.Attributes.Add("data-val-confirmvalue", ErrorMessage);
    context.Attributes.Add("data-val-confirmvalue-expectedvalue", _expectedValue.
    ToString());
}
```

At this point, you can run the application again and inspect the HTML to ensure that the attributes have been added as expected. You can do this in Microsoft Edge (and most other browsers) by right-clicking the AgreementAccepted check box and selecting Inspect Element. Listing 9-10 shows the generated HTML code.

***Listing 9-10.*** Generated HTML

```
<input name="AgreementAccepted"
        id="AgreementAccepted"
       type="checkbox"
       value="true"
       data-val="true"
       data-val- confirmvalue-expectedvalue="True"
       data-val-confirmvalue="Please accept the licensing agreement.">
```

## Adding the JavaScript

The client-side JavaScript that you will create will take advantage of two libraries, JQuery Validation and jQuery Validation Unobtrusive. The jQuery Validation library is a well-documented and full-featured jQuery plug-in. You can find documentation and videos for it at https://jqueryvalidation.org/. The jQuery Unobtrusive Validation library is a jQuery plug-in created by Microsoft whose sole purpose is to pull data from HTML 5 data attributes and use them to create rules in jQuery validation.

To begin, create a new JavaScript file under wwwroot/js named custom-validators.js. Inside the file create a self-executing function. Self-executing functions run as soon as they are loaded into the web browser. Self-executing functions in JavaScript use the following form:

```
$(function ($) {
    // code goes here
}(jQuery));
```

---

■ **Note**    Make sure you create a self-executing function and are not using the JQuery document ready function. jQuery validation registers its rules before the DOM is loaded. If you try to register your adapter after the DOM is loaded, your rules will not be processed.

---

Inside the self-executing function, you will need to perform two steps. First you will register a validation method with JQuery validation using the addMethod function. Next you need to add an adapter to unobtrusive validation.

## Registering the Validation Method with jQuery Validation

The addMethod function of the global validator object lets you define the function that will contain your validation logic. The addMethod function takes two parameters: the function name and the function to be executed. The function name must be a legal JavaScript identifier and should match the data-val-xxx attribute name that was created in Listing 9-9. The function passed as the second argument must have a signature that takes three parameters and returns a Boolean value. The function should return true if the validation condition was met and otherwise false. The three parameters are as follows:

- value: The current value of the HTML element that is being validated. Note that in the case of an unselected check box, value will be undefined.

- element: The HTML element that is being validated.

- params: Parameters to be passed to the method.

For this case, the method name will be confirmvalue to match the data-val-confirmvalue attribute that was added in Listing 9-9.

```
$.validator.addMethod('confirmvalue',
function (value, element, params) {
 // function body goes here
}
);
```

You expect that your params object will have a property named expectedvalue. The expectedvalue parameter should contain the value from the HTML attribute data-val-confirmvalue-expectedvalue. It is a best practice to always validate your input so that missing data does not cause an unexpected runtime error.

```
var expectedValue = params.expectedvalue;
if (!expectedValue) return false;
```

Even though you are using a check box in this example, the custom validator was designed to account for multiple scenarios and may not always be a check box. To account for different scenarios, an if statement checks to see whether the element type is a check box. If so, the checked property of the element will be evaluated, and the value of expectedValue will be converted to a Boolean value. For all other element types, the value property will be evaluated, and the expectedValue argument will not be altered.

```
var actual;
if (element.type === "checkbox") {
    actual = element.checked;
    expectedValue = expectedValue === "True" ? true : false;
} else {
    actual = element.value;
}

if (expectedValue === actual) {
    return true;
}
return false;
```

## Registering the Adapter with jQuery Unobtrusive Validation

Now that you have a validation method registered with the jQuery Validation library, you can use the JQuery Unobtrusive Validation library to wire up the form field with the validation method and pass the method the required parameters.

jQuery Validation by itself does not use the data-val attributes. It instead relies on the programmer to write code to wire up all the form fields to validation rules and then write a submit handler to call the jQuery Validation library's validate function in a submit handler. Submit handlers are JavaScript event handers that occur when a form is submitted. A submit handler can cancel the form submission if the validation fails.

jQuery Unobtrusive Validation uses a function called an *adapter* to harvest all the data from the data-val-xxx attributes and use them to write up the validation methods. You can add an adapter by calling the validator.unobtrusive.adapters.add function. The validator.unobtrusive.adapters.add function takes three parameters.

- adapterName: The name of the adapter to be added. This matches the name used in the data-val-xxx attribute (where xxx is the adapter name). In this case, the adapter name is confirmvalue since the attribute used was data-val-confirmvalue.

- params: An array of parameter names that are harvested from the HTML attributes. In the case of your adapter, you have a single parameter named expectedvalue. By passing the name expectedvalue in the params array, you are telling jQuery Unobtrusive Validation to look for HTML attributes named data-val-confirmvalue-expectedvalue on elements with data-val-confirmvalue attributes.

- fn: The function to call, which adapts the values from the HTML attributes into jQuery validate rules and/or messages. In your adapter, you will map the expectedvalue parameter to the matching parameter in the confirmvalue validator function that was added using the validator.addMethod function.

Listing 9-11 shows the custom-validators.js file.

***Listing 9-11.*** Custom-validators.js

```
$(function ($) {
    "use strict";
    $.validator.addMethod('confirmvalue',
        function (value, element, params) {
            var expectedValue = params.expectedvalue;
            if (!expectedValue) return false;
            var actual;
            if (element.type === "checkbox") {
                actual = element.checked;
                expectedValue = expectedValue === "True" ? true : false;
            } else {
                actual = element.value;
            }

            if (expectedValue === actual) {
                return true;
            }
            return false;
        });

    $.validator.unobtrusive.adapters.add('confirmvalue',
        ['expectedvalue'],
        function (options) {
            // Add validation rule for HTML elements that contain data-confirmvalue attribute
            options.rules['confirmvalue'] = {
                // pass the data from data-confirmvalue-expectedvalue to
                // the params argument of the confirmvalue method
                expectedvalue: options.params['expectedvalue']
            };
            // get the error message from data-confirmvalue-expectedvalue
            // so that unobtrusive validation can use it when validation rule fails
            options.messages['confirmvalue'] = options.message;
        });}(jQuery));
```

There are a few general JavaScript best practices that have also been implemented in Listing 9-11. First, the self-executing function does not have any dependencies on any global variables. It instead imports them as parameters. In this case, jQuery is passed in as an argument named $. Another best practice is the use of use strict. This puts the document in strict mode, which protects you from many of JavaScript's pitfalls such as accidentally creating a global variable by mistyping a variable name. You can find a good description of all the features of strict mode at https://developer.mozilla.org/en-US/docs/Web/JavaScript/Reference/Strict_mode.

## Adding the Script to the View Page

The last step of the custom validator process is to add a script reference to the view, as shown in Listing 9-12.

***Listing 9-12.*** Adding the Custom-validators.js Script Referance to the Index View

```
@section scripts{
    @Html.Partial("_ValidationScriptsPartial")
    <script src="~/js/custom-validators.js"></script>
}
```

You should now be able to test the application and see the custom validator working on both the client and the server.

# 9-3. Processing Custom Business Rules on an Entity by Implementing IValidatableObject

## Problem

You are creating a form for your application that requires the customer to enter a pair of dates to define a date range. You need to prevent the customer from choosing an end date that is before the start date. If customers can do this, then they must have a flux capacitor and could create a paradox that can destroy the universe. You must prevent this evil at all costs.

## Solution

When you need to create a validation rule that needs to consider more than one value on a model, you can have the model class implement the IValidatableObject interface. The IValidatableObject interface defines a single method called Validate. The Validate method returns an IEnumerable of ValidationResults and takes a single argument of the type ValidationContext. Since the method is part of the model class, it has access to all the members of the class. This makes it ideal for cases where you need complex validation rules involving multiple properties.

## How It Works

To demonstrate how to use the IValidateObject interface on a model, you will create an application that allows customers to create hotel reservations.

## Creating the Project

Create a new ASP.NET Core Web Application (.NET Core 1.1) project using the Web Application template. Name the project and the solution **Recipe03**. Ensure that No authentication is selected and Docker support is not enabled.

## Creating the Model

Add a folder called Models under the root of the Recipe03 project. Add a class to the folder named HotelReservation. The class should have two DateTime properties, named StartDate and EndDate. It should also have properties for Name and Room  Number. Standard data annotations, such as Required, DataType, and Display, can be added to the properties.

Next, change the signature of the class so it implements IValidatableObject. You can have Visual Studio automatically stub out the IValidatableObject.Validate message by hovering your mouse over the IValidatableObject in the code editor, clicking the yellow light bulb that appears next to it, and selecting "Implement interface" from the pop-up menu. You can then add code to the Validate method that uses the DateTime.CompareTo method to compare EndDate to StartDate. CompareTo will return -1 if EndDate is earlier than StartDate.

The yield keyword is used to return each of the elements of the ValidationResults enumeration one at a time. When completed, the code should match Listing 9-13.

***Listing 9-13.*** The HotelReservation Model

```
using System;
using System.Collections.Generic;
using System.ComponentModel.DataAnnotations;

namespace Recipe03.Models
{
    public class HotelReservation : IValidatableObject
    {
        [Required]
        [DataType(DataType.Date)]
        [Display(Name = "Start Date")]
        public DateTime StartDate { get; set; }

        [Required]
        [DataType(DataType.Date)]
        [Display(Name="End Date")]
        public DateTime EndDate { get; set; }

        [Required]
        [StringLength(50)]
        public string Name { get; set; }

        [Required]
        [Display(Name = "Room Number")]
        [Range(1,250)]
        public int RoomNumber { get; set; }

        public IEnumerable<ValidationResult> Validate(ValidationContext validationContext)
        {
            if(EndDate.CompareTo(StartDate) <= 0)
            {
                yield return new ValidationResult("The end date must be after the start
                date.");
            }
        }
    }
}
```

## Updating the Home Controller

To test that the validation works as expected, you will modify the Index action of the Home controller so that it has an HttpPost version that takes a HotelReservation object as an argument. The Index action will check the ModelState.IsValid property and then redirect the customer to the ReservationSuccess action if validation passes. Listing 9-14 shows the updated Home controller.

*Listing 9-14.* Home Controller Modified to Support a Hotel Reservation Form

```
using Microsoft.AspNetCore.Mvc;
using Recipe03.Models;

namespace Recipe03.Controllers
{
    public class HomeController : Controller
    {
        public IActionResult Index()
        {
            return View();
        }
        [HttpPost]
        public IActionResult Index(HotelReservation model)
        {
            if (ModelState.IsValid)
            {
                return RedirectToAction("ReservationSuccess");
            }
            return View("Index", model);
        }

        public IActionResult ReservationSucess()
        {
            return View("ReservationSucess");
        }

        public IActionResult Error()
        {
            return View();
        }
    }
}
```

## Updating the Index View

To finish up, delete the boilerplate code from the Index view and replace it with a form that uses Tag Helpers to render the form field and validation properties. Be sure to include a validation summary Tag Helper. The Validation Summary Tag Helper is required in this case since the error is with the form rather than a single form field. Listing 9-15 shows the updated view.

**Listing 9-15.** The Hotel Reservation Form

```
@model Recipe03.Models.HotelReservation
@{
    ViewData["Title"] = "Home Page";
}


<h1>Chapter 9 - Recipe 03</h1>
<form asp-action="Index">
<div class="form-horizontal">
    <h4>HotelReservation</h4>
    <hr />
    <div asp-validation-summary="ModelOnly" class="text-danger"></div>
    <div class="form-group">
        <label asp-for="StartDate" class="col-md-2 control-label"></label>
        <div class="col-md-10">
            <input asp-for="StartDate" class="form-control" />
            <span asp-validation-for="StartDate" class="text-danger"></span>
        </div>
    </div>
    <div class="form-group">
        <label asp-for="EndDate" class="col-md-2 control-label"></label>
        <div class="col-md-10">
            <input asp-for="EndDate" class="form-control" />
            <span asp-validation-for="EndDate" class="text-danger"></span>
        </div>
    </div>
    <div class="form-group">
        <label asp-for="Name" class="col-md-2 control-label"></label>
        <div class="col-md-10">
            <input asp-for="Name" class="form-control" />
            <span asp-validation-for="Name" class="text-danger"></span>
        </div>
    </div>
    <div class="form-group">
        <label asp-for="RoomNumber" class="col-md-2 control-label"></label>
        <div class="col-md-10">
            <input asp-for="RoomNumber" class="form-control" />
            <span asp-validation-for="RoomNumber" class="text-danger"></span>
        </div>
    </div>
    <div class="form-group">
        <div class="col-md-offset-2 col-md-10">
            <input type="submit" value="Create" class="btn btn-default" />
        </div>
    </div>
</div>
</form>
```

```
<div>
    <a asp-action="Index">Back to List</a>
</div>

@section Scripts {
    @{await Html.RenderPartialAsync("_ValidationScriptsPartial");}
}
```

You should now be able to test the form and confirm that the validation rules work as expected. Note that, in this recipe, the custom validation is on the server side only.

# 9-4. Using Remote Validation

## Problem

You are creating an application that allows musicians to register their band names. The application needs to ensure that the band name is not being used by someone else before it permits the name to be chosen. You want to have a good user experience and not force the user to submit the form to the server before seeing whether the name is available.

## Solution

ASP.NET Core has a new feature called RemoteAttribute. It allows you to specify an action and controller name of a Web API that returns a JSON object containing a validation result. Remote validation is performed only on the client.

## How It Works

To demonstrate RemoteAttribute, you will create a web application that contains a Web API controller with an action called ValidateBandName. A model class named BandViewModel will contain a specific property, BandName, that will be decorated with RemoteAttribute. You will then modify the Home controller and Index view to contain a form that allows users to check whether a band name is available.

### Creating the Project

Create a new ASP.NET Core Web Application (.NET Core 1.1) project using the Web Application template. Name the project and solution **Recipe04**. Ensure that No Authentication is selected and Docker support is not enabled.

### Creating the Model

The model used in this recipe contains a single property named BandName. To create the model, first create a new folder under the root of the Recipe04 project named Models. Add a class named BandViewModel to the folder. Use some of the built-in data annotation attributes to customize the display of the model and to ensure that BandName is required, has sensible string length limitations, and can contain only numbers, letters, spaces, and underscores.

The BandName property should also be decorated with the Remote attribute. The Remote attribute requires two properties, the action and the controller. The action and controller properties should point to a Web API controller in your web application that returns JSON. The completed model should match Listing 9-16.

*Listing 9-16.* The BandViewModel Class

```
using Microsoft.AspNetCore.Mvc;
using System.ComponentModel.DataAnnotations;

namespace Recipe04.Models
{
    public class BandViewModel
    {
        [Required]
        [StringLength(30, MinimumLength =3)]
        [Display(Name ="Band Name")]
        [RegularExpression("^[A-Za-z0-9 _]*[A-Za-z0-9][A-Za-z0-9 _]*$")]
        [Remote(action: "VerifyBandName", controller: "Band")]
        public string BandName { get; set; }
    }
}
```

# Creating the Web API

Add a new controller under the `Controller` folder named `BandController`. Note that in ASP.NET Core Web API, controllers are derived from `Controller`, not `APIController` as they were with ASP.NET Web API. To make it clear that this controller is an API controller, you will apply two attributes to the controller class. First, `[Produces("application/json")]` will have all actions in the controller generate JSON. You also add an attribute route using `[Route("api/Band")]`. It is generally a good practice to have all your APIs under /api if your web application is hosting both server-generated HTML and RESTful web services. While it is possible to have actions that return views and JSON in the same controller, it is not a good practice because it is mixing concerns under a single class.

The controller will have a single action called `VerifyBandName` that accepts a string argument called bandName. The action should accept both GET and POST HTTP verbs and needs to return JSON.

The JSON response needs to be in the format {`data: true`} when validation passes and {`data: "Error Message"`} when validation fails.

The action will first check whether the bandName arguments contain a value. If not, it will return a Bad Request response. If the bandName value is valid, then the action will make a database call to see whether the band name exists in the database. Listing 9-17 shows the completed controller.

*Listing 9-17.* The BandController API

```
using System.Linq;
using Microsoft.AspNetCore.Mvc;
using AspNetCoreMvcRecipes.Shared.DataAccess;

namespace Recipe04.Controllers
{
    [Produces("application/json")]
    [Route("api/Band")]
    public class BandController : Controller
    {
        MoBContext _context;
        public BandController(MoBContext context)
        {
            _context = context;
        }
```

```
        [AcceptVerbs("Get", "Post")]
        public IActionResult VerifyBandName(string bandName)
        {
            if(string.IsNullOrWhiteSpace(bandName))
            {
                return BadRequest();
            }

            var bandsMatching = _context.Bands.Count(b => b.BandName.ToLower() == bandName.
            ToLower().Trim());
            if (bandsMatching > 0)
            {
                return Json(data: $"The Band Name {bandName} is already in use.");
            }
            else
            {
                return Json(data: true);
            }
        }
    }
}
```

## Modifying the Home Controller

In the Home controller, you will add an HttpPost version of the Index action that accepts a BandViewModel class as an argument. It will verify ModelState.IsValid and show the BandNameReserved page. Listing 9-18 shows the completed controller.

***Listing 9-18.*** The HomeController Modified to Support the Band Name Registration Form

```
using Microsoft.AspNetCore.Mvc;
using Recipe04.Models;

namespace Recipe04.Controllers
{
    public class HomeController : Controller
    {
        public IActionResult Index()
        {
            return View();
        }

        [HttpPost]
        public IActionResult Index(BandViewModel model)
        {
            if(ModelState.IsValid)
            {
                return RedirectToAction("BandNameReserved");
            }
            return View("Index" , model);
        }
```

```
        public IActionResult BandNameReserved()
        {
            return View();
        }

        public IActionResult Error()
        {
            return View();
        }
    }
}
```

## Creating the View

The view is just a simple form that replaces the default Index view created from the Web Application template. No special code needs to be added other than the _ValidationScriptsPartial partial view that contains links to the jQuery Validation and jQuery Validation Unobtrusive libraries. Listing 9-19 shows the code.

*Listing 9-19.* The Band Registration Form

```
@model Recipe04.Models.BandViewModel
@{
    ViewData["Title"] = "Home Page";
}

<h1>Chapter 09 - Recipe 4</h1>
<form asp-action="Index">
    <div asp-validation-summary="All"></div>
    <div class="form-group-lg">
        <label asp-for="BandName"></label>
        <input asp-for="BandName" class="form-control">
        <span class="text-danger" asp-validation-for="BandName"></span>
    </div>
    <br />
    <button type="submit" class="btn btn-primary">Register Band Name</button>
</form>

@section scripts{
    @Html.Partial("_ValidationScriptsPartial")
}
```

When you run the application, you will see that the validation runs on the client without posting back to the server.

# 9-5. Creating Complex Validation Rules Using Fluent Validation

## Problem

You are building a web site that allows users to build their own electric guitars. They pick the woods, body, pickups, strings, tremolo, and other parts, and then a robot will put the guitar together and ship it to them. Before the guitar is built, you need to ensure that the parts they selected are compatible. You want to be able to give the users feedback as they are filling out the form when they select a part that is not compatible.

## Solution

In the first four recipes, data annotations were used in combination with custom validators, remote validators, and models that implement the `IValidatableObject` interface to solve several common validation issues. While it is possible to create a solution for the business requirements described in the problem using the techniques you learned in the earlier recipes, it would not be easy. You would likely need to create many custom validators and would need to write complex business logic in the `Validate` method.

As an alternate to the data annotation approach, this recipe will demonstrate how to use the Fluent Validation package. Fluent Validation is a popular open source library for solving complex validation requirements written by Jeremy Skinner. You can find the source code and documentation for the library at `https://github.com/JeremySkinner/fluentvalidation`.

The Fluent Validation library uses a fluent interface and lambda expressions to allow you to write very readable and expressive validation rules. If you are interested in reading more of the theory behind fluent interface design, I recommend reading the article by Martin Fowler at `https://www.martinfowler.com/bliki/FluentInterface.html`.

## How It Works

To create this example, you will create a new ASP.NET Core web application. You will then add models to define a guitar and parts you will add to it. Next you will install the Fluent Validation for ASP.NET Core NuGet package and use it to create validation rules. Finally, you will add a view model, the controller, and the views that make up the new guitar form.

### Creating the Project

Create a new ASP.NET Core Web Application (.NET Core 1.1) project using the Web Application template. Name the project and solution **Recipe05**. Ensure that No Authentication is selected and Docker support is not enabled.

### Creating the Models

The models used for this example will be made up of four classes:

- `Guitar.cs`: Represents the guitar that will be built
- `GuitarBody`: Represents the main body of the guitar that houses all of the electronics including the pickups, input jacks, and volume controls

- GuitarPickUp: Represents the magnets that must be installed on a guitar to allow it to convert the vibrations of the guitar strings into electronic signals

- GuitarString: Represents the metal strings that will be installed on the guitar

To create the model, add a folder called Models under the root of the Recipe05 project. Add classes to the folder named Guitar, GuitarBody, GuitarPickup, and GuitarString. Listings 9-20 through 9-23 show the completed classes.

***Listing 9-20.*** Guitar.cs

```
using System.Collections.Generic;
using System.ComponentModel.DataAnnotations;

namespace Recipe05.Models
{
    public class Guitar
    {
        [Display(Description ="Name your custom guitar.")]
        public string Name { get; set; }

        public GuitarBody Body { get; set; }

        [Display(Name = "Bridge Pickup.")]
        public GuitarPickup BridgePickup { get; set; }

        [Display(Name = "Middle Pickup.")]
        public GuitarPickup MiddlePickup { get; set; }

        [Display(Name = "Neck Pickup.")]
        public GuitarPickup NeckPickup { get; set; }

        public IList<GuitarString> Strings { get; set; }
    }
}
```

Note that, in Listing 9-20, even though you will be using the Fluent Validation library for your validation rules, data annotations can still be applied to the model for display information.

***Listing 9-21.*** GuitarBody.cs

```
using System;

namespace Recipe05.Models
{
    public class GuitarBody
    {
        public string Name { get; set; }
        public string ToneWood { get; set; }
        public int NumberOfStringsSupported { get; set; }
        public bool AllowBridgePickup { get; set; }
        public bool AllowMiddlePickup { get; set; }
        public bool AllowNeckPickup { get; set; }
```

```
        public BodyType BodyType { get; set; }
        public BodyStyle Style { get; set; }
        public String Color { get; set; }
    }
}

// BodyType.cs
namespace Recipe05.Models
{
    public enum BodyType { HollowBody, Chambered, SolidBody}
}

// BodyStyle.cs
namespace Recipe05.Models
{
    public enum BodyStyle { LesPaul, SG, Strat,Telecaster, FlyingV, Jazzmaster,
    Explorer, Gem }
}
```

The GuitarBody class shown in Listing 9-21 makes use of two enums. Using enums helps to keep your code readable. This will be especially important when you start defining the validation rules using the Fluent interface.

***Listing 9-22.*** GuitarPickup.cs

```
namespace Recipe05.Models
{
    public class GuitarPickup
    {
        public string Name { get; set; }
        public PickUpType PickUpType { get; set; }
        public PickUpPosition RecommendedPosition { get; set; }
        public int NumberOfStringsSupported { get; set; }
        public int NumberOfConductorsRequired { get; set; }
    }
}

// PickUpTypes.cs
namespace Recipe05.Models
{
    public enum PickUpType { Humbucker, SingleCoil, Piezo}
}

// PickUpPosition.cs
namespace Recipe05.Models
{
    public enum PickUpPosition { Piezo, Bridge, Middle, Neck}
}
```

*Listing 9-23.* GuitarString.cs

```
namespace Recipe05.Models
{
    public class GuitarString
    {
        public string Name
        {
            get
            {
                return string.Format("{0} : {1}", NoteAtStandardTuning, Gage);
            }
        }

        public string NoteAtStandardTuning { get; set; }
        public int Gage { get; set; }
        public string Material { get; set; }
    }
}
```

The GuitarString class shown in Listing 9-23 uses a computed property to derive the name. The Name property will be used for display purposes.

# Installing the Fluent Validation NuGet Package

There are two steps required to integrate the Fluent Validation NuGet package with ASP.NET Core. First you must install the NuGet package using the Package Manager, and then you must configure Fluent Validation in Startup.cs.

To install Fluent Validation, open the Package Manager Console window in Visual Studio and enter the following command:

```
Install-Package FluentValidation.AspNetCore
```

After the installation has completed, modify the ConfigureServices method of Startup.cs so that it matches Listing 9-24. RegisterValidatorsFromAssemblyContaining<Startup>()) will use reflection to find all the classes in the current assembly that are derived from AbstractValidator<T> and then register all the validation rules defined inside them.

*Listing 9-24.* Startup.cs Modified to Configure Fluent Validation

```
public void ConfigureServices(IServiceCollection services)
{
    // Add framework services.
    services.AddMvc().AddFluentValidation(fv => fv.RegisterValidatorsFromAssemblyContaining
    <Startup>());
}
```

# Creating the Validation Rules

To create validation rules for a class using Fluent Validation, create a separate class that extends the `FluentValidation.AbstractValidator<T>` class, where T is the class where you want to apply the validation rules.

Each rule in the validation class's constructor uses calls to the `RuleFor` method. The `RuleFor` method takes a lambda expression as an argument that allows you to specify the property the rule is to be applied to. `RuleFor` returns an `IRuleBuilderInitial` object instance. The `IRuleBuilderInitial` interface exposes a set of built-in rules that can be applied to the model. The following is a list of built-in validators:

- `NotNull`: Invalidates the model when the property is `null`.

- `NotEmpty`: Equivalent to the `Required` data annotation; invalidates the model when the property is `null`, empty, or whitespace.

- `NotEqual`: Invalidates the model when the property does not match the comparison value.

- `Equal`: Inverse of the `NotEqual` rule. Invalidates the model when the property matches the comparison value.

- `Length`: Like the `StringLength` data annotation, invalidates the model when the property length is not in the specified range.

- `LessThen`: Invalidates the model when the property value is less than the comparison value.

- `LessThanOrEqual`: Invalidates the model when the property value is less than or equal to the comparison value.

- `GreaterThen`: Invalidates the model when the property value is greater than the comparison value.

- `GreaterThanOrEqual`: Invalidates the model when the property value is greater than or equal to the comparison value.

- `Must`: Allows you to create custom validators inline using lambda expressions. Invalidates the model when the property does not meet the criteria specified in the expression.

- `Matches`: Equivalent to the `RegularExpression` data annotation. Invalidates the model when the property value does not match the specified regular expression.

- `Email`: Invalidates the model when the property value is not a valid e-mail address.

Each of the built-in validation methods returns an instance of the `IRuleBuilder` interface. The `IRuleBuilder` interface exposes a secondary set of rules that either can add additional rules to the property specified in `RuleFor` or can add restrictions to when the first rule can be applied. For example, if you wanted to create a rule for the `Guitar` class that ensured that if that guitar body requires a neck pickup, the neck pickup cannot be empty, then you would write the following:

```
RuleFor(guitar => guitar.NeckPickup).NotEmpty().When(guitar => guitar.Body.AllowNeckPickup);
```

Listing 9-25 shows a set of rules defined for the `Guitar` class in a validation class named `GuitarValidator`. To create this class, add a folder to the root of Recipe05 named `Validation` and then add a class named `GuitarValidator`.

*Listing 9-25.* GuitarValidator

```
using FluentValidation;
using Recipe05.Models;

namespace Recipe05.Validation
{
    public class GuitarValidator : AbstractValidator<Guitar>
    {
        public GuitarValidator()
        {
            // guitar name cannot be null, empty, or whitespace and
            // must be at least 3 but no more than 40 characters long
            RuleFor(guitar => guitar.Name).NotEmpty().Length(3,40);

            // guitar must have a body
            RuleFor(guitar => guitar.Body).NotEmpty();

            // guitar must have a pickup installed in each slot available in the selected body
            RuleFor(guitar => guitar.NeckPickup).NotEmpty().When(guitar => guitar.Body.
            AllowNeckPickup);
            RuleFor(guitar => guitar.BridgePickup).NotEmpty().When(guitar => guitar.Body.
            AllowBridePickup);
            RuleFor(guitar => guitar.MiddlePickup).NotEmpty().When(guitar => guitar.Body.
            AllowMiddlePickup);

            // can't select more strings then guitar body supports
            RuleFor(guitar => guitar.Strings)
                .NotNull()
                .Must((guitar, strings) => strings?.Count == guitar?.Body?.
                NumberOfStringsSupported)
                .WithMessage(@"The number of strings selected {0}
                                        does not match the number supported by the
                                        guitar body {1}",
                guitar => guitar?.Strings?.Count,
                guitar => guitar?.Body?.NumberOfStringsSupported);

            // can't add a middle pickup if the guitar body does not support it
            RuleFor(guitar => guitar.MiddlePickup)
                .Null()
                .When(guitar => guitar.Body.AllowMiddlePickup = false);
        }
    }
}
```

# Creating the View Model

The guitar builder form will contain a set of drop-down lists that list the available parts for each of the required guitar components. The drop-down lists will be created using the Select Tag Helper. The Select Tag Helper takes two attributes, asp-for and asp-items. The asp-for attribute wires the generated HTML form field with a model property. The asp-items attribute contains the data used to generate the Options tags that make up the drop-down list. The items passed to the asp-items attribute must be of the type IEnumerable<SelectListItem>.

## Creating a Generic SelectListItem Adapter

Since SelectListItems objects are a concern of the view and do not naturally appear in the model, a view model is required to allow the select elements to be generated and to provide a translation between the properties of the model and items selected in the form.

To simplify the code in the view model and to reduce the need to duplicate code, you will build a utility class called SelectListAdapter. The SelectListAdapter class will contain a method called ConvertToSelectListItemCollection. ConvertToSelectListItemCollection will allow you to convert a collection from the model into the IEnumerable<SelectListItem> required by the view. ConvertToSelectListItemCollection also allows you to specify the properties from the model's collection to be used for the text and value properties of each SelectListItem.

To create the SelectListAdapter class, first create a folder under the root of the Recipe05 project called Util. Next add a new class file called SelectListItemAdapter.

Since the SelectListItemAdapter class will be stateless and does not use any instance properties, it will be defined as static. Inside SelectListItemAdapter, create a generic method named ConvertToSelectListItemCollection. Generic methods allow the method to be strongly typed while supporting many types. The ConvertToSelectListItemCollection takes four arguments.

- source: This is the source list from the model that will be converted to an IEnumerable<SelectListItem>.

- text: This is a lambda expression that takes an instance of the collection type used in the source and returns a string. This will allow developers to select a property to use for the Text property of the SelectListItem list items.

- value: This is a lambda expression that takes an instance of the collection type used in source and returns a string. This will allow developers to select a property to use for the Value property of the SelectListItem list items.

- createEmpty: If true, which is the default value, an empty SelectListItem will be added to the list that contains the text *Please Select*.

A second version of the ConvertToSelectListItemCollection is also added that allows a single property to be used for both the Text and Value properties of SelectListItem.

---

### DEMYSTIFYING FUNC

The Func<T, string> construct may look complicated if you have never used it but is quite simple. The Func keyword defines a delegate that takes one or more parameters. For the example shown in Listing 9-26, the delegate takes a single argument of the type T. The second argument in this example is the return type of the delegate. Func<T,string> is shorthand for defining a delegate with the following signature:

```
delegate string MethodName(T);.
```

When developers call ConvertToSelectListItemCollection, they will be able to implement the delegate inline using a lambda expression.

---

*Listing 9-26.* SelectListItemAdapter

```csharp
using System;
using System.Collections.Generic;
using Microsoft.AspNetCore.Mvc.Rendering;

namespace Recipe05.Util
{
    public static class SelectListItemAdapter
    {
        public static IEnumerable<SelectListItem> ConvertToSelectListItemCollection<T>
            (IEnumerable<T> source, Func<T, string> text, Func<T, string> value, bool
            createEmpty = true) where T : class
        {
            var selectListItems = new List<SelectListItem>();
            if (createEmpty)
            {
                selectListItems.Add(new SelectListItem { Text = "Please Select",
                Value = "" , Selected= true });
            }

            foreach (var item in source)
            {
                selectListItems.Add(new SelectListItem { Text = text(item),
                Value = value(item)});
            }

            return selectListItems;
        }

        public static IEnumerable<SelectListItem> ConvertToSelectListItemCollection<T>
            (IEnumerable<T> source, Func<T, string> textAndValue, bool createEmpty = true)
            where T : class
        {
            return ConvertToSelectListItemCollection(source, textAndValue, textAndValue,
            createEmpty);
        }
    }
}
```

## Simulating an Inventory Module

In a real system, you may have an inventory module that would call out to a back-end database to pull the list of available parts. For this exercise, you will simulate the database call with the Inventory class. The Inventory class will consist of a set of properties containing lists of the various parts that make up the guitar. To create the Inventory class, create a new folder called Data and within it create a new class called Inventory. Listing 9-27 shows the Inventory class.

***Listing 9-27.*** Simulated Inventory Module

```
using Recipe05.Models;
using System.Collections.Generic;

namespace Recipe05.Data
{
    public class Inventory
    {
        public IList<GuitarBody> GuitarBodies = new List<GuitarBody>
        {
            new GuitarBody {
                Name = "Red Les Paul",
                AllowBridePickup = true,
                AllowMiddlePickup = false,
                AllowNeckPickup = true,
                BodyType = BodyType.SolidBody,
                ToneWood = "mahogany",
                Color = "Red",
                NumberOfStringsSupported =6,
                Style = BodyStyle.LesPaul
            }
            // additional guitar body choices go here
        };

        public IList<GuitarPickup> GuitarPickups = new List<GuitarPickup>
        {
            new GuitarPickup{
                Name = "Imperium 7™ Neck",
                NumberOfStringsSupported = 7,
                PickUpType =PickUpType.Humbucker,
                RecommendedPosition = PickUpPosition.Bridge,
                NumberOfConductorsRequired = 4
            }
            // additional guitar pickup choices go here
        };

        public IList<GuitarString> GuitarStrings = new List<GuitarString>
        {
            new GuitarString { Gage=9, Material = "Steel", NoteAtStandardTuning = "E"},
            new GuitarString {Gage=10, Material = "Nickel", NoteAtStandardTuning = "E"}
            // additional guitar string choices go here
        };
    }
}
```

## Creating the GuitarBuilderViewModel Class

To simplify the view logic used inside the Razor views, you will create a view model named
GuitarBuilderViewModel. To help you differentiate models that are purely entities from models
that are bound to views, you will create a new folder called ViewModels and name each view model
class in the folder with the ViewModel suffix. The GuitarBuilderViewModel class will contain an

IEnumerable<SelectListItem> for each of the drop-down lists required on the form. It will also have a string value to represent the selected value from each of the drop-down lists. In addition, since you want to use the display metadata from the Guitar class to create the labels and descriptions used on the form, the view model class will also have a Guitar property.

In addition to the properties, the GuitarBuilderViewModel class contains a helper method that uses SelectListItemAdapter to create IEnumerable<SelectListItem>. Listing 9-28 shows GuitarBuilderViewModel.

*Listing 9-28.* The GuitarBuilderViewModel Class

```
using Microsoft.AspNetCore.Mvc.Rendering;
using Recipe05.Data;
using Recipe05.Models;
using Recipe05.Util;
using System.Collections.Generic;

namespace Recipe05.ViewModels
{
    public class GuitarBuilderViewModel
    {
        public GuitarBuilderViewModel()
        {
            // in a real app we would get the data via constructor injection
            PopulateFromInventory();
        }

        public Guitar Guitar { get; set; } = new Guitar();

        public IEnumerable<SelectListItem> BridgePickupList { get; set; }
        public string SelectedBridgePickup { get; set; }

        public IEnumerable<SelectListItem> MiddlePickupList { get; set; }
        public string SelectedMiddlePickup { get; set; }

        public IEnumerable<SelectListItem> NeckPickupList { get; set; }
        public string SelectedNeckPickup { get; set; }

        public IEnumerable<SelectListItem> BodyList { get; set; }
        public string SelectedBody { get; set; }

        public IEnumerable<SelectListItem> StringsList { get; set; }
        public IEnumerable<string> SelectedStrings { get; set; }

        private void PopulateFromInventory()
        {
            Inventory = new Inventory();
            BodyList = SelectListItemAdapter.ConvertToSelectListItemCollection
                    (Inventory.GuitarBodies, s => s.Name);
            BridePickupList = SelectListItemAdapter.ConvertToSelectListItemCollection
                    (Inventory.GuitarPickups, s => s.Name);
            MiddlePickupList = SelectListItemAdapter.ConvertToSelectListItemCollection
                    (Inventory.GuitarPickups, s => s.Name);
```

```
            NeckPickupList = SelectListItemAdapter.ConvertToSelectListItemCollection
                    (Inventory.GuitarPickups, s => s.Name);
            StringsList = SelectListItemAdapter.ConvertToSelectListItemCollection
                    (Inventory.GuitarStrings, s => s.Name);
        }
        // used by the GuitarBuilderToGuitarAdapter class shown in next section
        internal Inventory Inventory { get; private set; }
    }
}
```

## Creating the GuitarBuilderToGuitarAdapter Class

The GuitarBuilderViewModel class does not contain enough information to be used to perform the rules processing required to meet the business requirements. The only purpose of the view model is to collect the data submitted by the user back to the controller. The complex rules that were defined in Listing 9-25 were defined on the Guitar class. Even though a Guitar class was included in the view model, not enough information was passed to it to invoke the rules. For the rules to be processed, data from the view model needs to be used to create a fully populated Guitar object.

The GuitarBuilderToGuitarAdapter class performs the function of creating the Guitar object from the form data collected in the view model. It does this by querying the Inventory property of the view model and finding the matching item using the key saved in the view model for each select list. Listing 9-29 shows the GuitarBuilderToGuitarAdapter class.

***Listing 9-29.*** The GuitarBuilderToGuitarAdapter Class

```
using Recipe05.Data;
using Recipe05.Models;
using System.Linq;

namespace Recipe05.ViewModels
{
    public class GuitarBuilderToGuitarAdapter
    {
        public Guitar BuildGuitar(GuitarBuilderViewModel viewModel)
        {
            if (viewModel == null) return null;

            var guitar = new Guitar()
            {
                Name = viewModel.Guitar.Name,
                BridgePickup = SelectPickUp(viewModel.Inventory, viewModel.SelectedBridgePickup),
                MiddlePickup = SelectPickUp(viewModel.Inventory, viewModel.SelectedMiddlePickup),
                NeckPickup = SelectPickUp(viewModel.Inventory, viewModel.SelectedNeckPickup),
                Body = viewModel.Inventory?.GuitarBodies?.FirstOrDefault(a => a.Name ==
                viewModel.SelectedBody),
                Strings = (from gs in viewModel.Inventory.GuitarStrings
                        where viewModel.SelectedStrings!=null && viewModel.SelectedStrings.
                        Contains(gs.Name)
                        select gs).ToList()
            };
            return guitar;
        }
    }
```

```
private GuitarPickup SelectPickUp(Inventory inventory, string pickupName)
{
    if (string.IsNullOrEmpty(pickupName)) return null;

    return inventory?.GuitarPickups?.FirstOrDefault(a => a.Name == pickupName);
    }
  }
}
```

## Creating the Controller

For this recipe, the Home controller that is created by Visual Studio will be modified to support the guitar builder form. First, modify the Index action so that it is passed a GuitarBuilderViewModel class to the view. Next, create an HttpPost version of the Index action that accepts GuitarBuilderViewModel as a parameter. Change the signature of the action to be asynchronous.

Inside the action, create an instance of GuitarBuilderToGuitarAdapter and then use the BuildGuitar method to create an instance of Guitar from the GuitarBuilderViewModel class passed into the action.

In the next line, call TryUpdateModelAsync with the Guitar object created by the adapter. TryUpdateModelAsync will cause the validation rules attached to the Guitar class from GuitarValidator to be run against the current state of the object. TryUpdateModelAsync will update the ModelState value of the controller with results of the validation and add any validation errors to the controller's model error list. This will allow validation errors to appear on the view when the Validation-Summary and Validation-For Tag Helpers are used. Listing 9-30 shows the updated Home controller.

*Listing 9-30.* Home Controller Modified to Support Guitar Builder Form

```
using System.Threading.Tasks;
using Microsoft.AspNetCore.Mvc;
using Recipe05.ViewModels;
using Recipe05.Models;

namespace Recipe05.Controllers
{
    public class HomeController : Controller
    {
        public IActionResult Index()
        {
            var model = new GuitarBuilderViewModel { Guitar = new Guitar { Name = "My New
            Guitar" } };
            return View("Index", model);
        }

        [HttpPost]
        public async Task<IActionResult> Index(GuitarBuilderViewModel model)
        {
            var adapter = new GuitarBuilderToGuitarAdapter();
            model.Guitar = adapter.BuildGuitar(model);
            await TryUpdateModelAsync(model.Guitar);
```

```
            if (ModelState.IsValid)
            {
                return RedirectToAction("OrderRecieved");
            }
            return View("Index", model);
        }
        public IActionResult OrderRecieved()
        {
            return View("OrderRecieved");
        }
        public IActionResult Error()
        {
            return View();
        }
    }
}
```

## Creating the Views and Testing the Application

The final step is to modify the Index view of the Home controller to host the guitar builder form. First, remove all the boilerplate code that was added by Visual Studio when the project was created. Next, use the @model directive to make the view strongly typed to Recipe05.ViewModels.GuitarBuilderViewModel.

Then create a FORM element with an asp-action attribute set to index. The asp-action attribute will render the FORM attributes necessary to post the form back to the Index action. Finally, add all the required form elements needed for the guitar builder form, as shown in Listing 9-31. Don't forget to include the _ValidationScriptsPartial view at the bottom of the page.

*Listing 9-31.* The Guitar Builder Form

```
@model Recipe05.ViewModels.GuitarBuilderViewModel
@{
    ViewData["Title"] = "Home Page";
}


<h1>Chapter 9 - Recipe 05</h1>
Use this form to build the guitar of your dreams and our robots will build it for you.

<form asp-action="index">
    <div asp-validation-summary="All" class="text-danger"></div>
    <div class="form-group">
        <label asp-for="Guitar.Name"></label>
        <input class="form-control" asp-for="Guitar.Name" placeholder="Name for your custom guitar">
        <span asp-validation-for="Guitar.Name" class="text-danger"></span>
    </div>
    <div class="form-group">
        <label asp-for="Guitar.Body"></label>
        <select class="form-control"
        asp-for="SelectedBody"
        asp-items="Model.BodyList">
        </select>
        <span asp-validation-for="Guitar.Body" class="text-danger"></span>
    </div>
```

```
    <div class="form-group">
        <label asp-for="Guitar.BridgePickup"></label>
        <select class="form-control"
                asp-for="SelectedBridgePickup"
                asp-items="Model.BridgePickupList"></select>
        <span asp-validation-for="Guitar.BridgePickup" class="text-danger"></span>
    </div>
    <div class="form-group">
        <label asp-for="Guitar.MiddlePickup"></label>
        <select class="form-control"
                asp-for="SelectedMiddlePickup"
                asp-items="Model.MiddlePickupList"></select>
    </div>
    <div class="form-group">
        <label asp-for="Guitar.NeckPickup"></label>
        <select class="form-control"
                asp-for="SelectedNeckPickup"
                asp-items="Model.NeckPickupList"></select>
    </div>
    <div class="form-group">
        <label asp-for="Guitar.Strings"></label>
        <select class="form-control"
                asp-for="SelectedStrings"
                asp-items="Model.StringsList"></select>
    </div>

    <button type="submit" class="btn btn-default">Submit</button>
</form>

@section scripts{
    @Html.Partial("_ValidationScriptsPartial")
}
```

Run the application and try submitting the form using different combinations of the input. You will see that for most of the validation errors, the validation summary will be updated, but no validation error will appear on the form field. The exceptions to this rule are validation errors, such as when the guitar name field is left blank.

# CHAPTER 10

■ ■ ■

# Securing Your ASP.NET Core MVC Application

One of the most fundamental needs of every application is security. This chapter discusses some of the built-in features of ASP.NET Core that can help you verify the identity of your application's users and ensure that their data is protected.

## 10-1. Creating an ASP.NET Core Web Site That Uses ASP.NET Identity Core for Authentication and Authorization

### Problem

You are building a consumer-facing ASP.NET Core application that will be deployed to the Web. You have requirements for user registration that will capture the username and password as well as some demographic information about each customer. In addition, you want users to be able to register using their Facebook accounts. All this information needs to be stored in a custom database.

### Solution

ASP.NET Core comes with a set of templates that allow developers to easily add authentication to a new application. When creating a new project, developers can select the authentication mechanism that best meets the application's requirements. These options include the following:

- *No authentication*: No authentication code is added to the project. This is suitable for web sites that do not require knowledge of a user's identity.

- *Individual user accounts*: This option will add Entity Framework and ASP.NET Identity to the web site. It also adds controllers and views for login, registration, and account management. Having individual user accounts allows developers to customize the database so that custom fields can easily be added to the user model. In addition to built-in authentication, having individual user accounts also supports third-party identity providers including Facebook, Google, Twitter, and Microsoft.

- *Work or school accounts*: This means configuring the application to use Active Directory authentication with either a Windows Azure Active Directory account or an on-premise Active Directory installation.

- *Windows authentication*: This means configuring the application to use the Windows authentication IIS module.

© John Ciliberti 2017
J. Ciliberti, *ASP.NET Core Recipes*, DOI 10.1007/978-1-4842-0427-6_10

For this recipe, using individual user accounts best meets the needs stated in the problem. After creating an ASP.NET Core Web Application project and selecting the Individual User Accounts option, you can then customize the ApplicationUser model class added to the project to support ASP.NET Identity and then use the Entity Framework Code First tools to create the database.

To meet the requirements for allowing a user to log in using third-party providers, you can add additional authentication providers in the Configure method of the Startup.cs class.

## How It Works

In this section, you will learn at how to create an ASP.NET Core application that uses ASP.NET Identity for authentication.

## Creating the Visual Studio Project

Create a new ASP.NET Core Web Application project (.NET Core 1.1) using the Web Application template. Click the Change Authentication button and then select Individual User Accounts. Make sure Docker support is not selected. Name the project and solution **Recipe01**. The screen should match Figure 10-1.

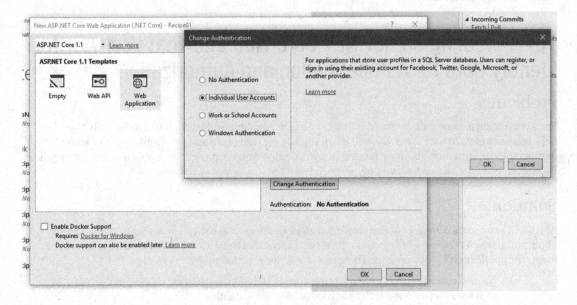

*Figure 10-1.  Creating a new project using the option Individual User Accounts*

## Exploring the Project

Selecting Individual User Accounts added many items to the project, including NuGet packages, controllers, views, data migrations, Entity Framework DBContext class, models, and app settings. You will briefly look at each of these items so that you can better understand all the moving parts of ASP.NET Identity.

## NuGet Packages

Table 10-1 briefly describes the ASP.Net Identity–specific NuGet packages that have been added to the project to support ASP.NET Identity and why they are needed.

*Table 10-1. Added ASP.NET Identity–Specific NuGet Packages*

| Package Name | Purpose |
|---|---|
| Microsoft.AspNetCore.Authentication.Cookies | This enables the application to use cookie-based authentication. In cookie-based authentication, a user supplies login credentials using a web-based form. The server then authenticates the credentials and passes an authentication cookie back to the user. The authentication cookie is used with each request and is validated by the authentication provider to ensure it is valid before the execution of the request can continue. If the cookie is missing or not valid, the user will be redirected to the login page. |
| Microsoft.AspNetCore.Identity.EntityFrameworkCore | This is the identity provider that uses Entity Framework. It contains common functionality such as the IdentityUser base class that is used to allow ASP.NET Identity to be used with Entity Framework Core. |

## Controllers and Views

Selecting the Individual User Accounts option adds two controllers to the project, AccountController and ManageController. The controller AccountController contains actions for registering and logging in and out of the web site. It also contains actions that are used for working with third-party authentication providers. The controller ManageController provides functionality that allows the user to add and remove third-party authentication logins. It also contains actions required to support two-factor authentication. With two-factor authentication, a user can add an extra level of security that will send an automatically generated passcode to the user's cell phone via a Short Message Service (SMS) message.

---

■ **Note**   The sample application generated by the template does not provide an implementation for SMS messaging but only a stubbed-out class. If you want to implement two-factor authentication, you will need to implement SMS messaging functionality in the application.

---

In addition to the controllers, selecting the Individual User Account option also adds all views required to implement basic login, registration, third-party authentication provider registration, and account management features such as password recovery.

## Data

The Data folder contains the ApplicationDbContext class and the Migrations folder. The ApplicationDbContext class is derived from IdentityDbContext<ApplicationUser>. You can find the source code for IdentityDbContext on GitHub at the following URL:

https://github.com/aspnet/Identity/blob/dev/src/Microsoft.AspNet.Identity.AspNetCoreCompat/IdentityDbContext.cs

In addition to defining several constructors, the `IdentityDbContext<TUser>` class on GitHub defines an `OnModelCreating` method that adds additional rules that are used by the Entity Framework Core tooling to create the database. It also contains a `ValidateEntity` method that provides validation rules that help prevent concurrent updates of user accounts and roles. Finally, the `IdentityDbContext` class defines `IDbSet<TRolesClaims>`, which is the parent object the ASP.NET Identity class hierarchy. `TRolesClaims` is a type derived by `IdentityRoleClaim<TKey>`, which by default is `IdentityRoleClaim <string>`. By including `IDbSet<TRolesClaims>`, Entity Framework will automatically also include these child classes:

- `IdentityUserClaim<TKey>`

- `IdentityUserRole<TKey>`

- `IdentityUserLogin<TKey>`

- `IdentityRole<TKey, TUserRole>`

- `IdentityUser<TKey, TUserLogin, TUserRole, TUserClaim>`

You will learn more about what these classes are and how to use them in recipes 10-2 and 10-3.

The `Migrations` folder contains data migrations that can be used by the Entity Framework tools to generate the database required to support the ASP.NET Identity schema.

## Models

Selecting the Individual User Accounts option adds a `Models` folder to the project. Under the `Models` folder you will find two subfolders: `AccountViewModels` and `ManageViewModels`. These folders contain classes that support the corresponding views.

At the root of the `Models` folder is a class named `ApplicationUser`. The `ApplicationUser` class represents a registered end user of your application. The `ApplicationUser` class is derived from `IdentityUser`, which is imported from `Microsoft.AspNetCore.Identity.EntityFrameworkCore`. The body of `ApplicationUser` is empty but can be modified so that you can add additional properties to describe your users. You are also free to refactor `ApplicationUser` and rename it to something that better suits your business domain. Be sure to use the refactoring features of Visual Studio if you rename `ApplicationUser` so that all the references to it are updated.

You can find the code for the `IdentityUser` class on GitHub at the following URL:

```
https://github.com/aspnet/Identity/blob/dev/src/Microsoft.Extensions.Identity.Stores/
IdentityUser.cs
```

---

■ **Note**   The link to the `dev` branch of the `IdentityUser` class is shown because at the time of this writing ASP.NET Identity is undergoing a major refactoring. In a future release, `IdentityUser` will be under the `Microsoft.Extentions.Identity.Stores` package.

---

Listing 10-1 shows the initial version of `ApplicationUser` that is added to the project.

***Listing 10-1.*** ApplicationUser.cs

```
using System;
using System.Collections.Generic;
using System.Linq;
using System.Threading.Tasks;
using Microsoft.AspNetCore.Identity.EntityFrameworkCore;
```

```
namespace Recipe01.Models
{
    // Add profile data for application users by adding properties to the ApplicationUser class
    public class ApplicationUser : IdentityUser
    {
    }
}
```

## IdentityUser Support for Different Data Types

The `ApplicationUser` class that comes with the ASP.NET Core Web Application template uses a string for the primary key. This string is initialized to a new GUID in the constructor of the parent base class `IdentityUser<string>`. The `IdentityUser` class that is used as the base class for `ApplicationUser` is derived from the class `IdentityUser<string>`. The class `IdentityUser<string>` is derived from the generic class `IdentityUser<TKey>`. The TKey generic type parameter represents the CLR type of the primary key. The goal of this design is to allow application developers the flexibility to choose the type used in the primary key.

If you want to use a different type for the primary key in your application, you can modify the `ApplicationUser` class to derive from `IdentityUser<TKey>` rather than `IdentityUser`. For example, if you want to use `Int64` as the type for your primary key rather than a string, you modify the `ApplicationUser` class so it is derived from `IdentityUser<Int64>`.

## Properties of IdentityUser<TKey>

Your `ApplicationUser` class inherits many properties from `IdentityUser<string>`. The properties of the `ApplicationUser` class and those inherited from `IdentityUser` will be added to a database table named `ApplicationUser` when you use Entity Framework to generate the database. All the properties of `IdentityUser` are virtual, which allows you to override them and use your own implementation of the getters and setters. In the following list, I identify each of the properties and describe their use:

- `Id`: The `Id` property represents the primary key of the database table. The `IdentityUser` class uses a string as the primary key.

- `UserName`: This is the unique name for each user.

- `NormalizedUserName`: This stores the `UserName` value as all uppercase to prevent users from registering use names that differ only by the letter casing.

- `Email`: This is the unique e-mail address for the user.

- `NormalizedEmail`: Like`NormalizedUserName`, `NormalizedEmail` prevents users from registering the same e-mail with different letter casing.

- `EmailConfirmed`: This returns true if the e-mail address has been confirmed and otherwise returns false. This field is useful if your application contains logic to prevent users from registering with fake e-mail addresses or e-mail addresses that do not belong to them. This is usually done by requiring users to click a link from an e-mail sent to them as part of an e-mail verification workflow.

- `PasswordHash`: This is the hashed and salted password. Passwords should never be stored in the database as clear text. If the database were ever compromised, the clear-text passwords could be stolen and used for nefarious purposes. It is a standard practice to use a one-way encryption function called a *hashing algorithm* to generate a fixed-length fingerprint or hash of the password. This technique is usually enhanced by adding some random text called a *salt* to the password before the hash algorithm is applied. Using a salt is recommended to protect against common hash-cracking techniques such as lookup tables, reverse lookup tables, and rainbow tables.

- SecurityStamp: This is a random value that must change when a user's credentials change or login is removed.

- ConcurrencyStamp: This is a random value that must change whenever a user is saved to the database. It is used to prevent multiple updates to the same user at the same time to avoid scenarios where two or more admins are updating the same user and end up overwriting each other's changes.

- PhoneNumber: This is the user's phone number. Phone numbers can be used with two-factor authentication where SMS messages are sent to the phone number with a random code that can be used in addition to the password.

- PhoneNumberConfirmed : This gets or sets a flag indicating whether a user has confirmed their telephone number.

- TwoFactorEnabled: This is true if two-factor authentication is enabled and otherwise is false. Two-factor authentication uses a randomly generated code usually sent to the user via SMS message in addition to the password for the user to log in.

- LockoutEnd: This is a DateTimeOffset value that is used when an account has been locked out because of too many failed login attempts. If the value of this field occurs in the past, then the account lockout has expired.

- LockoutEnabled: If this is true and the LockoutEnd occurs in the future, then the user is locked out.

- AccessFailedCount: This displays the number of failed login attempts since the last successful login.

## Services

The Services folder contains the interfaces IEmailSender and ISmsSender as well as the stubbed-out implementation of the interfaces in the class MessageServices. The class MessageServices is only a stub and does not contain any functionality. For information on how to provide a working implementation for IEmailSender, please refer to recipe 6-7.

## appsettings.json

appsettings.json is the main configuration file for the application. As shown in Listing 10-2, in the appsetting.json file are settings for the database connection string and logging. The connection string uses LocalDB. LocalDB is a lightweight version of Microsoft SQL Server that is useful for application prototyping and light development. LocalDB runs under your user context, which means that the process will have the same system-level access as your account. Since LocalDB and IIS Express are both running under your account, in most cases LocalDB can be used without any configuration, which makes it ideal for prototyping. IIS Express and LocalDB are installed with Visual Studio.

***Listing 10-2.*** appsettings.json

```
{
  "ConnectionStrings": {
    "DefaultConnection": "Server=(localdb)\\mssqllocaldb;Database=aspnet-Recipe01-3eecf46d-
      8318-4423-ae06-1b3760c22afb;Trusted_Connection=True;MultipleActiveResultSets=true"
  },
  "Logging": {
    "IncludeScopes": false,
    "LogLevel": {
      "Default": "Warning"
    }
  }
}
```

If you do not want to use LocalDB, it is easy to change the connection string to point to another SQL Server instance. The connection string has the following parts:

- Server: This is the server name or IP address of the server and instance name. If you are pointing to the default instance of SQL Server, then you can omit the instance name. The server name can use a shorthand notation when pointing to certain types of databases.

  - (localdb): This communicates to a LocalDB instance running on the local machine.

  - .: This single period is used to point to SQL Server on the local machine. If you are pointing at the default instance, only the period is required. For a named instance, you can use .\instanceName.

- Database: This is the name of the database. By default, Visual Studio will use the name or the project with a GUID appended to the end. This is to guarantee that the database name is unique and that Visual Studio will not overwrite an existing database by mistake. If you want, you can change the name of the database.

- Trusted_Connection: When set to true, yes, or sspi, the application will attempt to connect to SQL Server using the Windows account credentials of the currently running process. Since the IIS Express account will be running under your account, this setting will use your Windows account to access the database.

- MultipleActiveResultSets: This allows the execution of many SQL batches on a single connection.

## Creating the Database Schema

If you run the application and attempt to use the ASP.NET Identity framework features such as registering a new user account, you will see an error similar to the one shown in Figure 10-2.

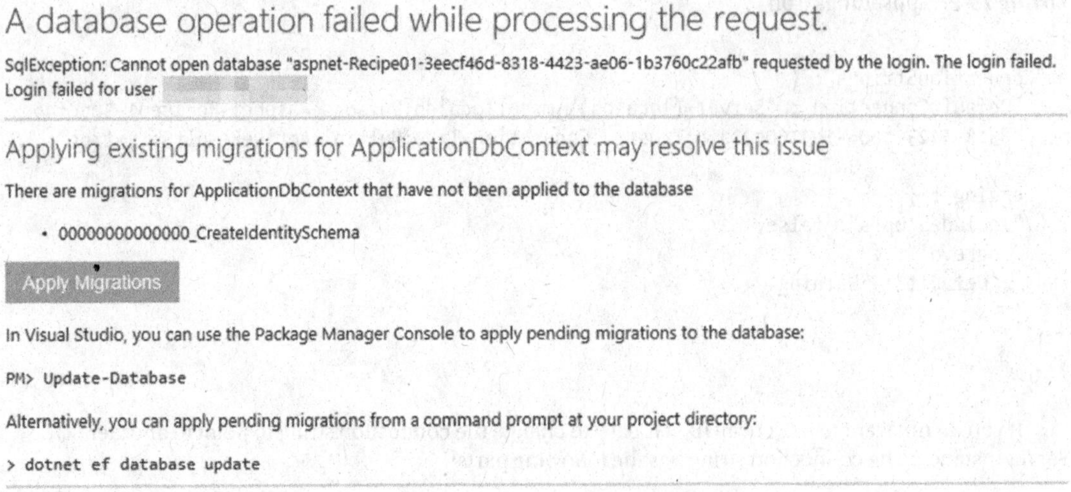

## A database operation failed while processing the request.

SqlException: Cannot open database "aspnet-Recipe01-3eecf46d-8318-4423-ae06-1b3760c22afb" requested by the login. The login failed.
Login failed for user ▓▓▓▓▓▓▓▓

## Applying existing migrations for ApplicationDbContext may resolve this issue

There are migrations for ApplicationDbContext that have not been applied to the database

- 00000000000000_CreateIdentitySchema

[ Apply Migrations ]

In Visual Studio, you can use the Package Manager Console to apply pending migrations to the database:

PM> Update-Database

Alternatively, you can apply pending migrations from a command prompt at your project directory:

> dotnet ef database update

*Figure 10-2.* *Database error page*

This error is a change in behavior from earlier versions of ASP.NET such as ASP.NET MVC 3 where the database migration was run automatically on the first use. Microsoft decided to remove this feature since many developers found this functionality confusing since this "magic" did not occur when the application was deployed to a production system. Fortunately, the error provides you with several options for creating the database. First there is an Apply Migrations button. If you click the button, the text in the button will briefly change to Applying Migrations, and then after about five seconds, the button will say Migrations Applied, and a message next to the button will prompt you to refresh the page.

The other two options listed in the error message show options for creating the database using the Package Manager Console in Visual Studio and from the command line using dotnet ef.

## How the Apply Migrations Button Works

The magic that is provided by the Apply Migrations button may seem a bit strange. If you right-click the Apply Migrations button in Microsoft Edge and select Inspect Element, you will see that the button has an onClick event that calls a JavaScript function called ApplyMigrations. If you expand the script block, you will see that ApplyMigrations makes an Ajax call to a service in your web application located on the route / ApplyDataBaseMigrations. Listing 10-3 shows the relevant sections of the source of the database error page.

*Listing 10-3.* Script Block from the Source of the Database Error Page

```
<script>
    function ApplyMigrations() {
        applyMigrations.disabled = true;
        applyMigrationsError.innerHTML = "";
        applyMigrations.innerHTML = "Applying Migrations...";

        var req = new XMLHttpRequest();

        req.onload = function (e) {
            if (req.status === 204) {
                applyMigrations.innerHTML = "Migrations Applied";
                applyMigrationsSuccess.innerHTML = "Try refreshing the page";
```

```
        } else {
            ErrorApplyingMigrations();
        }
    };

    req.onerror = function (e) {
        ErrorApplyingMigrations();
    };

    var formBody = "context=Recipe01.Data.ApplicationDbContext,%20Recipe01,
    %20Version%3D1.0.0.0,%20Culture%3Dneutral,%20PublicKeyToken%3Dnull";
    req.open("POST", "\/ApplyDatabaseMigrations", true);
    req.setRequestHeader("Content-type", "application/x-www-form-urlencoded");
    req.setRequestHeader("Content-length", formBody.length);
    req.setRequestHeader("Connection", "close");
    req.send(formBody);
}

function ErrorApplyingMigrations() {
    applyMigrations.innerHTML = "Apply Migrations";
    applyMigrationsError.innerHTML = "An error occurred applying migrations, try
    applying them from the command line";
    applyMigrations.disabled = false;
}
</script>
```

What may seem odd about the code shown in Listing 10-3 is that your application does not have an action named ApplyDatabaseMigrations in any of the controllers created by the template.

This functionality is provided by the DatabaseErrorPageMiddleware middleware that was added to your application in the Startup.cs class using the UseDatabaseErrorPage method, as shown in Listing 10-4. The DatabaseErrorPageMiddleware middleware is declared in a class named DatabaseErrorPageExtensions. It works by capturing database-related exceptions that may be resolved using Entity Framework migrations. Notice that this functionality is applied only when in development. In a production deployment, users would only see the error page at /Home/Error.

*Listing 10-4.* Configure Method in Startup.cs

```
public void Configure(IApplicationBuilder app, IHostingEnvironment env, ILoggerFactory loggerFactory)
{
            loggerFactory.AddConsole(Configuration.GetSection("Logging"));
            loggerFactory.AddDebug();

            if (env.IsDevelopment())
            {
                app.UseDeveloperExceptionPage();
                app.UseDatabaseErrorPage();
                app.UseBrowserLink();
            }
            else
            {
                app.UseExceptionHandler("/Home/Error");
            }
```

```
    app.UseStaticFiles();

    app.UseIdentity();

    app.UseMvc(routes =>
    {
        routes.MapRoute(
            name: "default",
            template: "{controller=Home}/{action=Index}/{id?}");
    });
}
```

## Exploring the Application

After the database migrations have been applied, you should now be able to perform activities including the following:

- Registering

- Logging in

- Changing the password

- Managing an external login (The page will be empty, however, since no logins have been configured. To learn how to add external logins to your application, see recipe 10-3).

- Logging out

Figure 10-3 shows the "Manage your account" page. In addition to the links provided for changing the password and managing external logins, the "Manage your account" page contains a placeholder for two-factor authentication support. Two-factor authentication requires additional configuration as well as integration with a third-party SMS provider, as described in recipe 10-4.

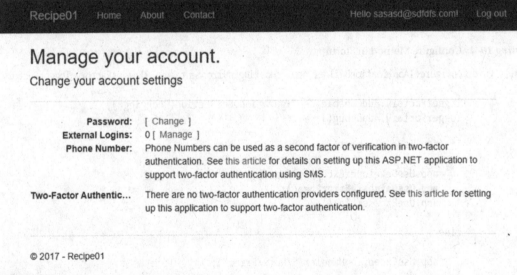

*Figure 10-3. "Manage your account" page*

344

# Exploring the Database

If you want to explore the database created using the Entity Framework migration, you have a few options such as opening the database in Microsoft SQL Server Management Studio or other database or third-party software such as Toad for SQL Server. In Visual Studio, you can use the SQL Server Object Explorer window to view the database. To do this, from the Visual Studio View menu, select SQL Server Object Explorer. The SQL Server Object Explorer will be displayed docked on the left side of Visual Studio. If your LocalDB instance is not shown, click the Add SQL Server button on the toolbar at the top of the SQL Server Object Explorer window. In the Connect window, expand the Local node and then select MSSQLLocalDB, as shown in Figure 10-4. Click the Connect button.

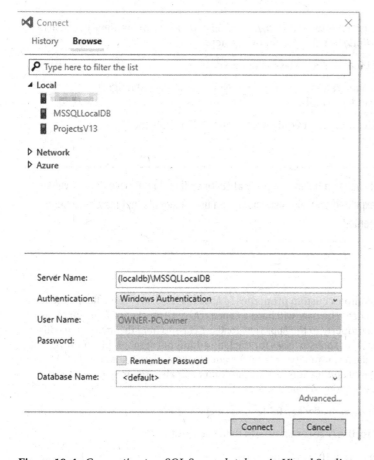

*Figure 10-4. Connecting to a SQL Server database in Visual Studio*

In Visual Studio Object Explorer, you can now expand (localdb)\MSSQLLocalDB, Databases, aspnet-Recipe01-(GUID), and then Tables. You should see eight tables. The first table, _EFMigrationsHistory, is created by Entity Framework to track changes applied by the migrations. The rest of the tables map to the classes under IdentityDbContext<TUser>.

# 10-2. Adding Custom Fields to the ApplicationUser Class

## Problem

You are building an application that will send alerts to your users when their favorite bands are playing in their area. You have created a new ASP.NET Core project as described in recipe 10-1, but you need to add some custom properties to the ApplicationUser object to track some additional demographics and preferences for receiving alerts. You want to understand how to change both the ApplicationUser class and the underlying database.

## Solution

ASP.NET Identity creates its database using Entity Framework Code First database migrations. Because of this, customizing the database can be done by using the following steps:

1. Add properties to the ApplicationUser class as required.

2. Run the command to add a migration by using either NuGet's Package Manager Console or dotnet command-line tools.

3. Run the Update Database command or equivalent command to apply the migration to the database.

---

■ **Note**    Be careful about adding non-nullable fields to ApplicationUser that do not have default values. The non-nullable fields can lead to unexpected behavior especially with user accounts that may have been created before the change was implemented.

---

## How It Works

To learn how to add both simple and complex custom properties to ApplicationUser, you will first create a new class called ConcertAlertPreference. The user will have a ConcertAlertPreference for each of his or her favorite bands. You will then add a property to the ApplicationUser class to hold the alerts. You will also add some simple properties to the ApplicationUser class for tracking additional demographic information required by the alert service. For the sake of simplicity, you will be adding these classes into the Models folder inside the web application. In a real application, you would want to create a separate class library project to act as a data access layer as you did in recipe 6-6.

1. In Solution Explorer, right-click the Models folder and select Add ➤ Class.

2. Name the class ApplicationUserPreferences and then click Add.

3. Modify the class to match Listing 10-5.

*Listing 10-5.* ApplicationUserPreference Class

```
namespace Recipe01.Models
{
    public class ConcertAlertPreference
    {
        public int ConcertAlertPreferenceId { get; set; }
        public string BandName { get; set; }
```

```
        public bool NotificationIsActive { get; set; }
        public bool NotifyViaEmail { get; set; }
        public bool NotifyViaSMS { get; set; }
        public bool ShowsOnWeekdays { get; set; }
        public bool ShowsOnWeekEnds {get; set;}
    }
}
```

4. In the ApplicationUser class, create properties for City, State, ZipCode, MilesFromCityCenter, and ConcertAlertPreferances, as shown in Listing 10-6, and then build the application.

***Listing 10-6.*** ApplicationUser.cs with Additional Properties

```
using System.Collections.Generic;
using Microsoft.AspNetCore.Identity.EntityFrameworkCore;

namespace Recipe01.Models
{
    public class ApplicationUser : IdentityUser
    {
        public string City { get; set; }
        public string State { get; set; }
        public string ZipCode { get; set; }
        public int MilesFromCityCenter { get; set; }
        public IList<ConcertAlertPreference> ConcertAlertPreferences { get; set;}
    }
}
```

Now that the ApplicationUser class has been modified, you need to create a migration. The migration will compare the current state of the application by examining the snapshot of the previous state and then generate new migration classes. To create the migration, open the Package Manager Console using View ➤ Other Windows ➤ Package Manager Console. In the Package Manager Console, enter the following command:

```
Add-Migration  "NewPropsForApplicationUser"
```

After running the command, you should see several new files added to the Data/Migrations folder alongside the existing migration classes that were created with the template. To apply the migrations to the database, run the following command:

```
Update-Database
```

If you explore the database as described in recipe 10-1, you will see that a new table named ConcertAlertPreference has been added to the database. Expand the Columns folder of the new table and then click a column name to select it. Information about the column will be displayed in the Properties window. You should also notice that the column ConcertAlertPreferenceId of the ConcertAlertPreference table is set as the primary key and is an Identity column with an Identity Seed value of 1. With this setting, the database will automatically generate a new numeric key and assign it to the ConcertAlertPreferenceId column when new records are added. This setting was applied automatically by Entity Framework since the ConcertAlertPreferenceId value follows the Code First convention of [ClassName]Id.

Another thing you should notice about the ConcertAlertPreference table is that a foreign key column called ApplicationUserId has been added to the ApplicationUser table. Entity Framework did this automatically because you added the ConcertAlertPreferences property to ApplicationUser. Because the list was added to ApplicationUser, it becomes the primary part of the relationship. Entity Framework then automatically adds a foreign key to the new table that links back to the primary key in ApplicationUser.

If you expand the Columns folder in SQL Server Object Explorer for the AspNetUsers table, you should see new columns for each of the properties you added to the ApplicationUser class.

Figure 10-5 shows a database diagram of the database generated for your project by Entity Framework.

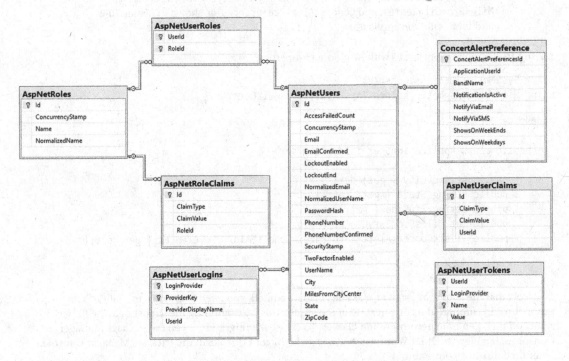

**Figure 10-5.** *Database diagram for application database with custom table and columns*

# 10-3. Allowing Users to Log In to Your ASP.NET Core Application Using Facebook

## Problem

You have created a new ASP.NET Core application with individual user account authentication as described in recipe 10-1. You have a business requirement for allowing users to log in to the application using their Facebook accounts and want to know how to implement this.

# Solution

ASP.NET Identity has built-in support for external authentication providers that includes Facebook, Twitter, Google, and Microsoft. To enable Facebook authentication, there are two major steps. First, you must create a new Facebook application using the Facebook developer tools on the Facebook web site. Second, you need to configure your ASP.NET Core MVC application to use the Facebook authentication middleware.

It is also highly recommended that you configure your application to use user secrets so that your Facebook application keys are not stored in your source control system.

# How It Works

As described in the solution, the first step will be to create a Facebook application. Once you have set up the Facebook application, you will be able to use the keys to configure your ASP.NET Core MVC application to use the Facebook authentication middleware.

## Creating a Facebook Application

For this first step, you will need to create a developer account on Facebook. If you have an existing Facebook account, you can extend that account to access the developer tools. You can find more information on how to become a Facebook developer at the following web site:

```
https://developers.facebook.com/docs/apps/register
```

Once your account has been set up, you can create a new application by first navigating to `https://developers.facebook.com/`. Once you are on the web site, you will see a drop-down menu in the upper-right corner of the web site, as shown in Figure 10-6.

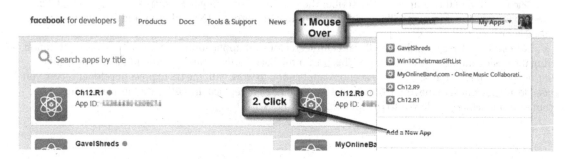

***Figure 10-6.*** *Creating a Facebook application, step 1*

After clicking the Add a New App link, a modal window will ask you for the display name and contact e-mail, as shown in Figure 10-7. Click the Create App ID button to create the application ID.

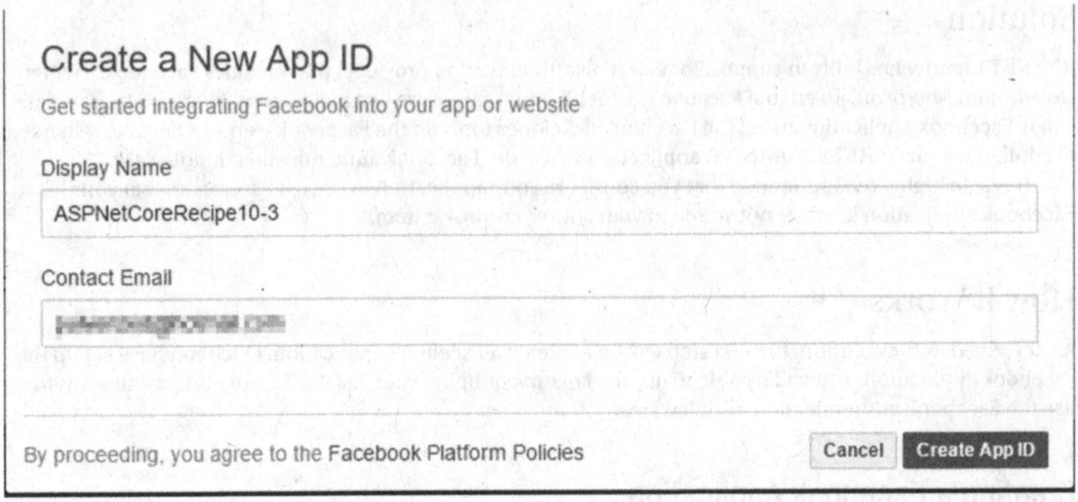

# Create a New App ID

Get started integrating Facebook into your app or website

Display Name

ASPNetCoreRecipe10-3

Contact Email

By proceeding, you agree to the Facebook Platform Policies          Cancel    Create App ID

*Figure 10-7.* *Creating a Facebook application, step 2*

After clicking the Create App ID button, you may be prompted to respond to a CAPTCHA image. A CAPTCHA image is an image of slightly obscured letters that most humans can read but fools most OCR applications. CAPTCHAs are designed to prevent automated form submissions.

The next screen in the Facebook application setup is the Product Setup page. Find the Facebook Login product. It should be the first item in the list. Click the Get Started button.

On the Choose a Platform page, select Web. You will then be prompted for the URL of the web site. If you know the URL, you can enter it now; otherwise, you can enter the URL of the developer server. On my machine, the URL is http://localhost:50183/.

The next part of the setup wizard describes the steps for connecting to Facebook using JavaScript. You can skip this section since you will be using the built-in features of ASP.NET Identity and not a JavaScript-based login.

Next you need to access the app ID and app secret for your application. You can access this information from the Basic settings page of your app. The link for the Basic settings can be found in the left navigation bar, as shown in Figure 10-8. For the Facebook application to work with the IIS Express developer server, you need to add localhost to the App Domains list. You will need to replace the URL with the actual domain of your web site before you deploy to production.

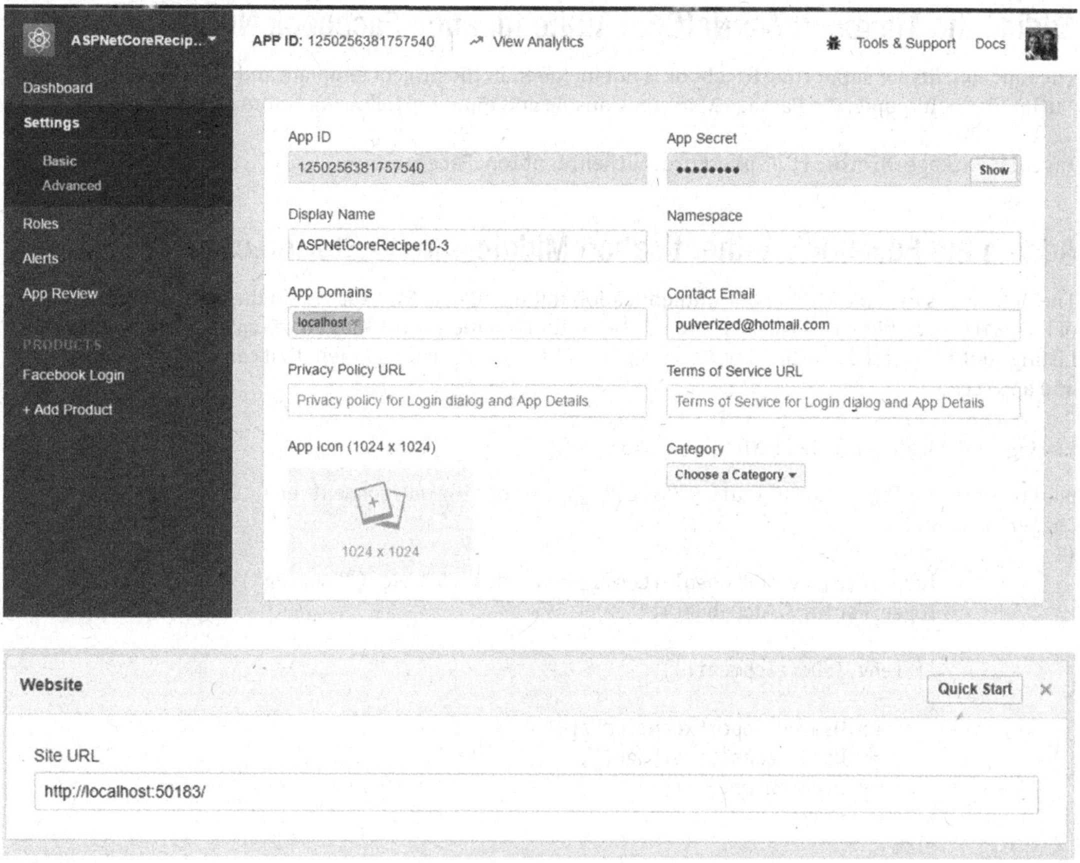

**Figure 10-8.** *Getting the Facebook app ID and app secret*

Make note of the app ID and app secret, but be careful not to expose your app secret since it is the password for your application.

## Adding the App ID and App Secret to the User Secrets Store

Since you do not want to risk accidentally uploading your app secret to your source control repository, it is highly recommended that you store the data in the app secrets store. To so this, right-click the project in Solution Explorer and select Manage User Secrets. An empty JSON file will open in the editor. You can then use standard JSON syntax to add the app ID and app secret that you received from Facebook to the app secrets store, as shown in Listing 10-7.

**Listing 10-7.** Adding App ID and App Secret to the User Secrets Store

```
{
  "FacebookAppID": "1250256381757540",
  "FacebookAppSecret": "05f7a1c86d1b87915ce64af80be6eeb8"
}
```

## Adding the Microsoft.AspNetCore.Authentication.Facebook NuGet Package

The functionality for supporting Facebook is not included in the project template and must be added using NuGet. To do this, open the Package Manager Console and enter the following command:

```
Install-Package Microsoft.AspNetCore.Authentication.Facebook
```

## Adding the Facebook Authentication Middleware to Startup.cs

The next step is to add the Facebook authentication middleware to Startup.cs. In the Configure method of the Startup.cs file, call the UseFacebookAuthentication method of IApplicationBuilder, as shown in Listing 10-8. UseFacebookAuthentication takes a FacebookOptions argument that can accept the app ID and app secret.

*Listing 10-8.* Adding Facebook Middleware to Startup

```
public void Configure(IApplicationBuilder app, IHostingEnvironment env, ILoggerFactory
loggerFactory)
{
        loggerFactory.AddConsole(Configuration.GetSection("Logging"));
        loggerFactory.AddDebug();

        if (env.IsDevelopment())
        {
            app.UseDeveloperExceptionPage();
            app.UseDatabaseErrorPage();
            app.UseBrowserLink();
        }
        else
        {
            app.UseExceptionHandler("/Home/Error");
        }

        app.UseStaticFiles();

        app.UseIdentity();

        app.UseFacebookAuthentication(new FacebookOptions()
        {
            AppId = Configuration["FacebookAppID"],
            AppSecret = Configuration["FacebookAppSecret"]
        });

        app.UseMvc(routes =>
        {
            routes.MapRoute(
                name: "default",
                template: "{controller=Home}/{action=Index}/{id?}");
        });
}
```

After making this change, you should be able to run the application. After logging in to the application, you should be able to navigate to the page for managing external logins at the path /Manage/ManageLogins.

You should now see a Facebook button on the external logins page. If you click the Facebook button, a Facebook page will appear asking you to confirm that you want to allow the application to access your Facebook information. After you click OK, you will be forwarded back to your application, and the "Manage your external logins" page will display a message stating that the external login was added successfully.

Another thing that has changed is that you now have a Facebook button on the "Log in" page, as shown in Figure 10-9. Clicking this button will allow you to log in to the web site using your Facebook credentials.

*Figure 10-9.* *The Facebook button now appears on the login screen*

# 10-4. Enabling Two-Factor Authorization in Your ASP.NET Core Application

## Problem

The security requirements for your application dictate that you need to include two-factor authentication in your application. You have set up an ASP.NET Core application with individual user accounts, as specified in recipe 10-1. You want to use the built-in features of ASP.NET Identity to enable two-factor authentication.

## Solution

The two-factor authentication features of ASP.NET Identity use SMS messaging to send a temporary code to your phone. The SMS code is used in conjunction with your password to provide an extra layer of security. With two-factor authentication, even if your password is compromised, an attacker would not be able to access your account unless they also have gained access to your phone.

Setting up two-factor authentication with SMS requires that you create an account with an SMS gateway service. For this recipe, you will use Twilio. Twilio offers a very flexible API for using SMS, Multimedia Messaging Service (MMS), and voice messages. Twilio is not free, but it offers a trial account that will allow you to get an SMS number and send sample messages.

Twilio has a NuGet package that makes it easy to interact with its services from your ASP.NET Core MVC application. Once your Twilio account has been set up, you can implement the ISmsSender interface in the MessageServices class to use the Twilio NuGet package. The ISmsSender interface is one of the files added to your solution by the ASP.NET Web Application template when the Individual User Accounts authentication option is selected.

Once you have set up the Twilio accounts and installed the Twilio NuGet package, you can then remove the code comments from Views/Manage/Index.cshtml to enable the management of phone numbers to be used with two-factor authentication.

## How It Works

In this recipe, you will first set up a Twilio account. Next, you will add the Twilio NuGet package to the project and implement the ISmsSender interface. You will then uncomment the HTML markup in the management view and verify that the solution works as expected.

## Setting Up a Twilio Account

To set up a new account on Twilio, open a web browser and go to https://www.twilio.com. On the home page, click the Get a Free API Key button. You will then be prompted to set up a new account. Ensure you have your cell phone handy when performing this step since Twilio uses two-factor authentication during the registration process.

After you complete the registration process, navigate to the Programmable SMS Dashboard and then click the Get Started button from the Twilio Programmable SMS Dashboard, as shown in Figure 10-10.

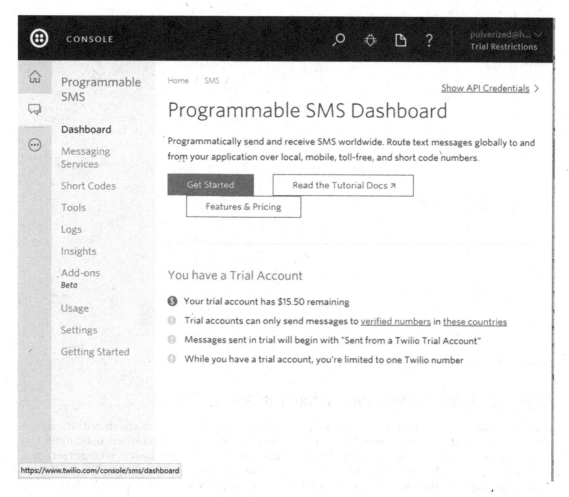

**Figure 10-10.** *The Twilio Programmable SMS Dashboard*

On the Build with Programmable SMS page, click the "Get a number" button. A modal dialog will pop up displaying a phone number. You have the option of either using the number displayed or searching for a different number. When you are happy with the phone number, click the Choose this Number button. A Congratulations window will appear with your new phone number displayed. Make note of the number. You will need to use it later when setting up the configuration of the application. Click Done to close the Congratulations window.

After you close the Congratulations window, a form will be displayed that allows you to send test messages. On the right side of this form a sample request is shown. This request, shown in Figure 10-11, contains your user ID and auth token as a multipart string delimited with a colon in the format USERID:AUTHTOKEN. You will need to check the Show your Auth Token check box to see the auth token. Make a note of these values since you will need them to configure your application.

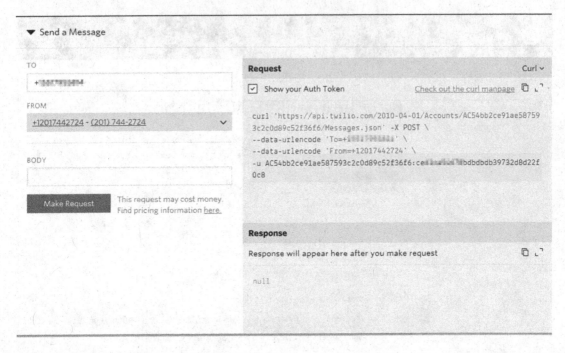

*Figure 10-11.* *Twilio sample request page*

## Adding the Twilio Configuration to the User Secrets Store

Your Twilio phone number, user ID, and auth token are unique to you and should not be shared on your source control system. To ensure these values are not shared on your source control system but can still be used for configuring your application in your development environment, add them to your user secrets store. To do this, right-click the project in Solution Explorer and select Manage User Secrets. The user secrets JSON file will appear in the editor window. Modify the user secrets JSON file to match Listing 10-9, but substitute the values with the ones you received from the Twilio web site.

*Listing 10-9.* Adding Twilio Configuration Data to User Secrets Store

```
{
  "FacebookAppID": "1250256381757541",
  "FacebookAppSecret": "05f7u1c86d1b87915se64af80be6eeb9",
  "TwilioPhoneNumber": "+12017442724",
  "TwilioUser": "AC54bb2ce91ae587593c2c0d89c52f36f6",
  "TwilioAuthToken": "ce01c054678b0bdbdb39732d8d00000"
}
```

## Installing the Twilio NuGet Package

To simplify working with Twilio, you will install the Twilio NuGet package. The Twilio NuGet package provides a light wrapper around the Twilio API and can be configured to use the ASP.NET Core configuration system.

To install the Twilio NuGet package, open the Package Manager Console and enter the following command:

```
Install-Package Twilio
```

## Creating a Configuration Class

As demonstrated in recipe 6-7, you will use the Options pattern for passing configuration data to the ISmsSender implementation. With the Options pattern, you will create a class for reading the configuration data and pass an instance of the class to the dependency injection system during the configuration method of the Startup class. To do this, create a new class under the Services folder named TwilioOptions. Add properties to the class that match the names used in the user secrets file, as shown in Listing 10-10.

***Listing 10-10.*** TwilioOptions Class

```
namespace Recipe01.Services
{
    public class TwilioOptions
    {
        public string TwilioPhoneNumber { get; set; }
        public string TwilioUser { get; set; }
        public string TwilioAuthToken { get; set; }
    }
}
```

## Implementing the ISmsSender API Using Twilio

Implementing the ISmsSender interface using Twilio is surprisingly simple. The ASP.NET Core Web Application template created a stub implementation of ISmsSender in the class MessageServices under the Services folder. You will complete this implementation.

First, you will need to add a constructor to the MessageServices class so the dependency injection system can supply the configuration data. You will also need to create a backing field for the configuration data so that it can be accessed from the SendSmsAsync method. Since you are using the Options pattern, you need to add a using statement for Microsoft.Extensions.Options so that you can use the IOptions interface. The class constructor will accept an argument of the type IOptions<TwilioOptions>. The Value property of the IOptions instance will be written to the backing field named Options.

To use the Twilio API, you need to add three namespaces to the class file: Twilio, Twilio.Rest.Api. V2010.Account, and Twilio.Types.

In the SendSmsAsync method, you first will need to initialize the Twilio client by calling the TwilioClient.Init method. You can then call the MessageResource.Create method to send the SMS message. Listing 10-11 shows the completed AuthMessageSender class.

***Listing 10-11.*** The Completed AuthMessageSender Class

```
using Microsoft.Extensions.Options;
using System.Threading.Tasks;
using Twilio;
using Twilio.Rest.Api.V2010.Account;
using Twilio.Types;
```

```
namespace Recipe01.Services
{
    public class AuthMessageSender : IEmailSender, ISmsSender
    {
        public TwilioOptions Options { get; } // set by the dependency injection system
        during startup
        public AuthMessageSender(IOptions<TwilioOptions> options)
        {
            Options = options.Value;
        }

        public Task SendEmailAsync(string email, string subject, string message)
        {
            // To see how to implement this method view recipe 6-7
            return Task.FromResult(0);
        }

        public Task SendSmsAsync(string number, string message)
        {
            TwilioClient.Init(Options.TwilioUser, Options.TwilioAuthToken);

            MessageResource.Create(
              to: new PhoneNumber(number),
              from: new PhoneNumber(Options.TwilioPhoneNumber),
              body: message);
            return Task.FromResult(0);
        }
    }
}
```

## Wiring Up the Configuration in Startup

For the configuration data to be passed to the AuthMessageSender class, you will need to wire it up in the
Startup.cs class's ConfigureServices method. To do this, in Startup, add a call to services.Configure, as
shown in Listing 10-12.

*Listing 10-12.* Wiring Up the Twilio Configuration Data in Startup

```
public void ConfigureServices(IServiceCollection services)
{
    // Add framework services.
    services.AddDbContext<ApplicationDbContext>(options =>
        options.UseSqlServer(Configuration.GetConnectionString("DefaultConnection")));

    services.AddIdentity<ApplicationUser, IdentityRole>()
        .AddEntityFrameworkStores<ApplicationDbContext>()
        .AddDefaultTokenProviders();

    services.AddMvc();
```

```
// Add application services.
services.AddTransient<IEmailSender, AuthMessageSender>();
services.AddTransient<ISmsSender, AuthMessageSender>();
services.Configure<TwilioOptions>(Configuration);
}
```

## Uncommenting the Code in Views/Manage/Index.cshtml

When the project was created, the ASP.NET Core Web Application template added a set of views for managing the credentials and phone numbers used for two-factor authentication. Some of this code is commented out by default since it would cause runtime errors if you attempted to use this functionality without the application being configured. Now that you have added the code required for using two-factor authentication, you can now uncomment the required blocks of code and remove the other unneeded boilerplate. When completed, Views\Manage\Index.cshtml should match Listing 10-13.

*Listing 10-13.* Removing the Commented-Out Code from Index.cshtml

```
<dt>Phone Number:</dt>
    <dd>
        @(Model.PhoneNumber ?? "None")
            @if (Model.PhoneNumber != null)
            {
                <br />
                <a asp-controller="Manage" asp-action="AddPhoneNumber"
                class="btn-bracketed">Change</a>
                <form asp-controller="Manage" asp-action="RemovePhoneNumber" method="post">
                    [<button type="submit" class="btn-link">Remove</button>]
                </form>
            }
            else
            {
                <a asp-controller="Manage" asp-action="AddPhoneNumber"
                class="btn-bracketed">Add</a>
            }
    </dd>

    <dt>Two-Factor Authentication:</dt>
    <dd>
        @if (Model.TwoFactor)
            {
                <form asp-controller="Manage" asp-action="DisableTwoFactorAuthenticati
                on" method="post" class="form-horizontal">
                    Enabled <button type="submit" class="btn-link btn-bracketed">Disable</button>
                </form>
            }
            else
            {
                <form asp-controller="Manage" asp-action="EnableTwoFactorAuthentication"
                method="post" class="form-horizontal">
                    <button type="submit" class="btn-link btn-bracketed">Enable</button>
                    Disabled
```

```
            </form>
        }
    </dd>
</dl>
```

You should now be able to run the application. On the "Manage your account" page, you should now see the option to add a phone number and to enable two-factor authentication, as shown in Figure 10-12.

| Chapter 10 | Home | About | Contact | | | Hello sdfsdf@dfdfdfg.com! | Log out |

## Manage your account.
Change your account settings

| | |
|---:|:---|
| Password: | [ Change ] |
| External Logins: | 0 [ Manage ] |
| Phone Number: | None [ Add ] |
| Two-Factor Authentic... | [ Enable ] Disabled |

*Figure 10-12.* "*Manage your account*" *page after enabling two-factor authentication*

To test the functionality, click the Add link for the phone number. On the Add Phone Number page, add the phone number you used when you set up your Twilio account. Since the Twilio account is in trial mode, it will only allow you to send SMS messages to verified phone numbers. Click the Send Verification Code button. After a short delay, you should see a SMS message on your phone with the security code. Once you enter the code and click Confirm, you will see the phone number appear on the "Manage your account" page.

Next, try enabling two-factor authentication by clicking the Enable link on the "Manage your account" page. After two-factor authentication has been enabled, log out. When you attempt to log in again, you will be prompted to send a verification code. You can enter the verification code on the Verify page, as shown in Figure 10-13. If you select the "Remember this browser" check box, you will not be prompted again when using the same web browser on the same computer.

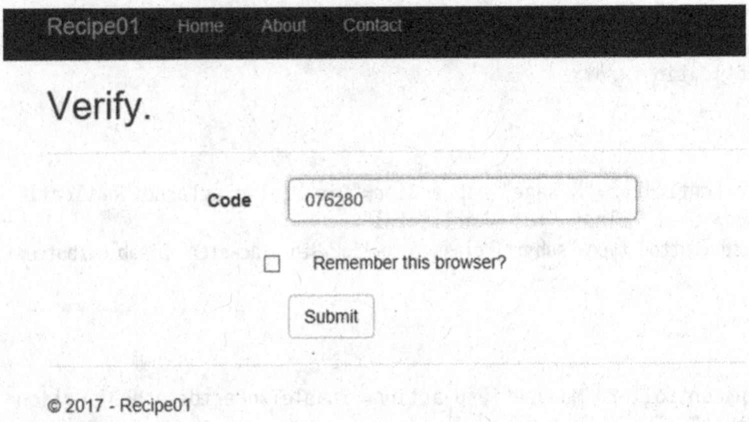

| Recipe01 | Home | About | Contact |

## Verify.

| | |
|---:|:---|
| Code | 076280 |
| | ☐ Remember this browser? |
| | Submit |

© 2017 - Recipe01

*Figure 10-13.* *Two-factor authentication in action*

# CHAPTER 11

■ ■ ■

# Creating Modern User Experiences Using React.js and ASP.NET Core

A revolution in web development has taken place over the past decade. While server-side rendering platforms such as ASP.NET Core, Ruby on Rails, and Spring MVC are still relevant and powerful, faster JavaScript engines, the emergence of ECMAScript 2015, and the evolution of front-end frameworks such as ReactJS and Angular 4 are allowing developers to create more immersive front-end experiences using JavaScript. In this new model, the role of the server has been increasingly limited to delivering RESTful services with most of the user interface being rendered on the client using powerful front-end frameworks. In this chapter, you will learn how ASP.NET Core embraces this new workflow. You will also learn how the new ASP.NET Core project format can be used in conjunction with complex JavaScript libraries to build next-generation user interfaces that interact with ASP.NET Core RESTful web APIs.

## 11-1. Understanding node.js and Bower Integration in the ASP.NET Core Project System

### Problem

You have just created a new ASP.NET Core 1.1 web application using the Web Application template. You want to get a better understanding of the new project structure and how it works out of the box and how you can customize it to better meet your needs.

### Solution

Many of today's JavaScript-based front-end frameworks have complex build workflows. The build workflows involve automated code analysis, unit testing, transcompiling, minification, optimization, and more. The build workflow is typically executed using command-line tools written in JavaScript running on the Node.js runtime.

ASP.NET Core web application projects have a new project system that includes a Node.js-based build workflow. The ASP.NET Core web application's new project structure was designed for "full-stack developers" who create both JavaScript-heavy front ends and the server-side components. The new project system creates a clean separation between client-side code and server-side code. This design allows "full-stack developers" to do all their development in Visual Studio under a single unified project system.

© John Ciliberti 2017

J. Ciliberti, *ASP.NET Core Recipes*, DOI 10.1007/978-1-4842-0427-6_11

In the ASP.NET Core web application project system, all client-side code is stored under the folder wwwroot. The ASP.NET Core web application build workflow downloads files from the Internet using the Bower package manager and optimizes files for improved performance using the BuildBundlerMinifier NuGet package. Visual Studio allows you to control the build workflow by modifying the contents of the following files:

- bower.json: This is the package manifest file for the Bower package manager. It allows you to specify which JavaScript libraries you want to include in your project.

- .bowerrc: This is the project-scoped configuration file for the Bower package manager. It allows you to change where Bower packages are copied after being downloaded from the Internet. It also allows you to specify a Bower server to use if your company has set up its own server.

- bundleconfig.json: This is the configuration file for Microsoft's bundling and minification tool. Bundling/minification makes your application faster by combining several JavaScript files into a single file and then compressing the file by removing whitespace and shortening variable names.

You can also extend or replace the JavaScript workflow added to your project by the ASP.NET Core Web Application project template by adding custom Node.js scripts or by using a JavaScript task runner such as Gulp.

## How It Works

In this section, you will look at each of the components of the built-in JavaScript workflow used by the ASP.NET Core Web Application template. You will then look at how you can extend and replace the components to create a custom build workflow.

## Node.js

Node.js is a JavaScript runtime environment based on Chrome's V8 JavaScript engine. You can think of Node.js as being the Common Language Runtime (CLR) for JavaScript. With Node.js you do not need a web browser to execute JavaScript. You instead can invoke scripts via the powerful Node.js command-line interface (CLI).

Visual Studio ships with a bare-bones installation of Node.js that offers enough functionality to perform the functions required for the build process. If you plan on performing significantly more with Node.js than is offered in the out-of-box experience with Visual Studio, it is highly recommended that you install the full Node.js. You can download Node.js from https://nodejs.org. Once installed, Node.js and Node Package Manager (NPM) will be added to your system's PATH environment variable and will be available in all console windows. The version of Node.js that comes with Visual Studio is not affected by the global installation. This will prevent new versions of Node.js from breaking the built-in functionality of Visual Studio while also allowing you to benefit from the full features of Node.js outside of Visual Studio when needed.

## NPM

The Node Package Manager, much like NuGet, is a package manager for Node.js packages. It can connect to the public NPM repository, which contains more than 465,000 packages including Bower and Gulp. NPM is included with Node.js but is often updated out of band with Node.js. NPM is also used to execute scripts and has been increasingly used as a build engine like MSBuild.

# Bower

Bower is a package manager for the Web much like NuGet is a package manager for .NET components and libraries and NPM is a package manager for Node.js packages. Bower is currently the preferred solution by Microsoft for managing web packages. You should not use NuGet to manage web packages for ASP.NET Core projects.

Bower consists of a public repository located at `https://bower.io/` but also allows you to have private repositories. Bower components are generally made up of HTML, CSS, JavaScript, fonts, and images. Bower differentiates itself from NPM in that it is designed to manage packages that are deployed as part of a web application that runs in the browser. NPM, on the other hand, is designed to manage packages designed to run on top of Node.js.

Visual Studio comes with a Bower package manager that allows you to browse, install, and manage the Bower packages from within Visual Studio. You can access the Bower package manager by right-clicking the project in Solution Explorer and selecting Manage Bower Packages from the pop-up menu. You can also edit the `bower.json` file directly in the code editor. Visual Studio offers statement completion for `bower.json` and will show you a list of available packages as you type. When you save the `bower.json` file, Visual Studio will automatically run a Bower package restore, which will download and install the packages you have selected. The default location for Bower packages in the Visual Studio project system is `wwwroot/lib`. While this configuration makes it easy to get started, it is not ideal because Bower will copy the entire source code of each of the Bower packages in addition to the files you need for your application. This path can be changed by modifying the `.bowerrc` file. The `.bowerrc` file can be found in Solution Explorer nested under the `bower.json` file. Recipe 11-2 shows how to change how Bower works with Visual Studio so that only the files you need are copied to the `wwwroot/lib` folder.

## Bower Depreciated

Bower has recently stopped active development and has moved to maintenance mode. The Bower team has recommended that you do not use Bower for new projects but instead use Yarn and Webpack. Yarn is an alternative package manager to NPM created by Facebook. Webpack is a module bundler like the one provided by Microsoft but is much more powerful and complex. Recipe 11-3 shows how to install Yarn. Webpack will be demonstrated in recipe 11-4.

Since Bower has been deprecated, I expect that Bower will be replaced in future versions of the Visual Studio tooling. No specific plans for replacing Bower have been announced from the Visual Studio team, however.

# BuildBundlerMinifier NuGet Package

The BuildBundlerMinifier NuGet package is a simple package bundler that is integrated with the ASP.NET Core project build system. It was designed to be easy to use and purposely avoids dependencies on other libraries and task runners such as Gulp. You can configure BuildBundlerMinifier using the `bundleconfig.json` file. The `bundleconfig.json` file included with the ASP.NET Core web application project, shown in Listing 11-1 contains two rules. The first rule takes a single input file, `wwwroot/css/site.css`; minifies it; and saves the minified version to an output file called `wwwroot/css/site.min.css`. The second rule takes the input file `wwwroot/js/site.js`, minifies it, and saves the minified output file to `wwwroot/js/site.min.js`. For the JavaScript file in the second rule, several options are specified for the minification process. First minify is enabled. This is the default value. The second option is `renameLocals`. The `renameLocals` setting tells BuildBundlerMinifier to rename all the local variables to a new shorter name to save additional space. The `renameLocals` setting is also enabled by default. The final setting, `sourceMap`, tells BuildBundlerMinifier not to create a source map. Source maps allow JavaScript debuggers to map lines of code in a minified file to a line of code in the original files. The generation of the source map file makes the build process take slightly longer but is very useful for debugging.

***Listing 11-1.*** Bundleconfig.json

```
// Configure bundling and minification for the project.
[
  {
    "outputFileName": "wwwroot/css/site.min.css",
    // An array of relative input file paths. Globbing patterns supported
    "inputFiles": [
      "wwwroot/css/site.css"
    ]
  },
  {
    "outputFileName": "wwwroot/js/site.min.js",
    "inputFiles": [
      "wwwroot/js/site.js"
    ],
    // Optionally specify minification options
    "minify": {
      "enabled": true,
      "renameLocals": true
    },
    // Optionally generate .map file
    "sourceMap": false
  }
]
```

# 11-2. Customizing the JavaScript Build Workflow in an ASP.NET Core Project

## Problem

You are implementing a new ASP.NET web application and have made use of several Bower components. In your build and deployment process, you are copying the entire contents of the wwwroot folder to your web servers. You have noticed that the deployment process is very slow and that thousands of files are being copied over on each deployment. After doing some investigation, you notice that for each Bower package you have added, the entire Git repository for the package is getting copied into the wwwroot/lib folder. This includes many files that you do not need to run your application. You want to find a way to change how Bower behaves so that only the files you need are copied to wwwroot/lib.

## Solution

The way that ASP.NET Core web application projects are configured out of the box is that all Bower components are copied to the wwwroot\lib folder. While this makes it easy to get up and running, it also causes many unneeded files to be added to the folder.

To correct this behavior, you can modify the Bower configuration file so that the files are written to another folder outside of wwwroot. You can then create an additional build step that copies only the needed files to the wwwroot/lib folder.

# How It Works

To demonstrate how to change the JavaScript build process, create a new ASP.NET Core 1.1 web application project using the Web Application template. Ensure that Authentication is set to No Authentication and that Docker support is not enabled. Name the project and solution **Chapter 11**.

After the project has been created, open the bower.json file and review the contents. The most important section of the file is the dependencies section. The dependencies section lists the Bower components that are installed in your application and allows you to specify the version of each Bower component. Bower.json also allows you to specify metadata for your application. You should see that the application name is asp.net. If you published your application to a Bower repository, the name listed in bower.json is what users would see while browsing the repository.

Try changing the name property in bower.json. You can also add additional metadata properties to the file, such as authors, description, and home page. For a full list of possible settings for bower.json, you can refer to the bower.json specification on GitHub here:

```
https://github.com/bower/spec/blob/master/json.md
```

Listing 11-2 shows a customized bower.json file.

***Listing 11-2.*** Bower.json Modified with Custom Metadata

```
{
  "name": "ASP.NET Core Recipes Chapter 11",
  "authors": [ "John Ciliberti" ],
  "description": "This is a chapter that shows how ASP.NET Core can work together with
  advanced front-end frameworks",
  "homepage": "http://ciliberti.info/",
  "private": true,
  "dependencies": {
    "bootstrap": "3.3.7",
    "jquery": "2.2.0",
    "jquery-validation": "1.14.0",
    "jquery-validation-unobtrusive": "3.2.6"
  }
}
```

## Changing the Bower Configuration

To change the location where Bower packages are downloaded to, you must modify the .bowerrc file. The .bowerrc file is the configuration file that controls how Bower works. To learn about all the available settings for .bowerrc, you can refer to the official documentation here:

```
https://bower.io/docs/config/
```

To edit the .bowerrc file, locate bower.json under the Chapter 11 project in Solution Explorer and then click the chevron to the left of the bower.json file name to expand the group, as shown in Figure 11-1.

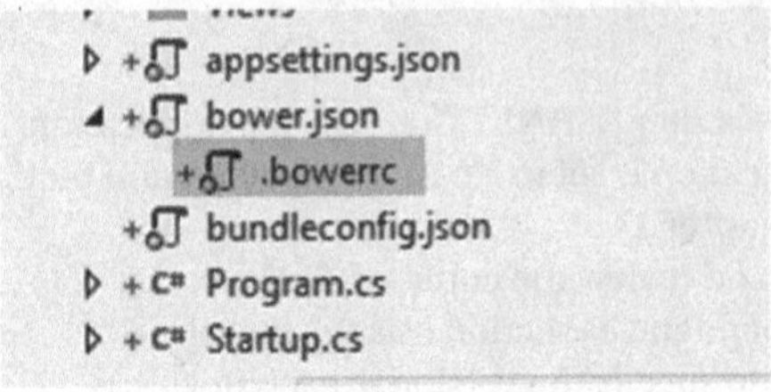

```
    ▷ + 🗊 appsettings.json
    ◢ + 🗊 bower.json
        + 🗊 .bowerrc
    + 🗊 bundleconfig.json
    ▷ + C⁎ Program.cs
    ▷ + C⁎ Startup.cs
```

*Figure 11-1.* *Locating .bowerrc in Solution Explorer*

Double-click .bowerrc to open it. Change the directory property from wwwroot/lib to bower_components. This change will make Bower download the components to the bower_components folder in the root of the web site project rather than under wwwroot. Later, you'll add a Gulp task to copy only the required files to wwwroot.

Listing 11-3 shows the modified .bowerrc file.

*Listing 11-3.* .bowerrc

```
{
  "directory": "bower_components"
}
```

## Adding Gulp to the Project and Automatically Running Tasks When the Project Is Built

Gulp is a toolkit written in JavaScript that runs on top of Node.js. Gulp is often used as a build tool for NPM projects since it makes it easy to automate tasks in your development workflow. Gulp can be installed using NPM.

The easiest way to install an NPM package with Visual Studio is to add a package.json file to the project and then edit the file to list the dependencies. NPM uses package.json to track dependencies, scripts, and metadata for a project. If you add a package.json file to a project in Visual Studio, Visual Studio will automatically watch changes to the file and download and install the listed packages.

To add a package.json file to the project, right-click Chapter 11 in Solution Explorer and then select Add ➤ New Item. Search for the NPM Configuration File template, ensure the file is named package.json, and then click the Add button. Modify package.json to match Listing 11-4. The code in Listing 11-4 defines some basic information about the project. You then add two NPM packages as development dependencies. The first is the Gulp task runner, and the second is a Gulp plug-in called Gulp Copy that you will use to define a copy task.

*Listing 11-4.* Package.json

```
{
  "version": "0.1.0",
  "name": "chapter11",
  "description": "Demonstration of how to modify Bower configuration",
  "private": true,
  "devDependencies": {
    "gulp": "3.9.1",
    "gulp-copy": "1.0.0"
  }
}
```

Now that Gulp has been added to the project, you can use it to define a few tasks. Gulp requires you to define the tasks you would like it to run in a JavaScript file called gulpfile.js. To add a new gulpfile.js file to your project, right-click the project in Solution Explorer and select Add ➤ New Item. In the Add New Item window, search for the Gulp Configuration File template. Ensure the file is named gulpfile.js and then click Add.

The Gulp file is typically made up of a set of require statements that load the components that will be used by the task runner. It then allows you to define one or more tasks. Listing 11-5 shows a simple Gulp file that defines a task called copyToWwwRoot. The copyToWwwRoot task uses the Gulp Copy plug-in to copy only the required files to the wwwroot folder.

***Listing 11-5.*** Gulpfile.js

```
var gulp = require('gulp');
var gulpCopy = require('gulp-copy');
var path_dest = 'wwwroot/lib';
var bower_components = 'bower_components';
gulp.task('copyToWwwRoot', function (){
    return gulp.src([
        bower_components + '/bootstrap/dist/**/*',
        bower_components + '/jquery/dist/*',
        bower_components + '/jquery-validation/dist/*',
        bower_components + '/jquery-validation-unobtrusive/*.js',
        bower_components + '/Respond/dest/*.js'
    ])
        .pipe(gulpCopy(path_dest, {prefix:1}));
});
```

The last step is to wire up the task with MSBuild. This will cause the task to execute each time the project is built. To set this up, open Task Runner Explorer by pressing Ctrl+Alt+Backspace. Task Runner Explorer automatically discovers that the project has a Gulp file and lists tasks found in it. You can bind a task to the After Build event in Visual Studio by right-clicking the task and then selecting Bindings ➤ After Build. You can test this by building the project using the Shift+F6 keyboard combination. The output of the script will be displayed in Task Explorer, as shown in Figure 11-2.

***Figure 11-2.*** *Gulp tasks run when the project builds*

# 11-3. Adding React to an ASP.NET Core Application

## Problem

Your team wants to build a state-of-the-art single-page application with a service tier created in ASP.NET Core. You see that it is possible to install React.js using Bower but are not sure if that is the correct approach. You are also concerned that Bower had been deprecated. A notice on the Bower website states the following: "...psst! While Bower is maintained, we recommend yarn and webpack for new front-end projects!"

Since you plan on putting a lot of effort into building this project, you want to make sure you are building on a solid platform and will not have to perform a major refactoring of the code to remove Bower in the near future.

## Solution

React is a UX library that makes it easy to build user interfaces made up of reusable components. If you plan on using React as a stand-alone library with most of your views rendered on the server, using Bower to manage it as a dependency is probably still a satisfactory solution.

If you plan on building a highly sophisticated single-page application, in most cases you will be using React in combination with several other components including React Router, Redux, and many other supporting libraries. You will also need to have a workflow for transcompiling and bundling your script modules. This is typically done using tools such as Babel and Webpack. Bower is not well-suited for this type of workflow.

A better solution would be to use Yarn for package management rather than Bower. It is also recommended that the front-end project be managed in a separate folder outside of your ASP.NET Core solution. A build step can be added to the React solution that can copy the bundled package to the wwwroot folder of the ASP.NET core application.

## How It Works

In this recipe, you will extend the solution created in recipe 11-2 so that it contains a web API that can be consumed by the React front end. You will then use the create-react-app NPM package to generate a new React application. The last step will be to modify the Webpack configuration of the React application so that the output of the Webpack compilation is copied to the wwwroot folder of the ASP.NET Core web application. In recipe 11-4 you will take a deeper dive into each of the components that make up the React application. In the remaining recipes in this chapter, you will use the foundation created in this recipe to build React components that will consume services created using ASP.NET Core.

## Why React

React is an open source JavaScript library for creating user interfaces that was originally created by Facebook. It has grown in popularity and has a strong community around it. React can be used as a stand-alone library but is more often combined with other components to form a complete front-end stack. The following are the key benefits of React:

- *Components*: React's component-based model makes it easy to decompose a user interface into reusable widgets. React components have life-cycle methods similar to ASP.NET web controls that give developers a high level of control over how the component behaves.

- *Virtual DOM*: React is fast. Much of its speed is a result of its virtual Document Object Model (DOM). The virtual DOM is updated automatically as the state of the component changes. React keeps track of the differences between the state of the virtual DOM and the browser's DOM and efficiently updates the browser's DOM in batches.

- *Testable*: Another advantage of the virtual DOM is that it makes React components easy to test. Facebook has a testing framework for React called Jest that allows you to write unit tests that only invoke the virtual DOM and do not require a web browser to be launched. This makes the test environment easy to set up and allows the tests to run very quickly.

## Installing the Required Software

Visual Studio comes with rudimentary versions of Node.js, NPM, and Git. These stripped-down versions are not sufficient for advanced front-end development. You will need to install the full version of Node.js and NPM to get the full functionality of the Node.js command-line interface and to ensure that the NPM packages work as expected. Since many of the Node.js tools are using Git behind the scenes, I also recommend installing the latest Git-SCM package. Installing the full Git-SCM package also installs MinGW and several Windows Shell extensions that can be useful for development. Minimalist GNU for Windows (MinGW) comes with many powerful Linux utilities including an SSH client, grep, vim, and more.

Another useful application for React development is Yarn. Yarn is a package manager created by Facebook as an alternative to NPM. Yarn is not required, but it is recommended since it is faster and more secure and reliable than NPM.

Table 11-1 contains the software packages you need to download and install.

*Table 11-1.* *Software Packages Required for Front-End Workflow*

| Package | URL | Purpose |
| --- | --- | --- |
| Node.js (LTS) | https://nodejs.org/en/ | JavaScript runtime environment and command-line tools. The Long-Term Support version is recommended since it is more reliable. I used version 6.10.3 when testing this recipe. |
| Git | https://git-scm.com/ | Version control system bundled with Unix command-line tools. Version 2.13.0 was used when testing this recipe. |
| Yarn | https://yarnpkg.com/en/ | Alternative to NPM created by Facebook. It is faster, more secure, and more reliable than NPM. Version 0.24.6 was used when testing this recipe. |

## Creating the React Single-Page Application Using create-react-app

React is a user interface library and not a full single-page application framework like Google's Angular. Creating single-page applications with React is possible only when React is used in combination with other tools. The flexibility of being able to assemble a stack from the best-of-breed solutions is one of the things developers love about React; however, this flexibility has led to massive fragmentation and the creation of hundreds of starter kits for React. This multitude of choices is intimidating for developers new to React. As a response to this problem, Facebook has created an officially supported starter kit for creating single-page applications with React called *create-react-app*.

create-react-app is a JavaScript application that runs on Node.js. It can be downloaded and installed using either NPM or Yarn. Although Yarn is generally better than NPM, I have found that on Windows, NPM does a better job for installing global packages such as create-react-app. Global packages are NPM packages that are installed alongside the Node installation and usually have their executables added to the PATH environmental variable.

To install create-react-app using NPM, enter the following command:

```
npm install -g create-react-app
```

If you are using a Mac or Linux PC, you can install create-react-app using Yarn rather than NPM by entering the following command:

```
yarn global add create-react-app
```

Once create-react-app is installed, open a new command window. It is necessary to open a new command window to access the changes in the PATH environmental variable performed by Yarn or NPM. In the new command window, navigate to the Chapter 11 folder. This should be one level up in the directory tree from the Chapter 11 Visual Studio solution. Enter the following command to create the React application:

```
create-react-app chapter11-react
```

create-react-app will take several minutes to run. It will use Yarn to download and install many NPM packages. The total number of packages required for the single-page application created by create-react-app was 860 at the time of this writing. Luckily, most of the packages are downstream dependencies that you do not need to worry about. When the installer process completes, you will see the following message in your command window:

```
Success! Created chapter11-react at C:\ AspNetCoreRecipes\Chapter11\chapter11-react
Inside that directory, you can run several commands:

  yarn start
    Starts the development server.

  yarn build
    Bundles the app into static files for production.

  yarn test
    Starts the test runner.

  yarn eject
    Removes this tool and copies build dependencies, configuration files
    and scripts into the app directory. If you do this, you can't go back!

We suggest that you begin by typing:

  cd chapter11-react
  yarn start

Happy hacking!
```

## Opening the React Project in Visual Studio

If you want to use Visual Studio to view and edit the files created by create-react-app, you can do so by using the Visual Studio Open Folder feature. Visual Studio 2017 allows you to open a folder without creating a solution or project file. Using this option will allow you to view the directory tree in Solution Explorer and edit the files. Many of the code-editing features such as statement completion, static code analysis, and code formatting will work as expected. Other features such as Visual Studio's build tools and the integrated test runner will not work unless a project file is created.

To open the folder, from the Visual Studio File menu, select Open ➤ Folder. You can then select the chapter11-react folder. You will see the folder tree displayed in Solution Explorer.

While Visual Studio 2017 is good as a basic React editor, there are other editors that offer more advanced features for front-end developers. I personally prefer to use JetBrains WebStorm for working on React projects. WebStorm costs $59 for the first year for individual developers but offers free subscriptions for developers working on open source projects, students, and educators. Visual Studio Code and GitHub's Atom editor can also be set up to support React development when coupled with the proper set of extensions. Visual Studio Code and Atom are free. If you want to try Visual Studio Code, I recommend installing the following extensions:

- *JSX*: This adds support for JSX development in Visual Studio Code.

- *ESLint*: This uses the ESLint installation and configuration from a local file to show code style problems and potential errors in the code editor.

- *EditorConfig for Visual Studio Code* : This adds the ability for Visual Studio Code to enforce standards defined in .editorConfig files. The .editorConfig file is a tool-agnostic standard for defining important editor defaults such as tabs versus spaces. This is essential when people on your team are using different editors but are sharing a common ESLint configuration.

- *Code Spellchecker*: This add-in is not React specific but makes it easy to detect and correct spelling errors in your code.

## Starting the React Development Server

Because create-react-app installed a development server that runs on top of Node.js, you can start the development server and interact with the React application by running the following commands:

```
cd chapter11-react
yarn start
```

After several seconds, your default web browser will open automatically and display a page similar to the one shown in Figure 11-3.

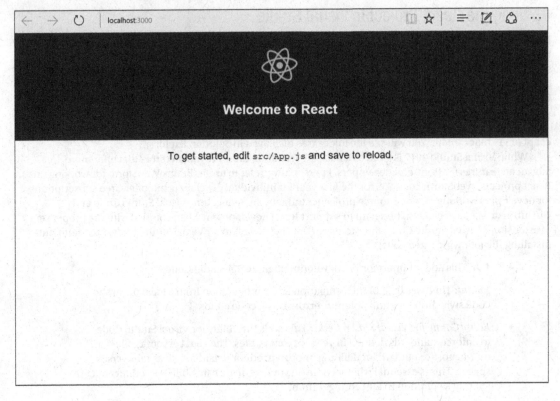

*Figure 11-3.* *React application created by create-react-app*

## Integrating the React Application with Your ASP.NET Core MVC Project

The React application you just created is a single-page application (SPA). An SPA can replace all or part of the user interface for your ASP.NET Core application. The React application has its own component model and routing engine. React component pages will be generated on the client rather the server like they are with ASP.NET Core MVC.

Client-side versus server-side rendering does not need to be an all-or-nothing decision. Most major web sites such as Facebook are not just one giant single-page application. In most cases, large web applications consist of several single-page applications in combination with traditional server-rendered pages. You will take this approach with your application. The home page will remain a server-rendered ASP.NET Core MVC view. You will also use server rendering to create the header and footer of the web site. The React SPA application will be embedded in a Razor view accessible from the path /profile.

To create this integration, you will first need to add the Profile action in the Home controller of the ASP.NET Core application, as shown in Listing 11-6.

*Listing 11-6.* Adding the Profile Action to the Home Controller

```
public IActionResult Profile()
{
    return View();
}
```

Next, you will add a new view in the Home folder called Profile. The Profile view will host the React application. For now, you will leave the view empty. The contents of this page will be generated using the React build process.

## Building the React App

To integrate the React application into the ASP.NET Core application, you will need to use the build script that has been added to the React application by create-react-app. The build script will generate the static assets. You can then copy the static assets into the folder wwwroot/lib/chapter11-react of your ASP.NET Core project. For the React application to work properly when deployed in that path, you need to modify the configuration of the React application. To update the configuration, open the package.json file in the chapter11-react folder and add a homepage property, as shown in Listing 11-7.

*Listing 11-7.* Updated homepage Property of package.json

```
{
  "name": "chapter11-react",
  "version": "0.1.0",
  "private": true,
  "homepage": "/lib/chapter11-react",
  "dependencies": {
    "react": "^15.5.4",
    "react-dom": "^15.5.4"
  },
  "devDependencies": {
    "react-scripts": "1.0.7"
  },
  "scripts": {
    "start": "react-scripts start",
    "build": "react-scripts build",
    "test": "react-scripts test --env=jsdom",
    "eject": "react-scripts eject"
  }
}
```

Next, you will run the build script. To do this, stop the React development server if it is still running by using the Ctrl+C key combination inside the console window.

If asked the following, enter Y:

```
Terminate batch job (Y/N)?
```

The server will stop. Next, enter the following command to build the React app:

```
yarn build
```

After several seconds, you will see the following in the command window:

```
yarn build v0.24.6
$ react-scripts build
Creating an optimized production build...
Compiled successfully.
```

```
File sizes after gzip:

  47.09 KB   build\static\js\main.23e5d2a8.js
  289 B      build\static\css\main.9a0fe4f1.css

The project was built assuming it is hosted at lib/chapter11-react/
You can control this with the homepage field in your package.json

The build folder is ready to be deployed.

Done in 11.62s.
```

## Copying the Contents of the React Build Folder to the ASP.NET Core Project

The React application is now ready to be copied into the ASP.NET Core application. In the next recipe, you will show how this copy step can be automated, but for now you will do it manually. To do this, create a new folder under the wwwroot/lib folder of the ASP.NET Core project and name it chapter11-react. Next, copy the entire contents of the build folder in the React project into the new folder.

The final steps in this process are to extract the generated HTML created by the React build process and use it to update the Profile view so that it loads the required JavaScript and CSS. You can find the generated HTML in the index.html file that has been added to the root of the React application's build folder. Copy the contents of this file into Profile.cshtml. Visual Studio will automatically format the HTML when it is pasted. Listing 11-8 shows the pasted contents. Note that the names of the JavaScript and CSS files will vary with each build. This is a feature that prevents cached versions of the files from causing issues.

***Listing 11-8.*** HTML Generated by React Build Process

```html
<!DOCTYPE html>
<html lang="en">
<head>
    <meta charset="utf-8">
    <meta name="viewport" content="width=device-width,initial-scale=1,shrink-to-fit=no">
    <meta name="theme-color" content="#000000">
    <link rel="manifest" href="/lib/chapter11-react/manifest.json">
    <link rel="shortcut icon" href="/lib/chapter11-react/favicon.ico">
    <title>React App</title>
    <link href="/lib/chapter11-react/static/css/main.9a0fe4f1.css" rel="stylesheet">
</head>
<body>
    <noscript>You need to enable JavaScript to run this app.</noscript><div id="root"></div>
    <script type="text/javascript" src="/lib/chapter11-react/static/js/main.148a30c4.js">
    </script>
</body>
</html>
```

There are several problems with the code you pasted. First, since the Profile view is using a layout page, it does not need the HTML, HEAD, and BODY elements. These elements can be deleted. Next, you need to make sure that the LINK and META elements are rendered inside the header of the page. To do this, you will need to create a new optional section in the ASP.NET Core _Layout.cshtml page, as shown in Listing 11-9.

***Listing 11-9.*** Adding the Head Section in _Layout.cshtml

```
@inject Microsoft.ApplicationInsights.AspNetCore.JavaScriptSnippet JavaScriptSnippet
<!DOCTYPE html>
<html>
<head>
    <meta charset="utf-8" />
    <meta name="viewport" content="width=device-width, initial-scale=1.0" />
    <title>@ViewData["Title"] - Chapter11</title>

    <environment names="Development">
        <link rel="stylesheet" href="~/lib/bootstrap/dist/css/bootstrap.css" />
        <link rel="stylesheet" href="~/css/site.css" />
    </environment>
    <environment names="Staging,Production">
        <link rel="stylesheet" href="https://ajax.aspnetcdn.com/ajax/bootstrap/3.3.7/css/
        bootstrap.min.css"
                asp-fallback-href="~/lib/bootstrap/dist/css/bootstrap.min.css"
                asp-fallback-test-class="sr-only" asp-fallback-test-property="position"
                asp-fallback-test-value="absolute" />
        <link rel="stylesheet" href="~/css/site.min.css" asp-append-version="true" />
    </environment>
    @Html.Raw(JavaScriptSnippet.FullScript)
    @RenderSection("Head", required: false)
</head>
<!-- The rest of the layout page is not shown -->
```

You will also need to make sure that the JavaScript file is loaded at the bottom of the page. The default layout page already has a `Script` section that you can utilize. Now you can modify the `Profile` view so that it uses the sections defined in `_Layout.cshtml`. The completed file should match Listing 11-10.

***Listing 11-10.*** Profile.cshtml

```
@section Head{
    <meta name="theme-color" content="#000000">
    <link rel="manifest" href="~/lib/chapter11-react/manifest.json">
    <link href="~/lib/chapter11-react/static/css/main.9a0fe4f1.css" rel="stylesheet">
}
<noscript>
    You need to enable JavaScript to run this app.
</noscript>
<div id="root"></div>
@section Scripts{
    <script type="text/javascript" src="~/lib/chapter11-react/static/js/main.148a30c4.js">
    </script>
}
```

You may have noticed that the links to the CSS and JavaScript files generated by the React compiler use a random sequence of characters between the file name and extension. This is an optimization added by the build script to help prevent problems caused by proxy servers caching outdated static content. Because of this, you will need to make sure that the `Profile` view is updated each time you build and copy the static assets from the React project. You will continue to build the functionality of the `Profile` React SPA in recipe 11-5.

If you are new to React, ECMAScript 6 (ES6), and JSX, I highly recommend that you read recipe 11-4 before moving on. Recipe 11-4 provides a brief overview of all the technology used in the React SPA application and the NodeJS build tool chain.

# 11-4. Understanding React, JSX, ES6, Babel, and Webpack

## Problem

In recipe 11-3, a tool named create-react-app was used to generate a single-page application based on React. The app contains hundreds of files and libraries. You need help understanding the React application before you can become productive in developing using this stack.

## Solution

React and its ecosystem are complex. This section provides a brief introduction to the major components of the React toolkit so that you will be able to better understand the contents of the rest of the recipes in this chapter.

## How It Works

Diving into React development requires gaining an understanding of many technologies that you may not be familiar with as an ASP.NET Core developer. While you do not need to be an expert at every component in the React toolchain, it is helpful to understand the major components. In this section, I will cover the following:

- *ECMAScript 6 (ES6)*: This is a major upgrade to the ECMAScript (aka JavaScript) language; it introduces many new features that make developing complex applications in JavaScript more practical.

- *React*: This is a user interface library created by Facebook. It provides a component-based model for creating user interface components.

- *JSX*: JSX is an ECMAScript 6 extension that simplifies the creation of components created with React by allowing you to easily mix ES6 code with HTML. You can think of JSX as the Razor view engine of the React world.

- *Babel*: Babel is a transpiler that is used to convert ES6 and JSX to ECMAScript 5. Babel allows you to use the latest ECMAScript innovations without compromising on browser compatibility.

- *Webpack*: Webpack is an advanced component bundler. It is responsible for generating the CSS and JavaScript files that you copied to the ASP.NET Core application in recipe 11-3.

## ES6

ES6 is a major upgrade to the ECMAScript language standard that was ratified in 2015. ES6 brings a new module system, new classes, better variable scoping, and new arrow functions. In this section, you will see the ES6 features that are the most critical to understand for React development.

## Module System

Modules are a foundational concept in computer science in which parts of a program are organized into independent units that can be linked together to work as a program. ES5 did not have a built-in module system, which made it difficult to develop complex JavaScript programs and led to an overreliance on global variables, which often resulted in difficult-to-solve bugs. As a result, the ES5 developer community began creating libraries that provided module-like functionality and eventually developed standard syntax for creating modules that could work across library implementations. Unfortunately, two competing incompatible standards, CommonJS and AMD, emerged from this evolution.

In ES6, a new built-in module system has been added that melds the best features of CommonJS and AMD. These features include the following:

- A compact, easy-to-understand declarative syntax for importing and exporting modules

- Support for configurable asynchronous module loading

- Support for cyclic module dependencies where module A imports module B and module B imports module A

Several new JavaScript keywords have been added to the language to support modules.

### export and export default

Functions and variables created in a module are hidden from other modules unless they are exported. The export keyword can be applied to objects, primitives, and functions to allow them to be imported into other modules. There are two types of exports, named export and default  export. Each module can have exactly one default export. Default exports differ from named exports in that developers can use a simplified syntax when importing them. Listing 11-11 shows examples of how the export keyword can be used.

*Listing 11-11.* Examples of the export and export default Keywords

```
// created named export for authorFirstName
// using new ES6 short hand equivalent to { authorFirstName : authorFirstName  }
const authorFirstName = 'John';
export { authorFirstName };

// declare and export variable name on one line
export const authorLastName = 'Ciliberti';

// export multiple objects
const arrayOfNumbers = [1, 2, 3, 4];
const someObject = {
  prop1: 'value 1',
  prop2: 'value 2'
};
export {
  arrayOfNumbers,
  someObject
};
```

```
// named export for a function
export function printWarning(message) {
  console.warn(message);
}

// default export function that returns string 'New ES6 return statement shorthand'
export default ('New ES6 return statement shorthand');
```

## import

The import keyword is used to make objects exported from other modules available in the current module. The functionality of import can be compared to how the using statement is used to import namespaces into a C# file. Listing 11-12 demonstrates some examples of how to use the import statement. In the first example, the React object, which is a default export, is imported from the React module. The React module was added to the application from NPM and is listed as an application dependency in the project.json file. It is referred to by name rather than by relative path. In the second import statement, two named imports, authorFirstName and authorLastName, are imported from a module located in the same directory. Notice that you use ./ to refer to a file in the current directory. You should also notice that the file extension is omitted from the path. In the third example shown in Listing 11-12, the default import and two named exports are imported. In the final example, the default export and all named imports are added. The notation * as mod2 is used to import all the named exports and make them accessible via the alias mod2. For example, the named exports food and animal from Module2 can now be accessed using mod2.food and mod2.animal.

*Listing 11-12.* Examples of the ES6 Import Statement

```
// import the default export from an external module
// defined as a dependency in package.json
import React from 'react';

// import the several named exports from
// module defined in same directory
import { authorFirstName, authorLastName } from './Listing11-9';

// import the default export as well as several named exports
// from module defined in directory Subfolder
import customName, { car, bike } from './Subfolder/Module1';

// import the default export as well as all named exports
// from module defined in directory Subfolder
import customName2, * as mod2 from './Subfolder/Module2';
```

## Classes

JavaScript has long supported object-oriented programing using a prototype-based inheritance model. ES6 does not change how inheritance behaves in JavaScript, but it does add some syntactical sugar that makes object-oriented JavaScript code much easier to read and understand. Several new keywords have been added to ES6 to support the new class syntax.

- class: This is used to define a new prototype. It should be noted that even though the syntax looks like the C# class definition, JavaScript remains prototype based.

- extends: This is used in class declarations to create a class that is a child of another class. It can be used to extend both custom and built-in classes as long as the type you are extending is an object or null.

- constructor: This is a method that can be defined inside a class that contains initialization logic that is executed when the object is created.

- super: This can be used inside a constructor function to call the constructor of the parent object.

- static: This is used to create methods that can be called directly on that class but not from instances of a class.

Listing 11-13 shows the new ES6 class syntax in action. First a class called Car is defined. Car has a constructor that accepts three arguments, year, make, and model, that it assigned to its context using this. Car also contains a method called printCarInfo that prints the car's year, make, and model. The printCarInfo method is using a new ES6 feature called *string interpolation*. With string interpolation, you can define a string using backticks instead of single or double quotes. You can then embed variables and expressions into the string by encapsulating the expression using ${expression}.

Next a class named Sedan is created that extends Car. The Sedan class has a four-argument constructor with an additional argument for color. The constructor calls super, which passes the year, make, and model to the parent constructor. Sedan also adds a static method called getYellowSedan for creating yellow sedans.

*Listing 11-13.* ES6 Classes

```
class Car {
  constructor(year, make, model) {
    this.year = year;
    this.make = make;
    this.model = model;
  }
  printCarInfo() {
    console.log(`The car is a ${this.year} ${this.make} ${this.model}`);
  }
}

class Sedan extends Car {
  constructor(year, make, model, color) {
    super(year, make, model);
    this.color = color;
  }
  static getYellowSedan(year, make, model) {
    return new Sedan(year, make, model, 'Yellow');
  }
}

const myCar = new Sedan(2016, 'BMW', '328i', 'Grey');
myCar.printCarInfo();

const yourCar = Sedan.getYellowSedan(1987, 'Dodge', 'Dart');
yourCar.printCarInfo();
```

## Variable Scoping with let and const

Variable scoping in ES5 is the cause of many bugs and errors. In ES5 you had two ways to declare a variable. The first and generally most recommended way was to use the var keyword when defining a variable. var creates a variable at the scope of the current execution context. Variables created using var inside a function are scoped to the function. Variables created outside a function are global. What is often misunderstood is that when you use var to create a variable inside a code block, the variable is still scoped at the function level.

The second way to create a variable in ES5 was not to use any initializer at all. When you create a variable without using var, the variable is always global regardless of where it is defined. This feature is very dangerous and can lead to mistyped variables being interpreted as new global variables. Thankfully, you could disable the ability to use undeclared variables by adding use strict at the top of your JavaScript file.

In ES6, it is possible to still use undeclared variables and variables defined using var, but it is discouraged for new code. Most possible static validation (*linters*) will show a warning when var is used. In the React build pipeline, use strict is automatically added when the ES6 code is cross-compiled to ES5 and the use of undeclared variables will result in build errors.

ES6 introduces two new variable declaration keywords, let and const. let and const both declare local variables scoped at the block level just like variable declarations in C#. const is used to create constants whose values cannot be reassigned.

Listing 11-14 shows several examples of how variables can be declared in ES6.

*Listing 11-14.* Behavior of let, const, var, and undeclared Variables

```
// following line of code will cause build to fail
global1 = 'this is a global variable';

var global2 = 'this is also a global variable';

function vars(){
    // this line will also cause a build error
    global3 = 'this is also a global variable';

    var varsScope1 = 'scoped at vars';
    if(1===1){
        var varsScope2 = 'Scoped in vars function (not the if block)';
        let scopedInIfBlock = 'This is scoped in the if block.';
        const constInIfBlock ='I am scoped to if block and cannot change';
        scopedInIfBlock = 'my value can change';
    }
}
```

## Arrow Functions

ES6 introduces a new shorthand syntax for creating functions known as *arrow function expressions*. Arrow function expressions follow the syntax patterns used in C# lambda expressions.

In Listing 11-15, an arrow function with no arguments and only one statement is created and stored in a constant called noCurlyBracesRequired. When only one statement exists in the function, the function body does not require curly braces. The noCurlyBracesRequired function can then be called just like any other function.

*Listing 11-15.* Arrow Function with No Arguments and Only One Statement

```
const noCurlyBracesRequired = () => console.log('This is an arrow function with no
arguments');
noCurlyBracesRequired();
// This is an arrow function with no arguments
```

In Listing 11-16 an arrow function that takes a single argument is created and assigned to a const called noParenthesisRequired. When you have only one argument, parentheses are not required for the argument list.

*Listing 11-16.* Arrow Function with One Argument and Only One Statement

```
const noParenthesisRequired = a => console.log(`The value of the a argument is ${a}`);
noParenthesisRequired('foo');
// The value of the a argument is foo
```

In Listing 11-17 an arrow function that takes three arguments is created and assigned to a const called requiresParenthesisAndCurlyBraces. When you have more the one argument, parentheses are required for the argument list. Curly braces are required when an arrow function contains multiple statements. In requiresParenthesisAndCurlyBraces, the first two arguments are expected to be strings, and the last is expected to be a function. In the call to requiresParenthesisAndCurlyBraces, an arrow function is used to define a function that is passed as the third argument.

*Listing 11-17.* An Arrow Function with Multiple Statements and Three Arguments

```
const requiresParenthesisAndCurlyBraces = (a, b, c) => {
  console.log(`The value of the a argument is ${a}`);
  console.log(`The value of the b argument is ${b}`);
  c();
};

requiresParenthesisAndCurlyBraces('foo', 'bar', () => console.log('bat'));
// The value of the a argument is foo
// The value of the b argument is bar
// bat
```

# React and JSX

React is a user interface library created by Facebook. React allows you to decompose your user interface into small, reusable components. React components are JavaScript functions that contain a render method that outputs HTML markup. React components can be nested into hierarchies in a comparable way as you would do with HTML elements. To simplify development, React supports the use of a JavaScript extension called JSX. JSX allows you to freely mix HTML and JavaScript, much like you can mix HTML and C# code in a Razor view. React components can be stateful and keep track of their own properties, or they can be stateless, with state information being managed in a parent component and changes to state being communicated via properties. When using JSX, properties of a React component can be passed using what look like HTML attributes, much like properties are communicated with Razor Tag Helpers.

Listing 11-18 shows the App.js component that is generated by the create-react-app NPM package. App.js is an ES6 module.

*Listing 11-18.* App.js

```
import React, { Component } from 'react';
import logo from './logo.svg';
import './App.css';

class App extends Component {
  render() {
    return (
      <div className="App">
        <div className="App-header">
          <img src={logo} className="App-logo" alt="logo" />
          <h2>Welcome to React</h2>
        </div>
        <p className="App-intro">
          To get started, edit <code>src/App.js</code> and save to reload.
        </p>
      </div>
    );
  }
}

export default App;
```

In line 1 of the module, React, the default export from the React package, is imported along with a named export called Component. Component is the base class for stateful React components.

```
import React, { Component } from 'react';
```

The second import statement does not import an ES6 module but rather an .svg image. This functionality is provided not by the ES6 module system but rather a loader plug-in for the Webpack module bundler. When Webpack processes the module, it will see the nonstandard import file and attempt to match it with a loader. If no matching loader is found, then the Webpack build will fail. If a loader is found, the loader plug-in will process logo.svg so that it is bundled into the script file generated by the Webpack build process.

```
import logo from './logo.svg';
```

In an equivalent way to logo.svg, a CSS loader plug-in from Webpack will package the CSS file App.css and make it available to the module.

```
import './App.css';
```

After the import statements is the App class declaration. The App class extends the Component class imported from the React package. The Component class contains rich functionality that includes a way to track component state and component life-cycle events. If you are familiar with the page life cycle from ASP.NET Web Forms, then the concept of component life-cycle events will feel very natural to you. In fact, a key feature of React is its one-way data flow that mimics the data flow of a server-side page rendering done by ASP.NET Web Forms. You will learn more about these features starting in recipe 11-5.

Inside the App class is the render method. The render method uses JSX syntax to render a header and "get started" message. For the most part, the content looks very much like standard HTML except for the src attribute of the img element.

```
<img src={logo} className="App-logo" alt="logo" />
```

The `img` element is using the `logo` object created from the second `import` statement and assigning it to the `src` attribute. JSX will treat the content inside the curly braces as a JavaScript expression. In this case, the curly braces contain the logo, but any valid JavaScript expression could be used.

## Webpack

As you may have guessed from the previous section, Webpack does much more than just simply combining and compressing script files. Webpack does complex build orchestration that begins with creating a graph of the application's dependencies and then intelligently including all of the required modules. Webpack treats every file in your JavaScript project as a module. It uses loaders to transform non-JavaScript files into a format that can be added to the dependency graph and then bundled into a script file. Webpack also supports the concept of plug-ins. Webpack plug-ins can be used to add custom functionality.

Webpack supports a concept called *hot module replacement*, which can add and remove modules while an application is running without reloading the entire application. This allows your app to retain state while updates to packages are efficiently replaced at the client.

You can find more information on Webpack at `https://webpack.js.org/configuration/`.

## Babel

A problem that has plagued front-end web developers since the dawn of the Web is cross-browser and backward compatibility. New language innovations are impossible to adopt because it takes years for the major browser vendors to implement the standards ratified by the W3C and ECMA and even longer for businesses and consumers to adopt standard-compliant browsers.

Babel helps to solve this problem by allowing you to use the latest innovations in JavaScript by transcompiling your ES6 into the equivalent backward-compatible code. In cases where no equivalent functionality exists in older versions of JavaScript, Babel provides a set of polyfill libraries that implement the new language features.

You can find more information about Babel at `https://babeljs.io/`.

# 11-5. Adding Unit Testing and Static Code Analysis to a React Project

## Problem

You are following test-driven development (TDD) using xUnit for your ASP.NET Core server-side code. You want to add the same level of test automation for your front-end code. You want to be able to add automated unit testing and static analysis to your build process. You also want to find problems early and have your IDE alert you as you are editing your code.

## Solution

The application created by create-react-app comes with ESLint static code analysis and the Jest unit test framework installed and set up to run automatically but with only a basic configuration. It is up to you add specific rules for ESLint and to create a full suite of unit tests. In this recipe, you will enhance the static code analysis by installing the Airbnb ESLint configuration, which will enforce rules created by the Airbnb development team. Airbnb was an early adopter of React and has created the ESLint rules to enforce best practices based on its experiences.

While the Jest unit testing framework is powerful, you can get additional benefits from adding the Enzyme test library. Enzyme was also created by the Airbnb team. Enzyme includes many features that substantially simplify writing unit tests with React. The most significant feature is shallow rendering, which allows you to test a React component without rendering all other components in the component hierarchy.

## How It Works

In this section, you will first install the Airbnb ESLint configuration and then customize it to meet your needs. Next, you will install several add-ons to Jest and the Enzyme library.

## ESLint Configuration

A *linter* is a tool that identifies code that does not follow best practices or has poor stylistic construction. The term *lint* was first used at Bell Labs in the 1970s to describe a tool that eventually was released as part of the Unix operating system. The Unix lint utility released in 1978 flagged suspicious and nonportable constructs that often were associated with software defects.

JavaScript contains many features that made it easy to learn for novice developers. These ease-of-use features unfortunately can make complex JavaScript applications error-prone and difficult to maintain. For example, with JavaScript, semicolons are optional, but when they are not used, you may sometimes have unintended results.

Linters are used to enforce rules that some developers feel should be enforced by the compiler. They are also used to enforce coding style standards across code bases. ESLint is a JavaScript linter for ECMAScript 2015. It is installed with create-react-app and will be run automatically when the application is built and then log any errors found to the console. ESLint results can also be seen in code editors such as Visual Studio and WebStorm. In some cases, the editor can correct the linting errors automatically. The application produced by create-react-app does not include any linting rules with the default configuration and leaves it to developers to add whatever rules they want. If you are using Visual Studio, a default ESLint configuration is included, but these setting are applied only within Visual Studio and will not be enforced on build servers such as TFS or Jenkins.

A popular ruleset is the one created by Airbnb. The Airbnb ruleset includes rules for ES6, React, and JSX. Installing the rules requires two steps. First you must install the eslint-config-airbnb package. You can add an .eslintrc file under the project root and set it so that it extends Airbnb. To install the Airbnb rules, enter the following at the command line:

```
npm install -g install-peerdeps
install-peerdeps --dev eslint-config-airbnb
```

Once installation has completed, add a file named .eslintrc to your project and then modify it to look like Listing 11-19.

---

Since Windows Explorer does not allow you to create files that begin with a dot, you will need to use a command-line utility such as the Unix touch command that is available with git bash to create the file. To do this, open the git bash shell, navigate to the directory of your project, and use the following command:

```
touch .eslintrc
```

---

*Listing 11-19.* Adding the Airbnb ESLint Rules to Your Project

```
{
  "extends": "airbnb"
}
```

After adding the ESLint configuration, you will notice that Visual Studio is showing many errors. The errors are caused by the fact that code generated by create-react-app does not comply with some of the rules created by Airbnb. For example, Airbnb's rules specify that all React components use .jsx extensions rather .js. Custom rules can be added to the .eslintrc file to override certain rules if you disagree with them.

## Adding Linting Rules for Jest Unit Tests

Since you will be using Jest as your unit test framework, you can add additional rules to your ESLint configuration that will help you ensure that your tests are created using best practices. To install the Jest ESLint plug-in, enter the following at the command prompt:

```
yarn add --dev eslint-plugin-jest
```

After the plug-in has been installed, you can add the plug-in and Jest rules to the .eslintrc file. It is also a good idea to add the Jest global variables to .eslintrc; otherwise, ESLint will mistakenly raise errors in all of your tests because it will not know that some of the Jest functions such as it and expect are valid global variables.

Listing 11-20 shows the .eslintrc file with the Jest plug-in configuration. Listing 11-20 also shows how certain rules such as the use of the .js extension can be overridden.

*Listing 11-20.* The Completed .eslintrc File

```
{
  "extends": "airbnb",
  "plugins": [
    "jest"
  ],
  "rules": {
    "comma-dangle": 0,
    "react/jsx-filename-extension": [
      1,
      {
        "extensions": [
          ".js",
          ".jsx"
        ]
      }
    ],
    "no-console": 0,
    "jest/no-disabled-tests": "warn",
    "jest/no-focused-tests": "error",
    "jest/no-identical-title": "error",
    "jest/valid-expect": "error"
  },
```

```
    "env": {
        "jest/globals": true
    }
}
```

# Types of Tests for Front-End Applications

When creating a test suite for the front end of your application, you will need to test several aspects of the application. Some tests, such as unit tests, are very much like what you do on the server with xUnit. Other tests will need to verify that the visual tree of the application is being rendered properly and that user interactions such as mouse overs and clicks have the desired effect. In this section, I will briefly describe the types of tests you will create. In recipe 11-6, you will build the tests as you create an SPA in React using the TDD methodology.

## Unit Tests

As you develop the React application, you will need to test nonvisual modules such as validation components, service proxies, and utilities. For nonvisual modules, you can create unit tests like you did in Chapter 7 with ASP.NET Core controllers. The main difference here is that rather than using xUnit as you did in Chapter 7, you will use Jest. Jest is a unit testing framework created by Facebook. Jest is used by Facebook to test all of Facebook's JavaScript applications. Since Facebook uses React as its main UI library, Jest offers many features specific to testing React. Jest is included with the application created using `create-react-app`.

## Snapshot Tests

Many React components will be stateless and will consist only of user interface components. Snapshot tests help you to verify that your UI does not change unexpectedly. The first time you run your snapshot tests, a snapshot of what the UI should look like will be recorded. If a modification to the application results in a change in the UI, the next test run will fail. Each time you make a change that should change the UI, a new snapshot can be recorded by running the following command:

```
jest --updateSnapshot
```

To enable Snapshot testing, you will need to add the react-test-renderer package to your project. To do this, enter the following command at the command prompt:

```
yarn add --dev react-test-renderer
```

## DOM Tests

With DOM testing, you can write tests that manipulate the rendered component and then use Jest assertions to verify the correct behavior. There are two popular libraries for implementing this DOM tests, React Enzyme and React's TestUtils. For this chapter, you will use Enzyme. To install Enzyme, enter the following command in the command prompt:

```
yarn add --dev enzyme
```

# 11-6. Creating an SPA Using ASP.NET Core and React

## Problem

You want to create an artist profile page for your web site. The page will show several pieces of information, including the artist name, biological information, and a list of collaboration projects the artist is engaged in. The page will combine the features and functionality of ASP.NET Core and React.

## Solution

Recipe 11-3 demonstrated how a React SPA application can be created at the command prompt and then integrated into an ASP.NET Core application by copying the bundled JavaScript and CSS files into the wwwroot folder of the ASP.NET Core project. In this solution, you will expand on that solution by creating several React components and then integrating them into the profile app. The process of creating the React SPA will require the following steps:

1. Create an HTML mock-up of the desired result.

2. Break the HTML mock-up into logical components and use these snippets as the basis of the React components.

3. Decide how data will be flow from the parent React component to the children using React props.

4. Create unit tests to verify both the front-end components and the ASP.NET Core services that you will create.

5. Create a controller in the ASP.NET Core application to supply the data to the React components.

6. Integrate the ASP.NET Core web services with the React front end.

## How It Works

This recipe will follow the test-driven development methodology described in Chapter 7. If you are unfamiliar with this approach, I recommend you read recipe 7-3.

### Creating the HTML Mock-Up of Your React SPA

Before diving into creating the React components, it is helpful to first create a mock-up of the intended output in standard HTML. To start this process, create a new folder called mockups under the chapter11-react folder created in recipe 11-3. Inside the mockup folder create a new file called profile-mock.html. Start the file by copying the contents of public/index.html and then replace the dynamic values such as the href properties of the LINK elements in the head of the document with hard-coded values. You should also remove any comments from the content since they are not needed. You can also remove the link to the manifest.json file.

When this step is completed, profile-mock.html should match Listing 11-21.

*Listing 11-21.* Profile.-mock.html Step 1

```
<!doctype html>
<html lang="en">
  <head>
    <meta charset="utf-8">
    <meta name="viewport" content="width=device-width, initial-scale=1, shrink-to-fit=no">
    <meta name="theme-color" content="#000000">
    <link rel="shortcut icon" href=" ../../public/favicon.ico ">
    <title>React App</title>
  </head>
  <body>
    <noscript>
      You need to enable JavaScript to run this app.
    </noscript>
    <div id="root"></div>
  </body>
</html>
```

At this point, the HTML page will not show any content. The next step will be to add some styling to the mock-up. Since the ASP.NET Core template uses the Bootstrap CSS library, you will need to add this to the mock-up page. This can be done by adding a LINK element to the HEAD section of profile-mock.html. You can obtain the HTML needed for adding the Bootstrap styling from https://www.bootstrapcdn.com/. The bootstrap CDN web site will generate the HTML, which includes the href to the Bootstrap CSS file and an integrity token, which when used with a supported browser can ensure that the file being pulled from the remote server matches the integrity token. Using an integrity token can help prevent your web site users from downloading malicious files if the CDN web site is compromised.

To support custom styles that may be required by the user profile mock-up, create a CSS file in the mockups directory called profile-mock.css. Add a LINK element to the HEADER of profile-mock.html so that any styles included in profile-mock.css can be applied to the page. Be sure that profile-mock.css appears after Bootstrap so that it will be possible for the custom styles to override styles from Bootstrap if required. When completed, the new LINK elements should appear in the header of profile-mock.html, as shown Listing 11-22.

*Listing 11-22.* Header of profile-mock.html After CSS Links Added

```
<link href="https://maxcdn.bootstrapcdn.com/bootstrap/3.3.7/css/bootstrap.min.css"
    rel="stylesheet"
    integrity="sha384-BVYiiSIFeK1dGmJRAkycuHAHRg32OmUcww7on3RYdg4Va+PmSTsz/K68vbdEjh4u"
    crossorigin="anonymous">
<link rel="stylesheet" href="profile-mock.css"/>
```

Next, you can add some content. The profile page will have a banner image that will cover the top 20 percent of the screen. This image will be something the users can customize to make their profile page more unique. You will also add a user profile picture. The profile picture will overlap slightly with the banner image. Directly to the right of the profile image and below the banner image will be page header with the artist first and last names. The artist biography will follow the header.

To start, you will add the CSS styles to profile-mock.css to support the design. Since you are using Bootstrap, only a small amount of custom CSS is required to cover your unique needs. The rest of the styling will be from the Bootstrap CSS.

To implement the banner, you will add a style rule that sets the width of the banner image to 100 percent. You will also add a margin to the bottom of the banner image so that the text will not be placed directly below it. Next, you will add a style for the artist profile image. To create the overlap effect, you will provide a negative top margin of 100px. Finally, you will add a media query to the style sheet so that you can adjust the margin of the profile image and the size of the header text for smaller screen sizes. CSS media queries allow you to specify styles that take place under only certain conditions, such as when a screen width is smaller than a certain size. Listing 11-23 shows the completed profile-mocks.css file.

***Listing 11-23.*** Custom Styles to Support the Profile Profile-mock.css

```css
.artist-profile img.artist-profile-banner {
  width: 100%;
  margin-bottom: 10px;
}

.artist-profile-image {
  margin: -100px 10px 0px 50px;
  z-index: 20;
  width: 20%;
}

@media (max-width:768px) {
  .artist-profile-text>h1 {
    font-weight: 600;
    font-size: 16px;
  }
  .artist-profile-image {
    margin: -45px 10px 0px 25px;
    z-index: 20;
    width: 25%;
  }
}
```

In the next step, you will add the HTML to profile-mock.html for displaying the banner image, profile image, artist name, and biographical information. The content will be added inside the root DIV element. The first element that you will add is a DIV styled with Bootstrap's container-fluid. This will allow the container to fill the entire page. Next a DIV with the style artist-profile is added. By applying this style, you can ensure that your style rules created in Listing 11-23 are scoped to the IMG elements inside the DIV scope rather than the entire document, which can provide a performance benefit. Inside the artist-profile DIV, you add the banner and profile images with the appropriate styles applied. Listing 11-24 shows the updated HTML.

***Listing 11-24.*** HTML Added to profile-mock.html to Support Banner and Profile Image

```html
<div id="root">
<div class="container-fluid">
    <div class="row">
      <div class="col-lg-12">
        <div class="artist-profile">
          <img align="left"
                 class="artist-profile-banner" src="SampleBackground1.jpg"
                 alt="Artist profile large background image" />
          <img align="left"
                 class="artist-profile-image img-circle img-thumbnail"
                  src="profileSample.jpg"
                  alt="Artist Profile image" />
```

```
            <div class="artist-profile-text">
              <h1>ArtistFirst ArtistLast</h1>
              <p>Artist Bio. Blaa blaa blaa ...</p>
            </div>
          </div>
        </div>
      </div>
   </div>
</div>
```

I have added a few sample images to the mockups folder to be used in the layout. In the actual application, these images and the other content will be added dynamically using data from your ASP.NET Core application.

The final edit for the mock-up will be to add some HTML for displaying the list of collaboration projects that the artist is involved in. To add the list, you will add a standard HTML table after the artist-profile DIV. The Bootstrap table and table-striped styles will be applied to the table so that alternate rows are given slightly darker colors to make them easier to read. Two sample rows will be added to the table so that you can verify the functionality of the striped rows. Listing 11-25 shows the sample table.

*Listing 11-25.* Table Added to Mock-Up

```
<table class="table table-striped">
    <thead>
      <tr>
        <th>
          Project Name
        </th>
        <th>
          Status
        </th>
        <th>
          Created
        </th>
        <th>
          Modified
        </th>
      </tr>
    </thead>
    <tbody>
      <tr>
        <td>Project 1</td>
        <td>Recruiting / Idea Exchange</td>
        <td>12/28/2016</td>
        <td>1/2/2017</td>
      </tr>
      <tr>
        <td>Project 2</td>
        <td>Mixing</td>
        <td>12/28/2016</td>
        <td>1/2/2017</td>
      </tr>
    </tbody>
  </table>
```

Now, if you view open `profile-mock.html` in a web browser, you should see something similar to Figure 11-4.

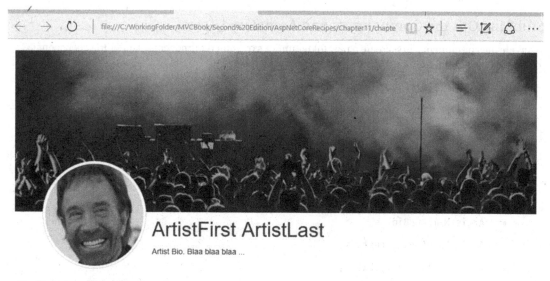

*Figure 11-4.* *Completed artist profile mock-up page*

## Creating React Components from the Mock-Up and Associated Unit Tests

Now that you have a working design, you can begin to decompose the mock-up HTML into React components. Since you will be following TDD, as you start creating the components, you will also create the tests for them. The test files will be placed in the same directory as the production code. Each test file will have a name that matches the production file but will have a `.test.js` file extension. Having tests in the same folder will make it easier to determine which files have tests associated with them. The Webpack configuration is set up so that it knows not to include files that end in `.test.js`. This is the default setting created by create-react-app.

The first step in the decomposition process is to determine the level of decomposition required to make the code easier to understand and test. I have decided to break this page up into a container component and five stateless components. The container component will contain all the logic and state management functionality. The stateless components, listed here, will only contain markup and will have all data and behaviors passed to them via properties:

- Banner
- Picture
- Name and Bio
- Collaboration List
- Collaboration List Row

As you create each of the components, you will also create a suite of tests that can be run automatically as you change the application. For each component, you will create several types of tests.

## Stubbing Out the Components and Associated Tests

To create the components, first create a new folder under src named components. Under the components folder, create a new folder named artist-profile. Under the artist-profile, create the following files:

- ArtistProfileContainer.js
- ArtistProfileContainer.test.js
- ArtistProfileBanner.js
- ArtistProfileBanner.test.js
- ArtistProfilePicture.js
- ArtistProfilePicture.test.js
- ArtistNameAndBio.js
- ArtistNameAndBio.test.js
- ArtistCollaborationList.js
- ArtistCollaborationList.test.js
- ArtistCollaborationListRow.js
- ArtistCollaborationListRow.test.js

After the files have been created, you can add the minimum amount of code to each of the React components to allow the application to build. You can then do the same for the test files. The stubbed-out tests should fail so that you do not accidentally mistake a test stub for a completed test that passes.

The first component that you will create will be ArtistProfileContainer. This component will be the top-level React component for artist profiles. You can think of a React container component as you do a web form created in ASP.NET. React components are ES6 classes that inherit from React.Component. React container classes can maintain state and usually implement one or more React life-cycle methods. If you have used ASP.NET Web Forms, the React page life cycle will sound very familiar.

To stub out the ArtistProfileContainer component, first add an import statement that imports React and Component from the React package. You can then implement a class that extends from React. Component. The class name should be ArtistProfileContainer to match the name of the file. Notice that the component begins with an uppercase letter as per the standard React component naming convention. Inside ArtistProfileContainer, create a method called render and have it return a JSX expression that creates a DIV element with the contents ArtistProfileContainer stub. You will then make the class available for import in other modules by exporting it as the default. When completed, your class should match Listing 11-26.

*Listing 11-26.* ArtistProfileContainer Stub

```
import React, { Component } from 'react';

class ArtistProfileContainer extends Component {
  render() {
    return (
```

```
    <div>
      ArtistProfileContainer Stub
    </div>
  );
  }
}

export default ArtistProfileContainer;
```

Next create stubs for the other components. The rest of the React components will be stateless functional components. Stateless functional components do not inherit from React.Component. They are simple modules that use an arrow function to return a JSX expression. Stateless functional components do not maintain state nor do they implement any life-cycle components. Everything they need to render will be passed to them using props. Props are arguments that are passed into JSX expressions as HTML attributes and consumed by components using arguments passed to the render method. I will go over this concept in detail later in this recipe.

For now, create stubs for each of the React components to match the pattern shown in Listing 11-27.

*Listing 11-27.* ArtistProfileBanner.js Stubbed as Statement Functional Component

```
import React from 'react';

const ArtistProfileBanner = () => (
  <div>ArtistProfileBanner Stub</div>
);

export default ArtistProfileBanner;
```

Once you have created a stub of each component, you can stub out each of the tests. The test stub will contain a single test that fails. For each test, you will call the describe function. The describe function takes two arguments; the first argument is a string that represents the name of the test suite, and the second argument is an arrow function that contains the test suite. Inside the arrow function, a call is made to the it function. The it function follows a similar pattern to describe. The first argument is the name of the test; the second argument is an arrow function that contains the test itself. Listing 11-28 shows the code for the test stub. You name the first test ArtistCollaborationList Renders without crashing. In the test body, you add the code, which will result in a failed test since you have not yet created the component.

```
expect(false).toBe(true);
```

The functions describe, it, and expect are global functions imported from Jest. You do not need to import Jest in the test module because it is done automatically when the tests are run. It should be noted that ESLint will normally raise an undeclared variable error if you use global variables in a module. The env setting that was added to .eslintrc in Listing 11-20 prevents ESLint from raising errors.

*Listing 11-28.* Stub for Tests That Will Fail

```
describe('ArtistCollaborationList', () => {
  it('ArtistCollaborationList Renders without crashing', () => {
    expect(false).toBe(true);
  });
});
```

After stubbing out the rest of the tests, you can run the following command from the command prompt to execute the tests.

```
yarn test
```

After a few seconds, you will see output like the following. The output includes the results for the test for App.js that is added by create-react-app in addition to the results for your new test.

```
FAIL src\components\artist-profile\ArtistCollaborationListRow.test.js
  - ArtistCollaborationListRow › ArtistCollaborationListRow Renders without crashing

    expect(received).toBe(expected)

    Expected value to be (using ===):
      true
    Received:
      false

      at Object.it (src/components/artist-profile/ArtistCollaborationListRow.test.js:3:19)
      at Promise.resolve.then.el (node_modules/p-map/index.js:42:16)

 PASS src\App.test.js

Test Suites: 6 failed, 1 passed, 7 total
Tests:       6 failed, 1 passed, 7 total
Snapshots:   0 total
Time:        0.604s, estimated 1s
Ran all test suites related to changed files.
```

## Implementing the "ArtistProfileContainer Renders without crashing" Test

Since you are following TDD, you will first write a set of tests for ArtistProfileContainer. The first test will verify that ArtistProfileContainer will render without crashing. To create this test, you will first add two import statements to the test so that React and ReactDom are added to the module. You also need to add an import statement for the ArtistProfileContainer component. Next, you will replace the body of the ArtistProfileContainer Renders without crashing test with two statements. The first statement will create a DOM element that you can use as a container. The second will call ReactDOM.render and attempt to render the ArtistProfileContainer inside the DIV element. When completed, ArtistProfileContainer. test.js should match Listing 11-29. This test should succeed.

*Listing 11-29.* ArtistProfileContainer.test.js

```
import React from 'react';
import ReactDOM from 'react-dom';
import ArtistProfileContainer from './ArtistProfileContainer';

describe('ArtistProfileContainer', () => {
  it('ArtistProfileContainer Renders without crashing', () => {
    const div = document.createElement('div');
    ReactDOM.render(<ArtistProfileContainer />, div);
  });
});
```

## Verifying That ArtistProfileContainer Contains the Expected Children

The next test will verify that ArtistProfileContainer renders each of the expected child components. As you add tests to your test suite that require rendering React components and then inspecting their state, the performance of the test suite may begin to degrade. To minimize the performance problems and to avoid having your unit tests fail because of an error in a nested component, you should test only the top-level component and not the children. However, you will need to use the shallow function from the Enzyme library. Add a new test called ArtistProfileContainer to render Banner, Picture, CollaborationList, and NameAndBio. In the test body, you will first use shallow to create a shallow representation of ArtistProfileContainer. You will then verify that the component renders at least one of each of the child controls. This test can be achieved using a function of the shallow component called contains. Listing 11-30 shows the completed test.

*Listing 11-30.* Verifying That the Container Has All the Child Components

```
import React from 'react';
import ReactDOM from 'react-dom';
import { shallow } from 'enzyme';
import ArtistProfileContainer from './ArtistProfileContainer';
import ArtistProfileBanner from './ArtistProfileBanner';
import ArtistProfilePicture from './ArtistProfilePicture';
import ArtistNameAndBio from './ArtistNameAndBio';
import ArtistCollaborationList from './ArtistCollaborationList';

describe('ArtistProfileContainer', () => {
  it('ArtistProfileContainer Renders without crashing', () => {
    const div = document.createElement('div');
    ReactDOM.render(<ArtistProfileContainer />, div);
  });

  it('ArtistProfileContainer should render Banner, Picture, CollaborationList and
  NameAndBio', () => {
    const wrapper = shallow(<ArtistProfileContainer />);
    expect(wrapper.contains([
      <ArtistProfilePicture />
    ])).toBe(true);

    expect(wrapper.contains([
      <ArtistProfileBanner />
    ])).toBe(true);

    expect(wrapper.contains([
      <ArtistNameAndBio />
    ])).toBe(true);

    expect(wrapper.contains([
      <ArtistCollaborationList />
    ])).toBe(true);
  });
});
```

If you check in the console window, you will notice that this new test fails. To make the test pass, you will modify the render method of `ArtistProfileContainer` so that it includes the child controls. To do this, follow these steps:

1. Add import statements for each of the child components, `ArtistProfileBanner`, `ArtistProfilePicture`, `ArtistNameAndBio`, and `ArtistCollaborationList`.

2. Use the HTML from the mock-up completed in Listing 11-21 to create the shell of the component. Remove the code that will be implemented in the child components. You will also not need the outer HTML structure, such as the HEAD and BODY elements that were created in the mock-up.

After you paste in the code from the HTML mock-up, you will see errors for each of the `class` attributes in the HTML elements. The errors are caused by the fact that JSX looks like HTML but is being converted into JavaScript under the covers. Since `class` is a JavaScript keyword, you cannot use it as an attribute in JSX. To correct the error, you must replace the `class` attribute with a `className` attribute. The updated `ArtistProfileContainer` should match Listing 11-31.

*Listing 11-31.* ArtistProfileContainer

```
import React, { Component } from 'react';

import ArtistProfileBanner from './ArtistProfileBanner';
import ArtistProfilePicture from './ArtistProfilePicture';
import ArtistNameAndBio from './ArtistNameAndBio';
import ArtistCollaborationList from './ArtistCollaborationList';

class ArtistProfileContainer extends Component {
  render() {
    return (
      <div className="container-fluid">
        <div className="row">
          <div className="col-lg-12">
            <div className="artist-profile">
              <ArtistProfileBanner />
              <ArtistProfilePicture />
              <ArtistNameAndBio />
            </div>
          </div>
        </div>
        <div className="row">
          <div className="col-lg-12">
            <h2>Collaboration Projects</h2>
            <ArtistCollaborationList />
          </div>
        </div>
      </div>
    );
  }
}

export default ArtistProfileContainer;
```

At this point, you should be able to run you tests again, and they should pass.

## Stubbing Out Tests for the Rest of the Components

The same process can now be followed for the child components.

1. Modify the test classes so that they contain similar logic as shown in Listing 11-28 to verify that the components can render without crashing.

2. Copy the HTML from the mock-up and paste it into the appropriate component. You will also need to change the `class` attribute to `className` as you did in the parent component.

3. Another change that will be required for the `ArtistProfilePicture` and `ArtistProfileBanner` components is that you will need to remove the `align="left"` attribute. The `align` attribute causes an error since it is not valid HTML 5. You will need to instead implement the alignment in the CSS by adding `float: left;` to the `.artist-profile img.artist-profile-banner` and `.artist-profile-image` styles.

Listing 11-32 shows the `ArtistProfilePicture` component.

*Listing 11-32.* ArtistProfilePicture.js

```
import React from 'react';

const ArtistProfilePicture = () => (
  <img
    className="artist-profile-image img-circle img-thumbnail"
    src="profileSample.jpg"
    alt="Artist Avatar"
  />
);

export default ArtistProfilePicture;
```

After you have added code to all the components and updated the unit tests, all tests should now pass. To verify that all the tests pass, return to the command window, which should still be running the test script but is waiting for input. Enter a to rerun all tests:

All the tests will run, and you should see output like the following:

```
PASS  src\components\artist-profile\ArtistProfileContainer.test.js
 PASS  src\App.test.js
 PASS  src\components\artist-profile\ArtistProfilePicture.test.js
 PASS  src\components\artist-profile\ArtistCollaborationListRow.test.js
 PASS  src\components\artist-profile\ArtistCollaborationList.test.js
 PASS  src\components\artist-profile\ArtistProfileBanner.test.js
 PASS  src\components\artist-profile\ArtistNameAndBio.test.js

Test Suites: 7 passed, 7 total
Tests:       8 passed, 8 total
Snapshots:   0 total
Time:        1.117s, estimated 2s
Ran all test suites.
```

## Adding the CSS

In ASP.NET Core, Razor views, and regular HTML, adding a style sheet to a page is done by adding a LINK element to the page with an HREF attribute that points to the style sheet. When creating React components, you cannot add styles in the same way since React components are JavaScript files. Webpack provides a solution to this problem by allowing you to use ES6 import statements to include CSS files into your components. To add CSS to your ArtistProfileContainer component, first create a new CSS file called artistprofile.css in the component/artist-profile folder. Copy the contents of the .css files that you created for the mock-up in Listing 11-22 into the new file.

In the ArtistProfileContainer.js, add an import statement.

```
import './artistprofile.css';
```

By adding the import statement, Webpack will automatically package the CSS file, add it to the CSS bundle, and then add the required JavaScript for loading the needed CSS for the component.

## Adding the Sample Images

In the final application, you will be using a web service to fetch the URLs for the images used in the artist profile from a web service. However, since you have not yet completed the services integration, it is helpful to have some test images to use when you are running the application with the React development server. To do this, in the public folder of the React application, create a subfolder called images. You can then copy both images that you used in the mock-up into the images folder. While in development, you will be able to access the images from the path ./images/profileSample.jpg. The images will not be added to the Webpack bundle.

## Replacing the Hard-Coded Values with Props and State

React uses *props* to pass data between components. Props are JavaScript objects passed to a component through its constructor. In the JSX code, properties can be passed to child components using what look like HTML attributes. To help developers who are consuming your components, React provides type checking for a prop using props validation. Props validation allows you to specify the expected data type of each property and whether it is required. It should be noted, however, that props validation is a help for developers only. It does not provide functionality for the users of your application. To enable props validation, you first need to add the prop-types library to your project. The prop-types library can be added to the project from the command line using the following:

```
yarn add prop-types
```

After adding prop-types, you can then add them to the ArtistProfileContainer component using the following:

```
import PropTypes from 'prop-types';
```

Next you can add the propTypes and defaultProps objects to the ArtistProfileContainer class. In the propTypes object, you will define the names and data types of the properties that you would like the component to support. The prop-types library helps you prevent errors in your program by verifying that the props you pass to a React component are of the expected type. Valid prop types include JavaScript primitives, such as a string, bool, or array; React components; or an instance or a JavaScript class. You can also verify that a JavaScript object adheres to a specific shape. You can find out more about the prop-types library at the following URL:

```
https://www.npmjs.com/package/prop-types
```

defaultProps allows you to specify default values for optional props. For ArtistProfileContainer, you will add default values so that the sample images can be loaded.

Listing 11-33 shows propTypes and defaultProps applied to the ArtistProfileContainer module.

*Listing 11-33.* propTypes and defaultProps

```
ArtistProfileContainer.propTypes = {
  profileImage: PropTypes.string,
  bannerImage: PropTypes.string,
  artistName: PropTypes.shape({
    firstName: PropTypes.string,
    lastName: PropTypes.string
  }),
  artistBio: PropTypes.string
};

ArtistProfileContainer.defaultProps = {
  profileImage: '/images/profileSample.jpg',
  bannerImage: '/images/SampleBackground1.jpg',
  artistName: { firstName: 'firstName', lastName: 'lastName' },
  artistBio: ''
};
```

Next, you will add a constructor to the ArtistProfileContainer class. The constructor will set the default state for the component. React components have an object called state that is tracked by the React framework. When changes are made to state, the React component will be rendered again, allowing changes to state that impact the UI to be displayed. The state object is only writable directly in the constructor. After that, changes to state must be handled using the setState method. Listing 11-34 shows the ArtistProfileContainer constructor.

*Listing 11-34.* ArtistProfileContainer Constructor

```
constructor(props) {
    super(props);
    this.state = {
      profileImage: props.profileImage,
      bannerImage: props.bannerImage,
      artistName: props.artistName,
      artistBio: props.artistBio
    };
}
```

The render method can now be updated so that the values in state are passed as props to the child components. JSX allows you to do this by applying custom HTML attributes to each of the React components. The HTML attributes can contain hard-coded values or JavaScript expressions wrapped in curly braces. Listing 11-35 shows the updated render method.

***Listing 11-35.*** Updated ArtistProfileContainer Render Method

```
render() {
    return (
        <div className="container-fluid">
            <div className="row">
                <div className="col-lg-12">
                    <div className="artist-profile">
                        <ArtistProfileBanner bannerImage={this.state.bannerImage} />
                        <ArtistProfilePicture profileImage={this.state.profileImage} />
                        <ArtistNameAndBio
                            artistName={this.state.artistName}
                            artistBio={this.state.artistBio}
                        />
                    </div>
                </div>
            </div>
            <div className="row">
                <div className="col-lg-12">
                    <h2>Collaboration Projects</h2>
                    <ArtistCollaborationList />
                </div>
            </div>
        </div>
    );
}
```

The unit tests will now fail since you are passing down props that they are not expecting.

## Updating the Child Components to Receive Props

Each of the child components can also be set up to receive props. In the `ArtistProfilePicture` component, you are using the ES6 deconstructor to break the props object into specific properties. This technique aids in readability and saves you some typing in the render method. Like the container component, you will also add props validation to `ArtistProfilePicture`. `ArtistProfilePicture` will require that the profileImage property is required and will not provide a default value. Listing 11-36 shows the completed `ArtistProfilePicture` component.

***Listing 11-36.*** ArtistProfilePicture Component Updated to Receive Props

```
import React from 'react';
import PropTypes from 'prop-types';

const ArtistProfilePicture = ({ profileImage }) => (
    <img
        className="artist-profile-image img-circle img-thumbnail"
        src={profileImage}
        alt="Artist Profile Image"
    />
);
```

```
ArtistProfilePicture.propTypes = {
  profileImage: PropTypes.string.isRequired
};
```

```
export default ArtistProfilePicture;
```

After making this change, you may notice some errors being displayed in the console that state the props validation is failing when running the unit tests for the child components. This is because you do not have default values for the props in the child components and the unit tests are not passing props when the components are being rendered. To fix the console messages, update the unit tests, as shown for ArtistProfilePicture.test.js in Listing 11-37. Similar changes will also be required in the other unit tests.

*Listing 11-37.* Updated Unit Tests to Avoid Props Validation Errors

```
describe('ArtistProfilePicture', () => {
  it('ArtistProfilePicture Renders without crashing', () => {
    const div = document.createElement('div');
    ReactDOM.render(<ArtistProfilePicture profileImage={'/images/profileSample.jpg'} />, div);
  });
});
```

Once the ArtistProfilePicture component has been updated, you can repeat the process with the other components.

## Viewing the Component in the Browser

Now that the structure of the React component has been created, you should be able to view it in the browser and verify that it matches the mock-up. First, you need to update App.js so that it is showing ArtistProfileContainer rather than the create-react-app boilerplate. To update App.js, follow these steps:

1. Open App.js and remove all the import statements except for React.

2. Add an import statement for ArtistProfileContainer.

3. Remove the content from the return statement of the render method.

4. Add <ArtistProfileContainer /> to the render method.

When done, App.js should match Listing 11-38.

*Listing 11-38.* App.js Updated to Include ArtistProfileContainer

```
import React, { Component } from 'react';
import ArtistProfileContainer from './components/artist-profile/ArtistProfileContainer';

class App extends Component {
  render() {
    return (
      <ArtistProfileContainer />
    );
  }
}

export default App;
```

After making the changes, verify that all your tests still pass.

The last component that is required in order for the React application to match the mock-up is to add the Bootstrap CSS. You do not want to add Bootstrap to any of the React components since you do not want it to be bundled by Webpack. The workaround is to add the LINK element to the index.html file in the public directory.

You can then use Ctrl+C to stop the test script in the command prompt and use yarn start to build the application and launch it in the web browser. The results should match the mock-up, as shown earlier in Figure 11-4.

## Creating a Snapshot Test

Now that your components look as you expect, you need to create a UI test that will verify that changes you make going forward do not create visual regressions. Jest snapshot tests allow you to do this without requiring that you launch a web browser. To create a snapshot test, follow these steps:

1.  In the ArtistProfileContainer.test.js file, import renderer from react-test-renderer.

2.  Inside the ArtistProfileContainer describe statement, add a new test using the it function named ArtistProfileContainer Matches Snapshot.

3.  Inside the new test, use the renderer.create function to render a copy of the component.

4.  Use the toJSON function to create a JSON representation of the component.

5.  Use the Jest expect.toMatchSnapShot function to test the current snapshot against the snapshot created the first time the function was run. The first time this test is run, the snapshot will be created, and the test will pass.

Listing 11-39 shows the snapshot test.

***Listing 11-39.*** Snapshot Test for ArtistProfileContainer

```
it('ArtistProfileContainer Matches Snapshot', () => {
    const component = renderer.create(<ArtistProfileContainer />);
    const tree = component.toJSON();
    expect(tree).toMatchSnapshot();
});
```

You can now rerun the test suite and all tests will pass. You should also notice that a new directory named __snapshots__ has been added to the components/artist-profile directory. A file named ArtistProfileContainer.test.js.snap has been added. If you examine the file, you will see that the snapshot contains the entire rendered HTML of the component complete with data.

## Creating the Artist Profile Service in the ASP.NET Core Application

So far, you have been using hard-coded values in your React components to simulate data. In this section, you will create a simple web service using ASP.NET Core that the React application can call.

# Creating the Model

The first step for creating the web service is to create a set of model classes to define the data model.

1.  In Visual Studio, open the Chapter 11 project.

2.  Create a new folder named Models.

3.  In the Models folder, create a new class named CollaborationProject and implement it so that it matches Listing 11-40.

4.  In the Models folder, create another new class named Profile and implement it so that it matches Listing 11-41.

*Listing 11-40.* CollaborationProject Model

```
using System;

namespace Chapter11.Models
{
    public class CollaborationProject
    {
        public string ProjectName { get; set; }
        public string Status { get; set; }
        public DateTime Created { get; set; }
        public DateTime Modified { get; set; }
    }
}
```

*Listing 11-41.* Profile Model

```
using System.Collections.Generic;

namespace Chapter11.Models
{
    public class Profile
    {
        public string ProfileImageUrl { get; set; }
        public string BannerImageUrl { get; set; }
        public string FirstName { get; set; }
        public string LastName { get; set; }
        public string Bio { get; set; }

        public IList<CollaborationProject> Projects { get; set; }

    }
}
```

## Creating the API Controller

You will create a new service that will return the data needed to populate the artist profiles. The service will use standard REST conventions to map a combination to URLs and HTTP verbs to create, read, update, and delete operations. The URL for the service will be the following:

```
/api/profile/{id}
```

To create the service, follow these steps:

1.  Create a new API controller by right-clicking the Controllers folder and selecting Add ➤ Controller.

2.  If prompted, add the minimum dependencies.

3.  In the Add Scaffold window, select API Controller with read/write actions.

4.  Click Add to create the controller.

5.  In the Add Controller window, name the controller ApiProfileController and then click Add.

6.  In the new file created by the template, change the Route attribute to [Route("api/profile")].

For this recipe, you will only be implementing the Get action. To simplify this example, you will be hard-coding some values to return from the service. Listing 11-42 shows the Get action.

***Listing 11-42.*** The Get Action in ApiProfileController

```
[HttpGet("{id}", Name = "Get")]
public Profile Get(int id)
{
        return new Profile
        {
            BannerImageUrl = "/images/SampleBackground1.jpg",
            ProfileImageUrl = "/images/profileSample.jpg",
            FirstName = "firstName",
            LastName = "lastName",
            Bio = "This is the Bio",
            Projects = new List<CollaborationProject> {
                new CollaborationProject {
                    ProjectName = "Project 1",
                    Status = "Recruiting / Idea Exchange",
                    Created = DateTime.Parse("12/28/2016"),
                    Modified = DateTime.Parse("1/2/2017")
                },
                new CollaborationProject {
                    ProjectName = "Project 2",
                    Status = "Mixing",
```

```
        Created = DateTime.Parse("12/28/2016"),
        Modified = DateTime.Parse("1/2/2017")
      }
    }
  };
}
```

You should now be able to run the ASP.NET Core application and verify that you can access the service and it is returning the correct values.

## Using the React Development Server's Proxy Setting to Avoid Cross-Domain Issues

The first problem you will face while developing a React SPA application is that React uses its own development HTTP server that runs on a different port than the IIS Express web server you are using with Visual Studio. Because it is running on a different port, security features in the web browser will prevent the Ajax calls to the ASP.NET Core web service from succeeding. There are several strategies that can be employed to get around the cross-domain issues such as JSONP, but you do not want to use them in this case since you are only going to have cross-domain issues while in development.

Thankfully, the React application created using create-react-app has a built-in feature that allows you to make proxy calls to the ASP.NET Core web service through the React development HTTP server. When the proxy is enabled and a request to the React development HTTP server does not match a path in the React application, the React development HTTP server will automatically forward the request to the server configured as the proxy. The result of this feature is that calls to the ASP.NET Core application appear as relative URLs to the browser and you do not have cross-domain errors.

To enable the proxy in the React application, follow these steps:

1.  Make note of the port being used by the ASP.NET Core application. You can find it under the project properties. To access the properties, right-click the project name in Solution Explorer and then select Properties. In the Properties window, click the Debug tab. The port number can be found under the Web Server Settings on the Debug tab. For my project, the port is 53017, but this will likely be different for the project you created.

2.  In the React project, open the package.json file, add a new item called proxy, and set it to the URL of the ASP.NET Core web server. Listing 11-43 shows the updated package.json file.

*Listing 11-43.* package.json updated with proxy Setting

```
{
  "name": "chapter11-react",
  "version": "0.1.0",
  "private": true,
  "homepage": "/lib/chapter11-react",
  "dependencies": {
    "react": "^15.5.4",
    "react-dom": "^15.5.4",
    "prop-types": "^15.5.10"
  },
```

```
"devDependencies": {
  "enzyme": "^2.8.2",
  "eslint": "3.19.0",
  "eslint-config-airbnb": "^15.0.1",
  "eslint-plugin-import": "2.2.0",
  "eslint-plugin-jest": "^20.0.3",
  "eslint-plugin-jsx-a11y": "5.0.1",
  "eslint-plugin-react": "7.0.1",
  "react-scripts": "1.0.7",
  "react-test-renderer": "^15.5.4"
},
"scripts": {
  "start": "react-scripts start",
  "build": "react-scripts build",
  "test": "react-scripts test --env=jsdom",
  "eject": "react-scripts eject"
},
"proxy": "http://localhost:53017"
}
```

## Creating the ArtistProfileAPI Class

To maintain a separation of concerns and to simplify unit testing, you will create a new module to make Ajax calls to the ASP.NET Core web API. The class will use the new Fetch API to make the Ajax calls. To create the ArtistProfileAPI class, follow these steps:

1. Create a new folder under the src directory of the React project and name it api.

2. Add a new JavaScript file called ArtistProfileApi.js.

3. Inside ArtistProfileApi.js define a class named ArtistProfileApi and define a static method called getArtistProfile that takes an argument called artistId.

4. The getArtistProfile should call fetch with the relative URL to the service as the URL.

Listing 11-44 shows the ArtistProfileApi class. The Fetch API is a bit different from the older APIs such as XMLHttpRequest or the Ajax methods used by libraries such as jQuery. The main difference is that it is based on ES6 promises. Promises are a similar concept to tasks in C#. Promises allow you to define an asynchronous function. Similar to the await keyword in C#, JavaScript has a .then function that will be called when an asynchronous operation is completed. The .then function takes a function as an argument. In Listing 11-44, you are using an arrow function to define the function anonymously. Just like using the await keyword in C#, using arrow functions in conjunction with the .then function simplifies asynchronous functions by making them look synchronous.

The second thing that may seem odd about the Fetch API is that the response argument that is passed to the .then function does not contain the data from the service call. It instead returns a response object that contains data about the response, such as if the request was redirected and the response code was returned by the server. If you want to access the contents of the response, you must call one of the transformation methods of the response object. In this case you are calling the json function, which will try to convert the response to JSON.

It should be noted that json() is an asynchronous method. It does not return the json object but rather another promise. The getArtistProfile method returns this promise to the caller. This will allow the caller to provide a callback function as an arrow function.

*Listing 11-44.* ArtistProfileApi Class

```
class ArtistProfileApi {
  static getArtistProfile(artistId) {
    return fetch(`/api/profile/${artistId}`,
      {
        method: 'GET',
        headers: {
          'Accept': 'application/json',
          'Content-Type': 'application/json'
        }
      }
    )
      .then(response => response.json());
  }
}

export default ArtistProfileApi;
```

## Calling the ArtistProfileApi When the ArtistProfileContainer Is First Loaded

In a similar fashion to ASP.NET Web Forms, React has a component life cycle. In ASP.NET Web Forms you have an OnLoad event that fires when the page first loads. This event is typically used for loading data from the back-end database and binding the data to controls. In React you have an event called componentWillMount that is called the first time a component is loaded by the application. You will use the componentWillMount event to trigger the web service call.

Since you defined getArtistProfile as a static method, you do not need to create an object instance. You can simply call ArtistProfileApi.getArtistProfile(1). Calling getArtistProfile will return a promise. You need to use the .then function to pass in a callback function that will process the data. Inside the callback function, you call this.setState. You can update all the objects in this state that were initially set in the component's constructor. After the state has been updated, React will add the changes to a queue and will apply changes to the UI by intelligently rerendering the component.

Listing 11-45 shows the completed ArtistProfileContainer class. It should be noted that you do not need to add any Ajax calls to the child components. The data is passed down to the children using props.

*Listing 11-45.* The Completed ArtistProfileContainer

```
import React, { Component } from 'react';
import PropTypes from 'prop-types';
import ArtistProfileBanner from './ArtistProfileBanner';
import ArtistProfilePicture from './ArtistProfilePicture';
import ArtistNameAndBio from './ArtistNameAndBio';
import ArtistCollaborationList from './ArtistCollaborationList';
import ArtistProfileApi from '../../api/ArtistProfileApi';
import './artistprofile.css';
```

```
class ArtistProfileContainer extends Component {
  constructor(props) {
    super(props);
    this.state = {
      profileImage: props.profileImage,
      bannerImage: props.bannerImage,
      artistName: props.artistName,
      artistBio: props.artistBio
    };
  }

  componentWillMount() {
    ArtistProfileApi.getArtistProfile(1)
      .then((data) => {
        this.setState({
          profileImage: data.profileImageUrl,
          bannerImage: data.bannerImageUrl,
          artistName: { firstName: data.firstName, lastName: data.lastName },
          artistBio: data.bio
        });
      })
      .catch((error) => {
        console.error(`There has been a problem with your fetch operation:
        ${error.message}`);
      });
  }

  render() {
    return (
      <div className="container-fluid">
        <div className="row">
          <div className="col-lg-12">
            <div className="artist-profile">
              <ArtistProfileBanner bannerImage={this.state.bannerImage} />
              <ArtistProfilePicture profileImage={this.state.profileImage} />
              <ArtistNameAndBio
                artistName={this.state.artistName}
                artistBio={this.state.artistBio}
              />
            </div>
          </div>
        </div>
        <div className="row">
          <div className="col-lg-12">
            <h2>Collaboration Projects</h2>
            <ArtistCollaborationList />
          </div>
        </div>
      </div>
    );
  }
}
```

```
ArtistProfileContainer.propTypes = {
  profileImage: PropTypes.string,
  bannerImage: PropTypes.string,
  artistName: PropTypes.shape({
    firstName: PropTypes.string,
    lastName: PropTypes.string
  }),
  artistBio: PropTypes.string
};
ArtistProfileContainer.defaultProps = {
  profileImage: '/images/profileSample.jpg',
  bannerImage: '/images/SampleBackground1.jpg',
  artistName: { firstName: 'firstName', lastName: 'lastName' },
  artistBio: 'Artist Bio. Blaa blaa blaa ...'
};

export default ArtistProfileContainer;
```

## Next Steps

You should now be able to start the React application and see that the profile page is getting data from the ASP.NET application. This is a good start, but the application is not complete. At this point, the unit tests you created earlier are broken and need to be updated. You will need to use Jest's mocking capabilities to override the getArtistProfile method with a mock implementation in the unit test. You will also need to update the snapshot so it properly reflects the new data that you will be providing in the mock service.

Once all the tests are working and you have added all the needed functionality to the application, you can follow the procedure shown in recipe 11-3 to copy the compiled components into the ASP.NET Core application.

The React ecosystem is complex. This chapter was only a brief introduction into what can be done with React. If you want to learn more about React, I highly recommend the book *Pro React* (Apress, 2015).

# Appendix

## A-1. Installing SQL Server 2016 Developer

Visual Studio comes with a basic version of SQL Server called SQL Server Express LocalDB. LocalDB is a great database to use for prototyping and basic development since it requires no configuration and does not require administrative rights on the computer to run. Unfortunately, LocalDB also has some limitations such as the following:

- LocalDB runs under your user account. This limitation may make it difficult to test application deployment scenarios where the application and SQL Server are running under different service accounts.

- LocalDB shuts down when not in use. LocalDB is a user process and not a Windows service. If you use LocalDB with the full version of Internet Information Services, it will not start automatically when you start the web application like it does when you launch IIS Express from Visual Studio.

- The instance collation for LocalDB is set to `SQL_Latin1_General_CP1_CI_AS` and cannot be changed.

- LocalDB cannot be a merge replication subscriber.

- LocalDB does not support some advanced SQL Server features such as `FILESTREAM`.

- LocalDB has limits on the number of CPU cores, memory, and size of the database.

An alternative to SQL Server Express LocalDB is SQL Server Developer. SQL Server Developer contains all the features of the SQL Server Enterprise edition but cannot be used in production. SQL Server Developer is run as a service and always available for your application. It also allows you to change the collation settings and can be a merge replication subscriber.

Another tool that you will likely find helpful on your developer workstation is SQL Server Management Studio. SQL Server Management Studio has several features that are not available in Visual Studio, including the ability to manage database backups, manage SQL Server Security, create database diagrams, and view the SQL Server logs.

### Downloading Microsoft SQL Server 2016 Developer

Microsoft SQL Server 2016 Developer is free and can be downloaded from the following URL:

```
http://go.microsoft.com/fwlink/?LinkID=799009
```

© John Ciliberti 2017
J. Ciliberti, *ASP.NET Core Recipes*, DOI 10.1007/978-1-4842-0427-6

# Installing Microsoft SQL Server 2016 Developer

After the download has completed, double-click the installer to launch it. Depending on your Windows settings, you may be prompted by Windows User Account Control. If prompted, click the Accept button.

In the SQL Server 2016 with SP1 Developer Edition install window shown in Figure A-1, click the Custom button.

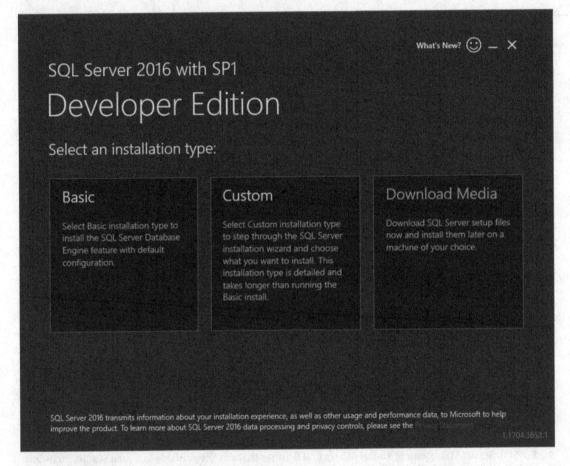

***Figure A-1.*** *SQL Server 2016 Developer edition install*

On the "Specify SQL Server media download target location" screen, use the default media location or select another location if the default location does not have available space. Click the Install button to begin downloading and installing SQL Server 2016. Depending on the speed of your Internet connection, this step may take a long time.

After the download phase has completed, the SQL Server Installation Center will open, as shown in Figure A-2.

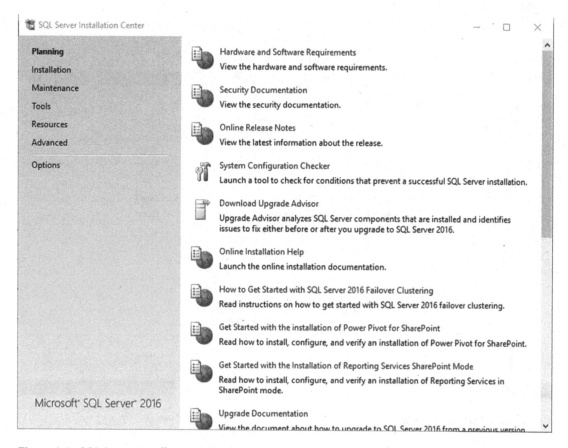

*Figure A-2.* *SQL Server Installation Center*

In the left panel of the SQL Server Installation Center, click Installation and then click "New SQL Server stand-alone installation or add features to an existing installation." After clicking, the SQL Server installer will run several checks to verify that your computer has the correct configuration to install SQL Server. In most cases, the check will not find any issues. If an issue is found, you can click the link under "status" and read the instructions on how to correct the problem. Figure A-3 shows the results on my PC. I had a warning regarding Windows Firewall. Clicking the Warning link under "status" showed that Windows Firewall was enabled but that I would need to make configuration changes to the firewall before SQL Server would be able to accept incoming connections. My SQL Server instance will not need to accept external connections because it is only for local development use, so I can ignore this warning.

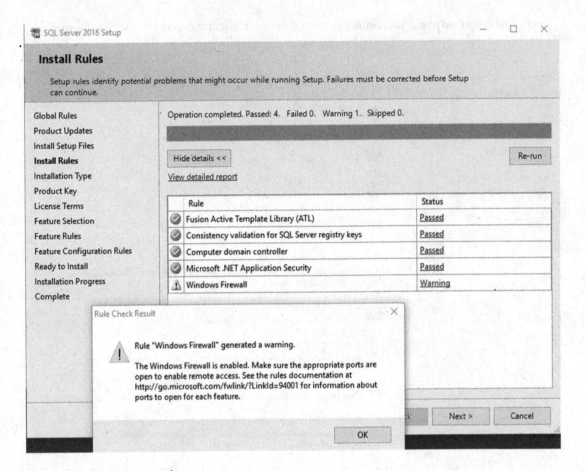

*Figure A-3. A common warning*

Click the Next button to move on to the next step in the installation process. On the Installation Type screen, ensure that "Perform a new installation of SQL Server 2016" is selected and then click Next.

On the Product Key screen, ensure that "Specify a free edition" is selected and that Developer is selected in the drop-down list, as shown in Figure A-4.

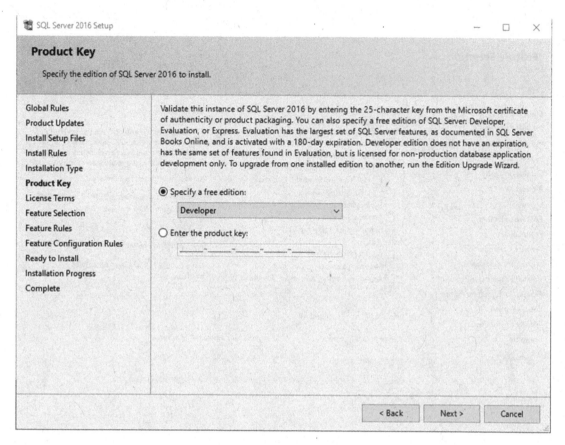

**Figure A-4.** *Ensure that Developer is selected for the product key*

Click Next to proceed to the License Terms screen. On the License Terms screen, select the "I accept the license terms" check box and then click Next.

On the Feature Selection screen, under Instance Features, select Database Engine Services, as shown in Figure A-5. You may optionally select other features, but they are not required for the examples in this book.

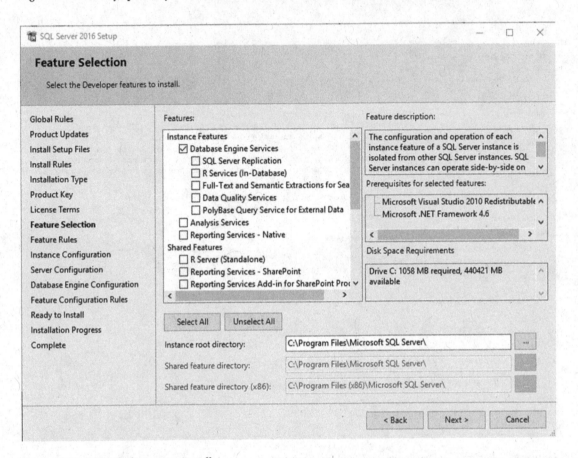

***Figure A-5.*** *Selecting features to install*

On the Instance Configuration screen, select "Default instance" and accept the default settings. Click Next to continue.

On the Server Configuration page, you can accept the default settings and click Next.

On the Database Engine Configuration page, ensure Windows Authentication Mode is selected and then click the Add Current User button to add your account as an administrator on the SQL Server instance. Click Next to move on. Another set of configuration rules will run and should pass. You will then be shown the Ready to Install screen.

Click Install to proceed with the installation. It may take as long as an hour for the installation to complete.

# Installing SQL Server Management Tools

After the SQL Server installation is completed, return to the SQL Server Installation Center. On the Installation section, click the Install SQL Server Management Tools link. This will open a browser window that will show a page with a link to download SQL Server Management Studio (SSMS). Click the link for downloading SSMS. Click Save in the browser when prompted. The installer will take a few minutes to download. After the download is complete, run the installer.

On the welcome screen, click the Install button. Depending on your computer's settings, you may be prompted by User Account Control.

A restart may be required to complete the installation. After the reboot is completed, click in the Windows 10 search bar and type **SQL Server Management Studio**. Click SQL Server Management Studio 17 in the search results. The first time you run SSMS, it may take a few minutes to start up, but eventually you will see a window like the one shown in Figure A-6. Type a single period, **.**, in the "Server name" text box to connect to the local SQL Server instance. A single period is shorthand for localhost. You can also enter **localhost**, the loopback address **127.0.0.1**, or **::1** if you prefer to use the IPv6 notation.

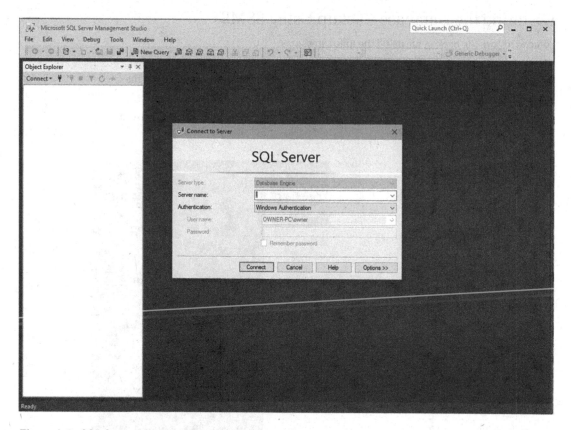

***Figure A-6.*** *SQL Server Management Studio after install*

# A-2. Downloading and Installing the Sample Database

Many examples in this book use a sample database. This database is based on de-identified data from a real production database. To install the database, you need to download the backup file of the database from the book's GitHub repository and then restore the backup to your local SQL Server.

## Downloading the Database Backup File

You can download the backup file from the following URL: `https://github.com/johnciliberti/AspNetCoreRecipes/blob/master/Shared/Database/mvcSharedDB.bak`.

On the GitHub web page, click the Download link. Click Save when prompted by the web browser.

Alternatively, you can use Git to clone the entire repository. This method is shown in the "Cloning the ASP.NET Core Recipes Git Repository" section A-5.

## Restoring the Database Backup Using SSMS

You can restore the backup file using the following steps:

1. Open Microsoft SQL Server Management Studio and connect to your local Microsoft SQL Server Developer instance. This technique was shown in the "Installing SQL Server 2016 Developer" section A-1.

2. In Object Explorer, right-click Databases and then select Restore Database, as shown in Figure A-7.

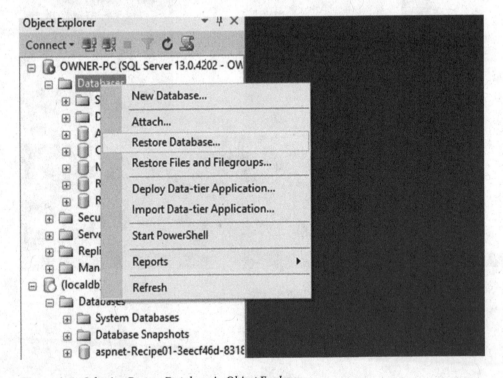

*Figure A-7. Selecting Restore Database in Object Explorer*

3. In the Restore Database window, select Device as the source.

4. Click the ellipsis button on the right side of the Device text box to open the "Select backup devices" window.

5. Ensure that the "Backup media type" is File and then click the Add button in the "Select backup devices" window.

6. Navigate to the file you downloaded from GitHub and then click OK. Figure A-8 shows the process of selecting the backup files.

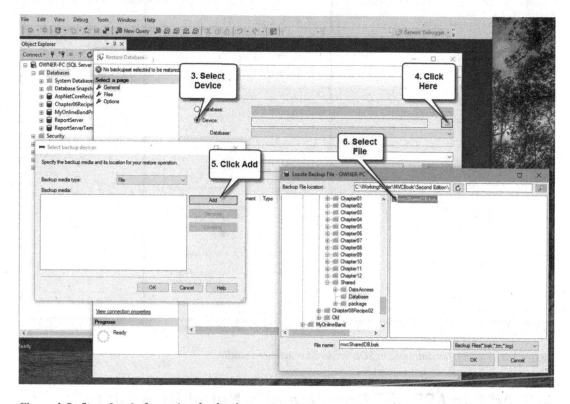

**Figure A-8.** *Steps 3 to 6 of restoring the database using SSMS*

7. Click OK to close the "Select backup devices" window.

8. In the Restore Database window, confirm the settings and optionally change the name of the destination database. You should also verify that the paths specified on the Files tab correspond to valid paths on your system. By default they will match paths used on the system that the backup was originally taken from.

9. Click OK to verify that the backup completed successfully.

10. After the restore is complete, you should be able to expand the database in Object Explorer and explore the data. Figure A-9 shows the database in Object Explorer and a query showing the contents of the Bands table.

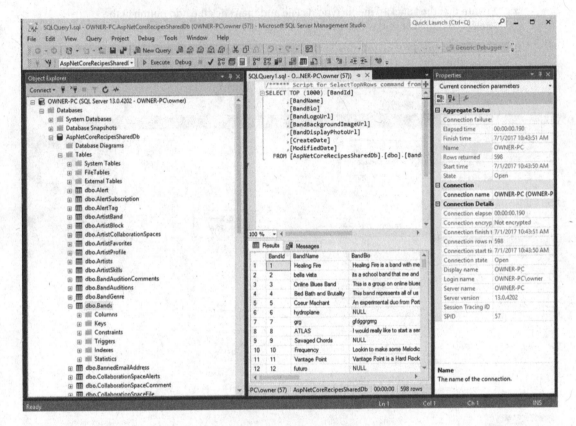

***Figure A-9.*** *Viewing the database in SQL Server Management Studio*

# A-3. Adding ASP.NET Core Recipe's NuGet Repository to Visual Studio

A custom NuGet repository has been set up to host the NuGet packages at MyGet.org. To add this repository to Visual Studio, you can perform the following steps:

1. Open Visual Studio 2017.

2. From the Tools menu, select Options.

3. Locate the settings for the NuGet Package Manager in the left pane of the Options window and then select Package Sources.

4. Click the Add button for "Available package sources" (the green plus sign).

5. Name the package source **ASPNETCore Recipes** and change the source to `https://www.myget.org/F/aspnetcoremvcrecipes/api/v3/index.json`, as shown in Figure A-10.

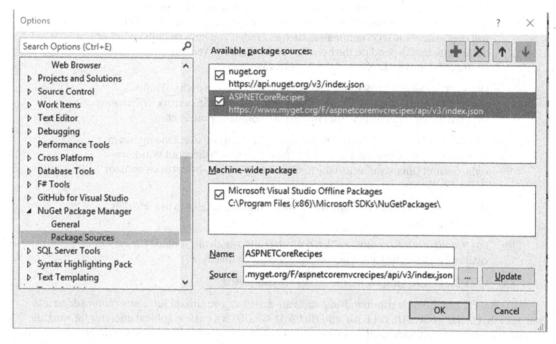

*Figure A-10.* *Adding the custom NuGet repo to Visual Studio*

6. Click OK to save your changes.

7. ASPNETCoreRecipes will now be available as a package source when you use the NuGet Package Manager.

# A-4. Installing Git

Visual Studio has built-in support for Git and can be configured to use GitHub. These features are great and make working with Git easy. Even with this great support, it can be advantageous to install the git-scm package from `https://git-scm.com/`. This package will install command-line utilities that can be used outside of Visual Studio and will install optional Unix utilities, a Unix-like command shell, and a shell extension that adds Git commands to Windows File Explorer.

To install the Git tools, follow these steps:

1. Go to `https://git-scm.com/`.

2. Click the Downloads for Windows button and then save the installer file.

3. After the download has completed, launch the installer. This step requires administrative access to your PC. Depending on your configuration, you may be prompted by Windows User Account Control to verify that you want to install the software. If prompted, select yes.

4.  In the Git setup, click Next after reviewing the GNU general public license.

5.  On the Select Components page, keep the defaults and then click Next.

6.  On the "Adjusting your PATH and environment" page, click "Use Git and optional Unix tools from the Windows command prompt." This will allow you to use Unix commands from any Windows command prompt. Note that this option will overwrite some DOS commands such as find. If you have custom scripts or use utilities that depend on the behavior of the Windows versions of these DOS commands, you can keep the default value. Click Next.

7.  On the "Choosing HTTPS transport" page, select "Use the native Windows Secure Channel Library." This option will help you avoid SSL errors when using Git from the command shell from inside your company's intranet.

8.  For the "Configuring the line ending conversions" setting, select the option that works best for your organization. The default setting of "Checkout Windows-style, commit Unix-style" is usually preferred in Windows-heavy development shops. Click Next.

9.  Use the default settings for configuring the terminal emulator to use with Git Bash. Click Next.

10. For "Configuring extra options," keep the defaults, which are "Enable file system caching" and Enable Git Credential Manager. Click Install.

11. Click the Finish button once the install has completed.

Now that Git and the Unix command-line tools are installed, you should see a new folder added into your apps that includes Git GUI, Git Bash, and Git CMD. Git GUI is a basic graphical interface for working with Git, Git Bash is a Unix-style shell based on the MING64 toolkit. Git CMD is a command prompt shortcut that contains some additional environment variables such as EXEPATH that lists the path to the Git home directory.

In addition, you will have new options in the Windows File Explorer window such as being able to select Git Bash Here when right-clicking a folder.

# A-5. Cloning the *ASP.NET Core Recipes* Git Repository

The fastest way to download the latest samples for this book is to clone the Git repository. The easiest way to do this is using the command window to perform a clone operation. A Git clone will give you a complete copy of the *ASP.NET Core Recipes* Git repository. To clone the repository, follow these steps:

1.  Open a command window.

2.  Navigate to the directory where you want to clone the repo. You can do this using the cd command. Here's an example:

    ```
    cd "My Documents"
    ```

3.  Enter the following command:

    ```
    git clone https://github.com/johnciliberti/AspNetCoreRecipes.git
    ```

After cloning, a new directory will be created called `AspNetCoreRecipes`. If you explore the directory, you will find a directory for each chapter and, for most chapters, a separate directory for each recipe in the chapter.

## Checking for Updates

I will continue to update the samples as new versions of ASP.NET Core are released and defects in the sample code are corrected. You can use the Git command-line tools to check whether you are running the latest copy. To do this, follow these steps:

1. Open a command window and navigate to the `AspNetCoreRecipes` folder where you cloned the repo.

2. Enter the following commands:

   ```
   git remote update
   git status
   ```

   The first command will update your remote references. The second will compare your local copy of the repository to the version on the remote server. If a new version is available, you will see a message such as the following:

   ```
   On branch master
   Your branch is behind 'origin/master' by 1 commit, and can be fast-forwarded.
     (use "git pull" to update your local branch)
   nothing to commit, working tree clean
   ```

3. If you have changed the code in the directory, you will need to stash your changes before you can bring down the latest changes to avoid merge conflicts. You can do this by using the `git stash` command.

4. To download the latest changes, you can use the following command:

   ```
   git pull
   ```

## Reporting Issues and Asking Questions

If you find a bug in the sample code or have a question or suggestion, you can contact me using GitHub by creating a new issue. Creating an issue requires that you create an account on GitHub. If you have an account, you can navigate to the following URL:

```
https://github.com/johnciliberti/AspNetCoreRecipes/issues
```

To create a new issue, click the New Issue button. Please give the issue a descriptive title and try to explain the issue in as much detail as possible. You can optionally tag the issue with a label. Valid labels include `bug`, `enhancement`, and `question`.

I try to answer questions as soon as I can and will usually respond within a few days.

# Index

© John Ciliberti 2017
J. Ciliberti, *ASP.NET Core Recipes*, DOI 10.1007/978-1-4842-0427-6

Simulating calls to external dependencies (*cont.*)
    mocking, 241
    Moq
        back-end database failure, 246–247
        data access component, 243–244
        ListAction_ReturnsListView, 242
        test project, 242
    no data found, testing, 245
Software license agreement forms
    client-side validation, 310
        AddValidation method, 308
        generated HTML, 308
        JavaScript, 309
        script reference to view, 312
    custom validation attribute, create, 304–305
    Home controller, 306–307
    index view, 307
    IsValid method, 304
    model, 303
SslActionLink, 85

## ■ T

Tag cloud
    CSS classes, 158, 160
    GetLinkItemClassName, 161
    project creation, 158
    Razor views, 160
    view component class, 162–166
Tag Helpers
    anchor
        action link creation, 107
        attribute, 105
        link to controller, 105–106
        route parameter, 106
        SSL, 107
    cache
        ConnStrings.json, 126
        controller, 130
        database connection, 125
        FormWithCacheViewModel, 130
        NuGet package, 125
        Shared.DataAccess, 126–127
        view, 127–129, 131
    class creation, 108
    controller, 108–109
    custom creation, 135–137
    custom Tag Helpers, 104
    drop-down list, 114–116, 118
    environment, 132
    fallback feature, 133
    HTML Helper, 102
    input validation
        class creation, 119
        controller, 120
        CSS, 122–123

error, 122, 124
        view, 120–121
    ITagHelperDescriptorResolver, 103
    Label and Input helpers, 107
    nullable bool type, 112–114
    script and link, 132
    view, 110–111
Telerik Fiddler, 46
Templated HTML Helpers, 97–99
Template engine, 40
Test-driven development (TDD), 22, 383
    controllers, 238–239
    design, 234
    ListAction_ReturnsListView, 239–240
    requirements, 234
    test class, 235–238
    TFD, 233
Test-first development (TFD), 233
T-shirts sale in online store
    data attributes, 297–298
    scaffolding
        controller, 299–300
        views, 300–302
    validation requirements, 296–297
    Visual Studio, 296
Twilio
    configuration data in startup, 358–359
    Congratulations window, 355
    create account, 354
    ISmsSender, 357–358
    NuGet package, 354, 356–357
    offers, 353
    options pattern, 357
    Programmable SMS, 355
    request page, 356
    User Secrets store, 356
Two-factor authentication
    in action, 360
    commented out code, 359–360
    manage your account, 360
    Twilio, 353, 355–359

## ■ U

Unit of Work pattern, 201
UrlHelper action, 78

## ■ V

View engines, 23, 30
    functional components, 40
    interface, 40
    IViewEngine interface, 40
    modular design, 40
    RenderAsync method, 42
    ViewContext, 42

# Get the eBook for only $5!

Why limit yourself?

With most of our titles available in both PDF and ePUB format, you can access your content wherever and however you wish—on your PC, phone, tablet, or reader.

Since you've purchased this print book, we are happy to offer you the eBook for just $5.

To learn more, go to http://www.apress.com/companion or contact support@apress.com.

# Apress®

Printed in the United States
By Bookmasters